STUDIES IN CHRISTIAN HISTORY AND THOUGHT

Reformation Faith

Exegesis and Theology in the Protestant Reformations

STUDIES IN CHRISTIAN HISTORY AND THOUGHT

Reformation Faith

Exegesis and Theology in the Protestant Reformations

Edited by Michael Parsons

Foreword by Dennis Ngien

WIPF & STOCK · Eugene, Oregon

Wipf and Stock Publishers
199 W 8th Ave, Suite 3
Eugene, OR 97401

Reformation Faith
Exegesis and Theology in the Protestant Reformation
By Parsons, Michael

ISBN 13: 978-1-62564-841-9
Publication date 4/15/2014
Previously published by Paternoster, 2014

Dennis Ngien
Friend, colleague and exemplary scholar

STUDIES IN CHRISTIAN HISTORY AND THOUGHT

Series Preface

This series complements the specialist series of Studies in Evangelical History and Thought and Studies in Baptist History and Thought for which Paternoster is becoming increasingly well known by offering works that cover the wider field of Christian history and thought. It encompasses accounts of Christian witness at various periods, studies of individual Christians and movements, and works which concern the relations of church and society through history, and the history of Christian thought.

The series includes monographs, revised dissertations and theses, and collections of papers by individuals and groups. As well as 'free standing' volumes, works on particular running themes are being commissioned; authors will be engaged for these from around the world and from a variety of Christian traditions.

A high academic standard combined with lively writing will commend the volumes in this series both to scholars and to a wider readership

Series Editors

CONTENTS

4. History

PREFACE

The title of this volume comes from a significant comment by Timothy George in his excellent work, *Theology of the Reformers* (Nashville: Broadman, 1988), 321, 'Reformation faith,' he says, 'was concerned with the whole of life, not merely with the religious or spiritual sphere. This was true because the sovereign God of the Reformation was concerned with the whole human being, body, soul, mind, instincts, social relations, and political affiliations.' This breadth of theological engagement is highlighted a little by the scope of interest in the following pages, from friendship and marriage to education and a person's physicality, from interpretation of scripture to the doctrine of Royal Supremacy, from doctrine to persecution, preaching and debate. Everything came under the scrutiny of reforming Protestants as they believed it did under the scrutiny of God.

Whilst two chapters have been written specifically for this volume (chapter 9, Michael Parsons, 'Calvin's letters to contemporary martyrs' and chapter 14, Martin I. Klauber, 'Edme Aubertin and the Eucharistic debates in 17th century France'), many of these essays started life at the Evangelical Theological Society's annual conference in Milwaukee, 2012—a conference I was privileged to attend. However, chapter 4, Carl Mosser, 'Calvin and the patristic doctrine of deification,' was given as a paper at the ETS conference in San Francisco in 2011. Peter Adam's chapter on Calvin's preaching is included, with permission, from its original journal location (*Churchman*, 2010) simply because of its continuing usefulness.

The chapters have been reworked, enhanced and enlarged to fit better into an academic book such as the present one. They demonstrate considerable attention to detail, a profound understanding of the subject matter — including both primary and secondary texts — and a commitment to the careful study of the Reformation period. I am grateful to the contributors who took the effort to produce such excellent work and who made the task of editing very straightforward indeed. I am grateful, too, to Dennis Ngien for taking the time and trouble to read the whole manuscript and for writing the Foreword. His understanding of the reformation is exceptional, with a much needed insistence on the reformers' pastoral calling. I am delighted to dedicate this volume to him as a friend and a colleague. He is also an editor to the series *Studies in Christian History and Thought* in which this book finds its place.

As always, particular thanks go to my wife, Becky, and our children, Chris and Katy, for their love, encouragement and support. The grace of God experienced in family life is no small matter.

I trust that this short volume might add to our growing understanding of the reformers and might provoke us to look again at what they said and did — not because they always got it right, of course, but more because they tried! Their determination to see the richness of divine grace in Jesus Christ, revealed in the Scriptures and through the Church is exemplary for the 21st century community of faith of which we are members by grace. My prayer, though, is that the Lord would cause us to keep reforming in response to the gospel he has so graciously given us in his Son.

Michael Parsons
Oxfordshire, 2014

FOREWORD

Why another volume on Reformation study? Simply because there are ample resources which can be reaped from it for faith and practice. This volume comprises of essays in the exegesis and theology of the Protestant Reformations, written by well-informed scholars of various traditions. It exhibits significant awareness of and ability to interact with related scholarly literature, ranging from the patristic via the medieval to the Reformation era and beyond. In fresh and lively presentation, yet in striking individual styles, major theological themes recur including the tensions between divine sovereignty and human free will, and the resolution of them, radical grace as divine remedy to the fall, God's knowledge as compared to human knowledge of events, the relationship between divine causality and human causality, how to espouse a theology of divine providence without being deterministic, the value of human body vis-à-vis Platonic denigration of it, Western doctrine of declaration or the Eastern doctrine of deification, biblical ground for belief in royal ecclesiastic authority, Christology of the Psalms in Hebrews 1-2, the messianic prophecy in Isaiah 52.13-53.12, marriage as a sacrament or not, martyrdom as God's gift and God's Word in action, the theology and practice of preaching, the importance of personal holiness and an educated, empowered laity, Eucharistic controversies and church unity, the need and significance of community life.

This volume of essays serves as an elucidation of these topics, and a corrective to one's faulty philosophical, theological and biblical notions about them. Broadly, this volume will engender not so much how rational faith in God is, but more how relevant God is in relation to the world, especially to human beings. Personal holiness and continual promulgation of ideas or beliefs are not to be viewed apart from the company of pastors and friends, whom God appoints as the instrument of power. The propulsion effect of friendship and collegiality for an ideological movement, which modern churches must heed to, is that which sustains one's doctrines and ensures its lasting piety.

However the most pertinent theme, which is still alive and much debated amongst the protestant circles, is whether deification is exclusively Eastern, largely removed from the Western theological tradition. Those who are unconvinced that divinization is part of the Reformation doctrine of justification, espoused by Luther and Calvin, will need to reassess the historical question of whether deification is a capitulation to Hellenism, a theological innovation which distorts Orthodoxy's fidelity to the biblical gospel, or whether it is constitutive of the faith of the United Christendom, well-attested in the patristic, medieval and contemporary writers.

Readers of *Reformation Faith* will discover gems which will water the root of faith, prick the conscience, bracket or re-examine their views, and nurture the soul.

Dennis Ngien
Professor of Systematic Theology
Tyndale University College & Seminary
Toronto, Ontario. Canada

CONTRIBUTORS
(in alphabetical order)

Peter Adam served, until recently, as the Principal of Ridley Theological College, Melbourne.

Suk-il Ahn is a PhD candidate (Old Testament) at McMaster Divinity College, Hamilton, Ontario, Canada.

Mark A. Blackwelder is Director of Graduate Studies in Bible, Freed-Hardeman University, Henderson, TN, USA.

Derek James Brown is the managing editor of *The Journal of Discipleship and Family Ministry* and web-editor for FamilyMinistryToday.com at the Southern Baptist Theological Seminary.

Jeff Fisher Jeff Fisher is Assistant Professor of Theological Studies at Kuyper College, Grand Rapids, Michigan, USA, and an ordained minister in the Christian Reformed Church in North America..

André A. Gazal is Professor of Historical Theology at Northland Graduate School, Northland International University, Dunbar, Wisconsin, USA.

David W. Hall is Senior Pastor at Midway Presbyterian Church, Powder Springs, GA, USA.

Lloyd A. Harsch is Professor of Church History at New Orleans Baptist Theological Seminary, USA.

Matthew J. Kasper is the Pastor of Grace Atlanta Bible Church, Georgia, USA.

Kevin D. Kennedy is Associate Professor of Theology and Chair of the Systematic Theology department at Southwestern Baptist Theological Seminary, Fort Worth, Texas, USA.

Martin I. Klauber is Affilliate Professor of Church History at Trinity Evangelical Divinity School, Deerfield, Illinois, USA.

Carl Mosser is Associate Professor of Biblical Studies at Eastern University; Visiting Scholar at the Center for Philosophy of Religion, University of Notre Dame, USA.

Dennis Ngien is Professor of Theology, Tyndale University College and Seminary, Founder of the Center for Mentorship and Theological Reflection, Toronto, Canada.

Michael Parsons is the Commissioning Editor for Paternoster, and an Associate Research Fellow at Spurgeon's College, London, UK.

Richard A. Shenk is an Adjunct Professor of Systematic Theology at Bethlehem College and Seminary and Pastor at Village Church, Minneapolis, MN, USA.

ABBREVIATIONS

AUSS	*Andrews University Seminary Studies*
AJT	*The American Journal of Theology*
ARG	*Archiv für Reformationsgeschichte/Archive for Reformation History*
ATR	*Anglican Theological Review*
BECNT	Baker Exegetical Commentary on the New Testament
CCSL	*Corpus Christianorum Series Latina* (Turnholti : Brepols, 1954-)
CH	*Church History*
CNTC	*Calvin's New Testament Commentaries* (edited by David W. Torrance and Thomas F. Torrance; Grand Rapids: Eerdmans, 1959-1972)
CO	*Ioannis Calvini opera quae supersunt omnia*, 59 volumes (edited by W. Baum, E. Cunitz, and E. Reuss; Brunswick and Berlin, 1863-1900)
COE II	*Calvini Opera Exegetica Series II* (Geneva: Librairie Droz, 1992-)
Comm	*Commentary*
CTJ	*Calvin Theological Journal*
CTQ	*Concordia Theological Quarterly*
DDSR	*Duke Divinity School Review*
EH	Ps. Dionysius, *Ecclesiastical Hierarchy*
EQ	*Evangelical Quarterly*
ET	English Translation
GO	*Textus Biblie cum Glossa Ordinaria et expositione Lyre litterali* (Basel: Froben & Petri, 1508)
GO (1601)	*Bibliorum Sacrorum cum Glossa Ordinaria* (Venice: Magnam Societatem, 1601)
GOTR	*Greek Orthodox Theological Review*
HTR	*Harvard Theological Review*
ICC	International Critical Commentary
IJST	*International Journal of Systematic Theology*
Inst.	John Calvin, *Institutes of the Christian Religion*, 1559
Int	*Interpretation*
JCS	*Journal of Church and State*
JEH	*Journal of Ecclesiastical History*
JLR	*Journal of Law and Religion*
JRH	*Journal of Religious History*
JTS	*Journal of Theological Studies*

LW	*Luther's Works* (edited by Jaroslav Pelikan and Helmut T. Lehmann; St. Louis: Concordia / Philadelphia: Fortress, 1955-)
OED	Oxford English Dictionary
NICNT	New International Commentary on the New Testament
NIGTC	New International Greek Testament Commentary
NPNF[1]	*Nicene and Post-Nicene Fathers*, first series (edited by Philip Schaff; Grand Rapids: Eerdmans, 1886-1890)
PG	*Patrologiae cursus completus: Series Graeca* (edited by J.P. Migne; Paris, 1857-1912)
PL	*Patrologiae cursus completus: Series Latina* (edited by J.P. Migne; Paris, 1844-1890)
PSB	*The Princeton Seminary Bulletin*
RefRev	*Reformed Review*
RHT	*Reformed Historical Theology*
RRR	*Reformation and Renaissance Review*
SBJT	*Southern Baptist Journal of Theology*
SJT	*Scottish Journal of Theology*
SRT	*Studies in Reformed Theology*
SVTQ	*St. Vladimir's Theological Quarterly*
T&T	John Calvin, *Tracts and Treatises on Reformation of the Church*, 3 volumes (translated and edited by Henry Beveridge; Edinburgh: Calvin Translation Society, 1851).
ThSt	*Theological Studies*
ThT	*Theology Today*
WA	*D. Martin Luthers Werke*: *Kritische Gesamtausgabe* (Weimar: Böhlau, 1883-)
WTJ	*Westminster Theological Journal*

1. Doctrine

CHAPTER 1

A comparison of Aquinas and Zwingli on the providence of God

Mark A. Blackwelder

One of the primary articles of the faith of Christians throughout the world relates to their understanding that they serve a God who is involved in the affairs of this world. Though some (notably the deists) have held the view that God simply created the physical universe and then disappeared from the scene, most Christians hold that God continued and continues to maintain contact with his creation. Two results of that continued contact are revelation (or communication) and providence (guidance and sustenance). This essay will focus primarily on the latter.

The concept of God's providence is found in the Bible from beginning to end. Before he created Adam and Eve, God prepared an ideal environment for them to live in. After humanity was created Genesis records God's awareness of their needs and ongoing concern for them—not merely in terms of providing for their physical needs, but also for their emotional needs and spiritual needs. God's statement that 'it is not good that the man should be alone' (Gen. 2.18)[1] demonstrates his attentiveness to the human psyche. Even after Adam's sin resulted in his expulsion from the Garden of Eden, God maintained a relationship with him. In fact, in the context of humanity's fall into sin there is a revelation of God's redemptive plan, suggesting his foreknowledge and anticipation of the spiritual need of his creatures and his willingness to meet that need (Gen. 3.15).

The actual terminology which underlies the idea of providence can be found as early as the story of Abraham's commission to sacrifice his son Isaac (Gen. 22). When Isaac asked what the sacrifice was to be, Abraham answered, 'God will provide for himself the lamb for a burnt offering' (Gen. 22.8). The Bible later records these words: 'So Abraham called the name of that place "The Lord Will Provide"' (Gen. 22.14). The Hebrew words in this passage are *Yahweh jireh* which were later translated by the Latin *Deus providebit*, from which we

1 Unless otherwise noted, all quotations from the Bible will be taken from the English Standard Version.

get the English term *providence* which means 'to provide for, to foresee'.[2] Georgia Harkness sees a dual meaning to the word providence; to look ahead (Latin *pro videre*) and to look after or provide for. 'In a word, to believe in divine providence is to believe that God sees the way before us and looks after us as we seek to walk in it.'[3]

There is no idea which has more far-reaching implications theologically. Yearley comments: 'In the sense that providence/predestination specifies the relation of God to the world, the concept becomes the most crucial and far-ranging human idea or question about the nature of God.'[4] The issue is related to one's understanding about God and his involvement with the world. At what level does God make decisions concerning his creation, specifically human beings? God's sovereignty and our free will hang in the balance. Yearley asks the simple yet powerful question, 'Does God control the actual happenings of the world?'[5] He continues:

> If it is held that he does not, then his lack of control makes him irrelevant to great sections of life, imperils the traditional doctrines of creation and the incarnation, means he is not omnipotent as there are powers which he cannot control, and radically changes the sense of justification and one of its corollaries, the theological virtue of hope. However, if it is held that he does, then large problems also arise. For if God rules effectively, free will appears to be a myth and moral responsibility a delusion; God causes evil and personally damns the reprobate; the incarnation is demeaned; nearly insolvable problems are raised about the nature and reason for the Creation; and, as all things happen of necessity, the obviously contingent causality of the world is denied.[6]

In recognition of this tension, through the centuries the concept of divine providence has been a prominent theme in religious conversation. The study is theologically loaded at the most foundational level. This is not the kind of issue that one can simply dismiss as esoteric, since the ripples from this discussion reach into almost every aspect of belief and practice.

The major part of this chapter will focus on the understanding of this idea by two major theologians; one from the medieval period (Thomas Aquinas), and the other from the Reformation (Huldrych Zwingli). These two men represent a polemic on the subject of divine providence which will be useful in uncovering the concerns and implications of this theological construct. We will outline the views of these two men and then compare and contrast their positions.

---

2 Benjamin Wirt Farley, *The Providence of God* (Grand Rapids: Baker, 1988), 16.

3 Georgia Harkness, *The Providence of God* (New York: Abingdon, 1960), 17.

4 Lee H. Yearley, 'St. Thomas Aquinas on Providence and Predestination,' *ATR* 49 (1967), 409.

5 Yearley, 'St. Thomas Aquinas,' 409.

6 Yearley, 'St. Thomas Aquinas,' 410.

Aquinas on providence

Thomas Aquinas (1225-1274) was a man for his time—a time when universities were being founded and questions about the relationship of faith and reason begged for answers. At a time when many in the religious world were prepared to reject philosophy as heretical, Aquinas sought to integrate the two in a coherent way. 'The result was a new *modus vivendi* between faith and philosophy which survived until the rise of the new physics.'[7] Unwilling to abandon either for the sake of the other, Aquinas emerged as arguably the greatest theologian since Augustine and a precursor to a way of thinking about religion that became dominant during the enlightenment.

An appreciation of Thomas Aquinas' view of providence must begin with his understanding of the sovereign knowledge of God. He argues that 'God's knowledge is the cause of all things.'[8] God's knowledge, however, is of an entirely different order than that of human beings. It seems to be the perpetual human inclination to anthropomorphize all living things—to project on them human qualities. Likewise we are often guilty of creating God in our own image. If people are not capable of doing a particular thing, it is difficult for them to conceive of the idea that God could do so. Of course, we expect him to be greater than us, but only in the sense that he is more of what we are, not entirely different than us. Certainly this is connected to the *imago Dei*, plainly affirmed in scripture. However, this perception of the deity can create a conceptual box too small to fit the God of the Bible into.

By contrast, in Aquinas' view the knowledge of God, both in scope and type, is incomparable to that of humanity. It is dissimilar to our knowledge in two basic ways. First, and most obviously, God's knowledge is boundless. He knows all which can be known. There is no information which God does not have at his disposal. This includes knowledge of both necessary and contingent events.[9] 'Nothing then escapes God's Providence, whether it is good or evil, whether it happens necessarily given the laws of nature, or contingently as a result of human choice.'[10] Though Aquinas' view of providence (and thus the doctrine of predestination) is not entirely deterministic, it puts no limits on divine awareness.

Second, and more important to this discussion, God's knowledge is not subject to the constraints of time. Human beings live in a 'reality' that is inherent, it seems, in the design of the physical world God created—a world that is well-suited to a finite physicality, but hardly capable of adequately encompassing eternity. Thus God, who lives in eternity, cannot be forced into conceptions of

---

[7] Ralph McInerny and John O'Callaghan, 'Saint Thomas Aquinas' in Edward N. Zalta (ed.), *The Stanford Encyclopedia of Philosophy* (Winter 2010 Edition). URL = <http://plato.stanford.edu/archives/win2010/entries/aquinas/>

[8] Thomas Aquinas, *Summa Theologica* I, q.14, art. 8.

[9] M.C. D'Arcy, *St. Thomas Aquinas* (Dublin: Clonmore & Reynolds, 1953), 139.

[10] George H. Tavard, 'The Mystery of Divine Providence,' *ThSt* 64.4 (2003), 710.

time designed for humans. To Aquinas, it is not entirely proper to say that God *knew* something or that he *will know* something. God, existing outside the boundaries of time, in eternity, perceives all events in an interminable present tense. He views the affairs of this world, according to Thomas, not in a linear fashion, as a person who cannot see beyond the horizon, but as one who sits on a mountain and 'sees the whole road from a height, sees at once all travelling by the way'.[11] This difference in perspective renders irrelevant even the term 'foreknowledge' and challenges the theologian to cast off a set of boundaries that constrict his perception of the possibilities.

Another important point in Aquinas' theology of divine providence relates to the distinction between necessary and contingent causes. God has made provision for the universe to function as it does. He has built the physical reality to operate in a sustainable and orderly fashion for its own coherence. He is, in fact, the ultimate antecedent cause of all things.[12] However, he has ordained that some things will be governed by necessary causes while others are the result of contingent causes. God's knowledge is perfect and identical with his essence. The plan of God, therefore, will be ultimately enacted. As Maurice De Wulf points out, the effect on lower beings is deterministic, 'but in the case of man [the plan of God] is known by the reason and it is in the power of human liberty to live in accordance with it or the contrary'.[13] This emphasis on our ability to make choices which affect our own destiny is one of the hallmarks of Thomas' theology of providence.

It is this last assertion that has been most often challenged by critics. The affirmation that God can lay claim to certainty while still allowing human actors the exercise of free will has challenged theologians (particularly some Protestant theologians) who view this point of view as incompatible with God's sovereignty. The tension between the sovereign will of God and human free was the focus of several objections anticipated and addressed in the *Summa Theologica*. Aquinas' answers to these objections are consistent with the three tenets of his doctrine of providence discussed above. First, he asserts that God does indeed know all things, even contingent future realities. 'Although the supreme cause is necessary, the effect may be contingent by reason of the proximate contingent cause.'[14] In other words, God as supreme cause empowers other (proximate) causes to bring about certain results, in full knowledge of what those results will be.

Unwilling, however, to 'weaken one truth in order more firmly to establish another,'[15] Aquinas turns to human freedom. 'At this very point, where St.

---

11 Aquinas, *Summa* I., q.14, art. 13.

12 Farley, *The Providence of God*, 129.

13 Maurice De Wulf, *The System of Thomas Aquinas* (New York: Dover, 1959), 97.

14 Aquinas, *Summa* I, q.14, art. 13.

15 Etienne Gilson, *The Christian Philosophy of St. Thomas Aquinas* (New York: Random House, 1956), 180.

Thomas seems to be dissolving beings in the divine omnipotence and submerging their activity in his efficacy, he turns brusquely against those irreconcilable enemies of his who would strip natural things of their own operations.'[16] God's use of agency (human or otherwise) to accomplish his over-arching intentions protects (in Aquinas' mind) the sovereignty of God, while asserting the possibility that he is not the immediate cause of every action. God's acting as supreme cause does not eliminate the agency of the proximate cause. In fact, not only can God allow contingent proximate causes, to claim that he cannot do so is to limit God himself. 'To deprive things of actions of their own is to belittle God's goodness.'[17] Those who argue for divine determinism would accuse Aquinas of positing a 'small God,' stripped of his sovereignty for the sake of human free will. Aquinas would argue, however, that his God is actually bigger, since he has the capacity to use other, proximate, causes to accomplish with certainty his divine will.

How is it possible to justify these apparently contradictory positions? Lonergan points out that in general 'St. Thomas always held that God was more a cause of the will's act of choice than the will itself.'[18] In other words, God is causing the ability to choose, not the choice itself. However, this falls short of addressing the concern, since it does not appear to insure the accomplishment of God's will. Empowered as he might be by God's purpose, it is still possible for Aquinas' proximate cause to choose poorly and thus subvert the divine intention. This is unacceptable to critics, and reasonably so, given their presuppositions about the nature of God's sovereignty. However, this is not the totality of Aquinas explanation.

While the empowerment of proximate causes is part of Aquinas' paradigm, a more important issue is that he sees God outside of time. 'Things reduced to act in time, are known by us successively in time, but by God [are known] in eternity, which is above time.'[19] As Sheed summarizes: 'God acts in the spaceless ness of his immensity and the timelessness of his eternity: we receive the effects of his acts in space and time.'[20] If God sees all things as an eternal present, he can know the outcome of actions which are future from our perspective without dictating those actions, foreknowing but not foreordaining.[21] In Aquinas' theology of providence God allows room for (in fact empowers, according

16 Gilson, *The Christian Philosophy*, 180.

17 Gilson, *The Christian Philosophy*, 182.

18 Bernard J.F. Lonergan, *Grace and Freedom: Operative Grace in the Thought of St. Thomas Aquinas* (edited by J. Patout Burns; London: Darton, Longman & Todd, 1971), 97.

19 Aquinas, *Summa* I, q.14, art.13.

20 Frank J. Sheed, *Theology and Sanity* (San Francisco: Ignatius, 1993), 117.

21 Anthony Kenny, 'Divine Foreknowledge and Human Freedom' in Anthony Kenny (ed.), *Aquinas: A Collection of Critical Essays* (Garden City: Anchor, Doubleday, 1969), 256.

to humanity's own nature)[22] our choices as contingent causes relating to his own destiny. What would happen if we made a choice that was not compatible with God's ultimate plan? Aquinas would consider that a logical impossibility or an affront to the omnipotent nature of God. It is inconceivable to Thomas that we could create a scenario in which it is impossible for God to use the results of our decisions to accomplish his ultimate goals. It is not necessary that we choose only one predetermined option in order that God's plans be accomplished. God is able to select from an indefinite array of 'subsequent' actions (since he has 'already seen' both the choices his creation will make and the end result) that will bring about his desired eventualities without throttling the human impulse in so doing.

Aquinas' ideas on providence are, therefore, predicated on the divine, unlimited knowledge of God coupled with human freedom. Human beings, according to God's good pleasure, have been endowed by their Creator with the privilege of limited self-determination. Men and women make decisions related to their destiny, though God is in control of the ultimate consequences and thus remains sovereign. With this Thomas attempts to strike a delicate balance: God sustains and is in control of his creation, yet the creature (specifically human beings) partakes of the divine essence, including the ability to make consequential choices. Elizabeth Johnson calls this 'a genuinely noncompetitive view of the world'.[23]

Zwingli on providence

Though perhaps eclipsed somewhat by his fellow reformers, Luther and Calvin, Huldrych Zwingli (1484-1531) was a powerful force in the Protestant Reformation of the sixteenth century. Whereas Thomas Aquinas promulgated his ideas within the relatively safe context of the medieval church (though not without some attacks),[24] Zwingli's theology was born in controversy. His ideas are conspicuous by their simplicity and consistency. More preacher than theologian, he nonetheless helped profoundly reshape the religious thought of his day. He approached theology with a view to the big picture; his works articulate one of the earliest expressions of what became Reformed Theology.[25] Helm

---

[22] John F. Wippel, *Metaphysical Themes in Thomas Aquinas*, volume 10, *Studies in the History of Philosophy* (edited by Jude P. Dougherty; Washington: The Catholic University of America Press, 1984), 263.

[23] Elizabeth A. Johnson, 'Does God Play Dice? Divine Providence and Chance,' *ThSt* 57 (1996), 12.

[24] In 1270 and 1277, Bishop Etienne Tempier issued a series of condemnations in which Aquinas was named. His reputation suffered and was badly damaged, though the church later exonerated him and canonized him. See Hans Küng, *Great Christian Thinkers: Paul, Origin, Augustine, Aquinas, Luther, Shleiermacher, Barth* (New York: Continuum, 1994).

[25] There remains debate as to the unique contributions of Zwingli, not because his writings are not extant, but because it is difficult to separate his ideas from his contempo-

states: 'If anyone can be said to develop a doctrine of providence/predestination in axiomatic fashion, Zwingli is a more likely candidate for this dubious honor than is John Calvin.'[26]

Though he was not as prolific with the pen as some of his contemporaries, Zwingli was the first of the reformers to devote a critical treatise to the subject of providence.[27] At the Marburg disputation (1529) Zwingli preached a sermon on the topic, which Philip of Hesse urged him to produce in written form. This he did, under the title 'On the Providence of God'.[28] His treatment of the subject is as much (or more) philosophical than theological. W.P. Stephens suggests:

> Zwingli expounds what providence is (and that it is eternal and unchangeable) and how it differs from wisdom (78.6-10; 83.19-23), using Moses, Paul, Plato, and Seneca as witnesses (83.15-16). He then discusses secondary causes, arguing that they are not properly called causes (83.24-25). This is important for his understanding of providence. It is only in the midst of this that Zwingli comes, as he has promised, to the biblical testimonies for what he has written (99.15-16).[29]

In his discussion of Zwingli's theology of providence, Stephens writes: 'Zwingli's entire theology, like his religious experience, is shaped by his sense of the sovereignty of God and man's utter dependence on him.'[30] Like Luther, Zwingli was convinced that nothing human beings could do would have any significant impact on their salvation. Beyond that, however, Zwingli maintained that men and women cannot affect the events of their lives in any way whatsoever, since this would diminish God's claims to certainty. This belief is a guiding principle for his view of divine providence and predestination.

The other underlying principle for Zwingli concerning the divine providence was that God is infinite in his goodness. In fact, it is not merely the case that God is infinitely good, but that he is exclusively good.

> The supreme good is not so called because it is above all goods, as if there were some goods that were good in their own nature but were surpassed by this good, just as gold surpasses silver though both are valuable. It is called the supreme good because it is the only thing good by nature, and every good that can be imag-

---

raries in the Zurich Reformation or from the articulation of his successor, Heinrich Bullinger. See Ulrich Gäbler, *Huldrych Zwingli: His Life and Work* (Philadelphia: Fortress, 1983) 155.

26 Paul Helm, 'Calvin (and Zwingli) on Divine Providence,' *CTJ* 29.2 (1994), 405.

27 Farley, *The Providence of* God, 143.

28 Farley, *The Providence of* God, 143.

29 W.P. Stephens, 'Election in Zwingli and Bullinger: a comparison of Zwingli's *Sermonis de providentia Dei anamnema* (1530) and Bullinger's *Oratio de moderatione servanda in negotio providentiae, praedestinationis, gratiae et liberi arbitrii* (1536),' *RRR* 7.1 (2005), 43.

30 W.P. Stephens, *The Theology of Huldrych Zwingli* (Oxford: Clarendon, 1986), 86.

> ined is itself really this supreme good. This Christ set forth by the words: 'Why callest though me good? There is none good but God.'[31]

Zwingli's conviction is that providence is not so much a reflection of God's power but of his goodness and perfection. According to Zwingli, 'providence must exist, because the supreme good necessarily cares for and regulates all things'.[32] God must remain aware of all things or else his goodness would be compromised; he must regulate all things or else his power would be in question.[33] Thus Zwingli's view of God's involvement with the world is one of absolute determinism. Any 'freedom of choice' which might be attributed to human beings would be an infringement on the sovereignty of the Almighty God. If anything is guided by its own power or will, God would not be all powerful, since 'there would be a might independent of [his] powers and therefore different from it'.[34] Or as Locher puts it: 'If there should be any area or any event, in time or in eternity, which lay outside God's providence, then it would mean that both his power and his goodness were limited.'[35] In Zwingli's concept of providence, humanity is simply a tool in the hand of God, which he picks up, uses, and lays down at his discretion,[36] even sometimes allowing it to rust before he picks it up again![37]

Also important in this connection is Zwingli's emphasis on God's immutability, particularly as it relates to the notion of the free will of human beings. If men and women can choose a particular course of action of their own volition, that course of action might be opposed to God's will. If that is the case, God is confronted with two options. Either he can allow his will to be subverted or he must make an adjustment. He cannot allow the former, therefore he must choose the latter. However, this would require that God change course, a change of mind which would violate his immutability. This Zwingli must reject, leading him to define providence as 'the enduring and unchangeable rule over and direction of all things in the universe'.[38]

Several issues rise to the surface in response to Zwingli's view of providence. Zwingli himself perceived these and attempted to address them, to a degree. First, if God is the direct cause of all things, then he is responsible for suffering and evil. To this Zwingli replied using, once again, the metaphor of the tool. 'If misfortune and sickness come, think always—God is casting you

---

31 Huldrych Zwingli, *On Providence and Other Essays* (edited by William John Hinke; Durham, NC: Labyrinth, 1983), 131

32 Zwingli, *On Providence*, 130.

33 Zwingli, *On Providence*, 130.

34 Zwingli, *On Providence*, 137.

35 Gottfried W. Locher, *Zwingli's Thought: New Perspectives* (Leiden: Brill, 1981), 125.

36 G.R. Potter, *Huldrych Zwingli* (New York: St. Martin's, 1977), 81.

37 Potter, *Huldrych Zwingli*, 82

38 Zwingli, *On Providence*, 136.

aside just as a locksmith rejects a worn-out tool. May be God will take you up again for his purpose. If not, you must not take it amiss but submit yourself patiently to his will.'[39] As usual, God is sovereign and must not be interrogated. The very idea that one would call God to account for his treatment of something which is his possession both by creation and by purchase is ludicrous in Zwingli's framework of understanding.

Zwingli's response to the contention that God is responsible for evil is unique. Citing Seneca, Zwingli also argued for the instrumental value of unrighteousness in making righteousness evident. In other words, one could not know and appreciate good if its opposite were not also present.

> And since the Deity could not possibly show us unrighteousness in His own person, inasmuch as He is by nature perfectly true, holy, and good, He produced an example of unrighteousness by means of a created being, not as if the created being produced it of itself, since it has neither being, life, nor activity without the Deity, but that the Deity is Himself the author of that which to us is unrighteousness, though not in the least so to him.[40]

Zwingli made no effort to dissociate God from the existence of evil. 'Ulrich refuses to accept the solution of Thomas Aquinas, for whom God determines man's fate in the sense that he knows in advance the use which man will make of his liberty.'[41] Instead, he asserted that though God is the direct cause of every action and event, he bears no moral responsibility for a human being's sinful actions since God is above the law imposed on humanity and has higher (and valid) reasons for causing them to commit acts which are sinful from our standpoint.[42] Goodness, as it describes God, is not defined according to our perception of it but by God himself. If God did it, it must be good. (This reasoning may seem somewhat circular unless one believes, as Zwingli did, that God's sovereign essence is the point of evaluation for all reality.) God defines what is good, both for humanity and for himself, but it should not be assumed that the definition is the same for God as it is for humanity.

Always, Zwingli affirms God's absolute sovereignty. By his definition, that would exclude the possibility that human beings could affect their own destiny in any way. God is in control and the very nature of his existence demands that all events be integrated in to a script of his own origin and design. Further, since he is sovereign, he cannot be called into account even for the existence of any negative realities he causes, since he is within his rights to have his way regardless of whatever undesirable consequences humans may experience—after all, he is God!

---

39 Potter, *Huldrych Zwingli*, 82.

40 Zwingli, *On Providence*, 175-76.

41 Jean Rilliet, *Zwingli: Third Man of the Reformation* (London: Lutterworth, 1964), 253.

42 G.W. Bromiley, *Zwingli and Bullinger* (Philadelphia: Westminster, 1953), 33.

Aquinas and Zwingli compared and contrasted

The discussion presented thus far is by no means an exhaustive or even comprehensive look at the theological positions on providence of these two men. For example, there has been little mention of a primary application of providence, predestination (which is of particular importance in the case of Zwingli, since he does not separate providence and predestination as Aquinas does). Nor have we dealt with election. These topics, though important, fall outside the scope of this study. However, the preceding observations do provide some basis for a comparison of the two perspectives.

There are several similarities between Aquinas and Zwingli on the subject of providence. First, both men begin with a recognition of the power of God. For Zwingli, God's power demands that he be in control of all events, great and small. Any event which God does not initiate robs him of his initiative and thus threatens his Godhood. Humanity's role is simply to accept God's will. Again, 'secondary causes are not properly called causes'.[43] Zwingli refers to language attributing causal agency to 'secondary causes' (which he indicates are not really causes but are 'instruments' of the only true cause) as metonomy[44]—ascribing to a part that which is actually the work of the whole. For Aquinas, God's power finds its greatest testimony in his ability to know all outcomes and accomplish his sovereign will regardless of who (or what) is the proximate cause of a given event. As Jill Raitt summarizes, 'God does not have to control every creature so directly that the causality of creatures is nullified.'[45]

Both men assert the graciousness and kindness of God toward human beings. For Zwingli, God's ultimate kindness is his taking the reigns and guiding individuals masterfully toward the undeserved reward to which he has called (elected) them. For Aquinas, God is kind in that he has bestowed upon his human creatures a measure of his own volitional ability and then given them a proper roadmap which will lead them to their undeserved and unattainable (ie. without his involvement) reward. Both men are committed to the need for God's sustaining kindness.

Despite certain similarities, the differences in the two regarding providence are profound. Aquinas emphasizes the free will of men and women to affect their destiny and holds them responsible for the consequences of their actions. Zwingli holds human beings responsible as well, not so much for individual actions and choices but for their inherent sinfulness, which is deserving only of punishment. God is sovereign and makes *all* the choices. Zwingli moves human responsibility to the corporate level; the fall of humanity is the locus of accountability.

---

43 Zwingli, *On Providence*, 138.

44 Iren Snavely, 'The Evidence of Things Unseen: Zwingli's Sermon on Providence and Colloquy of Marburg,' *WTJ* 56 (1994), 405.

45 Jill Raitt, 'St. Thomas on Free Will and Predestination,' *DDSR* 43 (1978), 190.

Aquinas places God outside of *time* in order to understand his ability to know all things without directly causing every action or event. This frees Aquinas from having to explain how God is responsible for the existence of evil and suffering. Zwingli places God outside of *law* so that, though he is the direct cause of every action and event, he is not morally accountable for the existence of evil and suffering.

Conclusion

What are the implications of this discussion for those who live hundreds of years after Aquinas and Zwingli? First, it is significant to notice the impact each of these men have had on those in their own traditions. Aquinas was both defined by and helped to define and clarify the doctrine of the Catholic Church on this as well as many other issues. Likewise Zwingli, along with Luther and Calvin, helped to make divine providence, with its constituent elements, election and predestination, a central element in the theology of Protestantism.

The final chapter of this debate has not been written. Charles Partee rightly says that 'as long as men believe in a God who cares for them directly and individually, some attention will be devoted to the doctrine of predestination'.[46] Certainly, far more questions than answers remain. Nevertheless, there are things that can be known. God is powerful, concerned and active in the lives of his creatures. Our response must be to emulate him in those aspects in which we see him clearly and allow him to have his way in our lives.

[46] Charles Partee, 'Predestination in Aquinas and Calvin,' *RefRev* 32 (1978), 21.

CHAPTER 2

Radical grace displayed in Martin Luther's doctrine of the Fall

Kevin D. Kennedy

A perennial theological question that Christians have asked for centuries is: 'How are we to understand God's relationship to the Fall?' Did God simply allow the Fall or was God's will in relation to the Fall more active than mere permission would imply? Further questions arise within this discussion. If human beings were created good, then how did a rebellious desire ever find a place in their heart such that they chose to disobey their creator? Does not the mere appearance of sin in humanity imply some sort of flaw in their nature? If God created men and women with a nature such that they could sin, then why is God not culpable for the results of his human creature's actions?

Perhaps an appeal to the presence of the serpent in the garden provides a solution. Upon reflection, however, this only moves the dilemma back a step. How did the serpent, identified in John's *Revelation* as the devil and Satan (Rev 12.9; 20.2), ever come to fall himself, given the fact that God declared all of his creation 'good?' Beyond this, we may ask as one of my former professors once asked: 'Is it even intelligible that an angel of light could ever form the thought of rebellion in his mind given the fact that he existed in the very presence and glory of God, essentially experiencing the beatific vision of God? How could any creature choose to rebel in such circumstances?'

It soon becomes clear that an answer to the question: 'How are we to understand God's relationship to the Fall?' will not be discovered in isolation from other theological questions. In fact, this question plunges the enquirer deeply into the larger debates concerning the sovereignty of God and the doctrine of providence. What is fascinating, however, is how often the question of God's sovereignty moves the inquiry almost immediately to the question of God's relationship to humanity's fall. Is it that we instinctively know that the appearance of sin in the human creature is the one event that our doctrine of providence must explain, otherwise our understanding of providence and God's sovereignty will be insufficient? Perhaps an investigation into the broader question of God's relationship to his creation might provide an explanation for humanity's fall, and perhaps even the fall of Satan.

This chapter explores one such explanation of God's relationship to the Fall as presented by Martin Luther in his treatise, *De Servo Arbitrio*, more commonly known to English speakers by the title, *The Bondage of the Will.* While explaining God's relationship to the Fall was not Luther's primary task in this treatise, Luther does make several telling remarks about both humanity's fall and the fall of Satan as a part of his larger explanation of God's omnipotence. Interestingly, it is in Luther's remarks about the Fall that we discover a striking perspective about the creator-creature relationship. According to Luther, humanity's fall and that of Satan came as a result of God 'deserting' his creatures through the withdrawal of his Spirit, whose accompaniment would otherwise have maintained his creatures in an upright status. However, with the withdrawal of the Spirit, both his human and his angelic creatures disobeyed their creator and fell irrevocably into sin and evil, thus losing their former upright standing before God and coming under bondage to sin and evil.

While this brief introductory description of Luther's explanation of the Fall seems at first to present God's actions as being directly responsible for the Fall, a closer examination shows this not to be the case. Furthermore, when one examines Luther's understanding of the Fall within the context of the larger argument in *The Bondage of the Will* one discovers Luther's radical understanding of grace. The implication of Luther's understanding of the Fall is that grace is not merely the divine response to creaturely sinfulness, but rather, grace, or its virtual synonym in Luther's mind—accompaniment by the Spirit[1]—is the necessary condition for proper human and angelic creaturely existence itself.

The process of explaining Luther's radical understanding of grace as displayed in the Fall will begin with an account of the relationship between God's sovereignty and creaturely actions in Luther's treatise *The Bondage of the Will.* Luther's explanation of the hardening of Pharaoh's heart requires particular attention since it is in the context of that discussion that we most clearly see Luther's portrayal of God's relationship to the actions of his creatures and it is also where we find Luther's remarks explaining how the Fall occurred. Finally, with these lines of evidence set before us we will come to see just how radical Luther's understanding of grace was.

Divine freedom and the necessity of human actions

The Bondage of the Will was Martin Luther's scathing response to Desiderius Erasmus' treatise *De Libero Arbitrio*, which Erasmus wrote in response to Lu-

[1] Luther uses accompaniment by the Spirit, or possession of the Spirit, almost interchangeably with the idea of the reception of grace, e.g. Martin Luther, *De Servo Arbitrio*, in *D. Martin Luthers Werke: Kritische Gesamtausgabe* [WA], vol. 18 (Weimar: Hermann Böhlaus Nachfolger, 1908). *The Bondage of the Will,* in *Luther's Works* [*LW*], ed. Jeroslav Pelikan (vols. 1-30) and Helmut T. Lehmann (vols. 31-55), vol. 33, *Career of the Reformer: III*, trans. Philip S. Watson, (Philadelphia: Fortress Press, 1972), 33:65, 124, 242.

ther's *Asertio* against the Papal Bull issued by Pope Leo X. In *The Freedom of the Will* Erasmus argues for the freedom of the human will against Luther's assertion that humans do not truly possess free will but rather do all things, whether good or evil, according to necessity. Despite the fact that Luther wrote *The Bondage of the Will* as a virtual point-by-point response to Erasmus' treatise, Luther claimed that *The Bondage of the Will* was one of only a handful of his writings that truly represented his thought.[2] Therefore, despite the fact that *The Bondage of the Will* was written as an occasional response to Erasmus, we have it on good authority that it accurately reflects Luther's thought.

Grasping two central elements, or even presuppositions, of Luther's argument is essential to understanding the overall presentation in *The Bondage of the Will.* First, on the question of freedom, Luther insists that 'free choice is plainly a divine term, and can be properly applied to none but the Divine Majesty alone; for he alone can do and does (as the psalmist says [Ps. 115.3]) whatever he pleases in heaven and on earth'.[3] Free choice, therefore, is improperly applied to any creature because first, all creatures are under the sway of the divine omnipotence, and second, both the human creature and Satan are in bondage to the evil into which they have been plunged by their own disobedience.

A second presupposition is related to the first. If we are indeed in bondage to sin as Luther argues, then left to ourselves, lacking the grace of God or the Spirit of God to aid us, we will unfailingly sin of necessity due to this bondage because we are only acting according to our very nature. Luther is quick to clarify that by necessity he does not mean compulsion, as the following quotation explains:

> Now, by 'necessarily' I do not mean 'compulsorily,' . . . That is to say, when a man is without the Spirit of God he does not do evil against his will, as if he were taken by the scruff of the neck and forced to it, like a thief or robber carried off against his will to punishment, but he does it of his own accord and with a ready will. And this readiness or will to act he cannot by his own powers omit, restrain, or change, but he keeps on willing and being ready; and even if he is compelled by external force to do something different, yet the will within him remains averse and he is resentful at whatever compels or resists it. He would not be resentful, however, if it were changed and he willingly submitted to the compulsion.[4]

Luther's central point is that fallen people do not do evil by force, but when moved to action they act according to their own nature. Even when that impetus to act comes from outside themselves, that impetus is still acting upon an evil nature. When an evil nature acts, it produces evil actions. Second, the necessity of our actions arises out of the fact that we are powerless to change our own

---

2 Martin Luther to Wolfgang Capito, July 9, 1537, *LW* 50.172-73.

3 *LW* 33.68.

4 *LW* 33.64.

nature or inclinations. If we are moved to action, we are no more able to act contrary to our natures than we are to resist the movement of divine omnipotence itself. Therefore, when spurred into action, our actions, apart from the Spirit of God, are evil necessarily. Finally, in the quotation above Luther identifies the factor which determines whether men and women do good or evil when moved into action. That factor is the presence or absence of the Spirit of God. When God withholds his Spirit, then the creature is unable to do the good commanded by God but instead does evil necessarily out of his evil nature. However, if the impulse to act is accompanied by the Spirit of God, the Spirit changes the person's heart and that person does the good and does so willingly.

This explanation of how God brings about certain actions in his creatures is intelligible considering the fact that God is dealing with fallen humanity. But how are we to understand God's actions in relation to humanity prior to the Fall? If human nature was not yet vitiated by sin, then there was no evil nature present in them to be spurred into action by God. If that nature was not yet present, then from where did the disobedient impulse arise? To answer this question, we must look more closely at Luther's portrayal of God's relationship to the actions of his creatures. This will be accomplished by examining Luther's explanation of how God hardened Pharaoh's heart. Luther's explanation of the hardening of Pharaoh's heart proves to be not just one example of God's relationship to the actions of his human creatures, but it actually seems to be paradigmatic of that relationship. Furthermore, within this explanation of the hardening of Pharaoh's heart, Luther seems to apply this paradigm to explain God's relationship to the first acts of disobedience committed by Satan and Adam. It is in this explanation that we also discover just how radical was Luther's conception of grace.

The movement of the divine omnipotence and the hardening of Pharaoh's heart.

An essential argument in the *Bondage of the Will* centers around the question of how God hardened Pharaoh's heart. Luther's description of the pattern of action on God's part displayed in the hardening of Pharaoh's heart seems to be paradigmatic for Luther's understanding of God's relationship to the actions of his creatures in general. In brief, Luther's explanation is that God, unwilling to allow his creature to remain static, moves his creature to action through his 'word and work'[5] and then controls the response of the creature to that word or work through either the granting or the withholding of the Spirit.

The movement of the divine omnipotence

Luther understands the omnipotence of God primarily in terms of the activity of God. It is God who works and moves, and in so moving, God stirs his creatures

5 *LW* 33.179.

into action. Indeed, Luther insists that God allows none of his creatures 'to be idle'[6] or 'to take a holiday,' but that God is 'unrestingly active . . . in all his creatures'.[7] When the creature is moved by the sway of the divine omnipotence, the creature must act, it cannot remain static. Therefore, clarifying how God acts upon evil creatures Luther explains that God acts upon them, 'as he finds them,'

> that is to say, since they are averse and evil, and caught up in the movement of this divine omnipotence, they do nothing but averse and evil things. It is like a horseman riding a horse that is lame in one or two of its feet; his riding corresponds to the condition of the horse, that is to say, the horse goes badly[8]

If God works accordingly through evil instruments, how is it that the evil committed by his creatures is not chargeable to God himself? Luther explains that although God brings about evil acts 'in and through evil men . . .yet God cannot act evilly . . . because one who is himself good cannot act evilly; yet he uses evil instruments that cannot escape the sway and motion of his omnipotence'.[9] Thus, not allowing his creatures to remain idle, God moves evil people to action. When they act, they act according to their natures, which are evil, and all the while God himself remains righteous in so moving them. The evil committed is clearly chargeable to the creature and not to God, as Luther explains:

> It is the fault, therefore, of the instruments, which God does not allow to be idle, that evil things are done, with God himself setting them in motion. . . . Hence it comes about that the ungodly man cannot but continually err and sin, because he is caught up in the movement of divine power and not allowed to be idle, but wills, desires, and acts according to the kind of person he himself is.[10]

God's omnipotence that does not allow any creature to remain idle, and our corrupt nature that can do no other than evil apart from the grace and Spirit of God, come together in such a way that evil people sin and do evil necessarily unless God intervenes with the addition of his Spirit when he moves his creature to action. Since 'God cannot lay aside his omnipotence on account of man's aversion, and ungodly man cannot alter his aversion, it thus comes about that man perpetually and necessarily sins and errs until he is put right by the Spirit of God.'[11] In this last quotation we discover the central factor that determines whether God works good or evil through his evil creatures—the Spirit of God. When God withholds his Spirit the creature acts according to its nature, which is evil, thus bringing about evil deeds. If God intervenes, however, and

---

6 *LW* 33.176.
7 *LW* 33.178.
8 *LW* 33.176.
9 *LW* 33.176.
10 *LW* 33.176.
11 *LW* 33.177.

adds his Spirit to the movement of the divine omnipotence, then the creature obeys God's will and willingly does the good which God intends. Therefore, God is able to bring about whatever God intends through either the granting or the withholding of his Spirit. It is in this very way that God is able to control the actions of his creatures, and it is also how God is able to bring about the hardening of Pharaoh's heart.

The hardening of Pharaoh's heart

The hardening of Pharaoh's heart begins when the movement of the divine omnipotence confronts the wicked heart of Pharaoh. God moves Pharaoh as he does all men, through his 'word and his work'.[12] God first confronts Pharaoh with his word in the command: 'Let my people go!' God then accompanies this word with the work of the miracles performed in the sight of all Egypt. However, God does *not* accompany this word and work with his Spirit. Therefore, when confronted with the word and work of God, Pharaoh acts according to his evil nature—he resists the command of God. In this way Pharaoh is hardened to disobey the command, 'Let my people go!'

Luther insists that in this work of hardening, God is not 'creating evil from scratch,' but rather that when God hardens (or makes evil, which Luther claims is the same thing), God works on the creature as he finds him:

> God works evil in us, i.e., by means of us, not through any fault of his, but owing to our faultiness, since we are by nature evil and he is good; but as he carries us along by his own activity in accordance with the nature of his omnipotence, good as he is himself he cannot help but do evil with an evil instrument, though he makes good use of this evil in accordance with his wisdom for his own glory and our salvation.[13]

When one considers Pharaoh, the mightiest man in the land, confronted with the lowly presence of Moses, the messenger of God, delivering the divine command—'Let my people Go!'—it is actually quite understandable that Pharaoh would not acquiesce to the command of God. Pharaoh's own exalted self-appraisal would never allow itself to be abased when so confronted. Therefore, as God presses harder and harder, Pharaoh resists all the more. By confronting Pharaoh with his word and work and at the same time withholding his Spirit whereby Pharaoh would have been able to obey, God affects the hardening of Pharaoh's heart. As Luther explains:

> It is thus that he hardens Pharaoh, when he presents to his ungodly and evil will a word and work which that will hates—owing of course to its inborn defect and natural corruption. And since God does not change it inwardly with his Spirit, but keeps on presenting and obtruding his words and works from without. . . . Pharaoh

[12] *LW* 33.179.
[13] *LW* 33.178.

> is puffed up and exalted by his own imagined greatness on the one hand, and moved to proud contempt on the other by the lowliness of Moses and the abject form in which the word of God comes, and is thus hardened and then more and more provoked and exasperated the more Moses presses and threatens him. Now, this evil will of his would not be set in motion or hardened if left to itself, but when the omnipotent Mover drives it along with inevitable motion like the rest of the creatures, it must of necessity will something. Then, as soon as [God] presents to it from without something that naturally provokes and offends it, it becomes as impossible for Pharaoh to avoid being hardened as it is for him to avoid either the action of divine omnipotence or the aversion or badness of his own will.[14]

By 'thrusting at [Pharaoh] through the word of Moses,'[15] by threatening to take away his kingdom, and at the same time withholding his Spirit, God achieved the hardening of Pharaoh's heart.

However, for Luther, Pharaoh's situation is not an isolated case. Luther seems to present the hardening of Pharaoh's heart as paradigmatic for God's dealings with all of humanity. While commenting on Pharaoh's hardening, Luther broadens the application to speak of all people generally:

> This provocation of the ungodly, when God says or does to them the opposite of what they wish, is itself their hardening or worsening. For not only are they in themselves averse through the very corruption of their nature, but they become all the more averse and are made much worse when their aversion is resisted or thwarted.[16]

This moving of his creatures to action and controlling the results of that movement through either the giving or withholding of the Spirit is Luther's explanation for how God works 'all in all'.[17] Therefore, Luther's explanation of the hardening of Pharaoh's heart is not merely the description of an isolated case. Rather, Pharaoh's situation reveals the paradigm of how God works 'all in all' and not merely 'all in some'.

This description of how God works 'all in all' is certainly coherent. It is rooted in the very narrative structure of the Exodus account. It is also able to explain how the Exodus account attributes Pharaoh's hardening both to God as well as to Pharaoh, while protecting God from culpability for the evil done by his creature. However, Luther's explanation also rests upon human sinfulness as a given. God is able to accomplish 'all in all,' both good and evil, *precisely because* God is dealing with sinful creatures. When God accompanies his word and work with the Spirit, God works good in his evil creatures. When God withholds his Spirit, God works evil *through* his evil creatures, all the while remaining good in himself. However, Luther's description presupposes an evil

---

14 *LW* 33.179.

15 *LW* 33.177.

16 *LW* 33.177.

17 *LW* 33.175, 242.

creature. How, then, are we to understand God's relationship to the actions of his creature before the advent of sin, the very question with which this chapter began? The answer, for Luther, is to recognize that God employed the very same method of working 'all in all' even before the advent of sin.

The fall of Adam and Satan: deserted by the Spirit of God

Luther's telling comments about the Fall occur in the midst of his response to a particular point made by Erasmus. Erasmus had argued that God could not have created Pharaoh evil because the creation account states that when God created, he pronounced everything in his creation 'very good'. Luther counters Erasmus' argument by making two points. First, the Exodus text does not say that God *created* Pharaoh in order to make his power known throughout the earth, but rather that God *raised him up* for that purpose (Rom. 9.17; Ex. 9.16). Therefore, Erasmus' appeal to the goodness of God's creation does not even apply in this case. Furthermore, Luther goes on to point out that the nature found in Pharaoh with which God deals is not the same 'good' human nature that God had originally created, but rather it is a nature that has been vitiated by sin through the Fall. It is in this context that Luther remarks on *how* the Fall occurred and human nature became corrupted by sin. Commenting on the statement that what God created was 'very good,' Luther explains that this 'was said before the fall of man. . . . But it soon follows, in the third chapter [of Genesis], how man became evil *when he was deserted by God and left to himself.*'[18]

There are three initial points to note regarding this language of divine desertion. First, Luther uses this language not to describe the human condition as a result of the Fall, but rather it describes the way in which the Fall actually occurred.[19] This fact is seen in Luther's comments soon after this statement. Luther explains that the reason Pharaoh is born with a corrupt nature is not because God directly created him corrupt, but that God 'does not cease to fashion and multiply the nature that has been *vitiated by sin through the withdrawal of the Spirit*, as a wood carver might make statues out of rotten wood'.[20] The withdrawal of the Spirit is the reason why human nature became vitiated by sin.

---

[18] *LW* 33.174, emphasis added. Even though this quotation from *The Bondage of the Will* mentions Genesis 3 as the context of God deserting his creature, Luther never mentions the idea of God deserting his creature in the *Lectures on Genesis* (*LW* Volume 1, *Lectures on Genesis Chapters 1–5*).

[19] Julius Köstlin correctly notes that this language of desertion is not referring to the condition of human beings after the Fall, but rather describes the way that they fell. 'The words "deserted by God," are not designed to indicate what man became through the fall, but how he came to fall. . . . That which God permitted, by leaving Adam to himself and denying him the further aid of His Spirit, could not, according to God's own appointment, have happened otherwise'—Julius Köstlin, *The Theology of Luther in its Historical Development and Inner Harmony* (Whitefish, MT: Kessinger, 2010), 2.489.

[20] *LW* 33.175.

It is the cause and not the result of the Fall. According to Luther, this corrupt nature is passed from parent to child because God continues to fashion his human creatures despite the fact that human nature has been vitiated by sin 'through the withdrawal of the Spirit'.

The second thing to note about this language of desertion is that this is not an isolated comment. In fact, Luther uses this language two more times to describe not only humanity's fall but also the fall of Satan. Commenting on the bondage of the wills of both human creatures and Satan, Luther says that '[n]ow Satan and man, having fallen from God and been *deserted by God*, cannot will good, that is, things which please God or which God wills'.[21] Later, when describing how God is in control not only of the actions of Pharaoh but also Satan, Luther states that God deals with Satan as he finds him. 'In this way he finds the will of Satan evil, not because he creates it so, but because it has become evil *through God's deserting it and Satan's sinning*; and taking hold of it in the course of his working he moves it in whatever direction he pleases.'[22] This fourth quotation is also further evidence that this desertion by God is the cause and not the result of the creature's fall since the desertion precedes Satan's sin. This language of desertion is used four times by Luther over the space of five pages in the English text. This language of desertion does not seem to be incidental to Luther's explanation of the Fall, but essential to it.

The third thing to note about this language of desertion is its relationship to the concept of the withdrawal of the Spirit. God's deserting his creatures seems to be *defined* in terms of God withdrawing his Spirit. Luther first explains that 'man became evil *when he was deserted by God and left to himself*'.[23] Luther then explains that God 'does not cease to fashion and multiply the nature that has been *vitiated by sin through the withdrawal of the Spirit*'.[24] This second statement comes almost immediately after and in the same context as the earlier statement that God deserted Adam and left him to himself. Presumably, according to the context, when Adam was left to himself, he was left without the Spirit.

Over the span of five pages Luther employs the language of desertion by God four times to describe the cause of the fall of Adam and the fall of Satan. Also within these pages, Luther seems to define this desertion in terms of God withdrawing his Spirit from his creature. How then are we to understand Lu-

---

[21] *LW* 33.175. Cameron MacKenzie, 'The Origins and Consequences of Original Sin in Luther's *Bondage of the Will*,' *Concordia Journal*, 31.4 (2005), 384-397, recognizes that Luther employs the language of desertion to describe the fall of Satan but does not mention the use of the same language in relation to the fall of Adam.

[22] *LW* 33.178, emphasis added.

[23] *LW* 33.174, emphasis added.

[24] *LW* 33.175, emphasis added. This language is similar to Luther's explanation of the Fall, where Adam is said to have disobeyed because the 'Spirit did not add [obedience] to him' (124).

ther's presentation of God's relationship to the Fall according to this description? Is there even enough information here to draw any conclusions?

Stephen Westerholm seems to think that Luther leaves the question of God's relationship to the Fall unanswered.[25] Westerholm recognizes that Luther works from the premise that God 'works all in all,' but he claims that Luther seems to treat the fall of Adam as an exception to this rule. While it is true that Luther never seeks to answer the question 'why?' God works the way that he does, Luther seems to present a consistent view of 'how' God works 'all in all,' even in relation to the fall of Adam. How is this so?

Remember that Luther discusses the fall of Adam and Satan within his discussion of *how* God's actions are related to the hardening of Pharaoh's heart. His discussion of the Fall is presented as part of that explanation. God is able to 'work all in all' in Pharaoh and all other sinful men and women through either accompanying his creature with his Spirit, or by withholding his Spirit from the creature. The case of Adam is just an extension of this same principle. If God accompanies his creature Adam by providing the Spirit, then Adam remains upright. However, as soon as God withdraws his Spirit Adam sins and loses his former standing before God and becomes inextricably bound to sin and evil. Therefore, the fall of Adam and of Satan are under the sovereign control of the divine omnipotence just as are the actions of his fallen creatures such as Pharaoh.

But does not this situation present a problem? When God is dealing with Pharaoh God is dealing with a nature already vitiated by sin through the Fall. In Pharaoh, sin is already a given. However, when God is dealing with Adam, God is dealing with a nature not yet touched by sin. How then do we account for the fall of Adam? Does not this situation seem to presuppose some seed of sin in the created nature of Adam? It is in the answer to these questions that we see how radical was Luther's view of grace.

If we assume that Luther's comments on the fall of Adam and Satan are coherent and consistent, which ought to be the assumption whenever one reads someone's work, then we must ask *how* it is that Luther's comments on the Fall are consistent with God working 'all in all'. The simplest solution seems to be to assume that Luther views 'accompaniment by the Spirit' as a necessary element of proper human and angelic existence itself. Luther seems to present God's human and angelic creatures as *needing* the presence of the Spirit in order for them to maintain their proper created existence. Luther's portrait of the falling creature is one of a creature who has lost something necessary to its proper existence. Were God to continue to accompany his creature with his

---

25 Stephen Westerholm, *Perspectives Old and New on Paul: The "Lutheran" Paul and His Critics* (Grand Rapids: Eerdmans, 2004), 39-40.n16, 'If Adam was "left to himself" to sin, this would, of course, appear to be an exception to Luther's understanding of divine omnipotence, by which God "works all in all"; Luther does not, however, address the issue.'

Spirit, then presumably the creature would remain upright. As soon as God withdraws his Spirit, however, the creature falls. This seems to be a description of a creature losing something necessary to its proper functioning.

At this point we must ask why it is that God did not continue to accompany his creatures and thus maintain them in their proper position and nature. We should also ask, If God's withdrawal of his Spirit would necessarily result in the fall of the creature, then how does God himself not become chargeable for the offense when he withdraws from the creature? Luther's response to the first of these questions would likely be to state that we are in no position to question *why* God does what God does in regard to his creatures. The reasons for God's actions, or even God's inaction, belong to the 'secrets of his majesty'.[26]

To answer how God is not chargeable for the offences of his creatures when it is God's withdrawal that results in those offences, I think that we must return to one of Luther's primary presuppositions—that only God is free. As Luther understands it, 'free choice is plainly a divine term, and can be properly applied to none but the Divine Majesty alone; for he alone can do and does (as the psalmist says [Ps. 115.3]) whatever he pleases in heaven and on earth'.[27] From this presupposition we might be able to find an explanation. God *freely* accompanies his creatures. Were God to be placed under some obligation to accompany his creatures, then God would be bound to his creatures and would not be free. Therefore, God's withdrawal of his Spirit from his creatures should not be viewed primarily as an act precipitating an evil act, but rather is an act demonstrating the divine freedom—this is simply one instance of God being God.[28]

Conclusion: radical grace

There is one final question left to answer: how is Luther's explanation of humanity's fall and that of Satan a display of the radical grace of God? Luther's doctrine of the Fall is a display of radical grace because his position seems to be intelligible only if we posit that accompaniment by the Spirit of God is a necessary component of proper creaturely existence itself. Without the Spirit, the creature has only itself on which to rely. Without the Spirit, the creature is powerless to remain upright on its own. Therefore, the grace of God, or its virtual synonym for Luther—the accompaniment of the Spirit—is not merely the divine response to creaturely sinfulness, but rather, grace is a necessary component of proper creaturely existence itself. Even a righteous man in paradise and an angel existing in the very presence of God needs the Spirit of God to maintain their standing *coram Deo*.

---

26 *LW* 33.180-81. Luther also states that we are wanting God to cease to be God when we ask why he continues moving his evil creatures to action through the movement of his omnipotence (180).

27 *LW* 33.68.

28 *LW* 33.180.

CHAPTER 3

'A prison house of riches': Calvin's theology of the human body

Derek J. Brown

Margaret Stiles is correct when she suggests that a study of Calvin's theology of the body must be approached by first considering Calvin's theological agenda and the context in which he wrote his theology.[1] This consideration is especially important in this case for Calvin did not write a separate volume dedicated to a theology of the body, nor did he designate a specific section of his major theological work, *The Institutes of the Christian Religion*, to a discussion of the human body. Thus, our study will draw upon statements made by Calvin about the body provided throughout the *Institutes* as they are given in the context of other important topics.[2]

The goal of this study, however, is not merely the recitation of texts from the *Institutes* related to Calvin's view of the body, organized under their respective categories. It is the argument of this essay that Calvin succumbed to some Pla-

---

1 Margaret L. Stiles, 'Theology, Anthropology and the Human Body in Calvin's *Institutes of the Christian Religion*,' *HTR* 74.3 (1981), 303.

2 Even in light of the fact that Calvin did not designate a section in his *Institutes* or set out to write a separate volume on a theology of the body, it is somewhat surprising to find so little written on this topic. For example, in secondary works that broadly examine Calvin's teaching, very little to no attention is given to Calvin's theology of the body. Books in which you might expect such discussion yield meager results. For example, John Leith's *John Calvin's Doctrine of the Christian Life* (Louisville: Westminster John Knox: 1989) says little about Calvin's view of the body or the physical aspects of life. Paul Helm's book, *John Calvin's Ideas* (Oxford: OUP, 2004), 129-32, provides a brief discussion of the body in relation to Calvin's view of the soul, but nothing beyond this short inquiry. A. Michael Hunter's *The Teaching of Calvin: A Modern Interpretation* (London: James Clarke, 1950) says very little and many biographies follow this same pattern. Mary Potter Engel, *John Calvin's Perspectival Anthropology* (Atlanta: Scholars Press, 1988), ix, confirms this observation when she notes that a study of Calvin's general anthropology, to say nothing of Calvin's view of the human body, 'has been one of the doctrines most neglected by scholars'. See also Jason Van Vliet, *Children of God: The Imago Dei in John Calvin and his Context* (Gottingen: Vandenhoeck & Ruprecht, 2009), 16.

tonic influence as he formulated his statements on the human body thus tarnishing—albeit slightly—his otherwise edifying and biblically faithful theology of the body. I will examine specifically this issue in the latter portion of this essay.

Accordingly, this study will proceed in three stages.[3] First, I will establish Calvin's general view toward the human body. In this section I will demonstrate the many ways in which Calvin valued and exalted the body and spoke positively about the physical character of earthly life. Second, I will examine the places in which Calvin demonstrates hints of Platonic influence with regard to the human body, noting especially Calvin's penchant for referring to the body as a 'prison house'. Finally, I will offer a brief biblical and theological evaluation of Calvin's theology of the human body.

A storehouse overflowing with inestimable riches: Calvin's positive view of the human body

As I have noted above, Calvin's view of the human body throughout the *Institutes* is largely positive. He speaks explicitly of the beauty of the body and defends the goodness of marriage and sex against the Roman Catholic Church's insistence on singleness and celibacy for members of the clergy. Calvin recognizes the necessity of food and drink for physical sustenance and rejoices in God's care for the body through the supply of its daily needs. He also condemns physical cruelty and exhibits compassion for those who are suffering persecution, while decrying not only laziness and gluttony but any spiritual activity that suppresses the impulse to serve others physically. Finally, Calvin exalts the humanity of Christ and the hope of the resurrection. We will examine each of these ideas more thoroughly under their respective headings.

The beauty and wonder of the human body

Calvin clearly recognizes the magnificence of the human body and the divine wisdom displayed in its configuration. To Calvin, the human body is a masterpiece—'a storehouse of inestimable riches'.[4] Indeed, Calvin views the human

---

3 The primary source for developing Calvin's theology of the body in this essay will be Calvin's *Institutes*, although some reference will be made to his commentaries as well. The method for choosing passages of Scripture upon which to concentrate in Calvin's commentaries will depend mainly on references made to Scripture in the text or footnotes of the *Institutes*.

4 John Calvin, *The Institutes of the Christian Religion* (translated by Ford Lewis Battles; edited by John T. McNeill; Philadelphia: Westminster, 1960), 1.5.4. See also *Inst* 1.5.2. Page 54n.7 directs us to Calvin's comments on Psalm 139.15 where he ponders God's immense wisdom in creating the human body. Calvin reminds us how fittingly the body has been made for the world in which we live. Any change in our bodily structure brings about serious inconvenience for life in this world as we see in those who have suffered major physical injury, such as an amputation or paralysis. See John Calvin, *Psalms 93-150* (Grand Rapids: Baker, 2003), *Comm. Ps.* 139.15.

person as the pinnacle of God's creation.[5] The very complexity and wonder of the human body is, according to Calvin, a '[sign] of divinity'.[6] For this reason, Calvin strongly condemns unbelievers for not recognizing the 'workshop' of God's creativity in their own bodies and for failing to praise God for his goodness and manifold wisdom apparent therein.[7] The refusal to recognize the hand of God in the intricate complexity of the human body, then, was inexcusable.[8] Nevertheless, the body is not to be worshipped, despite its glorious complexity and unfathomable intricacy; nor is it to become a representation for the invisible God. Calvin condemned all idolatry, especially worship of the human form.[9] Calvin's rejection of idolatry, however, did not stem from disdain for the human body in and of itself, but from the fact that God had forbidden any attempt to domesticate his divine nature by use of a human form.[10]

The goodness of marriage and sex

Although Calvin says little in the *Institutes* about sex specifically, he does speak often of marriage, upholding it as a sacred and honorable institution. For example, he acknowledges the kindness of the Lord in providing marriage for both companionship and for the promotion of purity.[11] Thus, lust and fornication are condemned with the latter viewed with stronger disdain than the former because fornication 'brands the body with its own mark'.[12] According to Calvin, fornication is most abominable since it is a sin committed against the body, whereas, echoing Paul, other sins are committed outside the body. Marriage, then, acts as a prophylactic, preventing men and women from indulging in sexual relations outside the marriage covenant by providing the proper context for sexual expression and enjoyment.[13]

In his censures against the Roman Catholic Church and their view of marriage, it is clear that when Calvin affirms the goodness of marriage, he includes

---

5 *Inst.* 1.14.20.

6 *Inst.* 1.5.4. See also Wilhelm Niesel, *The Theology of Calvin* (London: Lutterworth, 1956), 41-44.

7 *Inst.* 1.5.4.

8 See also Calvin, *Comm. Rom.* 1:19-20.

9 *Inst.* 1.11.1-2.

10 *Inst.* 1.11.2. Calvin has no problem with images and sculptures of the body as such—he views these forms of art as gifts from God that can provide legitimate pleasure (see 1.11.12). What Calvin is primarily concerned about here is the corruption of *worship* through the use of such images and sculptures. See also *Comm. Ex.* 20.4.

11 *Inst.* 2.8.41.

12 *Inst.* 2.8.41. See also Calvin, *Comm. 1 Cor.* 6:18.

13 Although there has been some speculation on whether or not Calvin himself enjoyed the sexual component of marriage, John Witte Jr. and Robert M. Kingdom set the record straight, noting that Calvin and his first wife enjoyed a 'very happy honeymoon,' while Calvin was known to repeatedly counsel couples to enjoy each other sexually. See *Sex, Marriage, and Family in John Calvin's Geneva* (Grand Rapids: Eerdmans, 2005), 1.99.

sexual intercourse between husband and wife within the scope of his blessing. For example, he strongly disapproves of the Catholic Church's 'rigid and inexorable'[14] requirement of celibacy for priests. This obligation for priests, according to Calvin, not only defies clear biblical teaching; it also exasperates sin among Catholic priests and pitches souls 'into a pit of despair'.[15] The Catholic Church even went so far as to label marriage 'uncleanness and pollution of the flesh'.[16] Calvin, on the other hand, elevated the institution of marriage to a place of high honor, affirming the biblical vision of marriage: that the earthly reality portrayed the spiritual reality of Christ's relationship with his bride, the church.

Furthermore, Calvin chastises individual clergy for their injudicious willingness to bind themselves to a vow of celibacy, reproving them for not only disregarding Scripture, but for the folly in thinking they are able to endure a celibate lifestyle. Those who enter rashly into vows of celibacy have not adequately considered their propensity to sin and, as a result, have developed an unrealistic view of their ability to resist temptation and remain pure. The gift of celibacy, according to Calvin, was usually temporary in nature and provided by God as particular occasions required it.[17] To resist marriage or to place the yoke of celibacy upon the clergy was, among other things, to misunderstand both Christ and Paul's teaching about such matters.[18] According to Calvin, marriage was not only to be held in high honor and viewed as a gift from God; it was a means by which God helps his people remain sexually pure.

God's providential care for the body

Throughout the *Institutes*, Calvin makes many references to both the necessity of food and drink for the nourishment of our bodies and to the kindness of the Lord in supplying these provisions.[19] In his lengthy discussion on the Lord's Supper, Calvin establishes Christ's spiritual nourishment of the believer through the table's elements upon a person's need of bread and wine for bodily sustenance.[20] In other words, Calvin does not disregard the body's need for physical nutrition or suggest that we should forego such provision in favor of a

---

14 *Inst.* 4.12.23.

15 *Inst.* 4.12.23.

16 *Inst.* 4.12.24.

17 *Inst.* 2.8.43. Calvin offers similar remarks in his commentary on Genesis, strongly reproving those who suggested that the celibate lifestyle is to be preferred above marriage. *Comm. Gen.* 2.18.

18 *Inst.* 2.8.42. In his comments on Matthew 19.12, Calvin strongly emphasizes the notion that voluntary celibacy was not something chosen or declined by one's own free will (like the Papists had suggested), but was something given by God to certain individuals. It is folly, therefore, for a man to remain unmarried if he has not received this gift. See Calvin, *Comm. Matt.* 19:12.

19 *Inst.* 1.16.3.

20 *Inst.* 4.17.1; 4.17.3; 4.17.5.

severe asceticism. For Calvin, the very meaning of the Lord's Supper hinges on the reality that God created a universe in which people need food and drink to live.

Calvin also speaks of God's providential care for the physical welfare of his creatures.[21] God's sovereign care for his creatures' safety and wellbeing is often expressed in the furnishing of secondary means by which people are able to guard and preserve their own life; the refusal of these gracious provisions is folly.[22] Indeed, human beings have the responsibility to make use of the wisdom and other advantages God gives his creatures in order to protect one's life and welfare.[23] Further, he recognizes the respect due to the body by his affirmation of the sixth commandment, 'You shall not kill.' Within the sixth commandment, Calvin saw the desire of God for the safety of all people,[24] yet he understood the underlying principle in this commandment to be God's concern, not merely for the safety of his creatures, but for the preservation of the image of God in humanity.[25]

Accordingly, people can freely give themselves over to God's care because God is concerned with both his spiritual and physical welfare.[26] Thus, by acknowledging and exalting God's care and provision for our physical wellbeing, Calvin demonstrates his own attitude toward the body: it is a gift from God, worthy of nurture and protection. This is not to imply, however, that Calvin condoned the preservation of life and health at all costs. Certain sections in the *Institutes* suggest that there are situations in which it is both good and right to give the body over to harm—and, quite possibly, to death—in order to fulfill God's will.[27] Yet, Calvin also observes that we tend to care more for our body

---

[21] Calvin saw the world as abundantly fitted for humanity's flourishing. See his helpful comments, *Comm. Ps.* 8.6. See also T.F. Torrance, *Calvin's Doctrine of Man* (Westport: Greenwood, 1977), 25.

[22] *Inst.* 1.17.4. See also, Niesel, *The Theology of Calvin*, 75.

[23] *Inst.* 1.17.4. Calvin practiced what he preached by attending to the means that God had given people to take care of their bodies. Calvin himself diligently sought the help of physicians for his many physical ailments, which included cancer, hemorrhoids, gout, kidney stones, and several other serious problems. See John Calvin, *The Letters of John Calvin* (Carlisle: Banner of Truth, 1980), 242-46. While thankful for the remedies God had provided his creatures to aid their various ailments, Calvin also believed that physical disease was a result of sin. See Davis Young, *Calvin and the Natural World* (Lanham: University Press of America, 2007), 146, *Comm. Isa.* 65.20. See Young's chapter, 'Calvin on the Human Body, Medicine and Origins,' 147-49, for an interesting survey of Calvin's discussion of various physical maladies in specific texts of Scripture.

[24] *Inst.* 2.8.39.

[25] *Inst.* 2.8.40.

[26] *Inst.* 3.20.44.

[27] *Inst.* 2.15.4. See also 1.8.13 where Calvin displays his admiration of the martyrs who died for true Scripture doctrine. Calvin, however, did not accept the idea that martyrdom was somehow meritorious, or that it purchased the forgiveness of sins (3.5.3). See chapter 9 of the present volume.

than we do for our soul,[28] much like the Israelites did to their own spiritual peril.[29] Hence, Calvin maintains that spiritual blessing is more important than physical blessing[30] and reminds his readers that their happiness does not consist primarily in an abundance of material blessings, but in the hope of a future heavenly life.[31]

Compassion for those suffering persecution, condemnation of physical cruelty

Calvin further demonstrates his esteem for the human body in his compassion for those suffering persecution and in his condemnation of physical cruelty. His concern for those suffering persecution first arises in the *Institutes*, not from explicit statements, but in his appeal to King Francis I in the introduction. One of the primary reasons for writing the *Institutes* was to promote the relief of suffering for persecuted evangelicals by quelling rumors about and establishing the soundness of Christian doctrine.[32] Inherent in the plea to King Francis to end the persecution against French Christians was Calvin's recognition that a desire for physical peace and health is a legitimate concern.[33] Thus, he diligently sought reprieve from physical suffering for his brothers and sisters in Christ. Calvin also demonstrated his regard for the human body by his disapproval of physical cruelty.

Calvin's condemnation of physical cruelty is found most overtly in the latter portions of the *Institutes* and specifically in his discussion of government. Although he maintained the government's divine right to exercise vengeance upon wrongdoers, he objected to cruel and unfair use of force. To Calvin's mind, rulers were to give the utmost attention to the issue of retributive justice so that they neither failed to exercise appropriate constraint when they executed punishment nor neglected their duty to castigate lawbreakers out of misdirected kindness.[34] Governments, according to Calvin, were also allowed to engage in lawful war. In the pursuit of just war, however, magistrates were to watch over themselves to ensure they acted with restraint and mercy toward their enemy.[35]

Criticism of monastic orders

In Calvin's criticism of the monastic orders, we find that he disapproved of laziness and gluttony as well as any spiritual practice that led devotees away from physical work or service. According to Calvin, the contemporary monas-

---

[28] *Inst.* 3.20.44.
[29] *Inst.* 2.9.23.
[30] *Inst.* 3.20.44.
[31] *Inst.* 2.15.4.
[32] See Calvin's 'Prefatory Address to King Francis I of France,' sections 1 and 2. For more on this, see T.H.L. Parker, *John Calvin: A Full Scale Life of the Controversial Reformation Leader and Influential Theologian* (Batavia: Lion, 1975), 40-43.
[33] See Calvin's 'Prefatory Address,' section 3.
[34] *Inst.* 4.20.10.
[35] *Inst.* 4.20.12.

tic order had degenerated from ancient practices—practices that he, for the most part, respected. In order to compare the present-day monastic order to the ancient practices, Calvin cites Augustine at length. According to Augustine, the early monastics were an example of true piety. In order to escape 'the allurements of the world,'[36] they had gathered together into a 'most chaste and holy common life,'[37] devoting themselves to the monastic community, to prayer, to readings, and to theological discussion. These men were not guilty of pride, laziness or materialism; they lived together, holding everything in common and feeding themselves only by what they had provided by their own hands. And although these men approved of fasting, they did not require those who were physically sick to abstain from food, nor did they advocate severe asceticism in order to attain holiness. Indeed, they rebuked those who promoted such restrictions.[38]

The present day monastics were, however, guilty of legalism, laziness and gluttony. In their observances and requirements, Calvin contends that the contemporary monks had departed from Augustine—although they claimed him as their predecessor—by obligating men to abide by extra-biblical constraints and by perverting the underlying purpose of the monastic lifestyle.[39] They had also failed to recognize that brotherly love and church unity were essential components to the monastic life.[40] Moreover, the contemporary monastics had fallen into the temptation of equating true spirituality with indolence—masking their laziness with appeals to meditation and other non-physical activities—and had also bound themselves to vows of perpetual virginity; a practice Calvin considered both dangerous and presumptuous.[41] On the whole, the existing monastic order had drifted so far from the ancient practice that it left no room for genuine comparison.

Yet, Calvin did not fully endorse the ancient practices either. While acknowledging many of the positive aspects of the ancient monastics, he disapproved of their overly rigid lifestyle and other significant elements of their praxis. He notes that although their lifestyle was not motivated by superstition, the ancient monks exhibited an 'immoderate affectation and perverse zeal'.[42] According to Calvin, the ancient monks had misunderstood the call to holiness insofar that they attempted to pursue piety detached from the world in which they lived. It was God's design that devotion to Christ and the pursuit of holiness would occur within the greater community of believers and the world. Thus, although he did not note any other practices among the ancient monastics

---

[36] *Inst.* 4.13.9—quoted from Augustine, *Morals of the Catholic Church*.
[37] *Inst.* 4.13.9.
[38] *Inst.* 4.13.9.
[39] *Inst.* 4.13.10.
[40] *Inst.* 4.13.10.
[41] *Inst.* 4.13.17.
[42] *Inst.* 4.13.16.

that were liable to correction, Calvin does go so far as to say their example in this respect was both useless and dangerous.[43] Here, in his critique of the ancient and contemporary monastic order, Calvin holds a view toward the body and to earthly life that rejected unnecessary rigidity and pseudo-spiritual sloth.

Calvin's defense of Christ's humanity

We learn much about Calvin's value of the human body from his discussion on the humanity of Christ. Calvin exalted the fact that the eternal Son of God had come to earth, not by taking on the appearance of human flesh as the Marcionites claimed, but by engrafting himself in a fully human nature. Nor did Christ take upon himself 'heavenly flesh,' as the Manichees asserted; on the contrary, he was truly human, susceptible to all the infirmities to which humankind is, by nature, disposed.[44]

Calvin goes to great length to defend the notion that Christ was fully human. He appeals to several biblical texts while affirming Christ's human decent from the line of David and, ultimately, the line of Adam. He sets his assertion of Christ's physical decent alongside his discussion of the virgin birth in order to demonstrate that Christ, though conceived miraculously, clothed himself in genuine humanity. The Marcionites had argued that Christ took his body 'out of nothing,' appealing to the fact that Matthew's genealogy only provided a list of Joseph's ancestors and that Mary, being a woman, was 'without seed,' and therefore unable to contribute to Christ's humanity. Calvin dismisses their argument and reaffirms the reality that Christ was, in fact, 'engendered by Mary from her seed'.[45] Thus Calvin concludes that Christ was not only true God, he was true man. The significance of this point for our purposes is the acknowledgment that Calvin esteemed the human body: it was, of all things, a suitable *telos* for the Son of God who will be embodied for all eternity.[46]

The resurrection of the body

Finally, Calvin's understanding of the resurrection confirms the notion that he greatly valued the human body. Practically, the resurrection from the dead was an appropriate, Spirit-guided hope for believers,[47] and Christian practice was incomplete unless the resurrection was the object of regular reflection.[48] Thus, Calvin pondered the truth of the resurrection at length in the *Institutes*, arguing for its biblical basis and defending it against both denial and misunderstanding.[49]

---

[43] *Inst.* 4.13.16.
[44] *Inst.* 4.13.16.
[45] *Inst.* 2.13.3.
[46] *Inst.* 4.17.29.
[47] *Inst.* 3.25.8.
[48] *Inst.* 3.25.1.
[49] *Inst.* 3, 25.3.

Against the Manichaeans, who could not countenance the idea of resurrection because they regarded the flesh to be 'consumed with rottenness', or who imagined that the resurrection would provide Christians with new bodies unlike our current, earthly bodies, Calvin argued for a resurrection not only of our flesh, but of the same flesh in which we were embodied while on earth. [50] While Calvin admitted that our bodies were not, in their fallen state, fit for heaven, he nonetheless recognized the intrinsic goodness of God's design and creation of the body by his assertion that we will receive the same bodies we once had (albeit glorified) at the resurrection.[51]

From this brief survey, we can clearly see that Calvin valued the human body as marvelous work of divine creativity, worthy of care, protection and, finally, resurrection. Earthly life is a blessing, while physical enjoyments—especially those found in food and marriage—were to be received with thanksgiving; abuse of the body through gluttony and neglect of the body from laziness were to be avoided. Nevertheless, Calvin's theology of the body is not entirely positive. Although he remains tethered to Scripture throughout the *Institutes*, thus forming a generally positive view of the human body, Calvin fails to separate himself fully from Platonic ideas about the body. It is to this issue I now turn.

Longing for escape from this prison? Platonic influence on Calvin's view of the body

Throughout the *Institutes*, Calvin clearly discerns two essential components in the human being: body and soul.[52] To Calvin, this is an issue to which Scripture and reason so clearly testify that it should be 'beyond controversy'. Furthermore, he saw the image of God residing in the composite human being—not exclusively in either body or soul, but in the whole person.[53] There is, however, a tendency in the reformer to value the soul over the body and, at some points, to view the body with contempt. For example, in the introduction to the section in which Calvin aptly defends the notion that we consist of two essential components, he also, in passing, ascribes greater honor to the immaterial part, call-

---

50 *Inst.* 3.25.7.

51 *Inst.* 3.25.7.

52 See Helm, *John Calvin's Ideas*, 129-132; John Cooper, *Body, Soul, and Life Everlasting: Biblical Anthropology and the Monism-Dualism Debate* (Grand Rapids: Eerdmans, 1989). For Calvin's own statements about Plato, see *Inst.* 1.5.11; 1.15.6.

53 See Torrance, *Calvin's Doctrine of Man*, 38-39; David Vandunren, 'The Content of Natural Law: Calvin's Doctrine of the Two Kingdoms,' *JCS* 46 (2004), 511. According to Vandunren, the placement of the divine image in the body in addition to the soul was a 'remarkable move' for Calvin's day. See also Engel, *Perspectival Anthropology*, 43-47.

ing it his 'nobler part'.[54] In a discussion on the image of God in human beings, Calvin designates the soul as the primary seat of the *imago.*[55]

Calvin further strengthens a disjunction between the body and soul with statements in which he classifies the body as a 'prison' or 'prison house'. The influence here in the use of this phrase is clearly Platonic.[56] He first uses these designations in reference to the body in his discussion and defense of humanity's immaterial nature.

> For even when these terms [soul and spirit] are joined together they differ from one another in meaning; yet when the word 'spirit' is used by itself, it means the same thing as soul; as when Solomon, speaking of death, says that then the 'spirit returns to God who gave it [Eccl. 12.7]. And when Christ commended his spirit to the Father [Luke 23.46] and Stephen to his to Christ [Acts 7.59] they meant only that when the *soul is freed from the prison house of the body*, God is its perpetual guardian.[57]

In this example, Calvin appears to access the phrase 'prison house' chiefly as a passing reference in his defense of the existence of the soul. Nevertheless, the very terminology of 'prison house' and Calvin's attachment of this phrase to the human body is somewhat unexpected, given what we have seen throughout the *Institutes* of his generally positive view of the body. Moreover, he continues in another paragraph to suggest that, 'we journey away from God so long as we

---

54 *Inst.* 1.15.2.

55 *Inst.* 1.15.3. In addition, in his discussion of the sixth commandment Calvin uses the fact that God has established rigorous laws for the protection of the body to infer that the soul is valued higher than the body in God's economy (*Inst.* 2.8.40). Although Calvin ties the image of God to both a person's material and immaterial aspects, he, like elsewhere, appears to place greater worth upon the immaterial. See also Engel, *Perspectival Anthropology*, 162-63, where she quotes from Calvin's remarks on Job 37, that 'our souls are more precious to [God] than our bodies'.

56 Helm, *John Calvin's Ideas*, 131. According to Francois Wendel, Plato's influence on Calvin appears to have come during subsequent publications of his *Institutes*. See, *Calvin: Origins and Development of His Religious Thought* (Grand Rapids: Baker, 1997), 115. See also Randall Zachman, *Image and Word in the Theology of John Calvin* (Notre Dame: University of Notre Dame Press, 2007), 15. Charles Partee, *Calvin and Classical Philosophy* (Louisville: Westminster John Knox, 2005), 51, suggests that Calvin's view of human beings is 'perhaps more indebted to the insights of the philosophers than any other area of his thought'. Partee, however, wants to avoid the conclusion that Calvin's anthropology is philosophical in its entirety. In this we are agreed. Calvin does depart from Plato in significant areas and tethers his doctrine of human beings to the Scriptures. The argument of this essay, however, is not primarily concerned with demonstrating that Calvin's anthropology was basically biblical, but that it retained some unhelpful vestiges of Platonism, especially in Calvin's discussion of the human body. See also Henri Blocher, 'Calvin's Theological Anthropology,' in Sung Wook Chung (ed.), *John Calvin and Evangelical Theology: Legacy and Prospect* (Louisville: Westminster John Knox, 2009), 75-76.

57 *Inst.* 1.15.2.

dwell in the flesh, but that we enjoy his presence outside the flesh [1 Cor. 5.6,8].'[58] In other words, not only did Calvin utilize the phrase 'prison house' to defend the notion that we possess an immaterial nature; he also viewed this 'prison' as something from which to escape in order to fully enjoy God's presence.

Accordingly, we find that Calvin uses the label of 'prison house' in reference to the body primarily in his discussion of the Christian's pursuit of holiness. Christians, though called and exhorted to pursue genuine purity of life, are unable to fully apprehend perfection this side of glory. In Calvin's judgment, the origin of righteous living was spiritual, located in the desires of the inner being. The body, on the other hand, was an encumbrance, hindering one's spiritual progress and obedience.[59] Thus, Christians were to remind themselves that perfection cannot be attained until they 'cast off the weakness of the body, and [are] received into full fellowship with [Christ]'.[60]

These passages seem to suggest that Calvin attributes, in some measure, spiritual inability and lethargy to the body. This inclination to view the body as impediment to spiritual progress increases his desire to break free from this prison so that he might enjoy unencumbered worship and enjoyment of God. Calvin is explicit at this point in his discussion of our inability to fulfill the law. While we are incarcerated in our bodies, we cannot wholly fulfill the commandments; it is not until we put off the weight of our bodies through death that we can do so.[61]

Thus, in light of these passages that suggest our current embodied condition provokes sin and hinders us from fulfilling the law in its entirety, it is not surprising to find Calvin, several sections later, instructing his readers to set their eyes upon their spiritual inheritance and to 'betake themselves wholly to mediate upon that eternal life to come'.[62] Given their current state of suffering and misery, Christians should look to their heavenly future for hope and encouragement. He explains,

> When it comes to a comparison with life to come, the present life can not only be safely neglected but, compared to the former, must be utterly despised and loathed. For, if heaven is our homeland, what else is the earth but our place of exile? If departure from the world is entry into life, what else is the world but a sepulcher? And death? *If to be freed from the body is to be released into perfect freedom, what else is the body but a prison*?[63]

58 *Inst.* 1.15.2.
59 *Inst.* 1.15.2.
60 *Inst.* 1.15.2.
61 *Inst.* 2.7.4; 2.7.13.
62 *Inst.* 3.9.4.
63 *Inst.* 3.9.4, emphasis added.

Calvin also admits that our current bodily condition disposes us to a situation in which we need to fight vigorously against our sinful flesh. 'Accordingly, so long as we dwell in the *prison house of our body* we must continually contend with the defects of our corrupt nature, indeed with our own natural soul.'[64] Deliverance from the body, then, was a welcome event.[65]

A failure to integrate: an evaluation of Calvin's theology of the body

As we saw in the first section of this essay, Calvin highly esteemed the human body as a work of wonder and earthly life was a blessing from the Lord to be received with gratitude and joy. Yet, in some sections of the *Institutes*, Calvin viewed the body as an impediment to spiritual progress and something that rendered Christians unable to fulfill the law of God. Here Calvin followed Plato in designating the body as a 'prison house,' from which escape was a welcome event.[66] In this way, Calvin's theology of the body falls slightly short of the biblical witness by failing to synthesize his statements that speak of our inability to fulfill the law together with statements that emphasize the dignity of the human body and the hope of resurrection.[67]

---

64 *Inst.* 3.3.20, emphasis added

65 Calvin's attitude here is further illustrated in a section from his sermon on Job 3, *CO* 33.170. See Engel, *Perspectival Anthropology*, 171.

66 Charles Partee, in his article, 'The Soul in Plato, Platonism and Calvin,' *SJT* 22 (1969), 278-295, admits that 'It might be argued that Calvin had a "spiritualizing tendency" and that Luther was more sensitive to the biblical antithesis of flesh and spirit as distinct from body and soul,' yet Partee wants to see this as 'a criticism of emphasis rather than of ignorance'. Partee desires to protect Calvin from the charge that he endorsed the entire Platonic tradition by noting the areas in which Calvin differed strongly with Plato and even qualified his overall commendation of Plato. (See also David Steinmetz, *Calvin in Context* (Oxford: OUP, 2010) for another affirmation that Calvin did not endorse Platonism in its entirety.) While Partee is correct to argue that Calvin departed from Platonism in significant portions of his theology—not the least of which was his teaching on the resurrection of the body and his rejection of the notion that the soul was self-perpetuating—it must still be maintained that Calvin's continual reference to the body as a 'prison house' from which escape was welcome, reflects a failure to fully correct Plato's view of the body. Nevertheless, both Partee (291, 292) and David Steinmetz, 'Calvin as the Biblical Interpreter Among the Ancient Philosophers,' *Int* 63 (2009), 145, remind us that Calvin endured terrible physical suffering throughout his life. While we cannot approve of his repeated references to the human body as a 'prison house,' we can sympathize with his desire for relief from his many bodily ailments. See Partee, 'The Soul in Plato,' 291; Steinmetz, *Calvin in Context*, 237. Bruce Gordon *Calvin* (New Haven: Yale University Press, 2009), 144, also reminds us of Calvin's many health problems.

67 As the subject matter of the first section of this essay affirms what William Davis asserts in his essay, 'Calvin's Legacy in Philosophy' in David W. Hall and Marvin Padgett (eds), *Calvin and Culture: Exploring a Worldview* (Phillipsburg: P&R, 2010), 131n.53, Calvin should not be accused of 'passing along an uncritically platonic hatred of the physical body'. It is true that Calvin *did* value the human body and

Certainly, Calvin follows the biblical model as he groans for a change in our current fallen condition. Indeed, in light of Calvin's consistency with Scripture at this point, one might contend that I am making too fine a distinction—that Calvin was expressing a desire for departure from *this* body, not *the* body as such, or that he was simply using the phrase 'prison house of the body,' as a kind of theological shorthand to denote our fallen condition. Yet, assuming the validity of this objection, an important question remains: is this longing for deliverance from our fallen state best expressed by classifying the body as a prison, especially in light of countless passages in Scripture that ascribe to the body great honor and designate the body an object of final redemption?

On the whole, the New Testament rejects the idea that escape from the body is an appropriate desire. Second Corinthians 5.1-10, for example, demonstrates that the apostle Paul did not rejoice in the fact that he will be *without his body*, but in the reality that he would be *with the Lord* (2 Cor. 5.6-10).[68] An unembodied state was not ideal, however—Paul longed for the resurrection so that he could be reunited with his body.[69] Paul considered the intermediate state, although better than his current condition (Phil. 1.21), far from ultimate. The apostle recognized that we do groan in our current fallen state—our groaning, however, is not a longing for an eternal immaterial existence, but for an eternal embodied existence (see also Phil. 3.1-21). Accordingly, Paul did not set his desires on an escape from the body in and of itself—he longed for the resurrection of his body.[70]

There is no doubt that in Romans 7.24 Paul saw our fallen condition as a hindrance to sanctification—this is affirmed not only in the immediate context (Rom. 7.13-25),[71] but in other Pauline texts as well (e.g. Gal. 5.16-26). Even so,

---

did not imbibe the whole of Plato's teaching concerning the body as seen in Calvin's arguments for the resurrection and for the goodness of marriage and sex.

68 See Paul Barnett, *The Second Epistle to the Corinthians* (Grand Rapids: Eerdmans, 1997), 255-67, esp. 262-63; Murray J. Harris, *The Second Epistle to the Corinthians* (Grand Rapids: Eerdmans, 2005), 365-86.

69 Calvin often appealed to this passage. We have already seen where Calvin refers to 2 Corinthians 5.1-10 in the *Institutes*, and he maintains a similar viewpoint in his commentaries when he says that there is 'nothing better than to quit the body that we may attain near intercourse with God, and may truly and openly enjoy his presence' (*Comm. 2 Cor.* 5.8).

70 Calvin comes close to integrating his desire for release from his current fallen condition with the hope of the resurrection in his comments on Philippians 3.21 (see *Comm. Phil.* 3.21). In this passage, it appears to me that Calvin is more careful to tie the solution to our current troubles to the hope of the resurrection, not merely our departure from our bodies.

71 I take Paul's description of his battle with sin in Romans 7.14-25 to be a description of his current experience as a believer, not an account of a religious Jew or of Paul's experience prior to his conversion to Christ. See C.E.B. Cranfield, *Romans 1-8* (New York: T. & T. Clark, 1975). One's decision on how to interpret Romans 7.14-25 in this regard, however, does not affect the overall argument that Paul, in Romans 7.24,

the apostle does not advocate the mere sloughing off of the body in order to remedy his fallen condition and his struggle with sin.[72] Rather, he grounds his hope of deliverance in the redemption of his body. The apostle even links our current suffering and groaning to this final redemption (see Rom. 8.18-23). Paul, then, is not looking for escape from the 'prison house of his body', but for the redemption of his body through the resurrection. Although Calvin adequately and helpfully describes the resurrection as the ultimate Christian hope, he fails to fully synthesize his belief in the resurrection with his statements about the dignity of the human body and the reality of our fallen condition. Rather than appealing to the Platonic notion of a 'prison house' in order to articulate the tension Christians feel in their current fallen state and the longing for heaven, Calvin would have been better served to place the resolution of this tension more squarely in the resurrection *of* the body, rather than in an escape *from* the body as such.[73] Calvin's misstep, here, mars slightly what is otherwise a robust and edifying theology of the human body. Although this oversight is far from rendering Calvin's theology of the body useless, it could serve to perpetuate an unhealthy disjunction between the body and the soul already apparent in some corners of evangelicalism.[74] Calvin must be commended for his efforts in cor-

---

is not condoning the idea that the body in and of itself is the source of our sanctification troubles. Tom Schreiner, in his commentary on Romans, helpfully observes that our understanding of the word 'body' used here should 'not be abstracted from the whole person, with the result that it is separated from it'. See Calvin, *Comm. Rom.* 7.24. Thus, it is incorrect to lay blame on the body per se for one's sanctification troubles.

72 Calvin seems to imply this in *Inst.* 2.7.5 when he comments, 'I further say that there will be no one hereafter who will reach the goal of true perfection without sloughing off the weight of the body.'

73 Dennis E. Tamburello, *Union with Christ: John Calvin and the Mysticism of St. Bernard* (Louisville: John Knox, 1994), 14-16, insists that contra Plato, it was *sin* that Calvin hated, not the body as such. Certainly we can affirm Tamburello's contention that Calvin's theology allowed for a distinction between the physical body as such and the reality of indwelling sin. Nevertheless, Calvin's reliance on the phrase 'prison house,' and his repeated assertion that release from this prison was a welcome event is, in my judgment, an example of a lack of precision at this very point.

74 See, for example, Gregg Allison's trenchant comments in, 'Toward a Theology of Human Embodiment,' in *SBJT* 13.2 (2009), 4-17, and Roger E. Olson, *Westminster Handbook to Evangelical Theology* (Louisville: Westminster John Knox, 2004), 204, when he describes the tendency among lay people to misunderstand the Scripture to teach that humans are 'godlike spirits imprisoned in physical bodies'. See. James K.A. Smith, *The Fall of Interpretation: Philosophical Foundations for a Creational Hermeneutic* (Downers Grove: InterVarsity, 2000), 142-43, observes a kind of 'dominant dualism' in much of Evangelicalism and uses Calvin's employment of the Platonic notion of 'prison house' as an example of such dualism. For a similar observation in a more popular work, see John M. Koessler, *True Discipleship: The Art of Following Jesus* (Chicago: Moody, 2003), 88-89. Koessler does, however, note later

recting faulty philosophical and theological notions about the human body that were predominant during his time, but his example here also compels us to continue to reform our doctrine of the body according to Scripture and to weigh carefully our own presuppositions as we do so.

that Calvin and the other reformers were responsible for reclaiming a more biblical, holistic view toward physical life generally and the human body in particular (92-93).

CHAPTER 4

An Exotic Flower? Calvin and the patristic doctrine of deification

Carl Mosser

In his commentary on 2 Peter 1.4, John Calvin stated, 'Let us then observe that the end of the gospel is to render us eventually conformable to God, and, if we may so speak, to deify us.'[1] I have argued that here and elsewhere Calvin affirmed the broad patristic consensus about the ultimate goal of redemption which some of the early Greek Fathers referred to as *theopoiēsis* (θεοποίησις) and some of the Latin Fathers as *deificatio*.[2] Several scholars agree that a doctrine of deification can indeed be found in Calvin's writings.[3] But others consider the idea inherently improbable despite what appears to be an explicit affirmation of the notion. Whatever Calvin meant in this passage, they insist, surely he could not have meant the same thing as, say, Athanasius or Cyril of Alexandria. Deification is an Eastern Orthodox doctrine and any attempt to find it in Calvin's theology is a misguided 'quest for an exotic flower'.[4]

Various more specific objections have been registered against the claim that Calvin affirmed the patristic doctrine of deification. They can be woven togeth-

---

1 *Comm 2 Peter* 1.4 (*CO* 55.446); John Calvin, *Commentaries on the Catholic Epistles* (translated by John Owen; Grand Rapids: Eerdmans, 1948), 371 [updated].

2 Carl Mosser, 'The Greatest Possible Blessing: Calvin and Deification,' *SJT* 55.1 (2002), 36-57. That essay occasionally used *theōsis* (θέωσις) as synonymous with *theopoiēsis* and deification. I am now convinced a distinction should be drawn between *theopoiēsis* and the later Byzantine doctrine of *theōsis*. The latter is a mystical, ascetical development of the patristic deification tradition.

3 J. Todd Billings, 'United to God through Christ: Assessing Calvin on the Question of Deification,' *HTR* 98.3 (2005), 315-34; idem, *Calvin, Participation, and the Gift: The Activity of Believers in Union with Christ* (New York: OUP, 2007); Julie Canlis, 'Calvin, Osiander and Participation in God,' *IJST* 6.2 (2004), 169-84; idem, *Calvin's Ladder: A Spiritual Theology of Ascent and Ascension* (Grand Rapids: Eerdmans, 2010); Myk Habets, '*Theosis*, Yes; Deification, No,' in Myk Habets (ed.), *The Spirit of Truth* (Eugene: Pickwick, 2010), 129-45; A.J. Ollerton, '*Quasi Deificari*: Deification in the Theology of John Calvin,' *WTJ* 73 (2011), 237-54.

4 The late David F. Wright reportedly gave this characterization during a Q&A session at the 2003 Rutherford House Conference in response to a question about 'The Greatest Possible Blessing'.

er to form a succinct critique that has considerable *prima facie* plausibility but which, I will argue, is built on faulty historical premises. It goes like this.

Those who claim Calvin affirmed deification have put an unpersuasive 'Eastern spin' onto Calvin's theology.[5] Their attempt to 'follow the Finnish misunderstanding of Luther into Calvin studies'[6] is questionably motivated by ecumenical interests, a desire to move away from 'cold' forensic understandings of justification,[7] or 'theosis-envy'.[8] It should be remembered that deification, originally a Greek idea, was baptized and embraced by the Eastern Fathers but never really took hold in the West. Though occasionally found among the mystics, the theme 'has often been overwhelmed in the West by an Augustinian emphasis on human sinfulness. For Augustine, Luther, Calvin, and others, human nature is so utterly corrupted that it can do nothing on its own but contribute to its own downfall.'[9] Thus, it 'was left to more radical strands within Protestantism to revive the theme of divinization'.[10] Moreover, Calvin's Christology and his doctrine of union with Christ preclude deification. His 'view of union with Christ is mystical union but not mystical experience'.[11] The redeemed are united to Christ only in his human nature and Calvin's understanding of the *communicatio idiomatum* prevents any transfer of properties from the divine to the human nature, much less to the redeemed.[12] Moreover, as François Wendel observed long ago, Calvin had a 'fear of anything that might have led to the admission of any deification of man, even by way of Jesus Christ and even in His person'.[13] Roland Bainton explains why: 'to Calvin the very notion of the deification of man was blasphemous'.[14] Calvin's polemic against Osiander

5 Hans Boersma, *Heavenly Participation* (Grand Rapids: Eerdmans, 2011), 94.

6 Mark A. Garcia, 'Imputation and the Christology of Union with Christ: Calvin, Osiander, and the Contemporary Quest for a Reformed Model,' *WTJ* 68.2 (2006), 239 n.55.

7 R. Scott Clark, '*Iustitia Imputata Christi*: Alien or Proper to Luther's Doctrine of Justification?' *CTQ* 70.3/4 (2006), 272 n.8.

8 This phrase was coined online by Orthodox philosopher Perry Robinson.

9 Linda Woodhead, 'Apophatic Anthropology' in R. Kendall Soulen and Linda Woodhead (eds), *God and Human Dignity* (Grand Rapids: Eerdmans, 2006), 237.

10 Woodhead, 'Apophatic Anthropology,' 237.

11 Charles Partee, *The Theology of John Calvin* (Louisville: Westminster John Knox, 2008), 169.

12 Jonathan Slater, 'Salvation as Participation in the Humanity of the Mediator in Calvin's *Institutes of the Christian Religion*: A Reply to Carl Mosser,' *SJT* 58.1 (2005), 39-58; Bruce L. McCormack, 'Union with Christ in Calvin's Theology: Grounds for a Divinization Theory?' in David W. Hall (ed.), *Tributes to John Calvin* (Phillipsburg: P&R, 2010), 504-29.

13 François Wendel, *Calvin: Origins and Development of his Religious Thought* (translated by Philip Mairet; Grand Rapids: Baker, 1997), 259; cf. 224, 235.

14 Roland H. Bainton, *The Reformation of the Sixteenth Century* (revised; Boston: Beacon, 1985), 125.

shows that he was 'utterly opposed to any form of deification'.[15] His forceful rebuttal of Servetus and role in that man's condemnation illustrate the depth of Calvin's opposition. As C.A. Patrides observes, the doctrine of deification's 'infrequent appearance in the West never managed to overcome the opposition of St. Augustine, and it was in time stamped to death by Calvin'.[16] Or so we are told.

For this essay the questions of whether deification can be found in Calvin's theology and, if so, whether it is consistent with other aspects of his theology will be set aside. Instead, my goal is to show that there is nothing historically unlikely about the thesis that deification was a component of Calvin's soteriology. Toward this end I will argue for the following contentions:

- Grand historical narratives that depict deification as a distinctively Eastern doctrine alien to the Western tradition are mistaken. There are no good historical reasons to assume deification would be an unlikely or exotic element in the theology of any Western theologian, including Calvin.
- Calvin's polemics against heterodox contemporaries in no way suggest that he would have opposed all forms of deification.
- Calvin was directly acquainted with the patristic doctrine of deification and did not consider it blasphemous.

My arguments should demonstrate that there is nothing farfetched about the possibility of 'Calvin's doctrine of deification'. Critics who dismiss the claim as a theological innovation thinly disguised as historical theology are invited to bracket out their own opinion of the doctrine's merits and reassess the historical question of whether Calvin affirmed it.

Neither absent from the West nor distinctively Eastern

The perceived *a priori* unlikeliness of deification in Calvin's theology is rooted in the commonplace that deification is an Eastern doctrine largely absent from and incompatible with the Western theological tradition. This commonplace was formulated by Ritschilian liberal Protestants to legitimate rejection of Trinitarian and Christological dogma. They depicted deification as proof of the Eastern churches' capitulation to Hellenism. Orthodox theologians who emigrated in the wake of the Russian Revolution subversively appropriated this commonplace, but for them the alleged absence of deification proves the Western churches' apostasy. For generations this commonplace has habituated scholars to see deification as a distinctively Eastern doctrine alien to the West. However, the historical narratives undergirding it are fatally flawed. Deification

---

15 Marijn de Kroon, *The Honour of God and Human Salvation* (translated by John Vriend and Lyle D. Bierma; Edinburgh: T & T Clark, 2001), 20.

16 C.A. Patrides, *The Cambridge Platonists* (Cambridge: CUP, 1980), 19.

is an ecumenical doctrine common to the East and West, as much the heritage of Catholics and Protestants as it is of the Orthodox.

Deification in rival accounts of the gospel's loss

Sixteenth-century anti-trinitarians claimed that the doctrine of the Trinity arose out of Greek philosophy and was foreign to both scripture and the early Church Fathers. Nineteenth-century liberal Protestants extended the argument in their 'scientific' histories of dogma. This literary tradition reached its climax with the publication of Adolf von Harnack's impressive *Lehrbuch der Dogmengeschichte*. A few years later Harnack popularized a Ritschilian modification to the argument in which deification is identified as the starting point of Christianity's Hellenization.[17]

Harnack's examination of primary sources did not support the claim that the Trinity was straightforwardly derived from Greek philosophy. Instead, he observed that debates which culminated in the formulation of Trinitarian and Christological orthodoxy were motivated by concern to preserve a particular soteriological vision, salvation as deification. Here it was easy to assert indebtedness to Greek philosophy because patristic writers frequently endorse Plato's statement that the goal for human beings is to 'become like God, so far as this is possible'.[18] The decisive moment in Christianity's abandonment of Jesus' message, then, was not Nicea. It took place in the second century when patristic writers imported the Hellenistic notion of deification into Christianity.

For example, Harnack notes that Irenaeus employed a variety of soteriological categories: humanity's restoration to the likeness of God, abolition of death, union of man with God, adoption as sons of God and 'gods,' impartation of a knowledge of God that culminates in beholding him, and bestowal of everlasting life. All these, he observes, are different aspects of the same blessing, which, 'being of a divine order, could only be brought to us and implanted in our nature by God himself'.[19] Thus, Christ's most important salvific work was not the works of his historical life but 'is contained in his constitution as the God-man'.[20] When patristic writers represented the Christian religion 'as the belief in the incarnation of God and as the sure hope of the deification of humanity, a speculation that had originally never got beyond the fringe of religious knowledge was made the central point of the system and the simple content of the Gospel was obscured'.[21] Harnack defines patristic deification as follows:

---

[17] Adolf von Harnack, *What is Christianity?* (translated by Thomas Bailey Saunders; Philadelphia: Fortress, 1986 [1900]).

[18] Plato, *Theaetetus* 176b.

[19] Adolf von Harnack, *History of Dogma* (ET. London: Williams & Norgate, 1894-99), 2.292.

[20] Harnack, *History*, 2.293.

[21] Harnack, *History*, 2.318.

> the highest blessing bestowed in Christianity is adoption into the divine sonship, which assured to the believer, and is completed in participation in the divine nature, or more accurately, in the deification of man through the gift of immortality. This gift includes the perfect knowledge and the lasting vision of God, in a blessedness devoid of suffering, but it does not do away with the interval between Christ and the believer.[22]

Harnack believed Trinitarian and Christological dogmas arose as a kind of logical implication from the soteriology of deification.[23] Once the incarnation and Trinity were firmly established, the simple gospel of Jesus was lost. Dogmatic Christianity would continue to obscure Jesus' message until it was unshackled by the insights of the Reformation and subsequent 'scientific' history of dogma.

Harnack caricatured deification as a subchristian 'pharmacological process' driven by 'the egoistic desire for immortal existence'.[24] It was an illicit aspiration for a higher form of life that leads to indifference toward daily life here and now.[25] As a result of adopting deification and its derivative dogmas, Christianity in the East degenerated into a rigid doctrinal system characterized by traditionalism, intellectualism and superstitious ritualism.[26] More pointedly, Eastern Orthodoxy represents a 'relapse into the ancient form of the lowest class of religion' and 'has absolutely nothing to do with the religion of Christ'.[27] In many respects it may 'be more appropriately regarded as part of the history of Greek religion than of the history of the Gospel'.[28] Harnack does not mince words: 'It was to destroy this sort of religion that Jesus Christ suffered himself to be nailed to the cross, and now we find it re-established under his name and authority!'[29]

In Harnack's view Roman Catholicism fared better up to the fourteenth century.[30] Primary credit goes to Augustine whose theology and religious fervor 'denote a special resuscitation of the Pauline experience and doctrine of sin and grace, of guilt and justification'.[31] Harnack concedes that deification is found in early Western writers, especially Augustine. 'But,' he goes on, 'if I am not deceived Augustine himself brought it to an edifying end.'[32] In subsequent centuries Augustinianism's 'sense and doctrine of sin and grace' stood in tension with the 'Church of rites, of law, of politics, of world-dominion'.[33] As the

---

22 Harnack, *History*, 3.164.
23 Harnack, *What is Christianity?* 234.
24 Harnack, *What is Christianity?* 232, 235, 236.
25 Harnack, *What is Christianity?* 193, cf. Harnack, *History*, 2.317.
26 Harnack, *What is Christianity?* 223-25, 228-29, 237-41.
27 Harnack, *What is Christianity?* 239, 241.
28 Harnack, *What is Christianity?* 263.
29 Harnack, *What is Christianity?* 238.
30 Harnack, *What is Christianity?* 247.
31 Harnack, *What is Christianity?* 258, cf. 257-62.
32 Harnack, *History*, 3.165.
33 Harnack, *What is Christianity?* 260-61.

Church became more entangled with the State during the fourteenth century, Augustinian religious fervor was subdued. Various individuals kept the Augustinian flame alive. Even so, the Roman Church began to catch up to the Greek.

Luther did much to restore the gospel by championing justification by faith alone. However, Luther 'had no means of distinguishing between kernel and husk, between what was original and what was of alien growth'.[34] Trustworthy knowledge of the history of dogma simply was not possible in the sixteenth century, so he understandably 'took the old dogmas of the Trinity and the two natures as part of the Gospel'.[35] However, it remains the case that these dogmas 'stand and fall' with salvation understood as deification.[36] Thus, Luther's insistence on justification by faith alone displaced their theological *raison d'être*. Recovery of the gospel begins with the experience and doctrine of justification by faith; it is completed in the repudiation of Christological and Trinitarian dogma.

When the Russian Revolution broke out in 1917, Harnack was the world's most celebrated historian of doctrine. Theologians who emigrated to the West found themselves confronted by his influential portrayal of Eastern Orthodoxy. In the 1930s and 40s Émigré theologians subversively appropriated Harnack's identification of deification as the hallmark of Orthodox theology. Combined with Theodore de Régnon's distinction between patristic and scholastic theological paradigms, they created a rhetorically powerful polemic against the entire Western tradition. De Régnon's distinction was meant to be chronological but it was taken up as a contrast between fundamentally incompatible Greek and Latin ways of doing theology.[37] The basic idea is that Latin theology after Augustine became a rationalistic, philosophical system with a deficient Trinitarianism that reduced soteriology to juridical categories and legal transactions. As a result, the gospel was fatally compromised. Orthodoxy, in contrast, upheld the gospel by preserving the patristic inheritance unchanged despite persistent attempts by the West to impose its theology, ecclesiology and way of life on the East.

In this narrative deification proves Orthodoxy's fidelity to the gospel and the genius of its distinctive theology. However, what is elevated is not the simple notion of *theopoiēsis* found in the early Fathers but the developed Byzantine doctrine of *theōsis* as articulated by Gregory Palamas during the fourteenth-century Hesychast controversy. This controversy is depicted as the archetypal struggle between Western scholasticism (represented by Barlaam) and the apophatic, mystical theology of the East (represented by Palamas). The particular way Palamas distinguished between the divine essence and energies to de-

---

[34] Harnack, *What is Christianity?* 290.

[35] Harnack, *What is Christianity?* 291.

[36] Harnack, *What is Christianity?* 234.

[37] See, further, Michel René Barnes, 'De Régnon Reconsidered,' *Augustinian Studies* 26.2 (1995), 51-79.

fend Hesychastic practices became the theological boundary between East and West, a *sine qua non* for true theology. Failure to properly distinguish the divine essence and energies along Palamite lines is evidence of deficient Christology and Trinitarianism.[38]

An ecumenical doctrine

Scholars influenced by the Ritschilian or Émigré narratives will be instinctively skeptical about the possibility of deification in the theology of Calvin or any other prominent Western theologian. But those narratives are contradicted by the facts. Deification is widely attested in both the patristic and medieval West.

Norman Russell's important study of the Greek Fathers includes an appendix surveying the Syriac and Latin traditions up through Augustine. It begins by matter-of-factly stating:

> The Christian understanding of deification was not confined to the Greek-speaking provinces of the Roman empire. Its fundamental tent, the Irenaean principle that the Son of God became as we are that we might become as he is, came to be more widely diffused.[39]

Deification is well attested in patristic writers who lived in both halves of the Roman Empire and, in a few cases, beyond its borders. Deification themes appear in second-century writings by Justin Martyr and Hippolytus, both working in Rome. They are found in Theophilus of Antioch and Tatian after returning to his native Mesopotamia. Irenaeus is widely credited with the first real exposition of the doctrine in *Adversus Haereses*. He spent most of his life as a priest and bishop in Lyons, 1500 miles to the west of Byzantium. The earliest developments of the doctrine are found in Clement, Origen, Athanasius and Cyril of Alexandria. Athanasius wrote some of his most important works touching on the subject during ten years exiled in Trier and Rome. The doctrine is a significant element in the theology of Ephrem the Syrian and attested in writers associated with the later Churches of the East.[40] Latin Fathers in which deification can be found include Tertullian, John Cassian, Hilary of Poitiers, Leo the Great

---

38 For critical exposition of this narrative, see Jeffrey D. Finch, 'Neo-Palamism, Divinizing Grace, and the Breach between East and West' in Michael J. Christensen and Jeffery A. Wittung (eds), *Partakers of the Divine Nature: The History and Development of Deification in the Christian Traditions* (Grand Rapids: Baker Academic, 2008), 233-49; Michael Gibson, 'Either/Or: The Question of Identity and Eastern Orthodoxy in the Thought of Christos Yannaras' (online: http://www.academia.edu/946991/) [accessed 1/11/2013].

39 Norman Russell, *The Doctrine of Deification in the Greek Patristic Tradition* (Oxford: OUP, 2004), 321.

40 Russell, *Doctrine*, 321-25.

and Ambrose of Milan.[41] On neither geographical nor linguistic grounds can deification be described as a distinctively Eastern or Greek concept. It was an ecumenical doctrine of the entire church.

Contrary to impressions created by some Protestant and Orthodox theologians, Augustine explicitly mentions deification with some frequency, elaborates on its significance and never repudiates it. Specialists make observations like the following. Deification occurs 'not as something added to his system as an afterthought, but as an integral part of the whole'.[42] For Augustine 'the deification of human beings is the purpose for which the Word became incarnate and is appropriated by them through baptism'.[43] He 'understands humanity's deification to be the primary purpose of Christian salvation'.[44] In concert with the Greek Fathers, the essence of Augustine's doctrine of deification can be summarized as 'man's participation in God through the humanity of Christ without any change in man's creaturely status'.[45] Contrary to portraits of mutual exclusivity, for Augustine deification and justification are not alternative soteriologies but linked corollaries: 'For He justifies, who is just Himself and not of another. Now He who justifies, Himself deifies, because by justifying He makes sons of God.'[46]

After Augustine deification continues to be attested in the Latin West, and not simply among fringe figures.[47] Scholars have identified it in the writings of

---

41 G. Bardy, 'Divinisation [III Chez les pères latins]' in M. Viller, F. Cavallera, J. De Guibert (eds), *Dictionnaire de spiritualité* (Paris: Beauchesne, 1935-95), 3.1390-98; Russell, *Doctrine*, 325-29.

42 Gerald Bonner, 'Deificare' in Cornelius Mayer (ed.), *Augustinus-Lexikon* (Basel: Schwabe, 1996), 2.265; cf. Bonner, 'Deification, Divinization' in Allan D. Fitzgerald (ed.), *Augustine Through the Ages: An Encyclopedia* (Grand Rapids: Eerdmans, 1999), 265-66.

43 Russell, *Doctrine*, 331.

44 David Vincent Meconi, *The One Christ: St. Augustine's Theology of Deification* (Washington: Catholic University of America Press, 2013), 234.

45 Bonner, 'Deificare,' 2.266. For exposition of the relevant texts, see Gerald Bonner, 'Augustine's Conception of Deification,' *JTS* 37.2 (1986), 369-86; Augustine Casiday, 'St Augustine on deification: his homily on Psalm 81,' *Sobornost* 23.2 (2001), 23-44; Mary Marrocco, 'Participation in Divine Life in the *De Trinitate* of St. Augustine,' *Augustinianum* 42.1 (2002), 149-85; Meconi, *The One Christ*, 79-174.

46 *Enar. in Ps. 49. 1.2*, as translated in Bonner, 'Augustine's Conception', 384. For the context see NPNF[1] 8.178.

47 Surveys include A. Speer, 'Vergöttlichung' in *Lexikon des Mittelalters* (Stuttgart: Metzler, [1977]-1999), 8.1531-32 in *Brepolis Medieval Encyclopaedias - Lexikon des Mittelalters Online*; A. Fracheboud, H-T. Conus, and R-L. Oechslin, 'Divinisation [IV Moyen âge]' in *Dictionnaire de spiritualité*, 3.1399-1445; Giles Constable, *Three Studies in Medieval Religious and Social Thought* (Cambridge: CUP, 1995), 145-68; Steven Botterill, *Dante and the Mystical Tradition: Bernard of Clairvaux in the 'Commedia'* (Cambridge: CUP, 1994), 203-221; Franz Posset, '"Deification" in the German Spirituality of the Late Middle Ages and in Luther: An Ecumenical Historical Perspective,' *ARG* 84 (1993), 103-26.

Boethius, John Scotus Erigena, Richard of St. Victor, Bernard of Clairvaux, Albertus Magnus, Bonaventure, Aquinas and Nicholas of Cusa. Medieval Latin theologians took for granted the basic Irenaean exchange formula at the heart of the Christian doctrine of deification. Some Latins had a more elaborate theology reflecting Byzantine influence. There is nothing surprising about this. Irenaeus' *Adversus Haereses* was disseminated whole in Latin translation; only scraps of the Greek text are extant, suggesting it was valued more in the medieval West than East. Direct acquaintance with early Byzantine formulations of *theōsis* could be had through Erigena's ninth-century translations of Ps. Dionysius and Maximus Confessor. Furthermore, by the mid-twelfth century several Latin translations of John of Damascus' *Exposition of the Orthodox Faith* were in circulation. While sustained reflection on the doctrine is rare (Erigena's *Periphyseon* excepted), Mary Marrocco is correct when she states, 'The history of Western theology does in fact involve deification, both explicitly and implicitly, much more than is commonly realized or studied.'[48]

Influential historical narratives use the alleged absence of deification in the West to measure fidelity to the gospel and define Eastern and Western theological approaches against one another. It comes as no surprise that discussion of deification in the theology of someone like Calvin is met with incredulity. It is also easy to understand why some Protestants and Orthodox faithful feel obligated to contest such claims. If the patristic doctrine of deification is found in the Western tradition after Augustine, then the boundary-marking claims derived from these narratives are undermined. Be that as it may, Daniel Keating is correct when he says 'the doctrine of deification is not the patrimony of the Eastern church alone, or an eccentricity of certain schools of Western theology. Rather, deification concerns the basic economy of God in Christ through the Spirit that is at the patristic root of both the Eastern and Western theological traditions.'[49] There simply is no historical reason why it could not have been known to and embraced by Calvin or any other Western theologian of his era.

An emerging doctrinal locus

Another point at which the Ritschilian and Émigré narratives falter is the prominence they assign to deification in the Eastern tradition. There are no patristic treatises devoted to deification like there are for Christology, pneumatology, Trinity, scriptural interpretation, wealth and poverty, asceticism, etc. Even Maximus Confessor, who elaborates on deification more frequently than any other late patristic or early Byzantine writer, does not really treat it as a doctrinal locus in its own right. Rather, deification is typically mentioned while elaborating on other doctrines, biblical texts, or spiritual disciplines. There were no debates such that deification was formalized as a discrete doctrinal locus. The

---

48 Marrocco, 'Participation in Divine Life,' 150.

49 Daniel A. Keating, *Deification and Grace* (Naples, Flor: Sapientia, 2007), 5-6.

closest that ever came to happening was the Hesychast controversy in the fourteenth century.

At most points of history deification has been no more prominent in the East than in the West. Consider the way Norman Russell characterizes the situation on the eve of the Hesychast controversy:

> Theosis did not mean much to most Byzantines in the early fourteenth century. Some writers referred to in passing. Anyone who was at all familiar with the Orations of Gregory of Nazianzus, or had dipped into the erudite discussions of Maximus the Confessor, could not have failed to have come across the term. But it was not widely used in later Byzantine writers. In patristic literature where theosis, or deification, was mentioned it was usually a metaphor for baptismal adoption by grace, or for the final consummation of the resurrected life.[50]

The Hesychast controversy certainly focused attention on deification in a new way, but that did not result in it becoming permanently prominent in Orthodox theology. Hilarion Alfeyev reports that Hesychasm was actually considered heresy by the Orthodox in Russia until the late nineteenth century and 'Palamism' continues to be little studied there.[51] According to Russell, at least as late as the 1950s, 'if you had asked the average Orthodox Christian . . . what theosis meant, you would probably have been met with a puzzled look'. More significantly, 'The word hardly featured in the standard theological handbooks. It was a technical term familiar only to monks and patristic scholars.'[52] Only in recent decades has the term become a common way to summarize the whole economy of salvation.

The situation is similar in the Western tradition. Patristic scholars, some theologians, and a few others have always been aware of deification. Recent decades have seen it discussed in Catholic and Protestant theology written for popular consumption. This is not the result of 'theosis-envy' tempting Western Christians to appropriate something alien to their own tradition. Rather, we are observing the retrieval, formalization and popularization of an ancient ecumenical theme to which all three branches of the Great Tradition can lay claim. The Orthodox have a few decades head start and possess a few more post-patristic formulations to work with, but the same process is taking place in all three communions. No longer does deification appear only in monastic or academic discussions or in passing during the exposition of other doctrinal loci, it is becoming a doctrinal locus in its own right.

---

50 Norman Russell, 'Theosis and Gregory Palamas: Continuity or Doctrinal Change?' *SVTQ* 50.4 (2006), 357.

51 Hilarion Alfeyev, 'The Patristic Heritage and Modernity,' *Ecumenical Review* 54.1 (2002), 108.

52 Norman Russell, *Fellow Workers with God: Orthodox Thinking on Theosis* (Crestwood: St Vladimir's Seminary Press, 2009), 13.

A note about terminology

Some scholars give the impression that they are willing to admit the presence of deification in a Western writer like Calvin if it can be demonstrated that he employs technical vocabulary frequently enough to establish that it was not used in a metaphorical sense. But such a standard conflates word and concept and reflects lack of first-hand familiarity with the patristic deification tradition.

Nearly all scholars who write on the subject identify Irenaeus as the first Christian to formulate a doctrine of deification. But Irenaeus nowhere uses technical terminology. He instead employs various forms of the exchange formula and speaks about adoption to divine sonship, being made 'gods', etc.[53] Christian writers, beginning with Clement of Alexandria, employ various 'technical' terms.[54] But they were never necessary to articulate developed versions of the concept. Cyril of Alexandria occasionally used *theopoiēsis* in his earliest works and then abandoned it because it was too easily misunderstood (especially after the outbreak of the Nestorian controversy). Nonetheless, a robust doctrine of deification permeates his later writings. Even without technical terminology Cyril and others could articulate deification by means of the Irenaean exchange formula and notions such as sharing divine life, participation in God, partaking of the divine nature (cf. 2 Pet. 1.4), being made immortal and incorruptible, and union with God. Just as Irenaeus and Cyril could write about deification in Greek without recourse to technical vocabulary, similarly 'It was perfectly possible to write about deification in Latin without exploiting the technical language represented by the group of words etymologically related to the basic verb *deificari*.'[55] The fact that Calvin only once uses this language to describe the gospel's end does not somehow make it unlikely that he really meant to affirm the broad patristic vision of salvation.

Calvin's polemics

Assertions that Calvin opposed *all* forms of deification as blasphemous can readily be found in older works by well-regarded scholars such as François Wendel, Wilhelm Niesel and Roland Bainton. Critics sometimes dismiss 'Calvin's doctrine of deification' by quoting these assertions. However, none of these scholars paraphrase anything Calvin himself said to this effect. Nor do they address the patristic doctrine. Their assertions are unwarranted inference drawn from (1) Calvin's disagreement with the Lutheran doctrine of the ubiquity,[56] (2) Calvin's polemics against Osiander,[57] (3) Calvin's opposition to the

---

[53] See further Carl Mosser, 'The Earliest Patristic Interpretations of Psalm 82, Jewish Antecedents, and the Origin of Christian Deification,' *JTS* 56.1 (2005), 41-54; Russell, *Doctrine*, 105-110.

[54] The terminology is helpfully surveyed in Russell, *Doctrine of Deification*, 333-44.

[55] Botterill, *Dante and the Mystical Tradition*, 203.

[56] Wendel, *Calvin*, 224.

teachings of Servetus,[58] and (4) a desire to differentiate Calvin's understanding of union with Christ from certain strands of medieval mysticism in which the human soul is thought to be absorbed into God.[59]

The heterodox divinizing notions Calvin attributes to Osiander, Servetus, the Libertines, 'certain fanatics' and others simply are not the same thing as *theopoiēsis* or *theōsis*. Nor is mystical absorption of the soul into God. Against the Lutheran doctrine of ubiquity, Calvin insists Christ's humanity did not cease to be corporeal and his flesh did not become omnipresent. But it does not follow that he would object to orthodox patristic teaching about Christ's 'deified' humanity.[60] To the contrary, he ascribes to Christ's exalted flesh the same properties patristic writers do when they say it was 'deified': holiness, glory, incorruption, immortality and life-giving power.[61] They, in turn, affirm the spatially circumscribed character of Christ's human nature—the mislabeled *extra Calvinisticum*.[62] Thus, the inference that Calvin rejected all forms of deification is a *non sequitur*.

Some recent critics assert Calvin's opposition to deification with patristic and Eastern Orthodox theology squarely in view. At least they *think* that is what they have in their sights. Charles Partee correctly defines deification (its core idea at least) as 'the believer's reception by grace of what the Christ is by nature,' yet associates it with 'participation in the divine essence' and mystical absorption into God's nature.[63] Andrew McGowan defines it as the 'doctrine that, in salvation, human beings are absorbed into the being of God' and claims this 'has long been the teaching of the Eastern Orthodox churches'.[64] Jason Van Vliet, referring to the teachings of the Fathers, states:

> Geneva's reformer decisively disagrees, though, with the notion of *theosis*. *Theosis*, or deification, was a somewhat tangential, yet tenacious, teaching that the restoration of the *imago Dei* would eventually allow human beings to participate in

---

57 Wendel, *Calvin*, 259.

58 Bainton, *The Reformation of the Sixteenth Century*, 125; idem, *Hunted Heretic: The Life and Death of Michael Servetus 1511-1553* (Boston: Beacon, 1960), 195-96.

59 Wilhelm Niesel, *Reformed Symbolics* (translated by D. Lewis; Edinburgh: Oliver & Boyd, 1962), 184-85; Wendel, *Calvin*, 235.

60 For discussion of key patristic texts, see George Dion Dragas, 'Exchange or Communication of Properties and Deification: *Antidosis* or *Communicatio Idiomatum* and *Theosis*,' *GOTR* 43.1-4 (1998), 377-99; Richard Cross, 'Perichoresis, Deification and Christological Predication and John of Damascus,' *Mediaeval Studies* 62 (2000), 69-124.

61 E.g., *Comm Matt* 3.13; *Comm John* 6.51; *Comm 1 Cor.* 15.47; *Comm Heb* 2.11, 5.7, 8.2; *Inst.* 4.17.8; 4.17.9; 4.17.24.

62 Cf. E. David Willis, *Calvin's Catholic Christology* (Leiden: Brill, 1966), 44-60.

63 Partee, *Theology*, 168, 172, 175.

64 Andrew McGowan, 'Colossians 3: Deification, *Theosis*, Participation, or Union with Christ?' in R. Michael Allen (ed.), *Theological Commentary: Evangelical Perspectives* (London: T & T Clark, 2011), 163.

the very essence and substance of God himself. Here is where Calvin drew a sharp line in the sand.[65]

Van Vliet repeatedly uses the term *theōsis* in reference to teachings of Osiander and Servetus, creating a false identification between their positions and the Fathers'. Elsewhere, he associates *theōsis* with the fusion of humanity and divinity, Manichaeism, and becoming 'part of God's eternal essence,' 'clones of God,' and 'divine beings'.[66]

These notions may apply to ancient ruler cults, hermeticism, theurgy, extreme forms of mysticism, the occult and certain new religious movements. However, the literature on Christian deification repeatedly emphasizes that those who are deified are deified in a manner appropriate to their creaturely status. They will ever remain human beings with distinct identities; they do not become deities or equal with God. It also highlights the essence/energies distinction which utterly precludes *theōsis* from being understood as participation in God's essence. Such egregious mischaracterization of Christian deification betrays insufficient familiarity with the relevant patristic and secondary literature.

Calvin's theology does indeed stand foursquare against any suggestion that human beings can participate in the divine essence, be absorbed into God's being, or become clones of God. He has no tolerance for any teaching that would obliterate the created human nature of Christ or those he redeems. Nobody suggests otherwise. Mainstream patristic and Eastern Orthodox theology is similarly opposed. The fact that Calvin argued against heretical divinizing notions does not make it probable that he would have opposed patristic and other mainstream doctrines of deification too. He had ample opportunity to do so but never did.

Calvin's response to mainstream expressions of deification

Deification is native to the Western tradition, widely attested in patristic and medieval sources. Any well-read theologian of the sixteenth century could have come across it. Calvin's responses to heterodox divinizing notions of his contemporaries and the ancient Manichaeans are well-known. We cannot, however, validly infer from them that he would have opposed the patristic doctrine as well. Nor can we assume he was unopposed simply because deification occurs in writers he especially valued (e.g. Augustine). Instead, we need to gauge his

---

65 Jason Van Vliet, *Children of God: The* Imago Dei *in John Calvin and his Context* (Göttingen: Vandenhoeck & Ruprecht, 2009), 127.

66 Van Vliet, *Children of God*, 91, 233, 249, 251, 254, 268, 269. Van Vliet also mentions *theōsis* in ways designed to distance Calvin's thought from it on pages 58-60, 62, 98, 116, 147, 159, 165, 235, 245-46, 248, 254, 255. Though nowhere cited, Van Vliet seems aware of my article and/or Billings' and seems concerned to undermine our claim.

reactions to orthodox conceptions of deification. In at least three cases we can do that.

Martin Bucer

For Martin Bucer, redemption was not restricted to atonement, reconciliation, or even the restoration of all things to their creational glory. We are, instead, restored to a more elevated and glorious position.[67] In his commentary on John, Bucer refers to this as the deification of the elect (*deificationem electorum*) through the incarnation of the Logos.[68] Lest there be doubt about his meaning, he also, somewhat surprisingly, employs the Greek term *apotheōsis* (ἀποθέωσις) as a synonym.[69]

According to Wendel, it is possible to pick up traces of Calvin's attentive reading of the second edition (1530) of Bucer's commentary in the 1536 *Institutes*.[70] Traces of the third edition (1536) 'reappear very plainly in the 1539 and 1541 editions of the *Institutes*'.[71] Did Calvin read this passage in particular? It occurs early in the work when Bucer discusses John 1.14, a key text in Trinitarian and Christological disputes. Furthermore, Calvin regarded Bucer as the foremost contemporary interpreter of Scripture and found his commentaries especially valuable.[72] So it is likely he read this passage while preparing edi-

---

67 Willem van't Spijker, *The Ecclesiastical Offices in the Thought of Martin Bucer* (translated by John Vriend and Lyle D. Bierma; Leiden: Brill, 1996), 39-40.

68 Irena Backus (ed.), *Martini Buceri Opera Latina vol. 2 Enarratio In Evangelion Iohannis (1528, 1530, 1536)* (Leiden: Brill, 1988), 44. The passage reads: Voluit nanque Pater ex hominibus deos facere [cf. Io 10,34], sed id per hominem qui Deus iam esset; ideo *Verbum* eius Deum *hominem fieri* [Io 1,14] oportuit. Cum iam arcanae literae ἀποθέωσιν, id est deificationem electorum ubique vel promittant vel doceant et illa nullis nisi per Verbum incarnatum contingat, nihil omnino in Scripturis legitur quod non suo modo ad Verbum respiciat, *finem* et perfectionem *Legis* [Rm 10,4]. Hoc siquidem autore et Mediatore divinitatis omnia ad nos perveniunt et perficiuntur [cf. Col 1,17]. Huius ergo admonere nos et in spem sortis divinae, penitus olim consequendae, erigere debet quod *Verbum caro factum est* [Io 1,14] quod in hoc ipsum assidue sane recogitandum pieque expendendum nobis fuerit.

69 This term is typically used in reference to pagan notions, but there is some precedent among the Fathers to use it in the context of Christian theology. See Russell, *Doctrine*, 337.

70 Wendel, *Calvin*, 139.

71 Wendel, *Calvin*, 140.

72 E.g., in October 1539 Calvin wrote: 'In addition to [Bucer's] profound learning, abundant knowledge, keenness of intellect, wide reading, and many other excellences in which he is surpassed by hardly anyone at the present day, this scholar, as we know, is equaled by few and is superior to very many. It is to his especial credit that no one in our time has been more precise or diligent in interpreting scripture than he'—John Calvin, *The Epistles of Paul the Apostle to the Romans and to the Thessalonians* (Grand Rapids: Eerdmans, 1960), 2.

tions of the *Institutes*, but if not then, then certainly while preparing his own commentary on John (Calvin explicitly cites Bucer on John 1.33).

Calvin does not comment on Bucer's affirmation of deification. We cannot read agreement into Calvin's silence.[73] However, his silence counts against the claim that Calvin opposed all forms of deification as blasphemous. If he held that view, then we could fairly expect evidence of dispute or censure in the record.

Cardinal Sadoleto

Calvin and Farel were banished from Geneva in April 1538. In March 1539 Cardinal Sadoleto wrote a letter to the citizens and council of Geneva hoping to win them back to Rome. Shortly thereafter Calvin was asked to write a response, which he did over the course of six days. Attempting to build on common ground with the Genevans, Sadoleto prefaces his main discussion with an oration on the nature and importance of salvation. He concludes by summarizing the doctrine of salvation with the Irenaean exchange formula, echoing its Athanasian formulation:

> So high is the excellence, so remarkable the price, so great the worth of this thing, viz., the soul of man, that, in order to its not being lost, but gained both to God himself and to us, the laws of universal nature having been utterly disturbed, and the order of things changed, God descended to the earth, that he might become man, and man was raised to heaven, that he might be a God.[74]

Sadoleto does not employ the exchange formula as if it is contentious, shocking, or exotic. Rather, he presumes agreement and wants to convince the Genevans that continued separation from the Roman Church endangers their shared hope for this salvation.

Twice Calvin's response specifically mentions Sadoleto's preface.[75] Calvin says it is unnecessary to spend much time in response despite the fact that it occupies about a third of Sadoleto's letter. Rather, he questions the Cardinal's motives for spending so much space rehearsing something that is not in dispute. Calvin agrees that what Sadoleto discusses 'deserves to be sounded in our ears

---

[73] Another passage from Bucer's (and Wolfgang Capito's) pen definitely known to Calvin that arguably teaches deification is found in chapter 4 of the Tetrapolitan Confession. The redeemed are said to show themselves to others 'as gods,' but more significant deification themes than that are present which cannot be exposited here. However, it is worth noting that Calvin likely subscribed to the Confession and certainly could not teach contrary to it during his years in Strasburg.

[74] *T&T*, 1.8. Latin: Tanta est nobilitas, tam insigne pretium, tam grandis aestimatio huiusce rei, quae anima hominis est, ut quo ne ea perderetur, sed et Deo ipsi et nobis lucrifieret, conturbatis penitus totius naturae legibus, atque ordine rerum permutato, et Deus descenderet in terras, ut fieret homo, et homo erigeretur in coelum, ut esset Deus [*CO* 5.373]. Cf. Athanasius, *De Inc.* 54.3.

[75] *T&T*, 1.29, 33-34.

by day and by night, to be constantly kept in remembrance, and made the subject of ceaseless meditation'.[76] Similarly, 'I readily agree with you that, after this sanctification, we ought not to propose to ourselves any other object in life than to hasten towards that high calling; for God has set it before us as the constant aim of all our thoughts, and words, and actions.'[77]

Accusing the Cardinal of blasphemy would have done much to make Calvin's case. However, Calvin registers no disagreement with Sadoleto's exposition. To the contrary, everything he says in reply presumes fundamental agreement. If Calvin considered deification blasphemous, then his failure to criticize Sadoleto on this point is inexplicable.

Cyril of Alexandria

Scholars identify Cyril of Alexandria as the theologian in which the early patristic deification tradition is summarized and brought to maturity.[78] This vision of redemption permeates his biblical commentaries in the form of a recurring 'narrative of divine life'.[79] This theme is especially found throughout his commentary on John. Calvin's use of this commentary and comments he makes about Cyril's theology are especially useful for gauging his reaction to the patristic doctrine of deification.

Sometime around 1540 Calvin wrote the preface for a proposed French translation of Chrysostom's homilies. There Cyril is praised as second only to Chrysostom among the Greek Fathers as an exegete of Scripture.[80] Calvin cites Cyril by name more than 50 times. But Cyril's influence on Calvin's exegesis and theology is deeper than the number of citations would indicate. Irena Backus observes that Calvin rarely refers to the Fathers explicitly in his commentaries but their influence can nonetheless be detected. She examines Calvin's commentary on the Johannine Prologue to illustrate the point. Backus finds that 'Cyril, although hardly ever mentioned explicitly, is found on closer inspection to be omnipresent, much more so than the modern editor's notes would lead us to believe.'[81] Similar results can be attained for other sections of John as well. In this context it is, of course, primarily Cyril's commentary that Calvin draws upon.

---

[76] *T&T*, 1.33.

[77] *T&T*, 1.34

[78] Cf. Daniel A. Keating, 'Divinization in Cyril: The Appropriation of Divine Life' in Thomas G. Weinandy and Daniel A. Keating (eds), *The Theology of St Cyril of Alexandria: A Critical Appreciation* (London: T & T Clark, 2003), 149.

[79] Daniel A. Keating, *The Appropriation of Divine Life in Cyril of Alexandria* (Oxford: OUP, 2004), 7.

[80] Irena Backus, 'Calvin and the Greek Fathers in Robert J. Bast and Andrew C. Gow (eds), *Continuity and Change: the Harvest of Late Medieval and Reformation History* (Leiden: Brill, 2000), 258.

[81] Backus, 'Calvin and the Greek Fathers.' 274.

Among the ways Cyril's commentary affirms deification are the exchange formula, reference to 'partaking of the divine nature,' discussion of union with God and describing the redeemed as being made 'gods by grace'. Calvin never censures Cyril's use of this deification language. Calvin even imports one of Cyril's distinctive deification images into his own sacramental theology, the Eucharistic communication of divine life through the flesh of Christ.[82] Calvin does, however, register a mild disagreement with some of Cyril's statements on union with Christ.

In a letter dated March 8, 1555, Peter Martyr Vermigli solicits Calvin's opinion of his position on the believer's union with Christ. Vermigli outlines three kinds of union: Christ's union with humanity in the incarnation, union effected by the Spirit in regeneration which makes believers capable of immortality and renewal into conformity with Christ's glory, and an intermediate 'secret' or 'mystical communion' between believers and the enthroned Christ. Vermigli says he understands and accepts these three kinds of union but does not understand 'that which some of the Fathers introduce, especially Cyril; who makes the substance of the Body and Blood of Christ in such wise our food, that they assert it to be really intermingled with our substance'.[83]

Calvin agrees with Vermigli's three levels of union and says of the fourth kind of union: 'But though I see that the ancients, especially Hilary and Cyril were carried much too far, yet I am not disposed severely to censure their hyperbolas, except when it is sought to prop up error by their authority.' Calvin ascribes to Hilary and Cyril the view 'that we also are of the same essence with Christ' and says that they 'fly' to this 'wretchedly obscure position' out of ignorance in an attempt to rebut Arian misinterpretations of John 10.30 and 17.21.[84] Hyperbolic language notwithstanding, elsewhere Calvin makes it clear that he has no fundamental disagreement with Cyril's overall position. In his dispute with Westphal he parenthetically comments:

> Here, however we must inform the reader, that, as Cyril was contending against the Arians, he is led into hyperbole, and teaches that believers become substantially one with Christ, just as he is one with the Father. The same was the case with Hilary, whose words, however, are so far from being contrary to our doctrine that I appositely retort them on the Magdeburgians.[85]

Calvin's reading of Cyril's commentary afforded repeated exposure to a mature soteriology of deification. The writing of his own commentary, polemics with

---

[82] E.g., *Inst.* 4.17.8; 4.17.19; 4.17.34; *T&T*, 2.541.

[83] Vermigli's and Calvin's letters are translated in George Corenelius Gorham, *Gleanings of a Few Scattered Ears* (London: Bell and Daldy, 1857), 340-52 (344).

[84] Gorham, *Gleanings*, 350-51. Cf. Cyril of Alexandria, *Commentary on the Gospel According to John*, vol. 2 *John 9-21* (translated by Thomas Randell; London: Walter Smith, 1885), 549-55.

[85] *T&T*, 2.435.

Lutheran critics and inquiries from friends gave Calvin ample opportunity to register any opposition to the doctrine he may have had. Yet, the most critical thing he says is that Cyril's notion of 'corporeal union' with Christ (to use Cyril's own phrase) is obscure and unnecessarily hyperbolic. Far from seeing Cyril's doctrine of deification as blasphemous, Calvin recapitulates some of its main elements in his own theology.

Conclusion

When Calvin dedicated his commentary on 2 Peter in 1551 he was familiar with erroneous divinizing notions propounded by Servetus, the Libertines, the ancient Manicheans and others as well as orthodox affirmations of deification. The fourth edition of the *Institutes* and his commentaries on the Pauline corpus were already published. It was a mature, informed Calvin who wrote of the gospel's end in terms of deification. But did he intend to affirm the broad patristic vision of salvation?

Calvin's additional comments on 2 Peter 1.3-4 suggest that deification is shorthand for such things as being clothed with God's glory, being endowed with God's power, restoration of God's glorious image, God himself being possessed by the redeemed such that what is his becomes theirs by grace, putting off the vices of the flesh, partaking of divine immortality and blessedness, and becoming 'one with God so far as our capacity allows'. In these themes we find nearly every element of John McGuckin's working definition:

> The concept of deification is the process of the sanctification of Christians whereby they become progressively conformed to God; a conformation that is ultimately demonstrated in the glorious transfiguration of the 'just' in the heavenly kingdom, when immortality and a more perfect vision (and knowledge and experience) of God are clearly manifested in the glorification (δόξα) of the faithful.[86]

Furthermore, Calvin's statement about union with God is strikingly similar to Ps. Dionysius' ancient definition: 'theosis is the attaining of likeness to God and union with him so far as possible'.[87] And, like many Church Fathers, Calvin regards his teaching as something which 'was not unfamiliar to Plato, because he defines the highest human good in various passages as being completely conformed to God'.[88] Calvin's comments on 2 Peter 1.3-4 certainly *look* like the patristic doctrine of deification.

---

86 J.A. McGuckin, 'The Strategic Adaptation of Deification in the Cappadocians' in Christensen and Wittung (eds), *Partakers of the Divine Nature*, 95.

87 *EH* 1.3, PG 3.376a, as translated in Russell, *Doctrine*, 248. Calvin was generally critical of Dionysius' speculations (cf. *Comm 2 Cor* 12.4; *Inst.* 1.14.4) but concedes that his writings 'contain some things not to be totally despised' (*Comm Acts* 17.34; *CO* 48.423).

88 *Comm 2 Peter* 1:4 (*CO* 55.446-47).

Those of us who are convinced on the basis of this and other passages that it is appropriate to speak of 'Calvin's doctrine of deification' are not attempting to import something exotic into Calvin's theology. Nor are we trying to put an 'Eastern spin' on it or radically redefine his doctrine of justification. In other words, we are not attempting to do with Calvin what some in the Finnish school do with Luther. Rather, we are trying to interpret Calvin within his context by means of a historiography of broad continuity.[89] This stands in stark contrast to the hermeneutic of discontinuity employed by some of our critics which portrays Calvin more like a Radical Reformation restorer of Christianity than as a reformer committed to the catholic faith of the early Church.[90]

Deification is a flower native to the soil of Western as well as Eastern Christendom. It is well-attested in patristic, medieval and contemporary writers Calvin read and valued. Calvin thought of himself as a 'catholic' theologian convinced that he was in agreement with the consensus of patristic theology.[91] Moreover, as Irena Backus reminds us, 'Calvin did not see the Greek Fathers he referred to as members of an alien Orthodox Church but as representatives of an United Christendom.'[92] So, when we see classic deification themes, formulas, and motifs permeate Calvin's writings, it is natural to conclude that he agreed with the broad patristic vision of salvation. While deification may sound strange to some modern Western theologians, it was familiar to Calvin. For him to affirm and presuppose the truth of this soteriological vision would not have been some kind of 'undignified flight to the East' but a rather predictable embrace of teachings from the 'purer church' of the first five centuries.

---

89 This approach is very nicely sketched in J. Todd Billings, 'The Contemporary Reception of Luther and Calvin's Doctrine of Union with Christ: Mapping a Biblical, Catholic, and Reformational Motif' in R. Grant Holder (ed.), *Calvin and Luther: The Continuing Relationship* (Göttingen: Vandenhoeck & Ruprecht, 2013), 165-82.

90 E.g., McCormack, 'Union with Christ in Calvin's Theology'.

91 I. John Hesselink, 'Calvinus Oecumenicus: Calvin's Vision of the Unity and Catholicity of the Church' in Eduardus Van der Borght (ed.), *Unity of the Church: A Theological State of the Art and Beyond* (Leiden: Brill, 2010), 69-93; J. Todd Billings, 'The Catholic Calvin,' *Pro Ecclesia* 20.2 (2011), 120-34; Tony Lane, 'Calvin's Attitude towards Catholicity' in Herman J. Selderhuis (ed.), *Calvinus Clarissimus theologus* (Göttingen: Vandenhoeck & Ruprecht, 2012), 206-27.

92 Backus, 'Calvin and the Greek Fathers,' 270.

CHAPTER 5

'A Christian prince hath charge of both tables.' John Jewel's biblical doctrine of royal supremacy[1]

André A. Gazal

When Parliament passed the Act of Supremacy in 1534, declaring the monarch 'Supreme Head' of the Church in England, it effectively made a theological statement which would change the character of the English Church. The Act of Supremacy in 1534 transferred the ecclesiastical jurisdiction held by the pope and exercised by legates to the monarch. It gave him/her the power not only to reform the Church, but also to determine doctrine and reprove heresy. No longer did the clergy derive their authority from the pope as the Vicar of Christ on earth, but from the monarch who claimed to rule the visible church in the temporal realm. While this statute enacted by Parliament served the personal and political purposes of Henry VIII (r.1509-1547), it would eventually provide the legislative basis for a national Evangelical Church, beginning in the reign of his son, Edward VI (r.1547-1553). With the death of Edward, evangelical advance by the government came to a stop under his Catholic sister, Mary Tudor (r.1553-1558). However, this seemingly certain return to Rome ended abruptly with the Queen's death in 1558. When Mary's younger half-sister, Elizabeth, ascended the throne on 17 November 1558, both England and its Church reached a critical impasse. In early 1559, after three attempts, Parliament passed a more detailed Act of Supremacy. Shortly after passage of the new Supremacy Act, Parliament enacted the Act of Uniformity which authorized the 1559 *Book of Common Prayer*. Both of these acts together served in part as the basis for the so-called 'Elizabethan Settlement' which became the legislative grounds for the Church of England.

During the reign of Elizabeth, a public theology of the ecclesiastical establishment emerged, which sought both to defend and define it. This was largely because now the Queen and Parliament declared the Church of England to be

[1] I would like to express my appreciation to the following for their constructive comments regarding this paper—the participants in our seminar on the theology of the English Reformers at Northland Graduate School—P.J. Wehry, Adam Pruden, Andrew Leaf and Christopher Howatt. My heart-felt thanks also go to my wife, Agata Gazal.

Protestant. But by what authority did the Queen decide the faith of the country, and moreover, what authority did Parliament have to give her this power? There had to be a definitive theology to answer these questions and thus to provide legitimacy to the legislative action taken with regards to the Church.

This emergent theology seems to have developed upon two main ideas: the supremacy of Scriptural authority and that of monarchical authority. John Jewel (1522-1571), Bishop of Salisbury (1560-71) and first major apologist of the Elizabethan Church, averred the supremacy of Scripture—in matters of doctrine and practice as well as the legitimate authority of the monarch to bring the Church into conformity with it—in his two official apologetic works, *The Apology of the Church of England* (1562) and the *Defence of the Apology* (1567, 1570).

There have been three major biographies of Jewel published in the last five decades.[2] While all three works mention Jewel's doctrine of Scripture and adherence to the Royal Supremacy, they do not explicitly discuss the relationship between the two. In the most recent of these biographies, Gary Jenkins reassesses Jewel's standing as a theologian. In so doing, he argues that Jewel employed a '*via negativi canonis*,' a set of parameters devised to assert what the Early Church did not believe or practice.[3] Jenkins further avers, 'This basic negative approach served more as a means to eradicate the whole edifice of traditionalism by embracing a minimum of fundamental dogmas, than as any positive platform on which to construct a purely positive theology.'[4] After allegedly demolishing the Catholic consensus resting upon the foundation of long-standing ecclesiastical tradition by means of his negative approach, Jewel erected two new canonical categories upon which he constructed his defense of the Elizabethan Settlement: the primacy of the godly prince within the national Church and the Protestant doctrine of *sola Scriptura*.[5] These two doctrines, however, for Jewel, were 'mutually incompatible beliefs and conflicting absolutes'.[6]

This revisionist reappraisal of Jewel has not gone unchallenged. In a later review article, Brett Usher savagely excoriates Jenkins' work.[7] In addition to noting Jenkins' omissions of relevant facts concerning Jewel's life and career, such as the fact that he was not the government's first choice for the see of

---

2 John E. Booty, *John Jewel: Apologist of the Church of England* (London: SPCK, 1963); W.M. Southgate, *John Jewel and the Problem of Doctrinal Authority* (Cambridge: Harvard University Press, 1962); Gary W. Jenkins, *John Jewel and the English National Church: The Dilemmas of an Erastian Reformer* (Burlington: Ashgate, 2006).

3 Jenkins, *John Jewel and the English National Church*, 73.

4 Jenkins, *John Jewel and the English National Church*, 73.

5 Jenkins, *John Jewel and the English National Church*, 242-43.

6 Jenkins, *John Jewel and the English National Church*, 243.

7 Brett Usher, 'John Jewel Junked,' *JEH* 59 (2008), 501-11. Brett Usher is Reader of Ecclesiastical History at the University of Reading, UK.

Salisbury,[8] he accuses Jenkins of merely regurgitating the arguments and characterizations of Jewel's Catholic opponents with 'no analysis' but 'simply strident polemic'.[9] Although scathing, Usher's critique is not without merit. Particularly problematic however, is Jenkins' contention that the two canons upon which Jewel maintained his defense of the Elizabethan Settlement, the primacy of the godly prince and the doctrine of *sola Scriptura*, were for this major apologist mutually contradictory. A careful reading of Jewel's works suggests just the opposite. This chapter will argue that Jewel, as the first official apologist for the Protestant Church of England, understood the doctrine of Royal Supremacy as deriving directly from the doctrine of *sola Scriptura*. Specifically, for the Bishop of Salisbury, the nexus between the formal doctrine of *sola Scriptura* and the material doctrine of Royal Supremacy was the interpretive priority he gave to Old Testament historical narrative. The interpretive primacy of Old Testament historical narrative in relation to other biblical passages made Royal Supremacy a biblical doctrine.

As the first major apologist for this reformed Church of England, Jewel wrote the *Apology of the Church of England* in response to the Council of Trent and his more voluminous *Defence of the Apology* as a reply to a formidable Catholic opponent, Thomas Harding. The central argument of both these works is that the reformed Church of England was established upon the Scriptures, the first four ecumenical councils, the early Church Fathers, and the example of the primitive Church. The councils, Fathers, and early Church were authoritative because they agreed with Scripture. Scripture's authority was supreme. Thus, by enacting the laws comprising the Elizabethan Settlement, Parliament returned England to the ancient and apostolic Church. This, for Jewel, provided the framework in which he defended the right of a state Church to regulate matters of doctrine and worship by means of its own regional and national synods apart from general councils. He particularly argued for the biblical duty of a godly prince to initiate national ecclesiastical reform. Jewel's belief in the divine authority of Holy Scripture was vital for his defense of this ecclesiastical establishment and particularly Royal Supremacy.

Jewel's biblical doctrine of Royal Supremacy: the primacy of Old Testament historical narrative

In a preface addressed to Queen Elizabeth I at the beginning of *A Defence of the Apology of the Church of England*, Jewel encourages her to continue

[8] The original choice for the see was William Bill, Elizabeth's first Almoner. The selection of Jewel came about largely after much intense negotiation in the Queen's Privy Council concerning episcopal finances. See Usher, 'John Jewel Junked,' 504. Also, for the significant role which the Privy Council played in ecclesiastical affairs, see Brett Usher, *William Cecil and the Episcopacy* (Aldershot: Ashgate, 2003).

[9] Usher, 'John Jewel Junked,' 507.

pursuing the righteous cause of ecclesiastical reform with the same zeal as her godly predecessors.

> God evermore inflame and direct your majesty with his holy Spirit, that the zeal of his house may thoroughly devour your gracious heart; that you may safely walk in the way of your father David; that you may utterly abandon all groves and hill-altars; that you may live an old mother in Israel; that you may see an end of all dissensions, and stablish peace and unity in the church of God. Amen.[10]

Even though Jewel, by means of this trope, might be referring to her actual father, Henry VIII, who appealed to Davidic kingship as the model for his exercise of ecclesiastical supremacy,[11] it is still significant that he eloquently summarizes Her Majesty's mission with this biblical panegyric. This benediction, consisting of a conflation of biblical tropes, expresses in metaphorical shorthand both the precise function and specific biblical basis of Royal Supremacy. As the monarch, she is to 'abandon all groves and hill-altars,' that is, remove all corruptions from the worship of God: she is to reform worship.[12] Next, the fact that the destruction by the kings of Judah of 'groves and hill-altars' because of their use in pagan worship provides divinely authoritative directive for present royal ecclesiastical action indicates the biblical material making such a prerogative a Scriptural mandate: the narrative literature of the Old Testament. In maintaining a biblical doctrine of Royal Supremacy Jewel directly appeals to Old Testament historical narrative in his two principal works, the *Apology of the Church of England* and *A Defence of the Apology of the Church of England.*

In the *Apology*, Jewel seems to express the underlying rationale for giving interpretive priority to Old Testament narrative as the basis for a biblical doctrine of Royal Supremacy.

> But lest some man should say that the foresaid things happened in the time of the Law only, of shadows, and of infancy, when the truth lay hid under figures and ceremonies, when nothing as yet was brought to perfection, when the Law was not graven in men's hearts but in stone (and yet is that but a foolish saying, for even at those days was there the very same God that is now, the same Spirit, the same Christ, the same faith, the same doctrine, the same hope, the same inheritance, the same covenant, and the same efficacy and virtue of God's word: Eusebius also saith, 'All the faithful even from Adam until Christ, were in very deed Christians)' . . .[13]

---

[10] John Jewel, *The Works of John Jewel* 4 volumes (edited by John Ayre; Cambridge: CUP, 1845-50), 3.118.

[11] See André A. Gazal, *Scripture and Royal Supremacy in Tudor England: The Use of Old Testament Historical Narrative* (Lewiston: Edwin Mellen, 2013), chapter 2.

[12] Earlier in the preface, Jewel makes it clear that to 'abandon' means also to remove all vestiges of false worship from the realm. See Jewel, *Works*, 3.118.

[13] John Jewel, *An Apology of the Church of England* (translated by Lady Ann Bacon; edited by John Booty; New York: Church Publishing, 2002), 70-71. The reference is

This statement by Jewel occurs in Part 4 in which he discusses inconsistencies between various papal actions and the teachings of Scripture, many of which have to do with attempts by popes to undermine and subjugate imperial and royal authority. The specific context in which he makes the above declaration is a description of how the 'church' had succumbed to corruption thus provoking the denunciation of the prophets. Notably, the period to which Jewel specifically refers in this discussion is that of the Old Testament. In commenting on this history, he frequently refers to the people of God at that time, ancient Israel, as 'the Church'. For instance, in citing Isaiah 1.22, Jewel specifically identifies his ancient audience as the Church. 'And when Isaiah said, "the silver" of God's people (that is, of the Church) was "become dross"; and that "the same city which aforetime had been faithful was now become an harlot"; and that in the same was "no part sound throughout the whole body, from the head to the foot?"'[14] This identification of ancient Israel as the Church is essential to understanding Jewel's normative use of the Old Testament and especially of Old Testament narrative. As evidenced in the first statement above, Jewel did not sharply distinguish between ancient Israel and the Church. Rather he conceived of one people of God beginning with Adam. This essential continuity of the people of God for Jewel entails the continuation of 'the same doctrine' and 'same covenant'. That the doctrine and covenant possessed by the ancient Israelites was identical to that of the present Church and Christian commonwealths enabled Jewel to regard Old Testament narrative as the chief source of doctrine concerning kingship with certain New Testament passages, such as Romans 13, functioning as secondary support with the command for all Christians to obey the 'higher powers'. Since the Old Testament narrative material granted to kings authority in cultic matters Romans 13.1 was read in conjunction with it to mean that Christians are to obey them as 'higher powers' in ecclesiastical affairs. This relationship between the Old Testament narrative and New Testament prescriptive passages based on the assumption of the continuity of doctrine shows itself to be apparent in Jewel's appeals to the former in Part VI of the *Apology*.

Part VI of the *Apology* comprises Jewel's main defense of the prince's power to reform the Church. It is a compendium on the doctrine of Royal Supremacy. The specific context in which Jewel makes his case for Royal Supremacy is a denunciation of the recent Council of Trent's exclusion of princes from participation in its deliberations and decisions.[15] It is in the midst of his impassioned accusation that Jewel declares the issue of the prince's role in ecclesiastical reform to be a Scriptural one.

---

to Eusebius, *Church History*, 1.4 (NPNF^2 1:87-88); Christian Classics Ethereal Library, http://www.ccel.org/ccel/schaff/npnf201.iii.vi.iv.html (10 September 2009).

[14] Jewel, *Apology*, 70.

[15] Jewel, *Apology*, 113.

> Or, if the said kings and princes happen to intermeddle in such matters and take upon them to do that they may do, that they be commanded to do, and ought of duty to do, and the same things we know both David and Solomon and other good princes to have done, that is, if they, whiles the Pope and his prelates slug and sleep or else mischievously withstand them, do bridle the priests' sensuality and drive them to do their duty and keep them still to it; if they do overthrow idols; if they take away superstition and set up again the true worshiping of God; why do they by and by make an outcry upon them that such princes trouble all and press by violence into another's office, and do thereby wickedly and malapertly? What Scripture hath at any time forbidden a Christian prince to be made privy to such causes? Who but themselves alone made ever any such law?[16]

By mentioning David and Solomon at the outset, Jewel sets Scriptural precedent over and against the papal contention that royal ecclesiastical reform constitutes an unlawful commingling of the magisterial and ecclesiastical offices. To show that he is establishing the duty of magisterial participation in church reform upon the Scriptures, the bishop states the biblical nature of princely ecclesiastical authority negatively for homiletic effect: Scripture nowhere prohibits a Christian prince from participating in church reform.

Jewel responds more specifically to the papal argument opposing royal involvement in ecclesiastical reform by evincing a mixture of temporal and spiritual offices in his *Defence*. He does this by answering two biblical objections leveled by his Catholic opponent, Thomas Harding. The first of these, often used by Catholic critics of Royal Supremacy, is the account in 2 Chronicles 26 of Uzziah's attempt to usurp the priest's office for which he was struck with leprosy. In reply, Jewel argues that this passage does not contravene Royal Supremacy because Royal Supremacy does not entail exercise of clerical functions by the monarch.

> Touching that ye write of the rash attempt of king Ozias, ye seem not to understand neither our words nor your own. For we teach not princes to offer up incense in sacrifice, as Ozias did, or by intrusion to thrust themselves into bishops' rooms, or to preach, or to minister sacraments, or to bind, or to loose; but only to discharge their own offices, and to do that duty that David, Salomon, Ezechias, Josias, and other noble and godly kings did, and evermore was lawful for the prince to do.[17]

The account of Uzziah does not serve the purpose of Harding and his fellow Catholics because their appeal to it evidences their misunderstanding of Royal Supremacy as taught in the Church of England. The doctrine of Royal Supremacy does not allow the monarch to preach, administer the sacraments, or practice church discipline; rather, it teaches that Christian princes have biblically

---

16 Jewel, *Apology*, 113.

17 Jewel, *Works*, 4:958.

mandated authority to make clerics faithfully and rightly discharge these sacred duties. What should be noted here is that Jewel strongly disagrees with Harding's application of the account of Uzziah, noting that his opponent appropriates the passage with an incorrect assumption about Royal Supremacy. Jewel refutes Harding's use of the Uzziah account with a direct appeal to four kings—David, Solomon, Hezekiah, and Josiah—who did indeed initiate ecclesiastical reform, thereby providing, by virtue of the presence of these accounts in Scripture, the biblical mandate for Christian princes to affect the same. Jewel's reference to these kings in upholding Royal Supremacy provides the necessary context for his response to Harding's use of Ephesians 4.11.

Ephesians 4.11 is the second biblical objection advanced by Harding in behalf of Catholic opposition to Royal Supremacy. It says that Christ 'gave some, apostles; and some, prophets, and some, evangelists; and some pastors and teachers'. In appealing to this passage, Harding, Jewel notes, attempts to argue against Royal Supremacy by negation. Christ instituted the offices in the church; absent from them are those of king and prince. Jewel's understanding of Harding's argument is that this obvious exclusion of kings and princes from this stated order of church offices necessarily prohibits them from exercising any ecclesiastical authority. To this Jewel replies by castigating Harding's reading of Ephesians 4.11. Very strikingly, here Jewel faults Harding for reading this passage separately from the rest of Scripture. As mentioned above, the primary material to which Jewel appeals to refute the Catholic appropriation of the Uzziah account were the narratives concerning David, Solomon, Hezekiah, and Josiah, which grant to kings the authority to reform the Church, thereby providing for the bishop the means of reading Ephesians 4.11 in a way that does not exclude kings from ecclesiastical governance. Jewel's main biblical argument buttressing Royal Supremacy in Part VI of the *Apology* is this: '. . . a Christian prince hath the charge of both tables committed to him by God, to the end he may understand that not temporal matters only but also religious and ecclesiastical causes pertain to his office.'[18] He expands on it in the *Defence* thus:

> Thus we say, the prince is put in trust, as well with the first as with the second table of the law of God, that is to say, as well with religion as with temporal government; not only to keep and perform the contents of both tables in his own person (for so much every private man is bound to do), but also to see that all others of his subjects, as well priests as laymen, each man in his own calling, do duly keep them. This is it that no private man is able to do.[19]

The summary biblical argument supporting Royal Supremacy was the monarch's role as enforcer of both tables of the Law, with the first governing the worship of God and the second regulating civil society. The distinctive charac-

[18] Jewel, *Apology*, 115.
[19] Jewel, *Works*, 4:974.

teristic of the doctrine is the monarch's scripturally mandated responsibility to enforce the first table; the monarch must see that God is worshiped according to his Word.

Jewel further develops the argument in the *Apology* by means of allusions taken directly from Old Testament narrative.

> Besides also that God by his prophets often and earnestly commandeth the king to cut down the groves, to break down the images and altars of idols, and to write out the book of the law for himself; and besides that the prophet Isaiah saith, 'A king ought to be a patron and nurse of the church.'[20]

The narrative material throughout both the historical and prophetic books of the Old Testament is replete with instances in which God indirectly commanded a king to eradicate from the kingdom all vestiges of idolatry. Jewel also references the command in Deuteronomy 17 for the king to write his own copy of the law, a passage frequently employed by Henrician and Edwardian apologists of Royal Supremacy as well as engaging in a rather extensive exegetical discussion of Deuteronomy 17 in the *Defence*.[21] Finally, Jewel quotes Isaiah 49.23 as a means of describing the nurturing function of the monarch's ecclesiastical position; this verse also serves as explicit testimony by the prophet to the monarch's direct responsibility for the well-being of the Church.[22]

Jewel then proceeds with an extensive recounting of Old Testament monarchical history beginning with Moses. He starts by describing the manner in which Moses was a magistrate. Immediately following Moses, Jewel touches on Joshua. 'Joshua also, though he were none other than a civil magistrate, yet as soon as he was chosen by God and set as a ruler over the people, he received commandments specially touching religion and the service of God.'[23] He com-

---

[20] Jewel, *Apology*, 115.

[21] See Jewel, *Apology*, 115; *Works*, 4:979; Gazal, *Scripture and the Royal Supremacy in Tudor England*, 70-76.

[22] Although Jewel does not say it here, his close friend from Zurich, Heinrich Bullinger took Isa. 49.23 as well as Ps. 2 to prophesy the future conversion of kings to the faith and their subsequent roles as caretakers of the Church. 'For the Prophetes, and among them specially Dauid in the 2. Psalme, and Esay in his 49. chapter and in other places, have foretold that kings should come into the Church of Christ, and that they should not onely lead their lives there after the maner of other Christen men, but also more over continue their will in governing, defending, [and] advauncing Church affaires, as kinges still executing kyngly power.' See Heinrich Bullinger, *A Confvtation Of the Popes Bull which was published more then two yeres agoe against Elizabeth the most gracious Queene of England, Fraunce, and Ireland, and against the noble Realme of England: together with a defence of the sayd true Christian Queene, and of the whole Realme of England* (London: John Day, 1572; STC (2nd ed.) / 4044. [Database online—subscription only]: Early English Books Online, http://eebo.chadwyck.com [13 August 2008]), 45r.

[23] Jewel, *Apology*, 115.

ments more on Joshua's magisterial role in the *Defence* in response to a formidable objection by Harding.

After Joshua, Jewel moves to David, the archetypal godly king for the doctrine of Royal Supremacy. In the *Apology*, he recounts the following concerning David's actions as king regarding worship.

> King David, when the whole religion was altogether brought out of frame by wicked King Saul, brought home again the ark of God, that is to say, he restored religion again, and was not only amongst them himself as a counselor and furtherer of the work, but he appointed also hymns and psalms, put in order the companies, and was the only doer in setting forth that whole solemn triumph, and in effect ruled the priests.[24]

Jewel marshals material from 1 Chronicles 13 to highlight the central role David played in Israel's religion. Jewel construes this episode as one of direct royal regulation of worship, another central feature of Royal Supremacy.

David receives additional treatment in the *Defence*. Jewel maintains that David affected reform by means of the priests.[25] He formulated the agenda and gave it to the priests to implement.

> David therefore called the bishops and priests together: he shewed them in what sort the religion of God was defaced: he willed them to bring the ark into Sion: he was present himself: he appointed and ordered the whole triumph: he assigned which of the Levites, and in what order they should serve before the ark: he allotted Aaron's children, which were the priests, to walk each man in his several office.[26]

Drawing from 1 Chronicles 16 and 24, Jewel notes that David appointed the priests and Levites to their specific ritual tasks. Moreover, David drafted the actual decree designating the specific duties of the priests and Levites according to their respective offices which his son, Solomon, followed in making his priestly assignments.[27] Despite the Catholic objection voiced by Harding that David instituted these measures by virtue of his office of prophet, Jewel insists that he did so as king on the basis of similar actions taken by his successors.[28]

Solomon exercised the same royal ecclesiastical authority as his father. To this effect Jewel says in the *Apology*: 'King Solomon built unto the Lord the temple which his father David had but purposed in his mind to do; and, after the finishing thereof, he made a godly oration to the people concerning religion and the service of God: he afterward displaced Abiathar the priest and set

[24] Jewel, *Apology*, 115-16.
[25] Jewel, *Works*, 4:987.
[26] Jewel, *Works*, 4:987.
[27] Jewel, *Works*, 4:987.
[28] Jewel, *Works*, 4:987.

Sadok in his place.'[29] Not only did Solomon actually construct the temple according to plans drafted by David, and admonished the people concerning their spiritual duty to God, he also exercised coercive authority over the priests as indicated by his deposition of Abiathar the high priest and replacement of him with Zadok. It is this coercive authority over priests which Solomon exerted that Jewel emphasizes in the *Defence*.[30] Jewel emphasizes Solomon's performance of specific ecclesiastical functions: ordering the removal the Ark of the Covenant into the temple; consecrating the temple; offering sacrifices; blessing the people; and directing the priests and Levites in their sacral duties. Moreover, Jewel stresses the meticulous obedience of the priests and Levites to his ritual commands. Solomon thus governed actively in ecclesiastical matters.

Jewel insists that the Old Testament narrative material gives the monarch authority to reform the Church by actively eradicating corrupt worship and restoring true devotion. Towards this end, he begins with the account of Hezekiah in the *Apology*:

> After this, when the temple of God was in shameful wise polluted through the naughtiness and negligence of the priests, King Hezekiah commanded the same to be cleansed from rubble and filth, the priests to light up the candles, to burn incense, and to do their divine service according to the old allowed custom. The same king also commanded the brazen serpent, which then the people wickedly worshiped, to be taken down and beaten to powder.[31]

Jewel clearly faults the priests for allowing and even encouraging the degradation of temple worship. When those charged with maintaining the sanctity of divine service proved derelict in their duty, especially to the point where they corrupted the rites, it was imperative for Hezekiah to initiate the necessary re-

---

29 Jewel, *Apology*, 116.

30 Jewel, *Works*, 4:988. Jewel's mentor, Peter Martyr Vermigli, explicitly emphasizes this account as giving kings the authority to depose bishops and even popes, observing that Christian emperors in turn exerted this same coercive ecclesiastical power. 'Annotabimus etiam regem Salomonem autoritate sua Pontificem deijecere, ateque ideo vanam esse nostrorum Episcoporum & Pontificum iaciantiem qua gloriantur se a laicis principibus non posse loco moueri aut attingi. At nunc Salomon regum omnium sapientissimus longe secus rem habere ostendit. In sacra porro Historia nusqua deprehendimus Pontifices aut sacerdotes deiecisse reges. At reges e diverso, Pontifices & sacerdotes in ordinem redegisse videmus. Quin & in orbe Christiano Iustinianus per Belisarium prius remouit Sylueriu, denide Vigillium Romanos Episcopos: quamuis aetate posteriori e diverso agitur. Romani siquidem Episcopi non verentur Imperatores loco mouere. Quod ideo fieri aliqui affirmant, quod Imperium Germanicum a Romana sede pendeat, & ideo eius longe aliam esse rationem, quam veteris imperij. Sed quam vere hoc dicitur, non est huis temporis excutere.' See Peter Martyr Vermigli, *Melachim, id est, Regvum Libri Dvo Posteriores et Commentariis* (Zurich: Christopher Froschouer, 1566); Zug, Switzerland: Inter Documentation Company, n.d., microfiche, 28v.

31 Jewel, *Apology*, 116.

forms. He did so first of all by compelling the priests to resume administering the sacred ordinances as originally received from God. Secondly, Hezekiah commanded the destruction of the bronze serpent, made by Moses, thus showing the monarch's authority to order the removal from the worship of God all elements defiling it.

Jewel responds to Catholic attempts to mitigate this account and its use to support Royal Supremacy in the *Defence*. Harding, representing the Catholic side, maintained that Hezekiah and other kings acted only on the advice of the priests and prophets.[32] The bishop counters that there is no evidence for this assertion.[33] Sharply distinguishing the roles of priests and prophets, Jewel notes that the latter had advised the king occasionally in such matters, but they did not exercise any direct religious governance. "For ye know that Esaias and Elizeus, notwithstanding, they were the prophets of God, yet were they neither priests nor bishops, nor had any manner of ordinary ministration in the church."[34] In fact, the priests who were there at the time caused much of the corruption in Israel's religion.[35] To prove that indeed the priests obeyed the king and not the other way around, Jewel appeals to two Latin renderings of the biblical text in 2 Chronicles 30.15.[36] Both renderings confirm for Jewel this conclusion: 'So ready were they to call upon and to further the king in his godly purpose! They held back what they could, and yielded to nothing but "with much ado" and "for very shame." They did nothing but by the king's commandment, and made him a reckoning of their doings.'[37] Ecclesiastical reform comes about when the monarch compels negligent clergy to implement it. The monarch devises the plan for reform and conscripts the clergy to activate it.

Jewel further supports the monarch's divinely mandated authority to reform by ridding the realm of all traces of false religion in the *Apology* by means of the recorded actions of Jehoshaphat. 'King Jehoshaphat overthrew and utterly made away the hill altars and groves whereby he saw God's honor hindered and the people holden back with a private superstition from the ordinary temple which was at Jerusalem, whereto they should by order have restored yearly from every part of the realm.'[38] To the example of Jehoshaphat, Jewel adds that of Josiah. 'King Josiah with great diligence put the priests and bishops in mind of their duty. King Josiah bridled the riot and arrogancy of the priests.'[39] Immediately after this statement concerning Josiah, Jewel mentions Jehu killing 'the wicked prophets' of Baal.[40] By these additional references and especially

32 Jewel, *Works*, 4:989.
33 Jewel, *Works*, 4:989.
34 Jewel, *Works*, 4:989.
35 Jewel, *Works*, 4:989.
36 Jewel, *Works*, 4:989.
37 Jewel, *Works*, 4:989.
38 Jewel, *Apology*, 116.
39 Jewel, *Apology*, 116.
40 Jewel, *Apology*, 116.

the last, Jewel reinforces the coercive power of the monarch over priests. He comments more on these references in relation to monarchical power over priests in the *Defence*.

Jewel begins this corresponding passage in the *Defence* by recounting the episode of Joash, who held back the offerings of the people in order to restore the temple. He describes this action by Joash in a way that discredits the priests. 'He sequestered the oblations of the people, which the priests had bestowed lewdly and wantonly upon themselves, and by his own authority turned the same to the reparations of the temple.'[41] In speaking about Josiah, Jewel cites 2 Chronicles 35.2 and immediately after part of 2 Chronicles 34.3.[42] In both instances royal ecclesiastical power is exerted in the redirection of money to temple restoration, assignment of specific ritualistic roles to the priests, and the purging of idolatry from religion. Once again, Jewel responds to a Catholic attempt to neutralize his appeal to the account of Josiah's reforms by arguing that he carried them out at the direction of the priests. Jewel reminds his opponents, Harding in particular, that upon learning what was written in the law, Josiah sent a priest, Hilkiah, to a prophetess, Huldah, to learn what needed to be done since Hilkiah apparently did not know what to tell the king.[43] Jewel, in this observation, accentuates the fact that Josiah 'was directed in matters of highest religion by a woman, and not by a priest'.[44] Given the fact that the monarch exercising Royal Supremacy at the time of the writing of both the *Apology* and *Defence* was a woman, it is more than likely that Jewel's emphasis given to Huldah did not pass without notice.

This completes the overview of Old Testament monarchical history employed by Jewel to construct a biblical doctrine of Royal Supremacy. The discussion of these passages makes up almost the entirety of the bishop's biblical case. That Jewel consciously gave hermeneutical priority to this narrative material in erecting the doctrine of Royal Supremacy was acknowledged by another one of his opponents, Thomas Dorman, whom he cites verbatim in the *Defence*.

> These examples be so manifest, that one of your fellows at Louvaine is fain thus to excuse the matter by over-much antiquity: 'If we would in these days,' saith he, 'use in all points the examples of the old law, there would follow an huge number of inconveniences.' 'It is no good reason to say that therefore our kings now-a-days must have the like authority.'[45]

---

41 Jewel, *Works*, 4:990.

42 Jewel, *Works*, 4:990.

43 Jewel, *Works*, 4:990.

44 Jewel, *Works*, 4:990.

45 Jewel, *Works*, 4:990. See also Thomas Dorman, *A Proufe of Certeyne Articles in Religion, Denied by M. Ivell* (Antwerp: Printed by John Latius, 1564; reprint, Ilkley: Scolar Press, 1976), folios 37.2, 39.2. For a detailed discussion of Dorman's objection, see Gazal, *Scripture and Royal Supremacy in Tudor England*, 365-417.

Jewel's reply to Dorman is quite telling:

> Thus saith he: as though the prince's right were now abated and altered, as the ceremonies of the law, and were otherwise now than it was before; or as if the coming of Christ into the world, and the preaching of the gospel, had purposely been to repress and pull down the seat of kings.[46]

In other words, while the coming of Christ did indeed either abolish or alter many of the ceremonies of the former economy, there are some that it did not, one of which was the ecclesiastical authority consigned by that same law to the godly prince. Royal Ecclesiastical Supremacy is one feature of the 'same covenant' which continues and therefore is normative in the time of the Gospel. What is significant about Dorman's comment and Jewel's response to it is that the bishop's opponents clearly understand the hermeneutical approach he takes. Jewel in turn acknowledges their correct description of his approach and justifies it. Indeed the cultic actions of Israel's and Judah's kings recorded in Holy Writ comprise the biblical mandate for godly princes in Christian commonwealths to oversee, regulate, and reform the national Church as the temple of God.

Conclusion

This study has endeavored to prove that contrary to Gary Jenkins' thesis, Jewel's two canonical categories of *sola Scriptura* and the ecclesiastical function of the godly prince were not contradictory in the reformer's thought. Rather for the first major apologist of the Elizabethan Church, royal ecclesiastical supremacy derived directly from *sola Scriptura*, making royal supremacy not merely an extraneous feature added to Protestant thought as propaganda for a politque regieme, but a doctrine averred clearly by the Word of God. Jewel's use of Scripture in support of royal ecclesiastical authority reveals the hermeneutic which enabled him to advance it as a biblical doctrine. This hermeneutic was the assignment of a normative, prescriptive function to the historical narratives of the Old Testament by the apologist. The acts of Moses, Joshua, and the kings of Israel and Judah in relation to the worship of

---

[46] Jewel, *Works*, 4:990. Bullinger makes an argument almost identical to this one in his defense of Elizabeth: 'And what man (except some giddybraynd and froward Anabaptist,) will say that Christian Princes have lesse authoritie and power in the Churches of Christenfolke, than the Jewish kynges had in the Synagogues? Can ye say, that the authoritie of these is diminished by Christ our Lord, or by his Apostles? Most certain it is, that it is not diminished by Christ.' See Bullinger, *A Confutation of the Popes Bull*, 45r. Also, in the *Decades*, Bullinger states, 'But wee on the other side will briefly shew that these auncient princes of Gods people, Iosue, Dauid, and the rest were Christians verilie and in deede, and that therefore the examples, which are deriued from them and applied to Christian princes, both are ought to bee of force and effect among us at this day'—cited from Torrance Kirby, *The Zurich Connection and Tudor Political Theology* (Leiden: Brill, 2007), 47.

God together formed a Scriptural mandate for Christian princes to lead the reforms of national churches in their realms. Moreover, since the New Testament did not abolish this feature of 'the old law' as it did others such as the Levitical sacrifices, it is still a divinely mandated component of the princely office. Thus, for Jewel, the scepter extended from the Word.

2. *Exegesis*

CHAPTER 6

Medieval and Reformation interpretations of Psalms quoted in Hebrews 1-2

Jeff Fisher

The book of Hebrews begins with the declaration that God has spoken in many ways and many times. The first two chapters of Hebrews are saturated with quotations from the Old Testament that the author uses to show the Son's superiority over angels. Throughout the history of biblical interpretation, there have been various approaches to understanding how the book of Hebrews uses the Old Testament, and many ways these passages have been interpreted. This essay aims to identify a significant component in the gradual shift away from medieval methods of interpreting Scripture at the time of the Reformation by comparing different interpretive explanations on the passages quoted from the Psalms in Hebrews 1-2. This comparative study reveals some of the continuity and discontinuity between medieval and Reformation interpretive methods. In order to provide focus to our study, we will compare the exegetical comments of the first-generation Swiss reformer, Johannes Oecolampadius (1482-1531) with his predecessors, contemporaries, and successors.[1]

Oecolampadius serves as a meaningful comparative point for this study because he was a transitional figure who taught in the early years of the Reformation, interacted with numerous prior and contemporaneous exegetes, and had his writings consulted by later interpreters. Oecolampadius had been ordained as a Roman Catholic priest around 1510, assisted Erasmus on the first edition of the *Novum Instrumentum* in 1516, and earned a Doctorate of Divinity in 1518. By at least May 1519, he began advocating Reformation teachings. Beginning in 1522, he was a pastor and theology professor in Basel, where he was recognized as the leading reformer—particularly when Basel officially em-

1 The standard biography of Oecolampadius is Ernst Staehelin, *Das Theologische Lebenswerk Johannes Oekolampads*, QFR 21 (New York: Johnson, 1939). Primary sources are found in Ernst Staehelin, *Briefe und Akten zum Leben Oekolampads*, QFR 10, 19 (New York: Johnson, 1971). The main English biographies are Diane Poythress, *Reformer of Basel: The Life, Thought, and Influence of Johannes Oecolampadius* (Grand Rapids: Reformation Heritage, 2011); Gordon Rupp, *Patterns of Reformation* (reprint: Eugene: Wipf & Stock, 2009), 3-46.

braced the Reformation in 1529. Oecolampadius lectured through books of the Bible from Spring 1523 until his death at the end of 1531. He taught in both Latin and German, and was among the few interpreters of the era who could utilize Greek and Hebrew. His lectures and some sermon series were published as 16 different commentaries, covering at least portions of 23 books of the Bible.[2] Oecolampadius lectured on Hebrews in 1529-1530. The commentary was published posthumously in 1534.[3] By focusing on the psalms quoted in Hebrews 1-2 the comparison of other exegetes with Oecolampadius will provide a better understanding of changing perspectives on the New Testament use of the Old at the time of the Reformation.

During the medieval period, the most common approach to interpreting the Bible was the fourfold sense of Scripture. Though there were various ways of applying this approach, exegetes generally espoused that in order to fully understand a biblical text, one must obtain the spiritual meaning(s) hidden in the literal meaning. The four senses were often referred to as the literal (historical), allegorical, tropological (or moral) and anagogical (or eschatological).[4] Throughout the centuries, however, the 'spiritual senses' became less dependent on the literal sense and commentators took particular liberties with the allegorical sense. The *Glossa Ordinaria* became an important means of transmitting this exegetical tradition by synthesizing the comments of previous Christian authors as interlinear and marginal glosses. Already in the twelfth century, though, a shift began taking place that focused less on the spiritual senses and more on the literal sense. Interpreters such as Hugh of St. Victor (ca. 1096-1141), Thomas Aquinas (1224/5-1274) and Nicholas of Lyra (ca. 1270-1349) gave greater attention to the literal sense while still offering explanations according to spiritual senses. The Renaissance movement further propelled a greater interest in the literal sense because of its focus on recovering original texts and original meanings. The Protestant reformers likewise placed a greater stress on the literal meaning of the text. However, many reformers still retained the *content* of the fourfold sense. They often relocated these meanings within a more expansive understanding of the literal sense.

---

2 For the most comprehensive bibliography of Oecolampadius' writings, see Ernst Staehelin, *Oekolampad-Bibliographie* (Nieuwkoop: de Graaf, 1963).

3 Johannes Oecolampadius, *In Epistolam ad Hebraeos, ut ex ore praelegentis exceptae, per quosdam ex auditoribus digestae sunt* (Strassburg: Mathiam Apiarius, 1534). On the background of the lectures and commentary, see Rupp, *Patterns of Reformation*, 19, 38, 42-43; Staehelin, *Das theologische Lebenswerk*, 566-67, 571; *Briefe und Akten*, 2.399, 756-58 (Nos. 706, 976).

4 A simple way of distinguishing the four senses was summarized in a short poetic verse in the Middle Ages: 'The letter teaches what happened // allegory what you should believe // the moral what you should do // anagogy to what you should aim.' See Henri de Lubac, *Medieval Exegesis: The Four Senses of Scripture* (Grand Rapids: Eerdmans, 1998), 1.1; 2.257.

For this study, we will primarily consider the most significant commentaries on Hebrews in the Middle Ages and at the time of the Reformation.[5] The most widely consulted writings on Hebrews included Chrysostom, Aquinas, Nicholas of Lyra and the *Glossa Ordinaria*.[6] Dionysius (or Denis) the Carthusian, Jacques Lefèvre d'Étaples and Erasmus provide us with a good representation of the general consensus of medieval interpreters and humanist interests.[7] Since Luther's lectures occurred in 1517/1518, his comments also provide a window into the shift taking place in the exegesis of the 'young Luther'.[8] Johannes Bugenhagen's commentary in 1524/1525 gives us a perspective on a 'Lutheran' interpretation.[9] The comments by Zwingli and Bullinger present an interesting comparison, since they were originally produced around the same time as Oecolampadius' lectures on Hebrews but none were published until after the deaths of Zwingli and Oecolampadius.[10] They each interpreted Hebrews around the same time without being able to consult the published works of one another. Finally, we will look at Calvin's commentary on Hebrews, which was first published in 1549.[11] Obviously, we cannot address all that each

---

5 See Kenneth Hagen, *Hebrews Commenting from Erasmus to Bèze, 1516-1598*, Beiträge zur Geschichte der biblischen Exegese 23 (Tübingen: Mohr, 1981), 99-111.

6 The editions cited in this essay are Chrysostom, 'Homiliae XXXIV in Epistolam ad Hebraeos' in PG 63.9-237, and *Homilies on the Gospel of St. John and the Epistle to the Hebrews* in NPNF[1] 14; Thomas Aquinas, 'Expositio super Epistolam S. Pauli Apostoli ad Hebraeos' in *In omnes d. Pauli Apostoli epistolas commentaria* (Leodii: H. Dessain, 1858), 3.191-406; Nicholas of Lyra, *Textus Bible cum Glossa Ordinaria et Expositione Lyre Litterali* (Basel: Froben & Petri, 1508), 6.132a-162b.

7 The editions cited in this essay are Denis the Carthusian, 'In Epistolam ad Hebraeos' in *In omnes Beati Pauli Epistolas Commentaria* (Cologne: Peter Quentel, 1538); Jacques Lefèvre d'Étaples, *Epistola ad Hebraeos* (Paris: Stephanus, 1512); Desiderius Erasmus, 'Annotationes in Epistolam Pauli Ad Hebraeos' in *Novum Instrumentum Omne* (Basel: Johannes Froben, 1516), 584-601; Desiderius Erasmus, 'Annotationes in Epistolam Pauli Ad Hebraeos' in *Novum Testamentum* (Basel: Froben, 1522), 561-89; Desiderius Erasmus, *In Epistolam ad Hebraeos paraphrasis* (Basel: Froben, 1523). Hereafter, these will be cited as Denis, Lefèvre and Erasmus, *Annotationes (1516)* and *Annotationes (1522)*. On the value of developing a composite picture of medieval interpretation, see David C. Steinmetz, *Luther in Context* (Grand Rapids: Baker, 1994), 99, 158, and G. Sujin Pak, *The Judaizing Calvin: Sixteenth-Century Debates over the Messianic Psalms* (Oxford: OUP, 2010), 6.

8 *WA* 57.III.97b-238; *LW* 29.109-242.

9 Johannes Bugenhagen, *Annotationes Io. Bugenhagij Pomerani in epistolas Pauli* (Basel: Adam Petri, 1525).

10 Ulrich Zwingli, 'In epistolam beati Pauli ad Hebraeos expositio brevis' in *Epistolasq[ue] aliquot Pauli, annotationes*, ed. Kaspar Megander (Zürich: Christoph Froschauer, 1539). Heinrich Bullinger, *In piam et eruditam Pauli ad Hebraeos Epistolam* (Zurich: Christoph Froschauer, 1532).

11 John Calvin, *Commentarius in Epistolam ad Hebraeos* (edited by T.H.L. Parker, vol. 19, Ioannis Calvini Opera Omnia, Series II, Opera Exegetica Veteris et Novi Testamenti (Geneva: Droz, 1996) and *The Epistle of Paul the Apostle to the Hebrews and the First and Second Epistles of St Peter* (edited by David W. Torrance and Thomas

of these theologians said on these verses, but we can identify some of the major emphases and approaches and see the ways in which they changed and remained the same.

Emphases in the exegetical tradition

Nearly all interpreters from the fourth century to the time of the Reformation explained Christ's superiority over angels in Hebrews 1-2 with reference to the theological controversies about the person and natures of Christ in the early church. The *Ancient Christian Commentary on Hebrews* makes the observation that '[t]he Fathers used these opening verses to comment on their doctrines of God, Christology, and the nature of angels'.[12] Most comments on these passages focused on how the words proved certain Christological views.[13] Cyril and the Alexandrian tradition emphasized the union of Christ's divine nature taking on flesh, while the Antiochenes highlighted the distinctions between Christ's human and divine natures.[14] Theodoret and Chryosotom, for example, articulated each instance where Hebrews referred to Christ according to his humanity or according to his divinity.[15] For centuries, most exegetes followed the approach of the Antiochenes by distinguishing the statements in Hebrews 1-2 that applied to the humanity of Christ and to his divinity.[16] Anselm, Aquinas, Denis and the *Glossa Ordinaria* all emphasized the importance of recognizing whether a certain statement about Christ was 'according to his divinity' or 'according to his humanity'.[17] Comments on the words from Psalm 45 in Hebrews 1.8-9, for ex-

---

F. Torrance, translated by William B. Johnston; vol. 12, Calvin's New Testament Commentaries (Grand Rapids: Eerdmans, 1994). Hereafter, these will be cited as *COE* II, 19 and *CNTC* 12.

[12] Erik Heen, Philip Krey, and Thomas Oden (eds.), *Hebrews*, Ancient Christian Commentary (Downers Grove: InterVarsity, 2005), 3.

[13] For example, Chrysostom dedicated an entire homily on Hebrews 1.3 to combat the heresies of Marcellus, Photinus, Sabellius, Arius, and Marcion (NPNF 1-14, 369-72).

[14] See Rowan A. Greer, *The Captain of our Salvation: A Study in the Patristic Exegesis of Hebrews*, Beiträge zur Geschichte der biblischen Exegese 15 (Tübingen: Mohr, 1973), 356-57. Greer notes that Cyril's explanation on Hebrews 1.3 presents a sharp contrast to the Antiochene interpretation (Greer, 322-23). Fragments of Cyril of Alexandria's comments on Hebrews are found in PG 76.385-452, 77: 401-982 and *Cyrilli Archiepiscopi Alexandrini Opera* (edited by P.E. Pusey; Oxford: Clarendon, 1872), 3.362-425.

[15] For example, see Chrysostom in PG 63.15; NPNF[1] 14.368.

[16] This is one of the reasons the oversimplified distinctions made in the past between an Alexandrian 'school' and an Antiochene 'school' cannot be maintained. While allegorical approaches, typically attributed to the Alexandrians flourished in the Middle Ages, most medieval exegetes actually followed the interpretive ideas of the Antiochenes in the way they explained these passages.

[17] *GO*, 793, 794-95. See also Thomas G. Weinandy, 'The Supremacy of Christ: Aquinas' Commentary on Hebrews' in Thomas Gerard Weinandy, Daniel A. Keating and

ample, almost entirely focused on Trinitarian arguments and distinctions about whether 'throne,' 'scepter,' and 'anointing' referred to Christ's human or divine nature.[18] This line of interpretation also appears in Reformation exegetes like Bugenhagen, Luther and Zwingli.[19] From Chrysostom forward, interpreters mainly emphasized how these passages refuted Christological heresy and articulated what they said about the human and divine natures of Christ.

At the time of the Reformation, a few exegetes like Oecolampadius moved away from primarily explaining these verses in light of Christology. While he acknowledged that these passages could be used to refute heresies about the Trinity and even quoted those who made such distinctions, he explicitly contended,

> There is nothing necessary to urge you to say that some things are to be understood about his humanity, other things about his divinity, and to reason about how a man created the world, or how God is an heir and predestined.[20]

He specifically rejected Augustine's idea that the quote from Psalm 2 in Hebrews 1.5 taught the 'divine begetting'.[21] He also rejected Cyril of Alexandria's denial that the pronoun in Hebrews 2.10 referred to the Son, because, he reasoned, those interpretations did not correspond to the meaning of the words, the context of the passages, or the custom of Scripture.[22] Similarly, Oecolampadius explicitly departed from interpretations that were based on speculation, such as

---

John Yocum (eds), *Aquinas On Scripture: An Introduction to his Biblical Commentaries* (London: T. & T. Clark, 2005), 226, 230.

18 Most exegetes maintained that Christ is heir of all things according to his human nature, but is creator of all things according to his divine nature. There were some differences among exegetes about which nature of Christ became less than the angels, became superior to angels, ascended to the right hand, and has an eternal throne. Cyril did not make these distinctions, but emphasized that the psalm quoted proves both the humanity and divinity of Christ (PG 70:375-76).

19 Bugenhagen, 263, 264; *WA* 57.^{3}.98.12-15, 99.1-10; Zwingli, 565. The distinctions are less pronounced in Bullinger, who emphasized the divinity of Christ and the unity of the Trinity 'without mixing or confusing the persons' (8b-10b).

20 Oecolampadius, 7b. Oecolampadius emphasized, 'These things should not disturb you at all . . . you should consider that the humanity and the divinity are included simultaneously . . . since those natures are undivided now, as much as they pertain to the union of the person . . . [Christ's] humanity was not secluded from nor separated from his divinity' (7b-8a). All translations from the Latin are my own.

21 Oecolampadius, 16a. Augustine's interpretation that the phrase, 'Today I have begotten you' teaches the eternal generation of the Son, was quoted in the *Glossa Ordinaria* and affirmed as the primary explanation of the verse by Anselm, Aquinas, Lyra, Dionysius, Lefèvre and Zwingli. See Augustine, *Enarrationes in Psalms* 2.6 in PL 36.71; 'Enchiridion' 49.14A in PL 40.255.

22 Oecolampadius, 29b. He appears to be referring to *Quod Unus sit Christus* (PG 75: 1333-40) since the Hebrews fragments do not contain Cyril's comments on 2:9-13. Oecolampadius was familiar with Cyril's views from his translation work on many of Cyril's writings.

the common way Christian exegetes had explained Hebrews 1.7 'to be about the order of angels . . . and the nature of angels'.[23] Oecolampadius reasoned that when these passages were rightly explained, making these kinds of theological distinctions were not necessary. This same perspective is evident in John Calvin, who denounced 'frivolous speculations' from these passages about the Trinity.[24] Calvin agreed that these verses sufficiently refuted heresies, but he also declared that there was 'no need to dispute too subtly' about the Trinitarian distinctions because 'there is a degree of impropriety in what is translated from created things to the hidden majesty of God'.[25] Calvin followed Oecolampadius in affirming that the kinds of distinctions that arose from the Christological controversies did not explain the Apostle's intention or the genuine meaning of the text.[26]

Use of Old Testament quotations in Hebrews 1-2

In contrast to the way previous exegetes had explained the first chapters of Hebrews, Oecolampadius took a particular interest in rightly understanding the frequent quotations of the Old Testament in Hebrews. Few exegetes prior to Oecolampadius had addressed this issue. Most interpreters did not even acknowledge all the phrases in Hebrews 1-2 that came from the Old Testament.[27] Those who did observe that the words were taken from the Old Testament most often assumed that when the Apostle quoted these verses they were clear, authoritative proof that Christ was superior over angels, without any concern for whether these passages referred to Christ in their original Old Testament setting.[28] Though nuances certainly existed, the view prevailed among medieval interpreters that whatever Old Testament text was chosen by a New Testament author its meaning was determined by the way the New Testament author used it. Sometimes this was 'proven' by interpreting the passage allegorically, and sometimes it was simply affirmed as the literal meaning.[29] Only rarely was the original Old Testament context actually considered.

We see some consideration of Old Testament context in Lyra, Denis and Luther. However, none of them commented on all the Old Testament passages quoted in Hebrews 1-2, and each rarely offered more than a cursory explanation of the original context before declaring that it rightly applies to Christ. Lyra and

---

23 Oecolampadius, 18b.

24 *COE* II, 1918.17-18; *CNTC* 12.8.

25 *COE* II, 19.18.11-14, 19.23-28; *CNTC* 12.7, 8-9.

26 See, for example, *COE* II, 19.18.24-28; *CNTC* 12.8.

27 For example, very few exegetes identify that the OT was quoted in Hebrews 1.6, 1.10-12 and 2.10-13. See Denis, 125a; PG 63.41; NPNF[1] 14: 384-85.

28 For a similar conclusion, see Hagen, *Theology of Testament*, 31-33, 60-61.

29 For a similar treatment with respect to how Justin Martyr, Chrysostom, Cyril of Alexandria, Aquinas and Lyra understood the New Testament use of Isaiah, see Brevard S. Childs, *The Struggle to Understand Isaiah as Christian Scripture* (Grand Rapids: Eerdmans, 2004), 39-41, 71, 93, 100, 112-17, 157-60, 163, 177-78.

Luther were the only major exegetes who provided any explanation about Psalm 97 in Hebrews 1.6 or Psalm 45.6-7 in Hebrews 1.8-9; but like most previous exegetes, they identified that these verses only spoke about Christ's kingdom and proved his divinity.[30] Luther provided more substantive reasoning for how these psalms applied to Christ, appealing to other verses in Psalm 97 and giving new explanations for 'throne' and 'staff' in Psalm 45 to conclude, 'Therefore this verse fits no one but Christ, because no one except Christ alone loves righteousness.'[31] Lyra, Denis and Luther on occasion identified David or Solomon as a type of Christ, but did not explain how they functioned as types.[32] A primary means of explanation for these passages was to cite Psalm 71 (72.17) as evidence that certain things were said about David or Solomon that could only refer to them as prefiguring Christ.[33] Both Lyra and Luther adopted this as their explanation for Psalm 2.[34]

Luther's hermeneutical grid of law and gospel allowed him to include the original historical context without others labeling his explanations as 'Jewish exegesis'. However, Luther's exposition of Hebrews confirms that he understood the psalms to be particularly about Christ unless there was a strong reason to indicate otherwise.[35] Lyra and Denis insisted that the Apostles often selected Old Testament passages based only on their sense and not the form of the words. When the New Testament quoted an Old Testament passage, it gave the literal meaning of both passages.[36] Lyra argued for a 'double literal meaning' (*duplex literalis sensus*) in Scripture which affirmed that 'the authority introduced by the Apostle is understood as the letter about Christ'.[37] Lyra specifically stated that his perspective on the use of the Old Testament in the New was patterned after Augustine's view that 'sacred scripture has a multiple sense, yet it is not considered an effective argument except by the literal sense, as Augustine says'.[38] Other interpreters, such as Bugenhagen and Lefèvre, operated from a similar assumption and thought that the way the Apostle used the Old Testament was the way everyone should understand the passages, including Jewish

---

30 Lyra, 6.135b; *WA* 57.[3.]104-105; LW 29.115.

31 *WA* 57.[3.]107-109; *LW* 29.117-19. Luther quoted from Psalm 97.1, 2, 3, 6, 10 to make the case that the entire psalm refers to the kingdom of Christ.

32 Denis, 124b; Lyra, 6: 135a-b.

33 See, for example, Lyra, 6.135a; *WA* 57.[3.]102; *LW* 29.114; Aquinas, 207.

34 *WA* 57.[3.]102-104; *LW* 29.113-15.

35 *WA* 55.I.6; *LW* 10.6. See Mark Thompson, *A Sure Ground on Which to Stand: The Relation of Authority and Interpretive Method in Luther's Approach to Scripture* (Eugene: Wipf and Stock, 2006), 152-63, 167-86; Childs, *Struggle to Understand Isaiah,* 185-91, 203-204.

36 Lyra, 6.135a-b; Denis, 124a, 124b.

37 Lyra, 6.135a. See also Pak, *Judaizing Calvin*, 28.

38 Lyra, 6.135a. Augustine famously asserted that 'the Old Testament revealed in the New is the New concealed in the Old' (CCSL 40.1567.9-10). For very similar comments, see also Denis, 124b.

interpreters.[39] Lefèvre even criticized Lyra's approach as a kind of 'Rabbinic exegesis,' because it didn't *directly* affirm that the Old Testament passages quoted spoke exclusively about Christ.[40] Most exegetes, including Lyra, Denis and Luther, did not observe the problem that some of these psalms, like Psalms 45 and 102, were written about God and not the Messiah.[41] Additionally, while there are some cases where these exegetes mentioned a Jewish interpretation of a specific psalm, nearly all of their responses are either a simple declaration that the Jews were in error or a brief refutation that did not directly engage how Jewish interpreters understood the psalm in its original context.[42]

Oecolampadius on Old Testament quotations in Hebrews 1-2

The comments made by Oecolampadius on Hebrews 1-2 demonstrate an important shift in the way these passages were explained. He continued the growing emphasis on the literal sense evident in exegetes like Lyra and Luther, but also added the specific dimension of insisting that the Old Testament passages must be understood in their original context in order to show *how* the New Testament author properly quoted them. Oecolampadius reasoned, 'Since the business for the Apostle is with Hebrews skilled in the law, he uses frequent and valid testimonies of Scripture, which ought to be treated diligently.' [43] He specifically expressed that one 'especially ought to be vigilant in our time, since the studies of the Hebrew language flourish'.[44] Oecolampadius remained in continuity with the exegetical tradition by affirming that every Old Testament passage quoted in the New Testament completely adhered to the meaning the New Testament authors found in them. However, he was among the few scholars of his day who interacted directly with Jewish interpretations in order to understand their explanations and to provide responses for how Hebrews properly quoted from the psalms and other Old Testament passages.[45]

---

39 Bugenhagen, 262–63; Lefèvre, 230b-31b.

40 Lefèvre, *Quincuplex Psalterium* (1513), A.iii. See also Thompson, *Sure Ground*, 40-41.

41 Anselm appears to be the only exegete who commented that 'in this *epistle* it is said to the person of the *Son*, not to the person of the Father . . . although in the *psalm* those things are said more suitably to the *Father*, or better to the entire Trinity'—*In omnes Pauli Epistolas ennarationes* (Coloniae: Gennepaeum, 1545), 455. Luther and Denis did not even discuss the use of Psalm 102 in Hebrews 1.10-12 (*WA* 57.³·8, 110-11; *LW* 29.119; Denis, 125a). Luther glossed that the psalm should be understood about Christ's incarnation (*WA* 57.³·8).

42 See, for example, Denis, 124a; Lyra 6.136a.

43 Oecolampadius, 14a. See also 31a.

44 Oecolampadius, 14a.

45 See Stephen G. Burnett, 'The Strange Career of the Biblia Rabbinica Among Christian Hebraists, 1517-1620' in Bruce Gordon and Matthew McLean (eds), *Shaping the Bible in the Reformation: Books, Scholars, and Their Readers in the Sixteenth Century* (Leiden: Brill, 2012), 71-73, 78.

Oecolampadius interacted with the interpretations of Rashi (Rabbi Shalomo Itzhaki, d. 1105), Rabbi David Kimhi (1160-1235), Rabbi Abraham Ibn Ezra (1092-1167), and Rabbi Saadia Gaon (ca. 882-942)—all medieval Jewish interpreters following the *peshat* method of exegesis.[46] He no doubt obtained much of his knowledge of Jewish interpretation from the *Biblia Rabbinica*, possibly both the 1517 and 1525 editions.[47]

Unlike those before him, Oecolampadius provided an explanation on the use of every Old Testament quotation in Hebrews 1-2 and directly interacted with Jewish interpretations and objections on eight of the nine quotations from the psalms. His first comments on the first quotation in Hebrews were a recounting of the Jewish interpretation—drawn from Kimhi and Rashi—that Psalm 2 referred to the day when David was anointed as king.[48] As part of his response, Oecolampadius accurately pointed out:

> Not all Hebrews separate this psalm from the Christ. Indeed [Ibn] Ezra and Kimhi say that there are those following the Talmud, who refer it to Gog and Magog as well as to the messiah. But Rabbi Schlomo [Rashi] instead advances his own [view] saying, 'Our teachers explained it to be about the king messiah, but although you may explain it that way, at its simplest, and to respond more fittingly to heretics, we observe [that it refers to David].'[49]

The general view of Jewish interpreters was that the 'begotten son' in Psalm 2.7 was the king whom God installed in Psalm 2.6, and this referred to David, though possibly the messiah. Oecolampadius agreed that 'according to the his-

---

46 Oecolampadius specifically named these Jewish interpreters (14b, 19a, 91a and 126a). Their comments on these psalms are found in Abraham ben Meïr Ibn Ezra, *Abraham Ibn Ezra's Commentary on the First Book of Psalms* (translated by H. Norman Strickman; Boston: Academic Studies, 2009); Rashi, *Rashi's Commentary on Psalms 1-89 (Books I-III)*, South Florida Studies in the History of Judaism 161 (translated by Mayer I. Gruber; Atlanta: Scholars, 1998); David Kimhi, *The Longer Commentary of R. David Ḳimḥi on the First Book of Psalms (I-X, XV-XVII, XIX, XXII, XXIV)* (translated by R.G. Finch; New York: Macmillan, 1919) and *The Commentary of Rabbi David Kimḥi on Psalms CXX-CL*, University of Cambridge Oriental Publications 22 (translated by Joshua Baker and Ernest W. Nicholson; Cambridge: CUP, 1973). For background on these Jewish interpreters, see Robert A. Harris, 'Medieval Jewish Biblical Exegesis' in Alan J. Hauser and Daune F. Watson (eds), *A History of Biblical Interpretation* (Grand Rapids: Eerdmans, 2009), 2.141-71; Uriel Simon, *Four Approaches to the Book of Psalms: From Saadiah Gaon to Abraham Ibn Ezra* (Albany: State University of New York Press, 1991).

47 The first edition of the *Biblia Rabbinica* in 1517 included Kimhi's commentary on Psalms and the second edition included Rashi and Ibn Ezra, but not Kimhi's. It is possible that Oecolampadius had access to both editions.

48 Oecolampadius, 14b, 16a. For the Jewish interpretations see Rashi, 53; Ibn Ezra, 30; Kimhi, *Longer Commentary*, 15-16.

49 Oecolampadius, 14b. See Kimhi, *Longer Commentary*, 18; Rashi, *Rashi's Commentary on Psalms 1-89*, 52, 54; Ibn Ezra, 25, 26, 29.

tory, we cannot deny that this happened to David'.[50] But he also affirmed, 'Yet far more dignified and loftier things are said in this psalm than are seen fulfilled in David.'[51] Using the same method as the Jewish interpreters, Oecolampadius considered how the rest of Psalm 2 supplied the essential elements to determine that 'at the same time we will be compelled to confess that the kingdom of Christ was foretold and sketched out under that shadow and David himself is called Christ by the prophets'.[52] Oecolampadius also responded to other Jewish interpreters 'who concede that this psalm was said about the Christ, but promise a temporary kingdom' by appealing to several other Old Testament passages to substantiate that an entirely different kind of king and kingdom is promised in Psalm 2.[53] He agreed with the Jewish view that the king installed in Psalm 2.6 is the 'begotten son' in 2.7, but deduced that if this king was 'to reside in Zion in the same way as any other mortal king' it would not explain the great honor and dignity which Psalm 2 extols.[54] He reasoned that in Hebrews, the Apostle recognized that 'to be begotten' was a 'trope of the Jews' that refers to a time when glory is revealed, which applied to David when he was anointed as king and to Christ when he was glorified in his resurrection.[55] Oecolampadius' approach and conclusion differed greatly from the exegetical tradition, which had primarily interpreted this as a reference to Christ's divine begetting or the incarnation, and had not engaged with Jewish interpretations.

Oecolampadius took a similar approach in his exposition of how Hebrews 2.5-9 used Psalm 8 to show that Christ is superior to angels.[56] He noted that 'with Basil, all the Hebrews said that this psalm was written about humankind. . . . So they interpret this psalm, and indeed, well enough what pertains to the letter.'[57] He again remarked, though, that 'something more lofty lies hidden' in Psalm 8 than the Jewish interpretation allowed.[58] He maintained that the Apostle

> at the same time does not deny this exposition [about humankind], but specifies something much more worthy. And since these things which the psalmist specifies

---

50 Oecolampadius, 14b.

51 Oecolampadius, 15a.

52 Oecolampadius, 14b-15a. Oecolampadius observed that verses 3, 6, 8 and 12, in particular, showed that David was not allowed to build the temple; his authority did not go beyond Judea and other kings did not honor him as the son of God.

53 Oecolampadius, 15a. Oecolampadius quoted from Zechariah 9.9, Hosea 1.7 and Isaiah 11.4.

54 Oecolampadius, 15b.

55 Oecolampadius, 15b-16a.

56 Oecolampadius, 25b-26b.

57 Oecolampadius, 26b-27a. For Basil's view, see PG 29.449 on Psalm 48.13-14 [49.12-13]. For the Jewish interpreters, see Kimhi, *Longer Commentary*, 51, 52; Rashi, 72.

58 Oecolampadius, 28a.

here cannot be said to be fulfilled in any human, it follows that these are fully fulfilled in Christ alone.[59]

His particular argument was that since humankind forfeited its power and dominion over creation at the Fall, the things declared in Psalm 8 could only apply to humankind imperfectly, but ultimately applied to Christ.[60] Previous Christian exegetes had almost entirely focused on and disputed about how each phrase from Psalm 8 specifically described Christ and his nature.[61] Luther, for example, criticized three views that differed from his own, because the passage 'can only be interpreted to refer to Christ; otherwise the context is distorted'.[62] One of the views he criticized was Chrysostom's teaching that 'although these things were spoken of human nature generally, they would nevertheless apply more properly to Christ according to the flesh'.[63] Oecolampadius' conclusion was similar to that of Chrysostom, but his approach included affirming the Jewish interpretation and providing reasons why Hebrews properly applied it to Christ.

In his exposition of on the three quotations in Hebrews 2.11-13, Oecolampadius likewise engaged with various Jewish interpretations.[64] He accurately described Kimhi's reporting that some rabbis interpreted Psalm 22 to refer to the ten tribes in exile and their 'brothers'—the Edomites, the Ishmaelites, and the children of Hagar—while other rabbis, like Kimhi himself, affirmed that it applied to the 'whole congregation of Israel while in exile'.[65] Oecolampadius affirmed the view that Psalm 22 'can be explained about David—but as a type. For quite clearly David presents himself as a type of Christ.'[66] Most Christian interpreters who commented on 2.10-13 directly equated the quotation with Christ standing 'in the midst' of his disciples after his resurrection without any connection to its original context in the life of David or Israel.[67] Bugenhagen represented the prevailing view that these Old Testament passages simply predicted Christ's suffering and glory.[68]

A significant difference in Oecolampadius' comments is his interest in addressing the issue that Hebrews applied certain psalms to Christ that only referred to God. In his comments on Hebrews 1.6, he recognized that 'the judaizers could be offended here, because in this psalm [97.7], no mention is made of

---

59 Oecolampadius, 27a, 28b.

60 Oecolampadius, 27a.

61 See Anselm, 458; Lyra, 6: 137b-38b; Denis, 124a, 125b, 126a; Lefèvre, 233a-34a; Erasmus, *Annotations* (1516), 585; *Annotations* (1522), 562-63.

62 *WA* 57.[3.]116-17; *LW* 29.125-26.

63 NPNF[1]14.383.

64 Oecolampadius, 31a-32b.

65 Oecolampadius, 31a; Kimhi, *Longer Commentary*, 97, 104.

66 Oecolampadius, 31b.

67 See NPNF[1] 14.384-85; PG 63.41; Lyra, 6.138a; *GO*, 6.138a-b; Denis, 126a-b; Anselm, 459; Aquinas, 232-33.

68 Bugenhagen, 268.

the Son, or of the Christ, but only God is introduced, as if this testimony pertains in no way to Christ'.[69] Likewise, with regard to the quotation of Psalm 102.25-27 in Hebrews 1.10-12, he acknowledged that 'the Jews again will oppose [this] as if it is simply about God and not about the Son of God, who is the Christ'.[70] Oecolampadius specified that the Apostle properly used Psalm 97 by connecting it to parallel passages, like Daniel 7, which 'plainly apply to the Christ, and show him to be the judge who is going to come, as this psalm has'.[71] Likewise, he pointed to other promises in Psalm 102 to confirm that this passage rightly applied to Christ and shows he is eternal, immutable, immortal by nature, and unlike any created being.[72] In his comments on the use of Psalm 45.6-7 in Hebrews 1.8-9, Oecolampadius explicitly reproved Rabbi Saadia's claim that the psalm did not address the messiah *as* God, but rather said *to* the messiah, 'God *will establish* your seat forever.'[73] Oecolampadius stated,

> by the consensus of all the Hebrews, it was written about the messiah, although they still seek to modify it, so they don't have to accept Christ as God and heavenly judge, even though those things are more obvious than their evasion allows.[74]

He reasoned that even if Saadia's addition to the text were legitimate, the psalm still teaches that the Christ is God, because only God can have an *eternal* throne and be the *eternal* judge.[75] He affirmed that the Apostle properly used Psalm 45 because it 'attributes judicial power and peaceful authority to Christ'.[76] While Oecolampadius was not primarily a literal-historical interpreter, he seems to be the first major exegete who engaged substantially with Jewish interpretations and insisted that the Old Testament passages quoted in Hebrews must first be understood in their original context in order to show how the New Testament author properly used them as proof of Christ's superiority over angels.

Other Reformed interpreters

When we compare Oecolampadius' comments on Hebrews with other contemporary Reformed interpreters, we see that his approach differed greatly from

---

69 Oecolampadius, 17b.

70 Oecolampadius, 20b.

71 Oecolampadius, 17b-18a.

72 Oecolampadius, 20b.

73 Oecolampadius, 19a.—my emphasis for clarity. Oecolampadius was likely aware of Saadia's view from Kimhi's comments on Psalm 45.7—*Rabbi Davidis Kimhhi Commentarii in psalmos Davidis* (translated by Ambrosio Ianvier; Paris: Billaine, 1666), 203.

74 Oecolampadius, 19a. Though Oecolampadius claimed that this view was the consensus of all Jewish interpreters, Rashi actually interpreted this psalm as a metaphor about following Torah and not about the messiah (*Rashi's Commentary on the Psalms*, 213, 214).

75 Oecolampadius, 19b.

76 Oecolampadius, 19a.

Zwingli and Bullinger. Zwingli, for example, did not even observe that Psalms 97, 104, 45 and 102 were quoted in Hebrews. He maintained that these Old Testament passages were used 'like a shield' to defend the excellence of Christ over angels.[77] He stated that it was not difficult to see that 'with many citations of testimonies of Scripture, he diligently teaches that Christ according to his human nature is more excellent and inferior to angels'.[78] Only in his expositions of Hebrews 2.5-9 do we see much similarity to the conclusions of Oecolampadius. There he commented, 'although [Psalm 8] may have been said about the common humanity of all mortals . . . the apostle properly applies it to the humanity of Christ'.[79] However, even in this case, Zwingli simply appealed to an anagogical interpretation of the passage, and continued in the exegetical tradition of making distinctions about Christ's humanity and his divinity.[80]

Bullinger also took a very different overall approach to explaining the quotations in Hebrews. Like Zwingli, Bullinger did not comment on many of the Old Testament passages. Where he did comment on a quotation, he only identified the location of the quote and then moved immediately to the New Testament meaning. For example, he stated that the identification of the 'only-begotten' in Psalm 2 proved Christ's divinity, and that the prediction that all angels would worship the 'firstborn' in Psalm 97 showed his true humanity.[81] Bullinger specifically articulated that several Old Testament passages, such as Psalms 2, 8, and 18, only applied to Christ allegorically.[82] Similarly, he specified that the quotation from Isaiah 8 in Hebrews 2.13 was 'according to the same use of *Catachresis*'—a rhetorical term that carried the sense of misuse.[83] But Zwingli and Bullinger did not express the same interest as Oecolampadius about how the Apostle properly used the psalms, but rather continued to explain these verses in ways that were similar to the exegetical tradition.

The most striking similarity to Oecolampadius' explanations of these passages is found in John Calvin.[84] A few scholars have noted that 'without a

---

77 Zwingli, 567. He also did not identify any of the Old Testament passages quoted in Hebrews 2.11-13 (568).

78 Zwingli, 566.

79 Zwingli, 567.

80 Zwingli, 567.

81 Bullinger, 18a.

82 Bullinger, 17b, 25b, 28a, 35a, 35b.

83 Bullinger, 28a. The basic definition of *Catachresis* was given by Quintilian and often repeated in the sixteenth century as the practice of adapting the nearest available term to describe something for which no proper term exists. See John Bender and David Wellbery, *The Ends of Rhetoric: History, Theory, Practice* (Stanford: Stanford University Press, 1990), 60-61.

84 Martin Bucer also took an approach similar to that of Oecolampadius, but Bucer did not write a commentary on Hebrews. His explanations for how the book of Hebrews used specific psalms can be found in his Psalms commentary of 1529. For a good summary of Bucer's interpretive approach, see Sujin Pak, *Judaizing Calvin*, 59-61, 68-69. Konrad Pellikan's commentary on Hebrews published in 1539 includes nu-

doubt, Calvin had Oecolampadius' exegetical works beside him and consulted them with reasonable frequency'.[85] Calvin not only recommended the work of Oecolampadius, but also permitted the entire corpus of his commentaries on Old Testament books to be republished in Geneva in 1558.[86] Of all the exegetes considered in this study, only Calvin and Oecolampadius directly commented on every quotation from the Old Testament. And only these two demonstrated a strong interest in explaining how Hebrews properly quoted the Old Testament.

One of Calvin's primary concerns in his Hebrews commentary was making sense of citations from the Old Testament which seem to be 'out of context or contorted'.[87] Calvin admitted there were places where the Apostle's use of Scripture 'still seemed insufficiently founded'.[88] He raised the same problem that Oecolampadius had observed with certain psalms that 'may seem unreasonable to apply to Christ what is spoken of God only'.[89] For example, he too observed that the quotation of Psalm 102 in Hebrews 1.10-12, 'may at first sight seem to be applied ineptly to Christ, especially in the doubtful way it is treated, for the discussion is not about the glory of God, but what properly applies to Christ. Yet there is no mention of Christ.'[90] Calvin also admitted that it 'would avail little in proving a doubtful point,' to simply *affirm* that when worship which only belongs to God is applied to Christ in Hebrews 1.6, it proves that he is eternal God.[91] Instead Calvin sought to explain *why* Hebrews properly used these Old Testament passages.

Calvin echoed Oecolampadius that the Old Testament passages quoted in Hebrews 1.5 were properly used because other elements in the rest of Psalm 2 showed that it had to refer to a kingdom greater than David's ever was and 2 Samuel 7 referred to Solomon and his kingdom as a type of Christ.[92] He even followed the same sequence as Oecolampadius when he criticized 'the frivo-

---

merous excerpts of the exact wording from Oecolampadius' commentary. See 'Commentarium in Epistolam D. Pauli Apostoli ad Hebraeos' in *Commentaria Bibliorum* (Zurich: Christoph Froschauer, 1539), 7.608-80.

85 For example, see Akira Demura, 'Two Commentaries on the Epistle to the Romans: Calvin and Oecolampadius' in *Calvinus Sincerioris Religionis Vindex*, 1997, 167; James Brashler, 'From Erasmus to Calvin: Exploring the Roots of Reformed Hermeneutics,' *Interpretation* 63.2 (2009), 165.

86 See the letter from John Calvin to Pierre Viret, dated May 19, 1540, in *CO* 11.36 (No. 217) where Calvin gives a qualified recommendation of Oecolampadius' Isaiah commentary. On publications in Geneva, see Jean François Gilmont, *John Calvin and the Printed Book* (translated by Karin Maag; Kirksville: Truman State University Press, 2005), 245-65.

87 Gary Neal Hansen, 'Calvin as Commentator on Hebrews and the Catholic Epistles' in Donald K. McKim (ed.), *Calvin and the Bible* (New York: CUP, 2006), 278.

88 See, for example, *COE* II, 19.22.7-31; *CNTC* 12.11.

89 *COE* II, 19.23.32-33; *CNTC* 12.12.

90 *COE* II, 19.26.27-30; *CNTC* 12.15.

91 *COE* II, 19.23.34-24.4; *CNTC* 12.12.

92 *COE* II, 19.21.26-29, 23.16–29; *CNTC* 12.10-12.

lous subtlety of Augustine, who imagines that "Today" is eternity and perpetuity,' and then affirmed, 'Certainly, Christ is the eternal Son of God. . . . But there is nothing about this in this passage.'[93] Calvin likewise quoted from the broader context of Psalms 102, 97 and 22 to show that even when 'Christ is not named in the whole psalm . . . his kingdom is commended to us,' and 'if you read the whole psalm, you will find nothing else but the kingdom of Christ'.[94] Calvin, though, did not identify David as a type in Psalm 22, like Oecolampadius had done, but rather asserted that 'Christ is the speaker, or David, in his name'.[95]

It is also apparent that Calvin observed the same Jewish interpretations that Oecolampadius had recounted about Psalms 45 and 102.[96] He echoed Oecolampadius' contention that the attempts by Jewish interpreters to explain Psalm 45 were 'mere evasions' and his conclusion that even if the word 'established' is added, only God's throne is established forever and so, 'the eternity of the kingdom is testimony of his divinity'.[97] Similarly, Calvin observed with regard to Psalm 8 that 'the Apostle seems to turn the words from the meaning in which David understood them,' because it was about 'the benefits which God bestows on humankind'.[98] Like Oecolampadius, he reasoned that 'by his own defection [humankind] deserved the loss of his dominion,' and so, Calvin concluded that Psalm 8 could only apply to Christ, because only Christ could restore what humanity lost.[99] Calvin constantly sought to explain 'why the Apostle applied this to Christ' and showed how each passage 'fittingly' and 'rightly applied to Christ'.[100]

Summary

This survey of comments on the psalms quoted in Hebrews 1-2 has shown that an important element in the gradual shift away from the traditional medieval

---

93 *COE* II, 19.22.34-23.1, 24.2-4; *CNTC* 12.11. By connecting this verse with Romans 1.4, Calvin also reiterated the conclusion of few other than Oecolampadius that 'begotten' here referred to the resurrection of Jesus (*COE* II, 19.23.5; *CNTC* 12.11).

94 *COE* II, 19, 26.31-27.11; *CNTC* 12.15. Compare with Oecolampadius, 20a-b.

95 *COE* II, 19.39.17, 40.1-2; *CNTC* 12.26, 27. Calvin also identified that David was 'speaking under a different person' in the second quotation in Hebrews 2.10-13, which he observed as being selected from Psalm 18.2 (*COE* II, 19.41.3-5; *CNTC* 12.27-28).

96 *COE* II, 19, 25.16-21, 27.11-12; *CNTC* 12.13-14, 15. Compare to Oecolampadius, 19a.

97 *COE* II, 19.25.25-27; *CNTC* 12.14. Compare to Oecolampadius, 19a. Calvin differed from Oecolampadius because he identified that Psalm 45 'was composed as a marriage song about Solomon,' whereas Oecolampadius had argued Psalm 45 showed Christ as judge (*COE* II, 19.25.13-16, 25.28-26.10; *CNTC* 12.13, 14).

98 *COE* II, 19.33.14-24, 34.34-35.9, 36.20-24; *CNTC* 12.22-23, 24.

99 *COE* II, 19.33.20-29, 34.25-28; *CNTC* 12.21. See Oecolampadius, 27a-b.

100 *COE* II, 19.41.21-23; *CNTC* 12.28.

fourfold approach was a new interest in reconciling the original sense of an Old Testament passage with its use in the New Testament. Brevard Childs summarizes Calvin's approach by observing that his 'marked reservations in exploiting a direct Christological application from the Old Testament set him apart not only from most of the Church Fathers, but also from the other Protestant Reformers, especially from Luther and his followers'.[101] It is evident that despite variations in their explanations, Calvin raised the same problems, mentioned many of the same Jewish interpretations, offered similar solutions and expressed many of the same conclusions as Oecolampadius had done twenty years earlier. Although Oecolampadius still offered many 'spiritual' interpretations that appear forced, he provided substantial explanations for how the Apostle properly applied each Old Testament passage to Christ. This particular interest of both Calvin and Oecolampadius differed greatly from most exegetes prior to the Reformation—and even many during the Reformation—who commented very little about the meaning of Old Testament passages or how they were properly used by the Apostle. Our interest today about the importance of understanding the use of the Old Testament in the New can be attributed to interpretive changes that took place during the Reformation, particularly in the exposition of John Calvin and Johannes Oecolampadius.

[101] Childs, *Struggle to Understand Isaiah*, 216.

CHAPTER 7

Luther and Calvin's understanding of Isaiah 52.13-53.12

Suk-il Ahn

The book of Isaiah contains a number of messianic prophecies, of which the most remarkable is the prophecy of the Suffering Servant in Isaiah 53. This prophecy has been understood as revealing Jesus Christ because he fulfilled the prophecy by suffering on the cross. To defend the messiahship of Jesus in prophecy, the early church had used the allegorical method of exegesis, while in the Reformation period the grammatico-historical method was employed, underlining the authority of Scripture.[1] And the foundation of the grammatico-historical method was laid by Luther and Calvin. However, it might be noted that both Luther and Calvin, as pre-critical interpreters, have more continuity with medieval theologians.[2] The basic concern of this essay, then, regards Luther and Calvin as biblical exegetes, as interpreters of the Bible. In this context, it is worth investigating their understanding of the messianic prophecy of Isaiah 52.13-53.12, for it demonstrates them to be biblical exegetes and interpreters. What is Luther and Calvin's interpretation of the messianic prophecy? How do they recognize it? What are the hermeneutic principles in their interpretation, and what are the similarities and dissimilarities between them?

First, I will briefly summarize Luther and Calvin's interpretive principles of the Old Testament, and then I will trace their understanding of Isaiah 52.13-53.12 by dealing with Luther's lectures and sermons on Isaiah 52.13-53.12 and Calvin's commentaries, sermons and the *Institutes of the Christian Religion*.[3]

---

1 Kemper Fullerton, 'The Reformation Principle of Exegesis and the Interpretation of Prophecy,' *AJT* 12.3 (1908), 424. This grammatico-historical method has two meanings: 'a given verse in a prophecy can have but one meaning' and 'the prophecy must be interpreted out of the historical situation which has given rise to it, so far as this can be discovered' (424). The principle of exegesis at that time was 'enunciated by Luther and Calvin in an intensely dogmatic interest, namely, to secure the perspicuity of the Bible and so protect it as a final authority against the claims of the pope' (442).

2 For discussion of Luther and Calvin as pre-critical interpreters, see David Steinmetz, 'The Superiority of Pre-Critical Exegesis,' *ThT* 37 (1980-81), 27-38.

3 Richard A. Muller, *The Unaccommodated Calvin: Studies in the Formation of a The-*

As a result, the similarities and the dissimilarities in their interpretation of Isaiah 52.13-53.12 will be proposed. Consequently, I will argue that the two reformers have understood Isaiah 52.13-53.12 in the frame of promise–fulfillment based on Christ-centeredness and that their understanding reflects their *Sitz im Leben*.

The reformers' Old Testament hermeneutics

Luther's Old Testament hermeneutics

Luther's method of interpretation of the Bible can be represented in five principles. First, Luther's interpretation emphasizes the authority of Scripture. In *the Freedom of a Christian* (1520) he asserts that there is only one thing necessary for Christian life, righteousness, and freedom: 'the most holy Word of God, the gospel of Christ'.[4] In this respect, Althaus indicates that 'All Luther's theological thinking presupposes the authority of Scripture.'[5] Smith says that 'Luther often wished that all the commentaries, including his own, would perish, so that men might have nothing to read but the plain word of God, for, said he, the Bible explains itself better than any gloss.'[6]

Second, Luther's method of interpretation is dialectic. For example, Luther stresses law and gospel. 'Almost all Scripture and the understanding of all theology hang on the proper understanding of law and gospel.'[7] In the commentary on Galatians (1531), Luther says, 'Whoever knows well how to distinguish the Gospel from the Law should give thanks to God and know that he is a real theologian.'[8] Luther thinks law and gospel works together as God's word for 'the same word strikes sinful man both as law and as gospel' and the word of the cross as the center of gospel performs 'the function of the law,' revealing 'man's sin and lost condition in a deeper and more painful way than any "law" in the narrower sense can do'.[9] Thus Childs indicates that 'opposing terms are juxtaposed and held in tension,' so that a peculiarity in Luther's interpretation is dialectic as seen in the terms such as 'spirit and letter, gospel and law, spiritual and physical kingdoms, external and internal, old and new creation, sin and righteousness, faith and works,' and so on.[10]

---

ological Tradition (New York: OUP, 2000), 182. Muller indicates that we should deal with Calvin's commentaries, sermons and the *Institutes of the Christian Religion* together in order to gain a whole picture of him.

4 *LW* 31.345.

5 Paul Althaus, *The Theology of Martin Luther* (Philadelphia: Westminster, 1966), 3.

6 Preserved Smith, 'The methods of Reformation Interpreters of the Bible,' *The Biblical Word* 38.4 (1911), 245.

7 *WA* 7.502, 34-35: '*pene universa scriptura totiusque theologiae cognito pendet in recta cognitione legis et Euangelii*'.

8 *LW* 26.115.

9 Althaus, *The Theology*, 264.

10 Brevard S. Childs, *The Struggle to Understand Isaiah as Christian Scripture* (Grand Rapids: Eerdmans, 2004), 195.

Third, Luther's interpretation emphasizes the literal sense. For Luther, the literal sense was correctly Christ-centered. Bornkamm explains it very well:

> Luther understood the 'literal' sense not as historical-factual interpretation, but as 'literal, prophetic sense,' namely, as the interpretation speaking out of the spirit of the prophets which pointed to the coming Christ. Each one of the exegetical methods is justified by this turning toward Christ; not just in the sense of a dogmatic presentation, but rather, in the sense that thereby Christ's call to decision in the life of the individual becomes, at the same time, visible tropologically.[11]

As such, for Luther the literal sense as Christ-centered was 'the whole basis of faith and Christian theology'.[12] In particular, Luther regards a combined literal-spiritual meaning by employing spiritual interpretation in opposition to allegorical. Bornkamm points out that for Luther the prophetic-tropological meaning is spiritual, that is, 'Scripture's pointing toward Christ as savior and judge.'[13] Luther does this because 'the allegorists (such as Jerome and Origen) miss the sense of Christ in Scripture'.[14] Accordingly, Luther's spiritual interpretation is distinguished from allegorical by 'the fact that it is grounded in the history of salvation and that it interprets the texts in terms of their relationship to Christ'.[15]

Fourth, Luther recognizes God's word in the Old Testament as Christ-centered. As Pelikan contends, Luther's argument against legalism 'enabled him to discern the redemptive theme in Old Testament history. Because he did not identify the Old Testament with the Law, he was able to find the Word of God as Gospel in the Old Testament.'[16]

Fifth, Luther interprets the Old Testament in the frame of promise-fulfillment. Luther interpreted the gospel as the new law in contrast to the law given at Sinai. In his lecture on Isaiah 2.3 Luther plainly states that he was involved in a new law, as a universal word, in contrast to the law given at Sinai, which is 'a prophecy about the dissemination of the gospel through the apostles'.[17] Thus Bornkamm indicates that 'Luther claimed the right to interpret those passages of the Old Testament in which reference is made to law in a prophetic context in terms of the "new law," the gospel.'[18] This points to the frame of promise-fulfillment in that the gospel as a new law has fulfilled the law in a prophetic context.

---

11 Heinrich Bornkamm, *Luther and the Old Testament* (Philadelphia: Fortress, 1969), 88-89.

12 Bornkamm, *Luther*, 91.

13 Bornkamm, *Luther*, 89.

14 Bornkamm, *Luther*, 89. Bornkamm quotes *LW* 35.247.

15 Althaus, *The Theology*, 96.

16 Jaroslav Pelikan, *Luther the Expositor: Introduction to the Reformer's Exegetical Writings* (St. Louis: Concordia, 1959), 57. See also 59-60.

17 Bornkamm, *Luther*, 154-55. Bornkamm quotes *WA* 31^2.22.19.

18 Bornkamm, *Luther*, 154.

Calvin's Old Testament hermeneutics

Calvin's method of interpretation of Scripture also can be represented in five principles. First, Calvin emphasizes the verbal inspiration and the illumination of the Holy Spirit. Wood indicates that Calvin's interpretation was based on 'the assumption of verbal inspiration'.[19] And Childs maintains that Calvin's hermeneutics stresses the illumination of the Holy Spirit:

> [Even though] God has made himself clearly known in the scriptures, human sinfulness has prevented his revelation from being understood. Thus it is only by the illumination of divine grace, by the 'inner witness of the Holy Spirit,' that the word is heard and understood (*Inst.* I.7.12). Moreover, Calvin is at pains to make clear that word and spirit are not to be separated, but only through the biblical text does the Spirit illumine.[20]

Second, Calvin's method of interpretation is one of lucid brevity and literal sense. Calvin's method in his exegesis is displayed in the preface of the commentary of Romans, in which Calvin introduced a letter sent to his friend, Simon Grynaeus. Calvin says that his basic principle to construe the Bible is 'lucid brevity'.

> I remember that when three years ago we had a friendly converse as to the best mode of expounding Scripture, the plan which especially pleased you, seemed also to me the most entitled to approbation: we both thought that the chief excellency of an expounder consists in *lucid brevity*. And, indeed, since it is almost his only work to lay open the mind of the writer whom he undertakes to explain, the degree in which he leads away his readers from it, in that degree he goes astray from his purpose, and in a manner wanders from his own boundaries.[21]

Thus Leith showcases Calvin as an interpreter of the Bible by claiming that Calvin's work was guided by two basic principles: one was simplicity and brevity and the other was the fundamental significance of 'the "natural sense of a passage"'.[22] Gamble also indicates that in his commentary 'Calvin keeps his teaching style simple and that he generally abstains from refuting opponents,'[23]

---

19 Arthur Skevington Wood, 'Calvin' in *The Principles of Biblical Interpretation as enunciated by Irenaeus, Origen, Augustine, Luther, and Calvin* (Grand Rapids: Zondervan, 1967), 86.

20 Brevard S. Childs, *Biblical Theology of the Old and New Testaments* (Minneapolis: Fortress, 1992), 47-48.

21 John Calvin, *Commentaries on the Epistle of Paul the Apostle to the Romans*, xxiii, emphasis added. See also David Steinmetz, 'John Calvin as an interpreter of the Bible' in Donald K. McKim (ed.), *Calvin and the Bible* (Cambridge: CUP, 2006), 289.

22 John H. Leith, 'John Calvin—Theologian of the Bible,' *Int* 25 (1971), 331, 337. See also David Steinmetz, 'Calvin and Abraham: The Interpretation of Romans 4 in the Sixteenth Century', *CH* 57 (Dec. 1988), 443.

23 Richard Craig Gamble, 'Brevitas et Facilitas: Toward an understanding of Calvin's Hermeneutic,' *WTJ* 47 (1985), 3.

concluding with the statement that 'Calvin's method, *brevitas et facilitas*, is a conscious attempt to shape his method of exposition in conformity to his understanding of the Scripture's own style.'[24] Thus Kraus sums up Calvin's exegetical principles, including the principle of brevity and clarity, such as the intention of the author, the historical background, the literal and grammatical meaning, the context of a passage, exegesis going beyond the biblical wording, figures of speech and 'the scope of Christ' in finding Christ in the scripture.[25]

Third, Calvin's method of interpretation emphasizes the original historical context. Wood indicates that for Calvin the basic interpretative principle 'lies in adherence to what we now term the grammatico-historical method,' which was sought 'through an attempt to reach the mind and situation of the human author'.[26] Farrar notes Calvin's attention to the text's historical context with his rejection of allegorical interpretation, maintaining that 'the most characteristic and original feature of his commentaries' is Calvin's views about 'the Messianic prophecies'.[27]

Fourth, Calvin's method of interpretation is Christ-centered in relation to the Old Testament. Parker states that for Calvin Christ cannot be separated from his Church, stressing that 'The prophecies of Christ are always grounded in the Covenant, the Law, and the Kingdom.'[28] McNeill points out that for Calvin 'the significance of the Bible turns upon the Gospel of reconciliation in Christ'.[29] Muller also indicates, 'Calvin's Old Testament sermons often belie the Christological restraint of the Old Testament commentaries.'[30]

Fifth, Calvin interprets the Old Testament in the frame of promise-fulfillment. Muller speaks about Calvin's exegesis of the Old Testament as follows: 'Calvin's hermeneutic of promise and fulfillment might thus equally well be called a hermeneutic of multiple fulfillments' and 'The literal meaning of the text is the historical succession of the promise as it moves toward its highest

---

24 Gamble, 'Exposition and Method in Calvin,' *WTJ* 49 (1987), 165.

25 Han Joachim Kraus, 'Calvin's Exegetical Principles', *Int* 31 (1977), 12-17. Cf. Thomas F. Torrance, *The Hermeneutics of John Calvin* (Edinburgh: Scottish Academic, 1988), 70-71. See also Richard A. Muller, 'The Hermeneutic of Promise Fulfillment in Calvin's Exegesis of the Old Testament Prophecies of the Kingdom' in *The Bible in the Sixteenth Century* (Durham: Duke University Press, 1990), 68-82, 214-16; idem, 'Biblical Interpretation in the Era of the Reformation: The View from the Middle Ages' in *Biblical Interpretation in the Era of the Reformation: essays presented to David C. Steinmetz in honor of his sixtieth birthday* (Grand Rapids: Eerdmans, 1996), 8.

26 Wood, 'Calvin,' 89.

27 F.W. Farrar, *History of Interpretation* (London: E.P. Dutton), 342-52.

28 T.H.L. Parker, *Calvin's Old Testament Commentaries* (Edinburgh: T. & T. Clark, 1986), 199. See also 197.

29 John Thomas McNeill, 'The significance of the Word of God for Calvin,' *CH* 27 (1959), 145. See also David L. Puckett, *John Calvin's Exegesis of the Old Testament* (Louisville: Westminster John Knox, 1995), 18, 139.

30 Muller, *Unaccommodated Calvin*, 182.

fulfillment.'[31] Parker also indicates that Calvin has interpreted the prophecies related to Christ in numerous ways, stating that for Calvin 'Christ is promised as the one who would fulfill the Law.'[32]

The context of the two reformers

Luther's Sitz im Leben *in his lectures and sermons on Isaiah*

In a letter to his friend Wenzeslaus Link in Nürnberg, Luther wrote early in May 1527 that he intended to translate the Old Testament prophets into German and to begin lectures on Isaiah: 'I plan to lecture on Isaiah, to keep from being idle (*lecturus simul Iesaiam, ne otiosus sim*).'[33] The lectures began in July 1527 and continued until February 1530. There were two important interruptions. In that very year the university had to move to Jena on account of the plague in Wittenberg. Also in the fall of 1529 Luther was at Marburg for six weeks for conversations with Zwingli. The notes on *Luther's lectures on Isaiah* until 1914 were not published. The only available source for these notes until that time was an edition of *scholia*, which was first published at Wittenberg in 1532 (issued again in a revised and expanded version in 1534).[34] Interestingly, one of those who heard Luther's lectures on Isaiah testifies to the effectiveness of them. Johann Mathesius, who came to Wittenberg in 1529, heard Luther's preaching, especially the last 22 chapters of Isaiah and said, 'From these lectures I repeatedly returned home full of comfort and joy.'[35]

Luther, in the preface of his lectures on Isaiah, says that two kinds of knowledge are needed to interpret the Prophet: one is 'a knowledge of grammar,' and the other is 'a knowledge of the historical background'.[36] The most significant principle in his view, however, is the interpretation of Christ-centeredness, so that Luther says, 'The chief and leading theme of all the prophets is their aim to keep the people in eager anticipation of the coming Christ.'[37] Luther then summarizes the historical limit of Isaiah's message in three sections: 'namely, the prediction of the coming captivity in Babylonia, secondly, the return from this captivity, and thirdly, what it says about Christ'.[38] These three parts cover the whole prophecy of Isaiah and constitute the background of Luther's lectures on Isaiah 53.

---

31 Muller, 'The Hermeneutic of Promise Fulfillment,' 77.

32 Parker, *Calvin's Old Testament Commentaries*, 197-199.

33 *LW* 16.ix.

34 *LW* 16.x; 17.ix.

35 *LW* 17.ix.

36 *LW* 16.3. Luther considers a knowledge of historical background, 'not only as an understanding of the events themselves as expressed in letters and syllables but as at the same time embracing rhetoric and dialectic, so that the figures of speech and the circumstances may be carefully heeded'.

37 *LW* 16.3.

38 *LW* 16.5.

In addition to Luther's lectures on Isaiah (1527-30),[39] there are two later studies of Isaiah 9 and 53 (1543-44).[40] In the case of Luther's sermon on Isaiah, only one sermon on Isaiah 53 is found in Luther's works. That sermon, preached in the afternoon of the Saturday before Easter, 1531,[41] contains three major texts, one of which is Isaiah 52.13-53.12 (with Jn. 18.31-42 and Matt. 27.62-66). Luther regards the text of Isaiah 52.13-53.12 as showing the purpose of Christ's suffering clearly.

> The prophet describes the suffering of the Lord almost more clearly than the Evangelists in the New Testament. In the entire Scripture of the Old Testament there is no place where the purpose of Christ's suffering is so precisely and clearly delineated as in this text. Truly, we can say that this chapter of the Old Testament is an exemplary summary of that purpose, just as St. Paul's Epistles are in the New Testament.[42]

In any case, Luther is interested in Isaiah 53 representing Christ as the suffering servant. It seems that Luther wanted to refute papists who insisted on salvation by works. In fact, Luther's deeper study of Isaiah 9 and 53 (1543-44) testifies to his Christ-centered contention against papists because those chapters certainly contain the prophecies of Christ as the suffering servant for us. This means Luther wanted to show salvation by faith, based on his Christ-centered interpretation of Isaiah 53.

Calvin's Sitz im Leben *in his commentaries and sermons on Isaiah*

The commentaries on the prophetic books lie in the last of Calvin's expository publications. These commentaries began with one on Isaiah, which was written in 1550 (first published 1550; revised 1559) when Calvin was anxious and sick. He had lectured on this book before, and then this commentary was revised with the copy of the lectures. The first edition, as Parker indicates, was dedicated to 'King Edward VI, who repaid the compliment by sending him his treatise *A l'encontre les abus du monde* (Against the abuses of the world),' and the second edition (1559) was dedicated to 'Elizabeth, in a vain attempt to undo the harm caused by Knox's *The First Blast against the Monstrous Regiment of Women*'.[43] As for Calvin's sermons on Isaiah, Parker points out that according to Nicholas Colladon, 'Calvin began to preach on Isaiah in 1556,' and then Raguenier, Calvin's secretary, has provided 'the later series in six volumes of manuscript, with the date of their preaching'.[44]

---

39 *WA* 31² and *LW* 16 and 17.

40 *WA* 40³. See Childs, *The Struggle to Understand Isaiah*, 202.

41 Martin Luther, *Sermons of Martin Luther* (Grand Rapids: Baker, 1996), 1.435-51.

42 Luther, *Sermons*, 1.441.

43 T.H.L. Parker, 'Commentary on the book of the prophet Isaiah,' *EQ* 20 (1948), 297.

44 See Parker's comments in Calvin, *Sermons on Isaiah's Prophecy*, 13-14.

In any case, Calvin must be especially interested in Isaiah 53 because he dealt with the exegesis of Isaiah first of all the prophetical books.[45] It seems that Calvin recognized Isaiah (with Psalms) as one of the most important books in the Bible. He shows a Christ-centeredness in his interpretation of Isaiah 53, especially by relating it to Christ's kingdom and Church.

Similarities in the reformers' interpretation of Isaiah 53

Christ-centered interpretation

Luther asserts that the Suffering Servant will be glorious: 'when His first office and ministry have been accomplished, He will be in glory. He will bring it about even in this life.'[46] Luther understands the Servant's office in this way: 'Here, in the time of his earthly life, He will be Servant. After death He will be Lord. In His life He will be the most prudent Servant.'[47] Luther thinks, therefore, that when the office and ministry of the Servant have been completed, He will be glorious. Interestingly, Luther represents this servant as the King, Christ in his sermon of Isaiah 52.15.

> Even though this King, Christ, would be so disfigured and marred, yet will he sprinkle the nations, that is, his battered appearance would be proclaimed around the world. Gentiles would come to hear of his awful, tortured appearance, how he was piteously nailed to the cross and how his own people were shamefully angered and offended by him. Kings will hush before him and prostrate their wisdom under this King's feet. This king who was crucified shall be so exalted that the kings of the world will be pleased to hearken to this wisdom.[48]

Gentiles will be called to Christ, the King. The Jews, however, will not believe him as the promised Messiah because they cannot imagine the death of the Messiah, as expressed by the death of the cross. 'Yet this King will be exalted and his kingdom will sprinkle the Gentiles.'[49] In this regard, Luther's sermon on Isaiah seems to be more Christ-centered than his lectures.

Luther states in his lectures on Isaiah 53 that Christ's suffering is for us. According to Luther, the purpose of Christ's suffering in Isaiah 53.4 was not for himself but for our sins. Christ bore what we would receive.[50] Thus, Luther says, 'I delight in this text as if it were a text of the New Testament. This new teaching which demolishes the righteousness of the Law clearly appeared absurd to the Jews.'[51] Accordingly, Isaiah 53 'leads us so earnestly beyond all

---

45 See Peter Wilcox, 'Calvin as commentator on the Prophets' in Donald K. McKim (ed.), *Calvin and the Bible* (Cambridge: CUP, 2006), 107.

46 *LW* 17.215-16

47 *LW* 17.216.

48 Luther, *Sermons*, 1.441-42.

49 Luther, *Sermons*, 1.442.

50 *LW* 17.221.

51 *LW* 17.221.

righteousness and our rational capacity and confronts us with the suffering of Christ to impress upon us that all that Christ has is mine,' which is 'the preaching of the whole Gospel'.[52] As such, Luther believes God's righteousness is given through Christ's suffering.

On Isaiah 53.5 Luther speaks of Christ-centeredness in our justification. Christ alone saves us by bearing our sins, so that righteousness cannot be gained by works. In Luther's view, 'Surely none of the papists can escape this fact when he sees Scripture as a whole, that Christ has accomplished all things for justification.'[53] As such, Luther emphasizes that Christ alone justifies us. Luther's Christ-centered interpretation is clearly expressed in the interpretation of this passage, 'And with His stripes we are healed.'

> See how delightfully the prophet sets Christ before us. It is remarkable plaster. His stripes are our healing. The stripes should be ours and the healing in Christ. Hence this is what we must say to the Christian: 'If you want to be healed, do not look at your own wounds, but fix your gaze on Christ.'[54]

Furthermore, in his sermon on Isaiah 53.6 Luther claims that salvation is through Christ's suffering and death: 'The only way to salvation is through Christ's suffering and death, because our sins are placed on him and he is punished for them. Whoever strays from this way and does not look for peace in Christ is on the wrong road.'[55] In his sermon on Isaiah 53.11, Luther asserts that Isaiah indicates manifestly how we should grasp the salvation gained by Christ.

> Because we can only be justified and saved through him, it was necessary that he be more than a perfect man. Human power and might can justify and save no one. God alone can do this. Now since the prophet testifies of Christ, that he will justify all who believe on him, he is testifying that Christ is not only true man, but also true God.[56]

Luther holds that 'two truths are juxtaposed: that Christ died, and that he is Lord over all'.[57] Christ as true man as well as true God is the center of the whole of salvation. As such, for Luther the focus was on Christ-centeredness.

In the case of Calvin, he asserts that Christ as the Servant will be highly honored (on Isa. 52.13): 'Christ will be exalted and will be highly honored; but, by giving to him the title of "Servant",'[58] and in his commentary on Isaiah

---

[52] *LW* 17.222.

[53] *LW* 17.222.

[54] *LW* 17.225.

[55] Luther, *Sermons*, 1.445.

[56] Luther, *Sermons*, 1.450.

[57] Luther, *Sermons*, 1.451. In Luther's view, 'If he died, he must be a true natural man. If he is to bring people to receive him in faith and win many as his reward, snatching away the strong for his booty, then he must be true God.'

[58] John Calvin, *Commentaries on the Book of the Prophet Isaiah* (Grand Rapids: Baker,

52.14, Calvin indicates, according to Isaiah, that 'Christ must first be rejected and humbled, and anticipates that doubt which might have arisen from his singularly debased and unseemly condition.'[59] Calvin maintains that some commentators would not catch the meaning of this verse for Isaiah says that 'Christ will be such that all men will be shocked at him. He came into the world so as to be everywhere despised; his glory lay hid under the humble form of the flesh.'[60] Consequently, Calvin concludes that 'the shame of the cross was followed by a glorious resurrection attended by the highest honor'.[61]

Calvin also emphasizes Christ's death and resurrection in his sermon on Isaiah 52.13-53.1. These two cannot be separated: 'that Jesus Christ has voluntarily suffered in the infirmity that He has taken of us, and that He was quickened in the power of His Holy Spirit, and that thereby He is declared the true Son of God'.[62] According to Calvin, Christ's death and resurrection point toward his being the true Son of God through the power of the Holy Spirit. Calvin (on Isa. 53.5) refers to reconciliation by Christ as accomplished by Christ's death and resurrection. 'Christ was the price of "our chastisement,"' so that God's wrath was appeased and the peace through Christ as 'the Mediator' was given to us.[63] Furthermore, in his sermon of Isaiah 53.11, Calvin states that even though we are not worth receiving God's favor, Christ redeems and justifies us. 'Jesus Christ justified us, not only in that He was God, but by virtue of His obedience, in that He has taken our nature and in it wished to fulfill the Law, which was impossible for us and a burden crushing us all and breaking our necks.'[64] As such, for Calvin, Christ only laid the foundation of our salvation.

We can also find many sections that deal with Isaiah 53 in the *Institutes of the Christian Religion*, in which Calvin refers to Isaiah 53 as related to universal invitation and the particular election of God. '[A]lthough the voice of the gospel addresses all in general, yet the gift of faith is rare. Isaiah sets forth the cause: that "the arm of the Lord has" not "been revealed" to all [Isa 53.1] . . . . He only warns that, because faith is a special gift, the ears are beaten upon in vain with outward teaching.'[65] Calvin also indicates that the purpose of Christ's incarnation was our redemption. Jesus Christ was appointed by 'God's eternal plan to purge the uncleanness of men; for shedding of blood is a sign of expiation,' so that Christ was 'the reconciler of God and man'.[66] Calvin says, 'Of all the testimonies to this, Isaiah's famous one will be enough' (Isa. 53.5-

1979), 3.107.

59 Calvin, *Comm. Isa.*, 52.14.

60 Calvin, *Comm. Isa.*, 52.14.

61 Calvin, *Comm. Isa.*, 52.14.

62 Calvin, *Sermons on Isaiah's Prophecy*, 36.

63 Calvin, *Comm. Isa.*, 53.5.

64 Calvin, *Sermons on Isaiah's Prophecy*, 125-26.

65 *Inst.* 3.22.10.

66 *Inst.* 3.12.4.

6).[67] Isaiah's testimony is manifest: '"The chastisement of our peace was laid upon Christ, and with his stripes healing has come to us".'[68] This means the substitution of Christ. Accordingly, Calvin regards Christ's death as an expiatory sacrifice. 'Christ was offered to the Father in death as an expiatory sacrifice. . . . Now it is clear what the prophet's utterance means: "The Lord has laid on him the iniquity of us all"' (Isa. 53.6).[69] Thus, Calvin concludes that 'to perform a perfect expiation, he gave his own life as an Asham, that is, as an expiatory offering for sin, as the prophet calls it [Isa. 53.10; cf. v.5], upon which our stain and punishment might somehow be cast, and cease to be imputed to us.'[70] Calvin surely recognizes that Christ is the center of our redemption.

God's Word working with the Holy Spirit

Luther (on Isa. 53.1) emphasizes the Word in union with the Holy Spirit, pointing to the office of the Holy Spirit. It is only by the Holy Spirit and the Word that we believe in Jesus Christ as our Savior. According to Luther, 'No more loathsome kind of death can be read about than that which Christ suffered, and to believe in Him under that form as the Messiah and to die in that faith—this is the office of the Holy Spirit.'[71] On the foundation of the Word through the Holy Spirit Christ's Kingdom will be established. Accordingly, Luther says that 'after His death Christ will have an eternal kingdom'.[72]

Luther also speaks of the knowledge of God that is given by the word working with the Holy Spirit. Luther suggests on Isaiah 53.11 that 'the individual words must be pondered in supreme faith, and they must be read and considered with the most watchful eyes,' so that it is 'a knowledge that justifies, in opposition to other kinds of knowledge'.[73] This knowledge is attained by the Word working with the Holy Spirit. Luther concludes that 'this knowledge is the formal and substantial righteousness of the Christians, that is, faith in Christ, which I obtain through the Word' and that 'The Word I receive through the intellect, but to assent to that Word is the work of the Holy Spirit.'[74]

Calvin stresses the gospel of Christ, which is effective when accompanied by the Spirit (lecture on Isa. 53.1): 'Isaiah declares that there will be few that submit to the Gospel of Christ; for, when he exclaims, "Who will believe the preaching?" he means that of those who hear the Gospel scarcely a hundredth person will be a believer.'[75] It is noteworthy, for Calvin, that 'Isaiah does not

[67] *Inst.* 2.12.4.
[68] *Inst.* 2.17.4.
[69] *Inst.* 2.16.6.
[70] *Inst.* 2.16.6.
[71] *LW* 17.219.
[72] *LW* 17.219.
[73] *LW* 17.230.
[74] *LW* 17.230.
[75] Calvin, *Comm. Isa.*, 53.1.

include merely the men of his own time, but all posterity to the end of the world; for, so long as the reign of Christ shall endure, this must be fulfilled' and that even though 'it is sufficiently evident that all are called to salvation, yet the Prophet expressly states that the external voice is of no avail, if it be not accompanied by a special gift of the Spirit'.[76] Thus, Calvin states in his commentary on Isaiah 53.3 that 'no man will ever be able to comprehend it by his own understanding till the Lord correct and form him anew by his Spirit'.[77] In any case, Calvin understands that the gospel is effective to people when it is delivered through the Holy Spirit.

Calvin also indicates that we are enriched by the gifts of the Holy Spirit. In his sermon on Isaiah 53.12 Calvin says that 'the fruit of the death and passion of our Lord Jesus is undying' in that 'He provides our needs and remedies all our scarcities' and that 'all the graces of the Holy Spirit are a part of the plunder of our Lord Jesus Christ'.[78] As such, Calvin stresses the Holy Spirit for us—this demonstrates Calvin's pastoral concern for believers.

The Kingdom of Christ

The kingdom of Christ occupies a major concept in Luther's understanding of Isaiah 52.13-53.12. Luther in his lecture on Isaiah 52.13 indicates it as follows:

> Christ's kingdom is depicted in the cross and that it is carried forward by faith and the Word alone. Yet that leading of faith, the Word, and the cross is not without deliverance and protection. In this chapter the prophet speaks primarily of the Head of the Kingdom as he treats of the person of the King and the manner of His deliverance. This is the foremost passage on the suffering and resurrection of Christ, and there is hardly another like it.[79]

First, Luther contrasts a physical kingdom with the Christ's kingdom. Luther (lecture on Isa. 52.14-15), revealing recognition of Jewish interpretation, states that 'the glorious King described as a man of the most hideous appearance in opposition to the Jews, who look for Him in a glorious form,' so that 'the Messiah is not to be looked for as coming with a physical kingdom, since His appearance is so extremely marred'.[80] Luther's dialectical interpretation is displayed in that he contrasts Christ's kingdom with a physical one. The contrast is often shown in Luther's interpretation of Isaiah. For example, Luther (on Isa. 35) interpreted an earthly kingdom and the spiritual kingdom in terms of spirit and flesh.[81] For this reason, Luther stresses that 'Christ's kingdom is indeed

---

[76] Calvin, *Comm. Isa.*, 53.1.
[77] Calvin, *Comm. Isa.*, 53.3.
[78] Calvin, *Sermons on Isaiah's Prophecy*, 140.
[79] *LW* 17.215.
[80] *LW* 17.216.
[81] *LW* 16.299-307.

spiritual and ultimately beyond death.'[82] In addition, Luther (on Isa. 53.3) states that this verse constitutes 'the basis for the church's faith that Christ's kingdom is not of this world,' describing 'Christ's person with respect to His suffering and His glorification'.[83]

Second, Luther indicates that Christ's kingdom will be extended by preaching. For Luther, 'sprinkle' in Isaiah 52.15 is significant for he says that the gentiles are spiritually included in Christ's kingdom. Luther explains that 'Sprinkling in the Law denotes preaching, as if to say: "After Christ will have suffered, He will be proclaimed not only among the Jews but also among the Gentiles as water is thrown at and sprinkled on people."'[84] Accordingly, Christ is preached among gentiles and they will be included in Christ's kingdom. The spiritual kingdom 'does not move forward with weapons but with word,' so that 'this kingdom of Christ's suffering and resurrection was promoted in the church by preaching alone'.[85]

Third, Luther indicates that the kingdom of Christ will prosper regardless of Papists' interruptions. Luther (sermon on Isa. 53.2) says that the Christ's kingdom is 'a delicate shoot but soon it grows into a great tree by God's grace' and that both the kingdom and the gospel 'thrive in the midst of trouble and turmoil'.[86] The gospel is regarded as foolish and it suffers persecution, but it surely prospers. Luther states, 'All the world figured that after three days we would be as nothing; nevertheless, we are still here and growing.'[87] Luther here warns against the Papists who have deviated from the right way of understanding Christ's suffering.

> The prophet repeats the reason why Christ suffered when he says that he was wounded and bruised as one rejected by God, and that this happened to him on account of our sins This we must earnestly bear in mind, all the more so because under the papistry the suffering of Christ has been so obscured, that what the prophet Isaiah and the apostle Paul have written was largely lost sight of by us, who were led away from Christ's suffering to our own works.[88]

Therefore, Luther emphasizes that Christ's kingdom will prosper even though the Papists interrupt the gospel.

Calvin stresses the kingdom of Christ in his commentary and sermons on Isaiah. First, Calvin underscores that Christ is the Savior of the whole world. Calvin in his sermon of Isaiah 52.13-53.1 asserts that 'this word [sprinkle] is a simile meaning also "to speak"' and that the most natural interpretation is that 'Jesus Christ shall sprinkle many nations: that is to say, although He is a dry

---

82 *LW* 17.217.

83 *LW* 17.220.

84 *LW* 17.217.

85 *LW* 17.219.

86 Luther, *Sermons*, 1.442.

87 Luther, *Sermons*, 1.443.

88 Luther, *Sermons*, 1.444.

and sterile trunk of a tree, none the less the whole world will be sprinkled with His power.'[89] Calvin points out that Isaiah reveals that God will work 'in an incomprehensible way'[90] and that 'the whole world will be sprinkled by our Lord Jesus Christ—that is, by the preaching of the Gospel'.[91] The prophet broadens his scope and he reveals that 'our Lord Jesus would be sent from God His father, not only for the Jews—although He was expressly promised to them—but to be the Savior of all the world,' so that Calvin thinks that this passage should be 'like a key to open the kingdom of God to us'.[92]

Second, Calvin speaks of the method of building Christ's kingdom. In his commentary on Isaiah 53.2, Calvin indicates that if we consider

> the whole method of establishing his kingdom, and the agency which he employed, and how feeble were its beginnings, and how many foes it encountered, we shall easily understand that all these things were fulfilled as they had been foretold.[93]

Christ's kingdom must not be judged by human conceptions. It has 'nothing that could direct or captivate the hearts of men to it by its outward show'.[94] Rather, the kingdom of Christ will be set up according to God's plan to save us from our sins.

Third, Calvin relates Christ's kingdom to the Church. Calvin in his commentary on Isaiah 53.8 points out that the prophet Isaiah 'declares that he was *taken away*; that is, that he was rescued "from prison and judgment" or condemnation, and afterwards was exalted to the highest rank of honor'.[95] Calvin states that the prophet does not say 'Christ's person alone, but includes the whole body of the Church,' so that Calvin refers to it as 'a striking proof of the perpetuity of the Church'.[96] Christ who does live forever 'will not permit his kingdom to perish' and the same immortality ultimately will be given to every member.[97] Furthermore, in his sermon on Isaiah 53.7-8, Calvin says that our Lord Jesus gave permanent life to the Church. As the prophet has declared, Jesus Christ 'has gained an unending life' and 'this was not only for Himself, but for all His church'.[98] In Calvin's view, Christ's Church is indestructible. Calvin surely connects Christ-centeredness to the Church, which is demonstrated in his sermon on Isaiah 53.9-10:

---

89 Calvin, *Sermons on Isaiah's Prophecy*, 38
90 Calvin, *Sermons on Isaiah's Prophecy*, 38.
91 Calvin, *Sermons on Isaiah's Prophecy*, 39.
92 Calvin, *Sermons on Isaiah's Prophecy*, 39.
93 Calvin, *Comm. Isa.*, 53.2.
94 Calvin, *Comm. Isa.*, 53.2.
95 Calvin, *Comm. Isa.*, 53.8.
96 Calvin, *Comm. Isa.*, 53.8.
97 Calvin, *Comm. Isa.*, 53.8.
98 Calvin, *Sermons on Isaiah's Prophecy*, 92.

> In sum, the Prophet wanted in this passage to say that not only were the death and passion of our Lord Jesus Christ sufficient for the salvation of the world, but that God will make them efficacious and that we shall see the fruit of them and even feel and experience it. From this we must gather that there will always be a Church in the world and that though the devil will be able to plot and to make all his attempts to overthrow what God builds, yet in spite of everything, Jesus Christ must come out on top and the grace of which He was minister and dispenser must be efficacious and be fulfilled among men.[99]

The frame of promise-fulfillment

Jesus Christ has fulfilled the prophecy of the suffering servant in Isaiah 53, indicating the frame of promise-fulfillment between the Old Testament and the New. Christ's kingdom will be filled with those who have the knowledge of Christ. Luther says on Isaiah 53.10 that the prophet 'describes the fruit of His passion,' that is, 'He will have His future kingdom according to the statement: "He sits at the right hand of the Father, from thence He shall come."'[100] As such, Christ's passion eventually is for his future kingdom. This kingdom will be filled with those who know Christ. Luther states on Isaiah 53.11 that Christ's kingdom will proceed '*By His knowledge*': explaining, '[t]hose who confess that their sins have been borne by Him are the righteous. . . . Here he says that righteousness is the knowledge of Christ, who bears our iniquities.'[101] According to Luther, this knowledge of Christ is based on Christ's fulfillment of the prophecy of Isaiah 53. Luther's study of the suffering servant concludes with the statement: 'He did not die in vain, but all promises of Scripture have been fulfilled, and all our sins have been taken away. No, He did not toil in vain by His death, but He died to fulfill the promises and to set us free.'[102] Therefore, Luther interprets Isaiah 53 by the frame of promise-fulfillment. Luther finally says in his interpretation of Isaiah 53 that 'we would be blessed people if we could believe this most noble text, which must be magnified.'[103]

Calvin also says in his commentary on Isaiah 52.15 that the kingdom of Christ was fulfilled in the New Testament. The apostle Paul cites this passage as fulfilled and claims 'he proclaimed the doctrine of the Gospel to those who had never heard of it at all (Rom. 15:21).'[104] Calvin indicates that 'the kingdom of Christ is more extensive than merely to embrace Judea, and that it is not now confined within such narrow limits; for it was proper that it should be spread through all nations, and extended even to the ends of the world.'[105] According

[99] Calvin, *Sermons on Isaiah's Prophecy*, 116.
[100] *LW* 17.228.
[101] *LW* 17.228-29.
[102] *LW* 17.231.
[103] *LW* 17.233.
[104] Calvin, *Comm. Isa.*, 52.15.
[105] Calvin, *Comm. Isa.*, 52.15.

to Calvin, the gospel will be spread on the basis of the fulfillment of the prophecy of Isaiah 53. This shows the frame of promise-fulfillment.

In his commentary on Isaiah 53.12, Calvin also points out that what was shadowed out is fulfilled in Christ. Calvin interprets the promise in this passage in relation to the fulfillment in the New Testament, especially in Pauline epistles. The prophet Isaiah applauds the victory after Christ's death 'for "although he was crucified through the weakness of the flesh, yet by the power of the Spirit" he rose from the dead, and triumphed over his enemies (2 Cor. 13.4),' and the prophet 'now adds that Christ's humiliation was the beginning of this supreme dominion; as Paul also declares that Christ, "after having blotted out the handwriting which was opposed to us, triumphed on the cross" (Col. 2.14).'[106]

Calvin here understands the relationship of the Old Testament and the New by the frame of promise-fulfillment, which is shown in his *Institutes*. With respect to Isaiah 53, Calvin speaks of 'how Christ has fulfilled the function of redeemer to acquire salvation for us' (2.16). For instance, Calvin states, 'To take away our condemnation, it was not enough for him to suffer any kind of death: to make satisfaction for our redemption a form of death had to be chosen in which he might free us both by transferring our condemnation to himself and by taking our guilt upon himself' (Isa 53.5).[107] Calvin indicates that we received righteousness due to Christ's obedience as the prophet says in Isaiah 53.7: 'even in death itself his willing obedience is the important thing because a sacrifice not offered voluntarily would not have furthered righteousness.'[108]

In addition, Calvin maintains that Christ's dominion is permanent in relation to his Church and every member of it. Surely, God promises that 'through the hand of his Son he will be the eternal protector and defender of his church' and this prophecy was fulfilled 'in Christ alone'.[109] According to Calvin, 'Isaiah's exclamation means the same thing': for the prophet in Isaiah 53.8 declares that 'Christ will so survive death as to bind himself with his members,' so that Calvin says that 'whenever we hear of Christ as armed with eternal power, let us remember that the perpetuity of the church is secure in this protection'.[110] For Calvin, the eternal power of Christ is the reason for the permanency of the Church because Christ protects it. Consequently, Calvin speaks of Christ's fulfillment of the prophecy as follows:

> Here we must note two things that had been foretold by the oracles of the prophets, and which greatly comfort and confirm our faith. When we hear that Christ was led from the judge's seat to death, and hanged between thieves, we possess the

[106] Calvin, *Comm. Isa.*, 53.12.
[107] *Inst.* 2.16.5.
[108] *Inst.* 2.16.5.
[109] *Inst.* 2.15.3.
[110] *Inst.* 2.15.3.

fulfillment of the prophecy to which the Evangelist referred: 'He was reckoned among the transgressors.'[111]

Dissimilarities in the reformers' interpretation of Isaiah 53

Luther and Calvin have a few differences, even though they have many similarities, in their interpretation of Isaiah 53. First, Luther emphasizes the relationship of law-gospel, whereas Calvin stresses that of law-prophets. Apart from Luther's interpretive principle of law-gospel, Calvin refers to the unity of law-prophets, which was represented in the preface of Calvin's commentary.

> He says that the prophets derived their doctrine from the law, like streams form a fountain; for they placed it before them as their rule, so that they may be justly held and declared to be its interpreters, who utter nothing but what is connected with the Law. Now, the Law consists chiefly of three parts: first, the doctrine of life; secondly, threatenings and promise; thirdly, the covenant of grace, which, being found on Christ, contains within itself all the special promises.[112]

Second, Calvin connects the kingdom of Christ to the Church, in comparison to Luther's greater interest in justification or salvation by faith in Christ, even though both reformers share the same interest in the Christ's kingdom. As Wilcox argues, there are two concepts penetrating Calvin's commentaries on the prophetic book: 'the progress of the Kingdom of Christ' and 'the restoration of the Church'.[113] Christ's kingdom 'provides a framework for the exposition of salvation history'.[114] Even though Calvin's interpretation of Isaiah is focused on 'the prophet's own intention and the original historical context,' as Sawyer indicates, 'it was essential to ensure that every interpretation was both christocentric and relevant to the contemporary Church'.[115] Consequently, both reformers' interpretation of Isaiah 53 can be described as 'promise-fulfillment in Christ's Kingdom'.[116]

However, these differences do not show significant dissimilarities between them. Rather, these reflect their understanding of Isaiah 53, because for Luther his main concern was salvation by faith in Christ, while Calvin's main concern was a more pastoral interest toward the Church. Therefore, we can conclude

---

[111] *Inst.* 2.16.5.

[112] Calvin, *Commentaries on the Book of the Prophet Isaiah*, 1.xxvi.

[113] Wilcox, 'Calvin as commentator on the Prophets,' 121; idem, '"The Progress of the Kingdom of Christ" in Calvin's Exposition of the Prophets' in *Calvinus Sincerioris Religious Vindex: Calvin as Protector of the Purer Religion* (Kirksville, Missouri: Sixteenth Century Publisher, 1997), 315-22.

[114] Wilcox, 'The Progress of the Kingdom of Christ,' 322.

[115] John F.A. Sawyer, *The Fifth Gospel: Isaiah in the History of Christianity* (Cambridge: CUP, 1996), 128.

[116] Muller, 'The Hermeneutic of Promise Fulfillment,' 68-82. I employ Muller's term for Luther and Calvin's interpretation of Isaiah 53, even though Muller only speaks of Calvin's hermeneutics of promise-fulfillment.

that even though Luther and Calvin have a few differences, both of them have the same interest in the kingdom of Christ, emphasizing Christ's fulfillment of the prophecy of the suffering servant.

Conclusion

I have argued the similarities and the dissimilarities in Luther and Calvin's interpretation of Isaiah 52.13-53.12. Some similarities in their interpretation are focused on Christ-centeredness. First, the two reformers stress God's Word working with the Holy Spirit and the literal meaning of the text. Second, their main concern is centered on Christ's kingdom. Third, the two reformers interpret the prophecy of Isaiah 53 in the frame of promise-fulfillment. Luther and Calvin do have some different emphases: law-gospel and law-prophets, more interest in justification for Luther, and more concern about Christ's Church for John Calvin.

3. Social/Pastoral Matters

CHAPTER 8

Is marriage among the sacraments? Were Luther and Calvin wrong?

Richard A. Shenk

'Why would you want to change a perfectly good word like ordinance?' So a fellow theologian erupted when he heard my plans to write a paper challenging the exclusive use of 'ordinance' and re-considering the term, 'sacrament'. Among some, the causal *association* of sacraments with grace is so strong that the retreat to 'ordinance' continues without debate. Yet, many, if not most, within the Protestant Church value 'sacrament' as an apt term for baptism and the Lord's Supper. Toward the end of rehabilitating the term for the broader Protestant Church, I want to explore a definition of 'sacrament' that may be historical, biblically consistent and satisfying to Protestants, especially Reformed, evangelical Protestants. But, not only those. Since the Reformation, all Protestant Christians have accepted the exile of marriage from among the sacraments—even from the ordinances. If 'sacrament' is a worthy term, it may be that marriage should be included as a sacrament. I will argue that Luther and Calvin may have done us a disservice by removing marriage from among the sacraments and from the domain of the Church and explore terms of its return as a sacrament within the Church.

What is a sacrament?

'Sacrament' is an old word, with a rich, multidimensional meaning, attached to it from centuries of use. Its historic and common roots are well known: a military oath and the sum which litigants deposit with the courts.[1] Tertullian was perhaps among the first to use the Latin word, *sacramentum*, in a religious context referring to the deep mysteries of God which are associated with faith, in-

[1] See Louis Berkhof, *Systematic Theology* (Grand Rapids: Eerdmans, 1941 [1949]), 617. Tertullian, *The Ante-Nicene Fathers: Translations of the Writings of the Fathers Down to AD 325* (*ANF*) (edited by Alexander Roberts and James Donaldson; New York: Christian Literature, 1895), 3.chapter 19, reveals its etymology as a military oath and insists on a disjuncture between the divine and military use, though even in so doing, he reveals the relationship—referenced on www.ccel.org on 27 Aug 2012.

cluding baptism.[2] Later, in the early fifth century, the word was ordained by Jerome in the *Vulgate*. Specifically, he used the term eight times to translate the NT Greek word 'μυστήριον,'[3] but only one of these uses was in the context of any of the sacraments later enumerated by the church. This singular instance was in Ephesians 5.32 where he translated 'τὸ μυστήριον τοῦτο μέγα ἐστίν' as '*sacramentum hoc magnum est*'. Even more influential is Augustine whose definition is cross-claimed by many traditions: 'sacraments are the visible signs of invisible realities'. But there is no evidence that by this he made reference to a specific set of sacraments, nor does this common attribution exist in this simple form in his writings.[4] It is worth adding that Augustine insisted that what made the sign (sacrament) efficacious for the believer was the Word. He wrote of John 15.1-3,

> 'Now ye are clean through the word which I have spoken unto you.' Why does He not say, "Ye are clean through the baptism wherewith ye have been washed," but "through the word which I have spoken unto you," save only that in the water also it is the word that cleanseth? Take away the word, and the water is neither more nor less than water. *The word is added to the element, and there results the sacrament, as if itself also a kind of visible word.*[5]

In this he is followed by Calvin and others. So, what began as an oath (connecting us to the command of God), took on the added dimension of association of a sign which points to the deep mysteries of God, which is effective in the life of the believer, because of the Word preached.

'Ordinance' is also an old word referring to something commanded, and is, with regard to the sacramental rites of the Church, singly dimensioned. Many evangelicals, particularly those baptistic evangelicals of my tradition, have only

---

2 Eg., 'I see no coherence and consistency; no, not even in the very sacrament of his faith! For what end does baptism serve, according to him?' (*ANF*, 3.1.28—referenced on www.CCEL.org on 27 Aug 2012). 'Happy is our sacrament of water, in that, by washing away the sins of our early blindness, we are set free and admitted into eternal life!' (*ANF*, 3.1—referenced on www.CCEL.org on 27 Aug 2012). But it should be remembered that the meaning of *sacramentum* was not limited at this time to a specific set of religious practices, or even of religious practice.

3 The Vulgate translated the NT Greek, 'μυστήριον' as '*sacramentum*' eight times: Eph. 1.9; 3.3, 9; 5.32, Col. 1.27, 1 Tim. 3.16, Rev. 1.20 and 17.7. This was amended more precisely to *mysterium* in the *Nova Volgata* (1971).

4 See Augustine, 'On the Catechizing of the Uninstructed' in *A Select Library of the Nicene and Post-Nicene Fathers of the Christian church* (*NPNF*) (edited and translated by Philip Schaff and Henry Wace; New York: Christian Literature, 1890), 3.26.50—referenced on www.CCEL.org on 27 Aug 2012; idem, *Confessions*, NPNF 3.chapter 17—referenced on www.CCEL.org on 27 Aug 2012. Here and elsewhere this is a theme of his writing as he speaks primarily of creation and natural revelation, not 'sacraments,' perhaps based on Rom. 1.20. Still, he may be thinking, *sacramentally*.

5 *NPNF*, Volume 7, 'John's Gospel,' 80.3.344, emphasis added.

an implicit understanding of the word 'ordinance' which represents for us both the Lord's Supper and baptism. Historically, and in the English language, the OED testifies to the use of 'ordinance' as a synonym for 'sacrament'. That is, by referring to this one characteristic of 'sacrament'—God's command—'ordinance' made reference to the whole. The OED cites several examples of such usage from the 15th to the 20th century. But that changed in the last hundred years. In fact, during the 20th century the OED limits the use of the term 'ordinance,' to the 'baptistic church' as a substitute term—no longer a synonym, but as a replacement for the term 'sacrament'. Of course, many other Protestants do use the word 'sacrament,' including Anglicans and Lutherans. And Wayne Grudem is willing to use both terms synonymously.[6] But among baptistic evangelicals, the accepted term is 'ordinance': 'ceremonies that Jesus commanded his church to perform'.[7] Millard Erickson is conventional in this regard: 'Since [baptism] was ordained by [Christ], it is properly understood as an ordinance rather than a sacrament.'[8]

The Roman Catholic *New Advent Encyclopedia* defines sacraments: 'outward signs of inward grace, instituted by Christ for our sanctification'.[9] This definition echoes Augustine. However, the second edition of the Catechism defines sacrament: 'The sacraments are efficacious signs of grace, instituted by Christ and entrusted to the church, by which divine life is dispensed to us.'[10] While both definitions are still used, the emphasis in the second is that the sacraments *in themselves* effectively cause grace to flow to the recipient. This conferring of grace was codified about one year after Luther's death during the seventh session of the Council of Trent (March 1547). Then, and to this day, sacraments were declared to be seven in number and also to confer grace explicitly.[11]

---

6 'If we are willing to explain clearly what we mean, it does not seem to make any difference whether we use the word sacrament or not. . . . I will use both "ordinances" and "sacraments" interchangeably, and regard them as synonymous in meaning'—Wayne Grudem, *Systematic Theology* (Zondervan, Kindle edition), 966. Berkhof, *Theology*, 560, 631, also makes use of 'ordinance' and 'sacrament' as synonyms. As a Lutheran, he leans strongly to the use of 'sacrament'.

7 Grudem, *Systematic Theology*, 966.

8 Millard Erickson, *Christian Theology* (Grand Rapids: Baker, 1998), 1105. Interestingly, there is no explicit definition of the term 'ordinance' in his text.

9 This definition was referenced on the New Advent website http://www.newadvent.org/cathen/13295a.htm, referenced 31 Aug 2011.

10 This definition was referenced on the Vatican website http://www.vatican.va/archive/ENG0015/__P35.HTM, paragraph 1131, on 27 August 2012.

11 *The Canons and Decrees of the Council of Trent* (translated and introduced by H.J. Schroeder; Charlotte, NC: Tan Books, 1978), Session 7, 'Canons on the Sacraments in General,' canons 1, 5, 6, 7. Though Trent made explicit both the number of the sacraments and the conferring of grace through the sacraments, this was not a new idea. Peter Lombard (ca 1096-1164) had proposed both in *Sentences* (4.1.2; 4.2.1).

Martin Luther had no objection to the term 'sacrament' and it continues in general use today by Lutherans. He did reject most of seven sacraments of the RCC, accepting only the Lord's Supper, baptism, and penance, arriving at this list by the use of two filters—'a divine promise' and 'a sign':[12] a *sacrament* is 'a word of divine promise, which must be believed in by him who receives the sign'.[13] Fundamentally, this means Luther rejected the Roman understanding of the operation of faithless grace through the sacrament. He did not reject the sacraments as means of grace, but as either the unique means of grace, apart from the Word, or a means of grace which could be faithlessly received.[14] Berkhof offers a helpful definition: 'A sacrament is a holy ordinance instituted by Christ, in which by sensible signs the grace of God in Christ, and the benefits of the covenant of grace, are represented, sealed, and applied to believers,

---

And the Council of Florence (1439) enumerated seven. Interestingly, while Trent hardened the division with the Lutherans in regard to grace in the sacraments, Trent also reversed the position of the RCC on indulgences. Though indulgences themselves were retained, they 'absolutely abolished' the 'evil traffic' of indulgences, asserting that they are administered for piety, not gain, so relieving Luther's presenting concern (July 1562, Session 21, 'Decree Concerning Reform,' chapter 9 and later in December 1563, Session 25, chapter 21).

12 In regard to the rejection of seven, he writes, 'The first thing for me to do is to deny that there are seven sacraments, and, for the present, to propound three: baptism, penance, and the Lord's Supper. All these have been taken for us into miserable servitude by the Roman curia and the church has been robbed of all her liberty. If, however, I were to use the language of Scripture, I should say that there was only one sacrament [cf. 1 Tim. 3.16], but three sacramental signs of which I shall speak in detail in the proper place'—Martin Luther, *Selections from his Writings* (edited by John Dillenberger; New York: Anchor, 1962), 256. Later, he rejected penance from the list—John Witte, Jr., 'The Reformation of marriage Law in Martin Luther's Germany: Its Significance Then and Now,' *JLR*, 4.2 (1986), 312n.32. His rejection is based, as he anticipated even in *Captivity*, upon the lack of a *sign* in penance, unlike baptism and Lord's Supper which have water and the elements, respectively (*Selections*, 357). Arguing against the Book of James he writes, 'I should say that it was not lawful for an apostle to institute a sacrament by his own authority; that is, to give a divine promise with a sign annexed to it' (*Selections*, 351). He also writes, 'It follows that, strictly speaking, there are but two sacraments in the church of God: Baptism and the Lord's Supper, since we find in these alone a sign divinely instituted, and here alone the promise of the forgiveness of sins' (*Selections*, 357).

13 *Selections*, 326.

14 This understanding is reflected in Berkhof: 'The church is not a means of grace alongside of the Word and the sacraments, because her power in promoting the work of the grace of God consists only in the administration of these. She is not instrumental in communicating grace, except by means of the Word and of the sacraments. Moreover, faith, conversion, and prayer, are first of all fruits of the grace of God, though they may in turn become instrumental in strengthening the spiritual life. They are not objective ordinances, but subjective conditions for the possession and enjoyment of the blessings of the covenant' (*Theology*, 604).

and these, in turn, give expression to their faith and allegiance to God.'[15] It is worth noting that this definition maps well onto the fourfold definition of the *New Advent Encyclopedia*, quoted previously: a sign, of grace, a commandment, and sanctification. To see this we must understand, 'benefits . . . expression to their faith and allegiance to God' as, sanctification, distinct from justification.

In Book 4 of the *Institutes*, John Calvin distinguished between ordinances and sacraments. He writes,

> Marriage is a good and holy ordinance of God; and farming, building, cobbling, and barbering are lawful ordinances of God, and yet are not sacraments. For it is required that a sacrament be not only a work of God but an outward ceremony appointed by God to confirm a promise.[16]

This helps us see both terms in active distinction. For Calvin, much influenced by Augustine, a sacrament is: 'a testimony of divine grace toward us, confirmed by the outward sign, with mutual attestation of our piety toward him'.[17] And like Luther, Calvin rejects the idea that sacraments are a cause of grace apart from the work of the Holy Spirit to regenerate, citing Augustine for support. Calvin says that there is a parallel between the Word and sacrament, so that both are received with God's mercy and grace. But grace is received not merely because the sacrament is *received*, because they are received *in faith,* thus *confirming* our faith by grace, rather than *conferring* grace apart from faith.[18] This asserts significant distance in his thinking between the concepts of 'confer' and 'confirm'. Further, whatever profit we have from the sacraments is only by the power of God's Spirit[19] so that in no way do they impart grace *in themselves*, for he called such magical ideas, 'diabolical'.[20] So, for Calvin, sacraments do not confer grace by any means, *per se*, but rather sacraments act as mirrors in which we may contemplate God's grace.[21] Sacraments are wonderful

---

15 Berkhof, *Theology*, 617.

16 *Inst.* 4.19.34.

17 *Inst.* 4.14.1.

18 Calvin writes, 'It is therefore certain that the Lord offers us mercy and the pledge of his grace both in his Sacred Word and in his sacraments. But it is understood only by those who take Word and sacraments with sure faith, just a Christ is offered and held forth by the Father to all unto salvation, yet not all acknowledge and receive him. In one place Augustine, meaning to convey this, said that the efficacy of the Word is brought to light in the sacrament, not because it is spoken, but because it is believed' (*Inst.* 4.14.7). But sacraments are not only by faith. In keeping with his illustration of a mirror, *sacraments* also confirm our faith (*Inst.* 4.19.16).

19 *Inst.* 4.14.9.

20 *Inst.* 4.14.14.

21 In Calvin's understanding, this in no way diminishes the import of sacraments. He writes, 'We might call them "the pillars of our faith". For as a building stands and rests upon its own foundation but is more surely established by columns placed underneath, so faith rests upon the Word of God as a foundation; but when the sacra-

and rich, distinguished from ordinances, which are merely commanded by God for our good. Calvin would define them this way: sacraments are ceremonies confirming a promise, ordained by God, which reflect God's grace into the life of the believer by the action of faith, the Word and God's Spirit. In distinction, ordinances are singly-dimensioned, referring only to the command, when compared with the multi-dimensional concept of sacrament. Also, like Luther, Calvin restricted the number of the sacraments, retaining baptism and the Lord's Supper, and rejecting all others, including penance, which Luther also rejected later.[22]

In summary, 'sacrament' is a term which was retained by the Reformation and, when properly understood, offers a rich, multi-dimensional understanding of these treasures given to the Church by Christ. This is distinct from the term 'ordinance,' which came into use recently, is used only among a minority of Christians, and is singly-dimensioned (referring only to the command). As such, it ignores much of the richness of these gifts: the drama of the signs, the mirrors of God's grace, and their role in our sanctification. So, let me make a first approach toward a definition acceptable to evangelical Protestants: a sacrament is a sign which mirrors the grace of God, which is ordained by God for our sanctification.[23] Contra Trent, and faithful to the distinction of the reformers, sacraments do not confer grace in themselves. And sanctification may be understood in the words of Berkhof: 'the benefits of the covenant of grace, are represented, sealed, and applied to believers, and these, in turn, give expression to their faith and allegiance to God'. Or, said with a nod to Calvin, sanctification arises as the work of God in the life of the believer as he contemplates the grace of God in the sacraments as in a mirror. This seems to reflect the intent of the reformers without the explicit errors codified at Trent. I propose that the richer term is the more valuable. Now we turn to the historic Protestant exclusion of marriage as a sacrament.

The exile of marriage from the sacraments

The careful definition of 'sacrament' leads necessarily to a reconsideration of what actually should be numbered among the sacraments. Today, the seven

---

ments are added, it rests more firmly upon them as upon columns. Or we might call them mirrors in which we may contemplate the riches of God's grace, which he lavishes upon us' (*Inst.* 4.14.6)

22 *Inst.* 4.19.14-17.

23 Notice here that in my definition, in contrast to the New Advent, I have substituted 'God' for 'Christ'. That is not without intention. I do so in order to have access to the Old and New Covenants, the commands of God to his people, not only the Church. I do this with warrant: Christ is the Word of God. It does not stand, in light of John 1, Hebrews 1, and the witness of the whole of the New Testament, to make a sharp distinction between the 'command of God' and the 'command of Christ'. While this might require more in the way of exegetical substantiation, I offer it here, explicitly, as my warrant for this amendment of the historical definition.

sacraments of the RCC are superset of the Protestants' two: baptism and the Lord's Supper.[24] Let's consider here the specific judgment of both Luther and Calvin in regard to excluding marriage.

Luther understood marriage not as a sacrament, but as a public estate. Michael Parsons writes that Luther understood marriage as 'the word and ordinance of God within the temporal government of his rule. Its nature, therefore, is outward and physical. Its realm is not that of the church, but that of civil affairs.'[25] Luther rejected marriage as a sacrament in *Babylonian Captivity of the Church*, writing,

> Nowhere do we read that it was instituted by God in order to symbolize something, although we grant that all things done in the sight of men can be understood as metaphors and allegories of things invisible. Yet metaphors and allegories are not sacraments, and it is of sacraments that we are speaking.[26]

Here Luther distinguishes between a symbol and a metaphor. A symbol is explicitly made so by Christ, himself, whereas a metaphor is discerned by inference. Next, Luther objects:

> There has been such a thing as marriage itself ever since the beginning of the world, and it also exists amongst unbelievers to the present day. Therefore no grounds exist on which the Romanists can validly call it a sacrament of the new law.[27]

This point is not a minor one. First, marriage cannot be a sacrament if real marriages are engaged by believers and unbelievers alike. And marriage cannot be a sacrament if it was instituted under the Old Covenant, and not in the New.

John Calvin also rejected marriage as a sacrament. He did this on at least four grounds. First, it was lately adopted as a sacrament under Pope Gregory X (1210-1276). He writes, 'All men admit that it was instituted by God; but no man ever saw it administered as a sacrament until the time of Gregory.'[28] Se-

24 I acknowledge here the minority positions which retain Confession (or penance) or add foot-washing. While worthy of exegetical discussion, this is outside the scope and interest of this paper.

25 Michael Parsons, *Reformation Marriage: The Husband and Wife Relationship in the Theology of Luther & Calvin* (Eugene: Wipf & Stock, 2011), 146.

26 *Selections*, 326.

27 *Selections*, 326.

28 *Inst.* 4.19.34. This citation stands for the successive citations in the same paragraph above. In regard to Gregory, cited above by Calvin, the specific Gregory to whom he refers is unresolved. Gregory VII (c. 1025-1085), to whom this reference is sometimes attributed, reformed marriage and morals among the priests. Also, he was prior to Lombard, the generally agreed antecedent for both the number of sacraments and conferred grace in the sacraments. However, Gregory X (c. 1210-1276) was given such an enumeration by Michael VIII Palaiologos (1223-1282, the Emperor of the Byzantine Empire), at the Council of Lyons (1274, an attempt to unify the Eastern

cond, he rejects it as a sacrament because if marriage is a sacrament, then everything is: 'marriage is a good and holy ordinance of God; and farming, building, cobbling, and barbering are lawful ordinances of God, and yet are not sacraments'. Third, he rejects marriage because it is a ceremony without a promise: 'For it is required that a sacrament be not only a work of God but an outward ceremony appointed by God to confirm a promise.' And, finally, as Luther also objected, its inclusion by the RCC is based on the misapplication of Ephesians 5.32.[29] Marriage is not numbered among the sacraments for the Reformed.

While Luther and Calvin had differing understandings of the meaning of the sacraments, they retained two: baptism and the Lord's Supper. They agreed that marriage was not among the sacraments. Five hundred years later this position is a distinctive of the Protestant church over and against the RCC.

The exile of marriage from the domain of the church

But Luther and Calvin's work was not complete in regard to marriage. They also exiled marriage not only from the sacraments, but also from the domain of the Church. Luther declared marriage to be not of the divine estate, but of civil government. At a theological level, marriage is excluded because of his understanding of two distinct kingdoms: temporal and spiritual.[30] So John Witte writes that Luther came to see marriage as 'an outward, physical, and worldly station,'[31] and, also, 'marriage was subject to the state, not the church. Civil law, not canon law, was to govern marriage' and for Luther, 'marriage was subject to the prince, not the Pope'.[32] There were, perhaps, less theological forces at work. Among his reasons for this was the terrible state of marriage in Germany which occasioned the writing of 'On the Estate of Marriage'.[33] It was, perhaps, only reasonable to assume that the civil government which protected

---

and Western church). This makes Gregory X a more likely candidate for Calvin's reference.

29 *Inst.* 4.19.35-36. This was covered above and is explained by the inexact translation from Greek to Latin, but even more so of the application of *sacramentum* to marriage rather than to Christ and the Church.

30 This can be seen in Parsons, *Reformation Marriage*, chapter 5, especially 122n.74, which gives a clear tabular representation of the distinctions between the kingdoms.

31 Witte, 'Reformation of Marriage Law,' 311.

32 John Witte, Jr., *From Sacrament to Contract: Marriage, Religion, and Law in the Western Tradition* (Louisville: WJK, 1997), 5-6.

33 'I am reluctant to do it because I am afraid if I once get really involved in the subject it will make a lot of work for me and for others. The shameful confusion wrought by the accursed papal law has occasioned so much distress, and the lax authority of both the spiritual and the temporal swords has given rise to so many dreadful abuses and false situations, that I would much prefer neither to look into the matter nor to hear of it. But timidity is no help in an emergency'—accessed 27 Aug 2012: referenced on http://pages.uregon.edu/dluebke/Reformations441/Luthermarriage.htm

him would also be a good repository for reformed marriage. Calvin also divested the Church of the primary authority in marriage, investing it with the civil government. Witte writes that for Calvin, 'marriage required the coercive power of the state to preserve its integrity. But it also required the spiritual counsel of the church to demonstrate its necessity.'[34] This makes sense for Calvin who trusted his own civil government, for by 1555 in Geneva he had successfully purged the city council of opposition. Of course, he could have left marriage fully within the Church, notwithstanding that he had demoted it from sacramental status. But perhaps it seemed that the Church lacked the authority to govern and preserve it. Marriage, in exile from the Church to the state, came under great forces which were already moving to make government a poor choice to secure marriage. The Enlightenment would secularize all things in the public square, including marriage.[35]

It should also be observed that Luther and Calvin did something quite unprecedented in removing marriage from the Church and putting it under the state. The state's authority over marriage is quite new. Stephanie Coontz writes, 'Some things that people believe to be traditional were actually relatively recent innovations. That is the case for the "tradition" that marriage has to be licensed by the state or sanctified by the church.'[36] For the first time in history, marriage was no longer under the family or religious community, but under the governing authority of the state.[37] Whether this transfer was caused primarily as a result of the influence of the reformers is not essential to the point. There can be no doubt other cultural changes contributed. But they were very influential and accomplished their purposes. And with some irony, we should notice that the RCC made no movement in this direction, yet they were also caught up in this movement of marriage toward the state. So, over the next several hundred years, without the agreement of the RCC or other religious groups, the actions of Luther and Calvin led to, or were concurrent with, forces which removed marriage from the family and religious community and placed it in under the state.

Of course, the idea of governmental control of marriage was not wholly new at that time. What was new was that control *actually* passed to the state. For example, the West could look back to Rome, which made a significant attempt to require a state marriage license. Christian Emperor Justinian (527-565) required a state marriage license to protect inheritance when he allowed aristo-

---

34 Witte, *From Sacrament to Contract*, 111

35 Witte, *From Sacrament to Contract*, 39-40.

36 Stephanie Coontz, M*arriage, a History: from Obedience to Intimacy or How Love Conquered Marriage* (New York: Viking, 2005), 5-6.

37 For the sake of historical comparison over long periods of time, allow me to loosen the categories: government rather than state, and family and religious community rather than Church. So, it can be said that historically, marriage has never been under the authority of the government, but instead only under the family or religious community.

crats to marry between classes. However, he soon had to relax his own ruling as unenforceable.[38] In fact, marriage licenses, issued by Western governments, only became common after the middle of the ninetieth century.[39] Reasons for government involvement seem to include supporting parental authority over minors, enforcing racial purity,[40] and perhaps taxation. Until the middle of 19th century, the United States, cohabitation, with no license and no church ceremony, was recognized as a marriage.[41] What is new is that state authority over marriage has become law and seems normal to us. In the context of a Christian marriage the words, 'by the power vested in me by the state of Minnesota, I now pronounce you, man and wife' are so familiar that we forget how novel they are. And this has effects. As the state took greater responsibility, the Church's influence over marriage weakened. That is not to say that this change is fundamentally wrong. The state has provided protections for marriage partners and protection for the children of the marriage, and also for the inheritance of property.

Should marriage be restored among the sacraments?

I now ask, What if we evangelicals, who hold to the singly-dimensioned term 'ordinance,' revived the multi-dimensioned term 'sacrament'? And what if marriage was brought into the number of the sacraments by evangelical Protestants? I want to explore possible advantages of both.

As I propose reviving the term 'sacrament' and restoring marriage among the sacraments, let me state working definitions. A sacrament is a sign, a dramatic enactment, which mirrors the grace of God, which is ordained by God for our sanctification. Marriage is the unbreakable uniting of two, one man and one woman, into one, representing the image of the one-and-many God and the divine covenant-faithfulness.

First, it is not my desire to abolish the use of 'ordinance'; it is a perfectly good word. But let 'ordinance' be used as a part for the whole, and let 'sacrament' be revived as a synonym, which points to that larger picture, which is displayed in the definition above. And if we use the term 'sacrament,' we do so without the baggage of Trent, as did Luther and Calvin who resisted 'magical' reflections, which assume or claim that any sacrament could confer saving grace. We could do with clear teaching. But, someone could object, why consider a term in need of such pedagogical maintenance? The use of the richer

38 Stephanie Coontz, M*arriage*, 81. See also 79.

39 Coontz, M*arriage*, 66.

40 Stephanie Coontz, 'Taking Marriage Private,' New York Times Op Ed, 26 Nov 2007, referenced at http://www.nytimes.com/2007/11/26/opinion/26coontz.html?_r=2)on 1 Sept 2012.

41 Coontz, 'Taking Marriage Private,' writes, 'The American colonies officially required marriages to be registered, but until the mid-19th century, state supreme courts routinely ruled that public cohabitation was sufficient evidence of a valid marriage.'

term 'sacrament' *invites* explanation and teaching. Teaching is the opportunity, not the problem. 'Ordinance' may be too thin a description of so great a gift from God without the support of the richer term. And whichever term we use, let us engage each other with the sign and enact the drama of God's work in our lives.

Second, let me address my use of 'drama' in association with 'sign' in this definition. 'Drama' is not intended as the trivial use, which we associate with entertainment. Rather, its use is a rejection of the ordinances as mere religious remembrances. In this, I am deeply indebted to Kevin Vanhoozer, who explains how deep, rich and wonderful the word 'drama' is and how appropriate it is for us as a description of the Scriptures:

> The Bible is more than divine data. . . . Scripture makes 'tyrannical' demands on the reader: The Scripture stories do not, like Homer's, court our favor, they do not flatter us that they may please us and enchant us—they seek to subject us, and if we refuse to be subjected we are rebels. . . . Forms of exegesis that read the biblical texts as data rather than as bearers of divine discourse are distinctly undramatic.[42]

And how much more appropriate is the term 'drama' to describe the ordained acts of eating and drinking to display the death of Christ, immersion in water to enact his death, drawing up from the water to enact his resurrection, and living out the two-in-one display of God's covenant-faithfulness within the daily drama of marriage? In the sign, the drama, we mirror the grace that stands behind the sign and to which the drama gives witness. We do this because we are commanded by God to do so. And in participation, we are drawn into the sanctifying work that the Holy Spirit brings into our lives through these sacramental acts—they make demands of us.

These preliminary explanations, and the historical theology of the previous sections, may make us ready to answer the question above: is there any reason for those who have neglected this term, not to revive its use? This is not a theological shift, but a revival of a useful and biblical idea. Moreover, it is a pedagogical opportunity. I suggest that the use of 'sacrament' can enhance our understanding and exercise of the ordinances. I would argue that we have much to gain by reviving the use of the word 'sacrament,' or at least allowing 'ordinance' to stand in a larger and richer meaning.

That leaves us with the more difficult question: should marriage be numbered among the sacraments? If the term 'sacrament' is called to duty among evangelicals, as well as among all Protestants, would it make sense to include marriage among the sacraments? To address this I will consider the objections of the reformers and the apparent lack of symmetry between the two Protestant sacraments of baptism and the Lord's Supper, and marriage. As we consider

[42] Kevin Vanhoozer, *The Drama of Doctrine: A Canonical-Linguistic Approach to Christian Theology* (Louisville: WJK, 2005), 5, 19, 20.

these objections, I will be comparing marriage to our working definition of a sacrament, and propose a modification of this definition, which may actually be implicit in our understanding of 'sacrament' (or 'ordinance'), but not expressed.

Does marriage fail as a sacrament for lack of symmetry with baptism and the Lord's Supper?[43] This objection has several parts: marriage's lack of a sign, marriage lacks a promise, marriage is not given to all within the Church, and marriage is a creation ordinance which is not uniquely given to the Church.

First, let me consider Luther's objection that marriage, unlike baptism and the Lord's Supper, lacks a sign. He wrote,

> [N]or does the rite of matrimony contain any hint that the ceremony is of divine institution. . . . Nowhere do we read that it was instituted by God in order to symbolize something, although we grant that all things done in the sight of men can be understood as metaphors and allegories of things invisible. Yet metaphors and allegories are not sacraments, and it is of sacraments that we are speaking.[44]

Luther is not deprecating metaphors, but rather noticing that marriage (like penance) engages no sign or symbol such as water, bread, or wine. But is that the best way to understand the sign? Instead of considering a sign to be an earthly element, should we instead consider the elements to be properties, 'props' in a drama, and that the sign to be the drama, itself? The properties, or the elements, are the physical and tactile objects, which are indeed important. They are important because they can connect the physical to spiritual through the sensory. But while there is no such property in the marriage drama, the intimate physicality of marriage, distinct from the ceremony, may provide the same kind of sensory connection. Indeed this is hinted at even in the declaration of unity in Genesis 2. If this is so, then the *sign* in baptism is not water, but baptism, itself. Such seems to be the implication of Romans 6.1-3 which describes baptism as a drama of the death, burial and resurrection of us in Christ. Similarly, in the Lord's Supper the bread and cup are properties used by the Church to enact the drama of Christ's self-giving for us in which we must partake in order to live. The corporate enactment of the Lord's Supper is the sign, not the wine and the bread. If I am correct, then it would be the drama, and the physical experience of the drama, which is the sign, not physical properties themselves. And although marriage is an ordinance or sacrament between two people and God, it is also observed by all, and so sacramental for the whole

43 What of Calvin's and Luther's concern about the historical exegesis of Eph. 5.32? They were correct in saying that the incidental use of the Latin, *sacramentum*, does not indicate that marriage is a sacrament. However, this particular discussion is not over a biblical term, but rather for the most helpful category and term. I would also set aside their concern that marriage as a sacrament is either too old or too new. Luther objected that it was too old (the Old Covenant) and Calvin that it was too new (since Gregory). These arguments are only a distraction and not in itself an argument.

44 *Selections*, 326.

community, a sign of God's covenant-faithfulness. So then, marriage does not lack a sign, for when it is enacted by God's people, it *is* the sign, pointing to God's faithfulness.

Second, let me consider both Luther's and Calvin's objection that marriage, unlike baptism and the Lord's Supper, lacks a promise. The argument above tells here as well. The promise of baptism is that if we die with him we will live with him; the enactment in the water points to this promise. The promise of the Lord's Supper is our forgiveness in the new covenant; drinking his blood and eating his flesh point to this promise. But what is the promise in marriage? It is this: the promise of God's faithfulness to return for his Bride. This hardly needs support, but we could consider the intended confusion of terms among the prophets in their use of the words 'idolatry' and 'adultery,' the story and prophesy of Hosea, the description of Israel in Ezekiel 16 and then, again, as Oholah and Ohaliab in Ezekiel 23, the image of the Bride in the writings of John, and Paul's teaching on marriage in Ephesians 5. The promise of marriage is the covenant-faithfulness of God to his Church; the wedding ceremony and the marriage lived-out point to that promise.

Third, consider the objection that marriage, unlike baptism and the Lord's Supper, cannot be participated in by all. If the sign is the enactment, and not simply the physical properties, then those who witness the sign also gain much from the sacrament. This shifts the sacrament from the individualistic participants to the corporate witness. This is not a minor point and it may point to a deep connection between the sacraments: sacraments are not private, nor should they be considered to be so. They are always fundamentally community-oriented, signs of God's favor and reflections of great truth. The enactment (by the one baptized, or the two married) is not important apart from community participation. If so, the value of a sign is not limited to the participant(s), but extends to the witnesses. This is particularly so in regard to marriage. If marriage is a sacrament, it is participated in by two, but it is a testimony of God's faithfulness to the whole community—married, unmarried, single, widowed and divorced.

Baptism (like conversion) is by a single participant, and enacted once each, but it is publicly witnessed, and it is symbolic of our entry into the people of God. The Lord's Supper is individually prepared for, partaken of corporately (in communion) and repeated often, and so it is symbolic of our participation together in the life of Christ. Marriage is dual, performed once, but corporately witnessed.

Fourth, and last, in regard to the apparent asymmetry of marriage in relation to baptism and the Lord's Supper, if marriage is a sacrament, what do we say of the rest of the world who also marry? Certainly these marriages cannot be sacramental by intent or in effect. It must be agreed that marriage was given in Genesis 2 as a creation ordinance, so it is both a grace to the world and to God's people. Marriage is a common grace to the world, and where it is honored, it is God's ordained means of procreation, the community and the couple benefits from chastity, and it offers companionship. This was the common perspective of Luther and Calvin.[45] There is no tension in agreeing that Christian and non-Christian marriages are valid marriages before God and offer goods to the world. This is the implication of Paul's argument in 1 Corinthians 7.12-16. But this does not limit the possibility of sacramental reality for marriages of God's people. Baptism and the Lord's Supper are not given to the world as sacraments, but they are given to the whole world in a different way by God. Everyone takes baths, and all people consume bread and wine; so what distinguishes the Lord's Supper from a meal and baptism from a bath? The distinction is in the Spirit and the Word as the reformers said. Moreover, sacraments are distinguished by the gathering of the people of God and their intent. Is this not also what distinguishes the marriage contract from the covenantal sacrament of marriage of God's people?

This point must be taken further. Baptism was a significant sign in Christ's day of other things: John baptized, but this was not the Trinitarian baptism command by Christ as an ordinance or a sacrament. Paul himself makes a distinction in Acts 19 between John's baptism and that in which the Holy Spirit is central. And the Jews had their 'mikvot' before and after Christ. Though Jesus gave us a sacred meal of bread and wine, the evil spirits also gave people 'sacred' meals of meat and drink, which is one of the issues that seems to have prompted the writing of 1 Corinthians. Though baptism and the Lord's Supper are not unique to God's people, this parallel participation of others in the same activity resulted (and results) in no confusion as to the status of the Lord's Supper or baptism. So also, marriage can be sacramental for God's people, even though those outside of the people of God also marry. Marriage is a sign and contains a promise, and it comes by Word and the Spirit—for God's people. It displays the image of God as one-in-many and God's covenant-faithfulness to his people. So, marriage is a sign pointing to God's covenant-faithfulness and could be considered very much like baptism and the Lord's Supper, which share common practices with the world. Marriage is a sign which points to a promise, is sacramental to participant and witness, and while it is a creation ordinance for the whole world, it is also a sacrament for God's Church. In this, marriage is like the other ordinances; asymmetry fades.

Now we turn to the final concern: Is everything sacramental? If we include marriage among the sacraments, then is this category broadened beyond all bounds? Let me restate Calvin here,

> Lastly, there is matrimony, which all admit was instituted by God, though no one before the time of Gregory regarded it as a sacrament. What man in his sober senses could so regard it? God's ordinance is good and holy; so also are agricul-

[45] Parsons, *Reformation Marriage*, 165. Here Parsons is giving Calvin's position, having already established Luther's in quite similar terms. Moreover, their common understanding leans heavily on Augustine's sense of the 'good of marriage': procreation, chastity, and the bond of union (56).

> ture, architecture, shoemaking, hair-cutting legitimate ordinances of God, but they are not sacraments (*Inst.* 4.19.3).

He makes two arguments here: historical and definitional. I have responded to the historical argument above. In regard to Calvin's definitional argument, let us recall the terms Calvin used to define a sacrament: ceremonies, ordained by God which reflect God's grace into the life of the believer, the action of faith, the Word, and God's Spirit. If this is a fair representation of Calvin, the exemplar activities which Calvin brings forward as parallel to marriage do not track. They are not commands (not ordinances of Christ) but goods, and they are not associated with ceremonies, but activities and trades. As such, they seem to be straw-men in this regard. Marriage, as has been shown above, is a command, is initiated in a ceremony, and contains all the elements of a sacrament.

But if marriage is 'in' and 'shoemaking' is out, what other God-ordained dramas might be numbered among the sacraments? I suggest that the ordinances which we do recognize are the commands which are uniquely grounded in the great events of the salvation history of God's people. Each points to one or more of the three great acts of God in salvation history of creation, redemption and restoration. Each of these acts of God is spoken of as both an act of creation and a crisis (or turning point). Baptism rests on redemption and restoration: redemption because it connects us to the death of Christ in our immersion and restoration in the promise of resurrection in our coming up out of the water. The Lord's Supper connects us to the death of Christ (redemption) and also to the wedding feast of the Lamb (restoration). So, baptism and the Lord's Supper are not only ordained by God in Christ, but they connect us with the great turning points of salvation history, though not necessarily all three. The following chart displays the chiastic structure of these three events with the apostrophe (') representing the crisis in each of the three creation & crisis events.

Display of Chiastic Structure of Creation & Crisis Events		
1	Creation of Heaven & Earth	Old Covenant
1'	The Fall of Humanity	
2	Incarnation of Christ	
2'	Death of Christ	
2	Resurrection & Creation of New People	New Covenant
3'	The Judgment	
3	Creation of New Heavens and New Earth	

Marriage is just as deeply connected to these turning points, perhaps more so, for it connects to each of these creation-and-crisis events of redemption. The connection to creation has already been established (Gen. 2). Specifically, this seems to be a connection to our participation in the image of God, two becoming one, so reflecting God who is one-and-many, and also anticipates the biblical theme of God's covenant-faithfulness displayed in marriage. We can also see a deep connection to redemption which is displayed in the words of John the Baptist who calls Jesus the Bridegroom (Jn. 3) and Jesus' own parable of the wise and foolish virgins (Matt. 25). This is made more explicit in Ephesians 5. Here Paul commands men to 'love their wives as Christ loves the church and gave himself for her'. This is God's covenant-faithfulness to us and it invokes all that preceded it in the old covenant in this regard. Apart from any historical translation errors (*sacramentum*), marriage is still tied to redemption because it is intended to display the selfless love that Jesus has for his people. In fact, the concepts are so intertwined, Paul cannot (does not want to) keep them fully separate through any phrase within this text. Finally, marriage connects us sacramentally to renewal in the Revelation of John (19.7; 21.2-9; 22.17). When Christ returns, his people are to be joined to him as a virgin bride. And we will celebrate with him in the wedding feast! We will be the Bride. He will be the Groom. And we will be united with him forever. If ordinances are also sacraments, not only because they offer a sign pointing to a promise, mirror God's grace, and engage us in sanctification, but also because they connect us to the specific promises of creation, redemption and restoration, marriage may be the chief of the sacraments.

So, let me return to definitions: a sacrament is a sign, a dramatic enactment, which mirrors the grace of God, which is ordained by God for our sanctification, and which displays God's great acts of salvation history. So defined, I propose that 'sacrament' is a helpful term for the evangelical Protestant Church, along with the term 'ordinance'. Further, this definition of sacrament enriches the term 'ordinance,' which in modern usage was in danger of becoming too flat to contain the grandeur of these things. And how much more is this true in the case of marriage which in our tradition does not even aspire to ordinance, but is considered by evangelicals as an 'institution'. I propose that if we understand marriage as a sacrament (or an enriched ordinance), we will value God and marriage more highly.

Conclusion

I have attempted to revive, with amendment, the historical definition of sacrament: a sacrament is a sign, a dramatic enactment, which mirrors the grace of God, which is ordained by God for our sanctification, and which displays God's great acts of salvation history. I have suggested that 'sacrament' is a helpful term for the whole of the Protestant Church, along with the term 'ordinance'. I have also suggested that it could serve the gospel if we included marriage among the sacraments—not only the ceremony, but the daily drama, the 'sacrament' of living out the command of Christ in a way that displays his grace, not only for others, but for our own sanctification. We need no permission from the state to define and practice marriage. Marriage is what God says it is. We are free in Christ, as we have always been. We are free to display God's truth and grace through the sacrament of marriage by the power of the Holy Spirit and in the community of the Church. In this God will be glorified.

CHAPTER 9

'It is too late to think of shrinking back.' Calvin's letters to contemporary martyrs

Michael Parsons

In a significant article, the Lutheran scholar, Robert Kolb, makes the rather bleak statement that with the Protestant reformations of the sixteenth century 'the phenomenon of dying for the faith returned'. Christian Europe executed heretics throughout the medieval period, of course, but, as Kolb reminds us, 'they died largely alone, at the edge of Christendom, mourned by relatively few and remembered by fewer'.[1] More recently, in a short introductory article, Haruko Nawata Ward speaks of a 'renaissance' of Christian martyrdom in the Reformation period. Ward suggests that there were two distinct spheres of martyrdom at that time. First, martyrdom occurred in Europe 'due to conflicts among Christian groups'. Second, numerous Catholic missionaries, sent to Africa, Asia, and the Americas, for instance, 'became martyrs at the hands of the so-called "pagans"'.[2] It is with the former sphere of martyrdom that this chapter has to do; that of conflict among Christian groups. More specifically, we are concerned with the context of martyrdom within the Reformed Church and Calvin's epistolary response in two specific instances.

Following a brief introduction to the general theme, highlighting Martin Luther's understanding of martyrdom—an understanding that had significant, perhaps seminal, influence in protesting theology—the essay examines several of John Calvin's letters to those about to be executed for their faith: three letters to five students in Lyons (1553) and a letter to a small group in Chambery (1555).[3] Brief reflections on Calvin's theology and pastoral approach follow.

---

1 Robert Kolb, 'God's Gift of Martyrdom: The Early Reformation Understanding of Dying for the Faith,' *Church History* 64.3 (1995), 399.

2 Haruko Nawata Ward, 'Martyrdom' in David M. Whitford (ed.), *T & T Clark Companion to Reformation Theology* (Edinburgh: T. & T. Clark, 2012), 332. See also Auke Jelsma, *Frontiers of the Reformation. Dissidence and Orthodoxy in Sixteenth Century Europe* (Aldershot: Ashgate, 1998), 75-90.

3 The letters are found in *Letters of John Calvin*, 4 volumes (edited by Jules Bonnet; Philadelphia: Presbyterian Board, 1858), henceforth, Calvin, *Letters*. On Calvin's letters, generally, see Douglas Kelly, 'The Transmission and Translation of the Collect-

Protestant martyrdom

According to Kolb, during the sixteenth century, 'sufficient numbers of the persecuted existed to enable every Christian confession to celebrate martyred brothers and sisters'.[4] Persecution was one significant aspect of an extremely violent age.[5] Men and women died for their faith, believing that their form of confession was the true faith, over against those that were not.[6]

Ward, helpfully, lists three requirements necessary for a death to be considered martyrdom. First, martyrs had to be executed by secular authorities. Second, the martyrs had to have a certain self-perception. Generally, they believed that they belonged to the true Church. Third, the martyr's death was visualised and interpreted within a particular community. They were not isolated individuals, but members of communities of faith and, therefore, their deaths were 'interpreted through the lens of the community's shared beliefs'.[7] We might add another, I think: that the death of a martyr had to be seen as witnessing to divine truth, as the community saw it; after all, the word 'martyr' (μαρτύριον) literally means 'witness,' of course. This is the curatorial nature of faith, to protect and to defend truth against its adversaries.

According to Robert Kolb, Luther was the first sixteenth century reformer to develop a *theology* of martyrdom.[8] His understanding of martyrdom, Kolb insists, illustrates the reformer's theology of the cross because it reveals a para-

---

ed Letters of John Calvin,' *SJT* 30.5 (1977), 429-37; Henry F. Henderson, *Calvin in his Letters* (Eugene: Wipf and Stock, 1996).

4 Kolb, 'God's Gift,' 399. For a wider perspective of this subject, see the excellent study by Brad S. Gregory, *Salvation at Stake. Christian Martyrdom in Early Modern Europe* (Cambridge: Harvard University Press, 1999). Also, William Monter, 'Heresy Executions in Reformation Europe, 1520-1565' in Ole Peter Grell and Robert W. Scribner (eds), *Tolerance and Intolerance in the European Reformation* (Cambridge: CUP, 1996), 48-64; Peter Matheson, *The Imaginative World of the Reformation* (Edinburgh: T. & T. Clark, 2000), 77-82; Bernard Cottret, *Calvin. A Biography* (Grand Rapids: Eerdmans / Edinburgh: T. & T. Clark, 2000), 244-47.

5 See Thomas M. Safley (ed.), *A Companion to Multiconfessionalism in the Early Modern World* (Leiden: Brill, 2011), to nuance this remark in this context. Also, from a different perspective, see Benjamin J. Kaplan, *Divided by Faith. Religious Conflict in the Practice of Toleration in Early Modern Europe* (Cambridge: Harvard University Press, 2009).

6 'Martyrdom was not a matter of dying for just any faith but for what they regarded as the true faith. The truth, not heroic zeal for any cause, mattered'—Kolb, 'God's Gift,' 400.

7 Ward, 'Martyrdom,' 332-33.

8 It is worth remembering that Luther, himself, thought he might be martyred for his stand against the established Church. This is partly why he delayed his own marriage. See letter to Spalatin, Wittenberg, November 30, 1524, *LW* 49.93 (*WA Br* 3.393-94); letter to Amsdorf, Wittenberg, June 21, 1525, *LW* 49.117 (*WA Br* 3.541); *Comm. 1 Cor.* 7.25-26, *LW* 28.49 (*WA* 12.134-35); Michael Parsons, *Reformation Marriage. The Husband and Wife Relationship in the Theology of Luther and Calvin* (Eugene: Wipf and Stock, 2011), 173-77.

dox 'which equates God's wisdom with what seems foolishness to the sinner and God's power with what seems impotence to the sinner (1 Cor. 1.18-2.16)'.[9] Therefore, confession of, or witnessing to, the truth of God is, for Luther, a gracious gift of God.[10] Kolb says the following,

> Because [the theology of the cross] led him to see martyrdom in the context of God's working through his Word, which finds its power and wisdom in what the world considers to be impotence and foolishness, he could define martyrdom as a gift from God, to the martyr who proved the power and wisdom of God in this ultimate sacrifice, and to the surviving people of God, who beheld the paradox of God's revelation of his love in the martyr's confession of the faith unto death.[11]

This certainly makes a great deal of sense. Kolb's conclusions are confirmed by even a cursory glance at the reformer's letters to those who are about to die for their faith or to others involved in grieving for them. For example, in writing to the believers in the Netherlands after the imprisonment and execution in Brussels of Henry Vos and John van den Esschen (the first Protestant martyrs),[12] Luther encourages them to be full of joy.

> For it has been your privilege before all others in the world not only to hear the gospel and know Christ but also to be the first to suffer shame and injury, anxiety and distress, imprisonment and death, for Christ's sake.[13]

In this eschatologically-charged letter the reformer suggests that they look at the persecution and deaths as God giving to them 'a new and fresh illustration of his own life'—that is, the kingdom, 'not in word, but in power'. 'Let us renew our hearts,' Luther exhorts, 'and be of good courage and joyfully *allow the Lord to slay us*.'[14]

In his letter to the martyr, Lambert Thorn,[15] Luther assures him of Christ's identification with him in his suffering: 'He himself suffers in you and is *glorified* in you. He is taken captive in you and *reigns* in you. He is oppressed in you and *triumphs* in you.'[16] The rhetorical intensity of the sentence, together with

---

9 Kolb, 'God's Gift,' 401.

10 Kolb, 'God's Gift,' 402. 'Martyrdom was, for [Luther], literally witness to the faith, the Word of God in action' (403).

11 Kolb, 'God's Gift,' 411. For a brief, excellent introduction to this theme in Luther, see Gerhard O. Forde, *On Being a Theologian of the Cross. Reflections on Luther's Heidelberg Disputation, 1518* (Grand Rapids: Eerdmans, 1997).

12 See letter to the Christians in the Netherlands, August, 1523: Theodore G. Tappert (ed.), *Luther: Letters of Spiritual Counsel* (Vancouver: Regent College, 2003), 192-94; *WA* 12.73-80—hereafter, Luther: *Letters*.

13 Luther: *Letters*, 193.

14 Luther: *Letters*, 193, italics added.

15 See letter to Lambert Thorn, January 19, 1524, Luther: *Letters*, 197-99; *WA Br* 3.237-39.

16 Luther: *Letters*, 198, italics added. In a letter to Sibyl Baumgaertner, July 8, 1544; Luther: *Letters*, 225-27; *WA Br* 10.604-607, Luther speaks again of this identification

the italicised words indicate Kolb's thesis concerning Luther. While Christ has become 'a reproach of men and despised of the people,'[17] in and through the suffering and the oppression of believers, Christ is glorified, reigns and triumphs.[18] In a letter to believers in Leipzig[19] Luther speaks of Christ 'who suffers and is put to death among you, but who will certainly rise again and reign'. He concludes on the same note of triumph through suffering: 'One must smite the devil in his face with the cross and not whistle his tune or flatter him. He must be made to know with whom he has to do.'[20] In another letter Luther assures the recipient that Christ is in the cell with him and encourages him to call upon Christ and to 'defy and ridicule the raging and arrogance of Satan'.[21] Suffering and persecution are necessary for the gospel to exist and to spread, according to the reformer,[22] and oppression of true believers in their inherent weakness sees the power of God in Christ manifest and reign.

Calvin's letters to contemporary martyrs

Interestingly, Andrew Pettegree sees John Calvin as first and foremost an evangelist and a preacher: 'He aimed at the conversion of society, and inevitably pursued traditional conversion strategies: the call to repentance, the appeal to political elites, the call to witness and, if necessary, exile or martyrdom.'[23] On the other hand, when those who were converted to the Reformed faith witnessed that faith and were arrested and tried, Calvin, the pastor, supported and encouraged them—even from a distance, as we shall see. In that context, we now turn to examine some letters that John Calvin wrote to two groups of prisoners about to be executed, the five prisoners at Lyons in 1553, and those in Chambery two years' later, in 1555.[24]

---

of Christ with suffering believers, '[W]e visit the Lord Christ himself,' he says, 'imprisoned in the person of a true member' (227).

17 Luther: *Letters*, 199.

18 Luther: *Letters*, 198. The reformer quotes Ps. 91.14-15; Jn. 16.33.

19 Letter to the Evangelicals in Leipzig, April 11, 1533; Luther: *Letters*, 223-24; *WA Br* 6.448-50.

20 Luther: *Letters*, 224. See, also, letter to the Christians of Miltenberg, February 14, 1524; Luther: *Letters*, 203; letter to the Christians in Bremen, March, 1525; Luther: *Letters*, 209.

21 Letter to Leonard Kaeser, May 20, 1527; Luther: *Letters*, 214; for the whole letter see 213-15; *WA Br* 4.204-206.

22 See letter to Casper Loener and Nicholas Medler, June 7, 1531; Luther: *Letters*, 216.

23 Andrew Pettegree, 'The spread of Calvin's thought' in Donald K. McKim (ed.), *The Cambridge Companion to John Calvin* (Cambridge: CUP, 2004), 222.

24 These are not the only letters written in such circumstances. See, for example, Calvin's letter to Bullinger, Whitsunday, 1552 (Calvin, *Letters*, 2.349), in which he speaks of a student being burned in Bordeaux; and, a letter to Sulzer, September 8, 1553 (Calvin, *Letters*, 2.427-30), in which he speaks of four more.

Letters to the five prisoners of Lyons

Jules Bonnet, editor of Calvin's letters, describes the situation briefly as follows.[25] In April, 1552, five young Frenchmen, students of theology in Lausanne were returning to their own country. They are named by Bonnet as Martial Alba from Montauban, Peter Escrivain from Gascony, Charles Favre from Blanzac in Angoumois, Peter Navihères from Limousin and Bernard Seguin La Reole. After having spent some days in Geneva they were tricked and betrayed by a stranger they met on the road who insisted they visited him in Ainay. There, to their shock, they were arrested and led away to prison. Eventually, all five students were declared guilty of heresy and, forthwith, delivered to the secular Judge Ordinary of Lyons. From their imprisonment they appealed to the Parliament of Paris for clemency and their hoped-for release. The Reformed Church supported them, with the authorities of Berne, in particular, striving to have them released. Their long drawn-out trial lasted more than a year, during which time they were transferred from dungeon to bleak dungeon. Eventually, they were brought back to Lyons to await their sentence. On 1 March, 1553, they received the communication which gave them over to their execution at the stake. During this ordeal they were supported by the reformer, John Calvin, and by others. Several letters are of significance to our study.

1. to the five prisoners of Lyons, from Geneva, 10 June, 1552[26]

The first letter that Calvin wrote to the prisoners was written in response to a letter from one of the students. Calvin says that he had wished to write as soon as he had heard of their predicament, but admits that he had delayed somewhat in case his letter fell into the wrong hands in transit, fearing that it may have caused them greater harm by their resulting association with his name. The letter was written before sentence had been passed on them, and it appears from what he says that there was still room for hope of their release. Calvin writes, then, to assure them of his concern, but, also, to answer two questions that Bernard Seguin La Reole had asked, one concerning vows and the other, perhaps more understandably, about the nature of the glorified body.[27]

The major import of this letter is to assure them that God is intimately involved with them in their terrible situation. Calvin repeats what he has evidently heard, perhaps from John Liner (see below). 'I had been informed,' he says, 'how that God wrought so powerfully in you by his grace that you stood in no

---

[25] See Calvin, *Letters*, 2.350n.1; 2.391n.1. These prisoners became famous as martyrs, being cited, for example, in Sebastian Meyer, *In apocalypsim Johannis Apostoli* (Zürich: Froschouer, 1559), fol. 42r.

[26] Calvin, *Letters*, 2.350-53.

[27] We need not enter into detail. Suffice it to say, concerning vows, Calvin says that it is not lawful to vow to God anything but what he approves (Calvin, *Letters*, 2.351-52). Concerning the glorified body, the reformer argues that it is the 'corruptible and fading nature of the world' which will be changed in our bodies—quoting Phil. 3 (Calvin, *Letters*, 2.352-53).

great need of my letters.'[28] Their constancy in this affliction is enough to demonstrate divine presence and help. Upon this foundation, the reformer reassures the prisoners that God will give them strength to fulfil what they have begun. They can rest in the divine promises, 'we know from experience that he has never failed those who allow themselves to be governed by him'.[29] Calvin, later, makes the point that this comes to those who suffer through Jesus Christ and their establishment in him.[30]

A secondary, but important, theme of the letter is the identification of the Reformed community with them in their distress. They are not isolated, not alone in their trial.

> Meanwhile, all the children of God pray for you as they are bound to do, not only on account of the mutual compassion which ought to exist between members of the same body, but because they know well that you labour for them, in maintaining the cause of their salvation.[31]

Interestingly, the motivation runs in two directions, according to this paragraph. On the one hand, the Church has compassion on the prisoners in their misfortune and anguish, 'as they are bound to do'. On the other hand, the Church realises that the prisoners 'labour for them, in maintaining the cause of their salvation'. They are united, then, by both Christian love and the defence of what they consider to be biblical truth.

Calvin appears to draw the themes of God's and the Church's involvement together in his closing prayer for them.

> In conclusion, I beseech our good Lord that he would be pleased to make you feel in every way the worth of his protection of his own, to fill you with his Holy Spirit who gives you prudence and virtue, and brings you peace, joy, and contentment; and may the name of our Lord Jesus be glorified by you to the edification of his Church![32]

It is, of course, characteristic of the reformer to allude to the triune God in his prayers. Calvin is clear that it is the Lord who protects, it is the Spirit who is able to furnish them with the qualities of prudence and virtue, and to allow them, even in this awful circumstance, to experience peace, joy and contentment; and, it is Jesus Christ who will be glorified by their perseverance. In all of this, the consequence is that the wider Church will be edified and built up.

[28] Calvin, *Letters*, 2.350.
[29] Calvin, *Letters*, 2.351.
[30] Calvin, *Letters*, 2.351: '[B]ut the firmness which is in Jesus Christ is sufficient for this, and all else that might shake us were we not established in him.'
[31] Calvin, *Letters*, 2.350-51.
[32] Calvin, *Letters*, 2.353.

2. to the five prisoners of Lyons, March 7, 1553[33]

This letter, the second of the reformer to the prisoners, was written just six days after the sentence against them was passed. Calvin begins by confessing his own state of mind: 'We have been for some days past in deeper anxiety and sadness than ever,' he says, 'having heard of the resolve taken by the enemies of the truth.'[34] But, again, understandably, the theme of this short letter revolves around the presence and help of God.

Though he anticipates the worst, Calvin remains open to God's gracious providence, indicating that the Lord may yet dispose of the situation in an unexpected manner.[35] However, with that, the reformer speaks of continually praying to God 'to uphold you, and not permit you to fall away; in short, to have you in his keeping. I feel well assured that nothing shakes the firmness which he has put within you.'[36] God has given them constancy up to this point; Calvin's prayer is that he continues to do this. He exhorts them through consideration of the divine promises.

> If he has promised to strengthen with patience those who suffer chastisement for their sins, how much less will he be found wanting to those who maintain his quarrel—those whom he employs on so worthy a mission as being witnesses for his truth! You must therefore keep this sentence in mind, that 'He who dwells in you is stronger than the world.' We who are here shall do our duty in praying that he would glorify himself more and more by your constancy, and that he may, by the consolation of his Spirit, sweeten and endear all that is bitter to the flesh, and so absorb your spirits in himself, that in contemplating that heavenly crown, you may be ready without regret to leave all that belongs to this world.[37]

There are several points worth underlining in this important quotation. First, in encouraging the students to set their minds on the divine promise, Calvin speaks of them, not merely as believers, but as 'those who maintain his [God's] quarrel,' 'those whom he employs,' 'witnesses for his truth'. This clearly establishes their position as Christian or, more particularly, Reformed martyrs. The

---

33 Calvin, *Letters*, 2.391-93.

34 Calvin, *Letters*, 2.391.

35 It is worth noting that, when he writes to others at this time, Calvin is not optimistic in the least. Between the reformer's letters, dated March 7 and May 15 (1553), Calvin wrote to his friend Pierre Viret (22 April, 1553) in which he gives an account of the situation—see Calvin, *Letters*, 2.401-402. According to Calvin, the majority of judges 'were disinclined to agree to the condemnation of the brethren, inasmuch as the king had given no express orders respecting it' (2.401). The Constable, Anne de Montmorency, 'stood alone in opposing this' (2.401). The reformer, also, points out Cardinal de Touron as being particularly obstinate in the matter. Calvin expresses the feeling that, though some still attempt to gain their freedom, there is now no real hope for the prisoners.

36 Calvin, *Letters*, 2.391.

37 Calvin, *Letters*, 2.392.

work is God's, as is the truth and, consequently, so is the quarrel with the enemies of that truth, and the students have been called into this mission by God and for God. Second, Calvin suggests the second theme that pervades these letters, that of the Reformed community: 'We who are here shall do our duty in praying.' The prisoners are not alone in this situation, but have the Church supporting them in the difficult days that lie ahead. Third, Jesus Christ will be glorified by their constancy. Fourth, the Spirit, by absorbing their spirits in himself, will bring consolation to them in their anxiety. By this, Calvin appears to mean that the Holy Spirit will so encompass their troubled spirits that they will be comforted (see, perhaps, 2 Cor. 1.4; Rom. 8.26-27). Fifth, the reformer reminds the young men of that eschatological dimension and focus, speaking of them 'contemplating that heavenly crown'. This brings into focus the spiritual perspective, so vital in times of affliction and anxiety, in which believers may be ready to leave this transient world without remorse.

Calvin knows that, given the situation, the prisoners will have considered their deaths[38] and exhorts them to put their confidence in God alone, trusting that he will fill them with his Holy Spirit to the point of overcoming. Then comes the inevitable final prayer, together with a request that they pray for him—indicating their mutual dependence, even at this hour.

> And now, my brethren, after having besought our good Lord to have charge over you, to assist you in everything and through everything, to make you taste by experience how kind a Father he is, and how careful of the salvation of his own, I pray to be remembered in your prayers.[39]

Again, the understandable emphasis on the Lord's assisting presence. But, here is an interesting stress on experience, too. Calvin prays that, even in their distressing situation, they may *experience* 'how kind a Father he is and how careful of the salvation of his own'. Within the awful experience of imprisonment and waiting for execution, Calvin prays that they may experience something else, something greater and more comforting, even the fatherly love and grace of God.

3. to the five prisoners of Lyons, 15 May, 1553

Calvin's third letter to the prisoners was written a day before their execution.[40] The reformer commends the five men for never having wavered in their faith

---

[38] Calvin, *Letters*, 2.392, 'It cannot be but that you feel some twinges of frailty.'

[39] Calvin, *Letters*, 2.393. It might be noted, too, that Calvin suggests that the prisoners write, warning the church of the false and malicious conspirator of the church whom they have met. Knowing the current weight of their testimony, the reformer believes this will help others.

[40] Calvin, *Letters*, 2.404-408. Between this letter and the last, on 28 March (1553), Calvin wrote to Christopher and Thomas Sollicoffre, merchants of Gall, dwelling in Lyons. A messenger on behalf of the prisoners had been to the French court to solicit pardon from the king, Henry II. Calvin asks the merchants if they would give the ex-

and trust in God. He exhorts them at this last hour to look towards heaven, to subdue their passions and to be humbly ready. Calvin speaks of God using their deaths 'to sign his truth'.

> You know, however, in what strength you have to fight—a strength on which all those who trust, shall never be daunted, much less confounded. Even so, my brothers, be confident that you shall be strengthened, according to your need, by the Spirit of our Lord Jesus, so that you shall not faint under the load of temptations, however heavy it be, any more than he did who won so glorious a victory, that in the midst of our miseries it is an unfailing pledge of his triumph.[41]

Here are those characteristic comments. In seeking to encourage the prisoners in their last hours, Calvin identifies their misery with Christ's, only then to call attention to Christ's subsequent victory and their own triumph, through him. They are, he assures them, 'maintaining his [God's] quarrel'; their blood will *not* be spilt in vain. Their deaths will result in the name of Jesus Christ being 'powerfully' glorified.[42]

Calvin is sure that God will give to them the experience of his comfort and reminds them of the inheritance to which they go. Significantly, in this appalling context, the reformer speaks of them as martyrs: 'That God should have appointed you his Son's martyrs, is a token to you of superabounding grace.'[43] He continues the eschatological theme by asserting the truth of resurrection:

> And seeing that he employs your life in so worthy a cause as is the witness of the Gospel, doubt not that it must be precious to him. The time draws nigh when the earth shall disclose the blood which has been hid, and we, after having been disencumbered of these fading bodies, shall be completely restored.[44]

Further, reflecting something of Luther's approach, perhaps, he claims that the Son of God will be 'glorified by our shame'.[45]

---

penses of the messenger's journey. Of course, as we know, the journey, itself, was to no avail—Calvin, *Letters*, 2.396-97. Apparently, to the brethren in Berne they wrote that their blood would be soon 'shed for the confession of his [Christ's] holy name' and that they were ready to suffer and to be received into God's heavenly kingdom. See the short, moving account of their deaths, Calvin, *Letters*, 2.404-405n.2.

41 Calvin, *Letters*, 2.405-406.

42 Calvin, *Letters*, 2.406, emphasis added.

43 Calvin, *Letters*, 2.406.

44 Calvin, *Letters*, 2.407.

45 Calvin, *Letters*, 2.407. See the argument of Bonnie Pattison in her excellent essay, 'The suffering church in Calvin's *De Scandalis*: an exercise in Luther's *Theologia Crucis*? in Michael Parsons (ed.), *Since we are Justified by Faith. Justification in the Theologies of the Protestant Reformation* (Milton Keynes: Paternoster, 2012), 117-37, in which she concludes that Calvin resembles Luther in his approach and understanding of the suffering Church and that 'for Calvin as for Luther, there is no other way except through weakness and suffering to make manifest a knowledge of God in the lives of God's people' (137).

Calvin's final word to the prisoners, as one would expect, is a prayer. In it he asks God to protect them, to strengthen them 'more and more by his power,' 'to make [them] feel what care he takes of [their] salvation,' to increase the Spirit's gifts in them, and to let them serve 'his glory to the end'.[46] From the account of their death we know that this prayer was answered in good measure.

During the trial of these unfortunate students, Calvin wrote to John Liner, a rich merchant of St. Gall, who had settled in Lyons. Apparently, he often visited the men in their dungeon and, on occasion, undertook errands for them.[47] Some of the contents of this short letter are worth considering at this juncture, as they add to our understanding of Calvin's view of the prisoners, themselves, and of martyrdom.

Naturally, Calvin thanks Liner for the zeal he has displayed on their behalf. He comments that the tireless work of Liner is, in fact, God's work 'by the power of his Spirit'. By this, he means that the Spirit has disposed and directed Liner in his sacrificial efforts. He has been honoured by God and has been given grace and courage to perform his duty.[48] It is interesting, though, that the reformer speaks in this way more because of the Lord's high regard for the prisoners, than anything to do intrinsically with Liner and his efforts. Notice how he puts this.

> For however despised and rejected of men, the poor believers persecuted for the sake of the Gospel may be, yet we know that God esteems them very pearls; that there is nothing more agreeable to him than our striving to comfort and help them as in us lies.[49]

The gospel reverses perspective. In the eyes of the world and of 'the enemies of the faith'[50] they are 'despised and rejected'; in God's sight (*coram Deo*) they are precious jewels. They are God's 'agents, whom he appoints for the defence of his Gospel'.[51] Further, speaking of Liner's actions as 'fatherly,' Calvin cites Jesus' words about giving a cup of water to the least of his people (see Matt. 25.34-46): 'a cup of water given to them shall not be lost'. Significantly, the parable to which Calvin alludes suggests that water given to the least is water given to Jesus Christ, himself—such is his identification with those who suffer.[52] Then, in speaking of the prisoners as 'martyrs' Calvin, also, identifies Liner's efforts with theirs: 'It is said that they who comfort the children of God in their persecutions which they endure for the Gospel, are fellow-labourers for

---

46 Calvin, *Letters*, 2.407.
47 Letter to John Liner, 10 August, 1552, Calvin, *Letters*, 2.358-60.
48 Calvin, *Letters*, 2.358.
49 Calvin, *Letters*, 2.358-59.
50 Calvin, *Letters*, 2.358.
51 Calvin, *Letters*, 2.359.
52 Calvin, *Letters*, 2.359.

the truth.' And, more remarkably, he states that God upholds and approves *us* (Calvin and Liner, in this instance) as his martyrs, 'even though we do not personally suffer, merely because his martyrs are helped and comforted by us'.[53]

The theme of the Christian community is never far from the reformer's mind, in this or any other context. Again, he raises it here, reminding Liners that many believers glorify God for what he is doing. The prisoners are said to be encouraged and made more resolute in their stand because they can see God working in Liner's gracious actions on their behalf. 'Be of good courage, therefore, in this holy work, in which you serve not only God and his martyrs, but also the whole Church.'[54]

A letter to prisoners in Chambery, 5 September, 1555[55]

Again, Jules Bonnet gives us the names of four of the five individuals imprisoned for the sake of the gospel.[56] They are John Vernou, student, native of Poitiers; Anthony Laborie of Caiar (formerly the royal judge of that place); John Trigalet (licentiate of law) of Nismes, and Bertrand Bataille, student, of Gascony. These young men set out with the intention of preaching the Word of God but were arrested and imprisoned, later to face death for their faith.

Characteristically, the reformer expresses his sorrow for the situation which these prisoners face: '[W]ith what anguish our hearts are filled on account of your bonds,' he says.[57] Likewise, he assures them of the affection of 'the whole body of the church'—a poignant reminder that they are part of a wider community, the Reformed Church.[58] Indeed, he alludes again to this wider context in the following comment: 'Since then so many of the brethren pray fervently for you, I doubt not but our heavenly Father will listen to their desires and groanings, and I see by your letters how he has already begun to work in you.'[59] The use of the word 'groanings' is significant; perhaps, it indicates that Calvin and the others praying for these brethren did not know what to pray for but trusted in the Spirit to aid their agonised prayers (see, perhaps, Rom. 8.26).

There is in this letter a tacit understanding that the situation might end in execution for the prisoners. The reformer is quite open about this. He says, for instance, that he wishes they had, what he calls, 'worldly means' of deliverance; but encourages them to 'look higher' as he believes God urges them to do. He acknowledges their weakness and fear, but sees even in that the activity of divine grace: 'For if the weakness of the flesh will sometimes show itself in

---

53 Calvin, *Letters*, 2.359.

54 Calvin, *Letters*, 2.359. Calvin encourages Liner to persevere, speaking of the temptations involved: '[T]he devil,' he says, 'will not fail to whisper in your ear on many sides to divert you from it' (2.359).

55 Calvin, *Letters*, 3.220-23.

56 See Calvin, *Letters*, 3.220n.1.

57 Calvin, *Letters*, 3.221.

58 Calvin, *Letters*, 3.223.

59 Calvin, *Letters*, 3.221.

such a manner as that you shall have hard and difficult struggles to maintain, this is not to me a matter of astonishment, but rather of magnifying God, because he raised you above it.'[60]

Calvin then explicitly uses terms that situate the prisoners within the concept of contemporary martyrdom, reminding them that God has called them into his service. Speaking of the doctrines for which they make a stand, he tells them that divine providence will cause their present witness to be even more effective than their preaching or teaching: '[T]he testimony which you are about to bear will not fail to confirm them from afar. For God will bestow on it a virtue to resound further than voice of man can reach.' This is God's work, not theirs. But Calvin encourages them to practise what they have learned, to continue to do what they have begun.[61] The reformer continues in a similar vein,

> [R]epose in his paternal goodness, not doubting but he will take your bodies as well as your souls under his protection, and if the blood of his faithful followers is precious, will effectually show it in you, since he has chosen you to be his witnesses. And should it be his will to demand the sacrifice of your lives to approve his truth, besides that this is as you know an oblation well pleasing in his sight, let it console you that in surrendering the whole into his hands you will lose nothing; for if he kindly deigns to take us under his protection during this perishable life, much more, having called us away from it, will he show himself the faithful Guardian of our souls.[62]

Here we find the reformer's characteristic themes: the fatherhood of God, his choice of these men to witness to the gospel truth, the believer's eternal safety, and so on. Calvin seeks to confirm the prisoners' divine calling and their sense of worth within God's purposes. Even their deaths, should that be God's demand, are 'an oblation well pleasing in his sight'. Though the unimaginable situation must have challenged the faith of these men to the extreme, they are to cling tenaciously to the grace of God, 'the faithful Guardian' of their souls. Calvin's final exhortation, then, is this: 'Since God has brought you so far, it is too late to think of shrinking back. Cast all your cares on the providence of God.'[63]

---

60 Calvin, *Letters*, 3.221.

61 Calvin, *Letters*, 3.221.

62 Calvin, *Letters*, 3.222.

63 Calvin, *Letters*, 3.222. The prisoners had apparently written a petition against their imprisonment, which, except for a few minor things, had gained Calvin's approval. He graciously acknowledges that it had been God who had put this into their minds. 'If the world approve not so a just and holy protestation, at least it will be approved of by God and his angels, by his prophets, apostles, and the whole church. Nay, every true believer, on seeing it, will have cause to glorify him for having dictated it to you by his Holy Spirit'—again, reference to that broad community who support the prisoners in their time of difficulty; a community expanded to include the whole company of heaven, itself (see, perhaps, Heb. 12.22-24)—Calvin, *Letters*, 3.222.

Calvin's last comment, as always, concerns his prayer for them. It is noticeable that though the reformer is open about the very real possibility of their deaths, he prays that they may experience satisfaction in God during this terrible ordeal.

> I will pray our heavenly Father to have you in his holy keeping, direct you by his Spirit, arm you with courage and constancy, so to do battle that he may triumph in you either by your life or death, and that he would make you feel what it is to have our whole satisfaction in him alone.[64]

Reflections

John Calvin often comments on the difficulties that pastors face as they adhere to what he would term the truth of Reformed teaching. In his reply to Sadoleto, for instance, he speaks, not only of the work that pastors do inside the Church to edify believers, but, also, of their readiness to work *against* those who would destroy that Church: '[T]hey are also armed,' he says, 'to repel the machinations of those who strive to impede the work of God.'[65] But, one might argue that that is specifically an integral part of the pastor's calling, *as pastor*. Calvin thinks otherwise. He claims in *Concerning Scandals*, for example, that it is part of *every* Christian's calling, as *believers* in Christ.

> But the fact is that the heart of a Christian ought to be so fortified that no matter what scandals burst on the scene he never yields ground or turns aside a hair's breadth from Christ. The man who is not equipped for perseverance like this, so as to overcome all scandals victoriously, does not yet understand the power of Christianity.[66]

This appears a somewhat dogmatic stance, lacking both nuance and, perhaps, concrete reality and sensitivity. However, our examination of Calvin's letters has demonstrated that in the acute pastoral context, involving those who presently face execution for their faith, the reformer is quite different.[67]

Calvin, the pastor, is extremely aware of the situation which these prisoners encounter. He is open about the difficulties they endure, about the anxiety that

---

64 Calvin, *Letters*, 3.223.

65 Calvin's reply to Sadoleto—John C. Olin (ed.), *A Reformation Debate. Sadoleto's Letter to the Genevans and Calvin's Reply* (New York: Fordham University Press, 2000), 47. See, also, 86.

66 See *Concerning Scandals* (1550) (translated by John W. Fraser; Edinburgh: Saint Andrew Press, 1978), 10; OS 2.167.

67 W. Robert Godfrey, 'The Counsellor to the Afflicted' in Burk Parsons (ed.), *John Calvin. A Heart for Devotion, Doctrine and Doxology* (Lake Mary: Reformation Trust, 2008), 83-93, says, '[Calvin's] counsel had both a tough realism and a sensitive compassion to it. He faced the miseries and struggles of life straightforwardly, and he pointed Christians to God's fatherly care both in this life and in the life to come' (92).

this must cause them, about their weakness and frailty in the face of a painful, horrifying death. He is also open about his own feelings of anxiety for them, and tells them so. He sometimes hints at his longing for a hopeful outcome, but more often admits that this is unlikely. In this, he shows himself to be human and sympathetic, a pastor who feels their anguish. He clearly rests on the providence of God, but, importantly, not as a doctrine to be intellectually comprehended, certainly not understood as determinism, but as a truth to be taken in faith and prayerful trust.

We have seen that Calvin has several themes in his letters, themes by which he seeks to encourage the prisoners in these dreadful situations: the centrality of God in the situation, the importance of community and the prisoners' role as witnesses of God's truth.

The centrality of God in the situation

First, Calvin stresses the part God plays—he is central to the situation. For Calvin, God is absolutely pivotal to the circumstance, however difficult that is to grasp.[68] He emphasises divine involvement, stressing that God's engagement is seen both in the present and in the future. At this moment, they see his presence by the way the prisoners themselves remain constant in the faith, persevering in their trial—this is the current work of the Holy Spirit upon them. They are held closely by the Spirit and established in Christ. The Father has given them promises and protects and strengthens them, even now. We noted the Trinitarian nature of Calvin's words. And, though there is not so much comment on personal eschatology as in Luther's letters to prisoners in similar circumstances, Calvin, also, says that in the future God will call them away from this perishable life towards eternal life, to a heavenly crown and to victory in Christ.

A notable feature of this theme is the way in which Calvin stresses experience to those who are presently suffering a terrible experience in the gruelling ordeal they face. When speaking about the promises of God to those in Lyons, for instance, the reformer underlines that *from experience* they know that God never fails them. Further, he prays that they may be made to *feel* the divine protection; and, again, he prays that 'in everything and through everything' that God would 'make [them] taste *by experience* how kind a Father he is'.[69] For the prisoners in Chambery he prays that they may experience full satisfaction in God alone. This stress is entirely understandable, of course. Given that in their situation the experience through which they go is likely to press in upon them and overshadow all else, Calvin tries to direct their attention to the reality of spiritual experience that might get crowded out. The reformer attempts to cause

[68] However, see the critical comments, Matthew Myer Boulton, *Life in God. John Calvin, Practical Formation, and the Future of Protestant Theology* (Grand Rapids: Eerdmans, 2011), 193-99.

[69] Calvin, *Letters*, 2.393, emphasis added.

them to see by faith, not by sight; to realise the spiritual reality of a paternal God who cares for them, even though circumstances might persuade otherwise.

The importance of Christian community

Second, Calvin stresses the importance of Christian community. Into a context which evokes isolation and despair Calvin wishes to instil a sense of communal empathy, support and prayer. He does this in several ways. He assures the prisoners that the Church has compassion on them and that they show this concretely by praying for them and supporting them, for example, in the way that John Liner has been doing. Calvin is careful to suggest that the relationship is two-way. The prisoners, in their stand for the truth, bless the Church: they edify the community of faith. This emphasis on the community to which the prisoners belong identifies them with something outside of their narrow and frightening situation as well as encouraging them to see that they are actually standing for something much bigger than their own faith—that is, the faith of the Reformed community. This gives them a sense of purpose and of their own worth.

Witnesses of God's truth

Third, Calvin underlines the prisoners' role as witnesses of God's truth and stresses that they are to view themselves as martyrs and their situation as martyrdom. By doing this Calvin establishes an even greater sense of value to their present situation. They are martyrs, Calvin says, those who maintain God's quarrel, divinely chosen and called, employed by God, agents or witnesses 'whom he appoints for the defence of his Gospel'[70] and, further, those who are identified with Jesus Christ in his suffering and the victory of his resurrection. These powerful images connect the troubled prisoners with the Church's esteemed martyrs of the past but, more importantly, with Jesus, himself, in his sacrifice for others in the mission of God. Their humble status allows them to re-evaluate their situation against the backdrop of eternal truth and their relationship with God.

In the *Institutes* (1559), Calvin speaks of martyrs in the context of our acceptance of the credibility Scripture. It is worth quoting fully here:

> Now with what assurance ought we to enlist under that doctrine which we see confirmed and attested by the blood of so many holy men! They, having once received it, did not hesitate, courageously and intrepidly, and even with great eagerness, to suffer death for it. Should we not accept with sure and unshaken conviction what has been handed on to us with such a pledge? It is no moderate approbation of Scripture that it has been sealed by the blood of so many witnesses, especially when we reflect that they died to render testimony to the faith; not with fa-

[70] Calvin, *Letters*, 2.359.

> natic excess (as erring spirits are sometimes accustomed to do), but with a firm and constant, yet sober, zeal toward God.[71]

Martyrs confirm and attest scriptural doctrine to be true, according to Calvin. They died, he says, 'with a firm and constant, yet sober, zeal toward God'. The reformer's reassurance to these contemporary martyrs, through letters, is to encourage them to live and to die 'with a firm and constant . . . zeal toward God'. We have seen that Calvin does not enlist them as martyrs to glorify them in any way; nor to make them fanatical for Reformed doctrine, but, rather, to suggest to *them* (not to others) that they stand for truth, divine truth, and for the good and edification of the Church. They endure suffering and hardship, not for their own sakes, but for the sake of the gospel and the Church. They confirm the certainty of what that Church believes, and they encourage believers to fight for the Gospel of Christ and the cause of God. Notice how Calvin puts it in what follows,

> 'Was it unprofitable for them to glorify God through their death? to attest his truth by their blood? to bear witness by their contempt of the present life that they are seeking a better life? by their constancy, to strengthen the faith of the church but to break the stubbornness of its enemies? . . . But the church in general receives benefit great enough, when by their triumphs it is kindled with a zeal to fight.[72]

Through their suffering, martyrs, showing patience, fortitude, dignity, and, above all, faith, manifest the victory that is in Jesus Christ. They suffer as Christ's witnesses on account of righteousness.[73] They demonstrate the eschatological nature of the kingdom—in weakness is strength, in apparent defeat is triumph. Calvin, the pastor, assures them, ultimately, of the fatherly love of God. This, he knew, was the paramount encouragement for those facing death for Christ's sake, as it is today.

---

[71] *Inst.* 1.8.13; OS 3.81. This comes in a section in which Calvin lists reasons why 'the dignity and majesty of Scripture' are 'affirmed in godly hearts,' in which he seeks to establish the credibility of Scripture (see *Inst.* 1.8.1-13; OS 3.72-81). However, and importantly, Calvin concludes that 'Scripture will ultimately suffice for a saving knowledge of God only when its certainty is founded upon the inward persuasion of the Holy Spirit' (*Inst.* 1.8.13; OS 3.81).

[72] *Inst.* 3.5.3; OS 4.135-36.

[73] See Calvin, *Sermons on the Beatitudes* (translated by Robert White; Edinburgh: Banner of Truth, 2006), 61.

CHAPTER 10

Calvin's preaching and homiletic: nine engagements[1]

Peter Adam

We often think of John Calvin as a theologian, but the centre of his life was his ministry to the people of Geneva and especially his preaching.[2] Calvin wrote theology, but he also wrote commentaries, letters of pastoral encouragement, a catechism for children and church ordinances and instructions for the supervision of country churches. Calvin was also a teacher and preacher, and this was his daily task in Geneva, as he preached on average five sermons a week, and lectured three or four times. He also reordered the life of the church, worked to reform the society, provided pastoral care for individuals, taught in the Academy, took part in the ministry of the gospel in Geneva with its three parishes and large ministry team, trained and nurtured others in ministry in Geneva and beyond, engaged in theological debate and discussion with his fellow reformers, and with the Roman Catholic Church, and worked for the growth of Reformed Christianity in Europe, especially in his beloved homeland, France. Calvin was a man active in gospel ministry, and his preaching was a key ingredient in that ministry. We cannot understand Calvin without his preaching. 'Through the task of regularly preaching the Lord brought him at last into the heart of the Reformation movement in its battle for the soul of Europe, for it was more through his preaching than through any other aspect of his work that he exercised the extraordinary influence everyone has acknowledged him to have had.'[3]

---

1 This chapter was first published as 'Calvin's Preaching and Homiletic: Nine Engagements, Part 1,' *Churchman* 124.3 (2010), 201-16; 'Part 2', *Churchman* 124.4 (2010), 331-42 and is used with permission.

2 This is based on '"Preaching of a lively kind"—Calvin's engaged expository preaching' in Mark. D. Thompson (ed.), *Engaging Calvin* (Nottingham: Apollos, 2009). This present essay was given in an earlier form at a meeting of the Australasian Academy of Homiletics, Sydney (April, 2009).

3 Ronald S. Wallace, *Calvin, Geneva, and the Reformation* (Edinburgh: Scottish Academic, 1988), 17.

Calvin helped to create a powerful pattern of vernacular expository preaching, with a new homiletic, a new rhetoric, a new 'art of preaching'. He influenced preaching in Europe by the people he trained in Geneva, especially those training for France, and by ministers who found refuge in Geneva and then returned home. Knowledge of his preaching spread through his published sermons, especially in French and English.[4]

The homiletic styles available to Calvin

Here are the three main models of preaching available to Calvin.

(1) The formal medieval Latin sermon. Its outline is as follows.

Theme.	The text from the Bible, including three significant words.
Ante-theme.	Introduction and prayer for the sermon.
Introduction.	A way into the theme, using Scripture, a theologian, a pagan writer, a proverb, or an illustration.
Division.	This was always in three parts, each of which had to have rhyming endings, such as, in English, crea*tion*, participa*tion* and satisfac*tion*.
Declaration.	Justification of the three-fold division of the theme.
Confirmation.	Demonstration that the three-fold division was scriptural.
Development.	The theme was supported by appeals to theologians, reasonable arguments, stories and illustrations, then the people urged to respond.[5]

Smyth comments, 'The text from Scripture is supposed to be the preacher's theme: it is in fact merely the peg on which he hangs an academic exercise.'[6] Calvin would have been familiar with this style of preaching. However, it was too artificial, too clever and too distracting for ordinary people. No wonder that he did not use it in preaching in Geneva.

(2) The popular style of vernacular preaching.
Popular vernacular preaching was developed by the Preaching Orders. It was not always based on Scripture. It was typically the preaching used by mendicant preachers when preaching in the countryside, at Preaching Crosses. It was plain, easy to understand, it used simple vivid language, humour, satire, moral tales and illustrations, and it was moralistic rather than biblical or theological. There are many references to biblical words and expressions, but the Bible is assumed, not taught. Calvin did attempt popular vernacular preaching, but transformed this style to teach people the content and meaning of the Bible.

---

4 T.H.L. Parker, *Calvin's Preaching* (Edinburgh: T. & T. Clark, 1992), 72, 108-27, 188-94.

5 See Charles Smyth, *The Art of Preaching: 1747-1939* (London: SPCK, 1940), 19-35.

6 Smyth, *Art of Preaching*, 53.

(3) Expository preaching.

Calvin found examples of expository preaching in Augustine and John Chrysostom.[7] He prepared a preface for an edition of Chrysostom's sermons[8] to provide biblical teaching for lay people, and show expository preaching in the Early Church.[9] Such expository preaching in the Early Church died out for four reasons: the demands of theological controversy, the presence of many ignorant people required simpler sermons, more complex services meant that sermons had to be shorter, and low standards of clergy-training meant that many were unable to preach biblical sermons.[10] Expository preaching was also found in monasteries in medieval times. *Homilia* was used for this verse-by-verse exposition of Scripture and *Sermo* for more popular, non-exegetical preaching.[11]

There were vernacular Bible translations and sermons before the Reformation.[12] The Franciscans and Dominicans used some biblical exposition in vernacular preaching.[13] Wycliffe had used vernacular expository preaching.[14] Early humanists and reformers Wimpfeling, Geiler and Surgant were pioneers of an expository style that became common in Zurich, Strasburg and Geneva.[15] Another source could have been the late medieval innovation of teaching books of the Bible in universities.[16] Luther lectured for ten years at Wittenberg on Genesis and Thomas Cranmer and other reformers studied the Bible this way.

---

7 Parker, *Calvin's Preaching*, 79-80.

8 Randall C. Zachman, *John Calvin as Teacher, Pastor, and Theologian* (Grand Rapids: Baker Academic, 2006), 59.

9 There are also examples of expository preaching from Bernard, Anselm, Bonaventura and Aquinas. See Parker, *Calvin's Preaching*, 80.

10 Thomas K. Carroll, *Preaching the Word: The Message of the Fathers of the Church* (Wilmington: Michael Glazier, 1984), 63, 197, 206, 220.

11 A.G.P. van der Walt, 'Calvin on Preaching' in B.J. van der Walt (ed.), *John Calvin's Institutes: His Magnum Opus* (Potchefstroom: Potchefstroom University for Christian Higher Education, 1986), 328.

12 G.W.H. Lampe (ed.), *The Cambridge History of the Bible* (Cambridge: CUP, 1969), 2.338-491; A.G.P. van der Walt, 'John Calvin and the Reformation of Preaching' in B.J. van der Walt (ed.), *Our Reformational Tradition: a rich heritage and lasting vocation* (Potchefstroom: Potchefstroom University for Christian Higher Education, 1984), 199.

13 Hughes Oliphant Old, *The Reading and Preaching of the Scriptures in the Worship of the Christian Church* (Grand Rapids: Eerdmans, 1999), 3.185-292, 341-440. Wycliffe and Bishop Grosseteste of Lincoln used vernacular preaching—see G.W.H. Parker, *The Morning Star: Wycliffe and the Dawn of the Reformation* (Grand Rapids: Eerdmans, 1965), 43-51, Smyth, *Art of Preaching*, 54, respectively.

14 See Parker, *Wycliffe*, 43-51.

15 John H. Leith, 'Calvin's Doctrine of the Proclamation of the Word and its Significance Today' in Timothy George (ed.), *John Calvin and the Church: A Prism of Reform* (Louisville: Westminster John Knox, 1990), 209.

16 David Steinmetz, 'John Calvin as an Interpreter of the Bible' in Donald McKim (ed.), *Calvin and the Bible* (Cambridge: CUP, 2006), 289.

Among Calvin's contemporaries, Zwingli was the first to preach through books of the Bible, and began his sermons on Matthew in Zürich in 1519.[17]

What had been done in Latin in monasteries and universities was now being done in churches. Calvin used vernacular expository preaching as the almost universal diet for the ordinary people of the church.

Nine demanding engagements

Calvin's preaching was marked by nine engagements. Any one of them is demanding; it was the genius, strength and vitality of Calvin's preaching that he attempted all of them. Calvin helped his hearers engage with God, with the Bible and with theology. He engaged his own humanity in his preaching. Calvin engaged with his congregation in his preaching. Calvin engaged in training the congregation and, also, future preachers. In these engagements he challenges our preaching today. We recover Calvin's homiletic not in order to reproduce it in our different contexts, but so that we can be stimulated by his engagements, understand his methodology in its historical and theological context and benefit from his example.

Engage with God who is present and powerful

The preacher and the congregation must engage with God, because God is present and active in his majestic splendor and saving power and compassion in the Scriptures, in the congregation, in the preacher and in the sermon. Calvin does not preach as if God is absent. He preaches because God is present. '[God] has ordained his Word as instrument by which Jesus Christ, with all his benefits, is dispensed to us.'[18] For 'the preaching of the Gospel . . . is the spiritual sceptre of Christ, by which he displays his power'.[19]

The present secret work of the Spirit is to change us, not to make the Scriptures powerful. By the Spirit's power inherent in God's words and by the same Spirit's secret internal work within us, God affects hearing, faith, obedience and transformation: 'God works by his words that are preached to us. It is not a bare voice that sounds in the air and disappears. For God puts into his words the power of his Holy Spirit.'[20]

In the Scriptures the living words of God are heard,[21] and because the Scriptures have flowed to us from the very mouth of God,[22] preaching which ex-

---

[17] T.H.L. Parker. *The Oracles of God: an Introduction to the Preaching of John Calvin* (London: Lutterworth, 1947), 18.

[18] John Calvin, *Theological Treatises* (translated by J.K.S. Reid; London: SCM, 1954), 143.

[19] *Comm. Isaiah* 54.14.

[20] *Serm. 2 Tim.* 1.1-2 (665). With regard to Calvin's sermons, all references have been modernized; brackets after the biblical text indicate page numbers—see bibliography.

[21] *Inst.* 1.7.1.

[22] *Inst.* 1.7.5.

pounds and applies the Scripture means that God's voice sounds in his Church: 'God would even have his living voice to resound in his church . . . [so] preaching is inseparably united with Scripture.'[23] It, therefore, follows that 'as often as the Word of God is set before us . . . God is present and calling us'.[24] So, Calvin taught the congregation to hear God's voice through the preacher.

> Therefore if a person claims to be a believer and a member of God's flock, and comes to hear a sermon either in a house or from a pulpit, should think like this: 'Our Lord wants me to hear this man as my father, and receive doctrine and counsel and warning at his hands.'[25]

God is present and his words are an effective means of grace.

> God calls out that morning and evening his arms are stretched out to receive us and call us from afar. He wants nothing more than to have us under his wings, and peaceably to enjoy us. So, for our part, we must take pains to run to him to hear him, and cut off all hindrances that would hinder us from hearing the preacher.[26]

He set aside time during the sermon to encourage people to feel the presence of God.

> It is certain that if we come to church we shall not only hear a mortal man speaking, but we shall feel [even by his secret power] that God is speaking to our souls, that he is the teacher. He so touches us that the human voice enters into us and so profits us that we are refreshed and nourished by it.[27]

He helped them expect to meet with God. 'Where there is preaching, there God's voice rings in our ears.'[28] 'When we speak, behold God, who wishes to be heard in our persons.'[29] Preachers are responsible: 'Then let them work hard to ensure that their hearers feel the power that is in God's word. That it may be received as it should and everyone may submit to it, so that God may be worshipped by all.'[30]

What a contrast to the view that a sermon is merely a study of the Bible, that our focus is only on the Bible and that the church is the people of God gathered around the word of God, and that our task is merely to teach the Bible. The Bible and preaching are means to an end: our purpose is that people meet God in Christ.

---

23 *Comm. Lev.* 10.9
24 *Comm. Acts*, 10.33.
25 *Serm. 1 Tim.* 3.3-5 (284).
26 *Serm. 2 Tim.* 4.2-5 (959).
27 *Serm. 2 Tim.* 1.1-2 (665).
28 *Serm. Deut.* 33.9-11 (1206).
29 *Serm. Job* 32.1-7 (575).
30 *Serm. Deut.* 1.42-46 (56).

Engage with the sixty-six texts of Scripture

It is possible to help the congregation to engage with God and yet to fail to engage in any significant way with Scripture. Calvin worked hard to help his congregation to engage with Scripture. He wanted the congregation to learn to understand the Bible, to meditate on the Bible, to receive God's words in the Bible, to be moved and transformed by the Bible, to learn to interpret the Bible, to remember the Bible and to be able to explain and teach the Bible to others. This involved a commitment to the 'texts' of the Bible. He wanted to avoid 'taking a text,' in the sense of taking one or two verses of Scripture out of context, paying scant attention to their original purpose. In his letter to Seigneur of Peidemont, he warned of the emptiness of those preachers who have only 'snatched in a passing way a few words of Holy Scripture'.[31] A text (that is, one or two verses) without a context is a pretext. It is, of course, a very idiosyncratic understanding of the word 'text' to describe one or two verses of the Bible.

Calvin wrote of the commentator on Bible texts: 'It is almost his only task to unfold the mind of the writer with whom he has undertaken to expound, he misses the mark, or at least strays outside his limits, by the extent to which he leads his readers away from the original meaning of his author.'[32] We have 66 'texts' in our Bible and we should treat each text with respect and integrity. Expository preaching attempts to do this.

During his ministry in Geneva from 1549-1564 he preached Sunday series on Hebrews, Acts, Psalms, Thessalonians, 1 and 2 Timothy, Titus, Corinthians, Galatians, Ephesians and the Gospels. On weekdays he preached from Jeremiah, Lamentations, Micah, Zephaniah, Hosea, Joel, Amos, Obadiah, Ezekiel, Job, Deuteronomy, Isaiah, Genesis, Judges and Samuel. This model of preaching was particularly helpful for people who did not know their Bibles, as it is the natural way to read and understand a text or book.

Calvin wanted to convey God's words as clearly as he could, by preaching them in the shape in which they were found in the Bible. He explained when he began his sermons on Psalm 119:

> For my own part, because I will frame myself to that manner and order which the Holy Ghost has here set down, I shall enforce myself to follow as briefly as I can the plain and true meaning of the text . . . for performance thereof I determine by the grace of God to finish eight verses apart in every sermon, and to hold myself within such compass, so that the most ignorant shall easily acknowledge and confess that I mean nothing else but to make open and plain the simple and pure substance of the text.[33]

---

31 Wallace, *Calvin, Geneva*, 171.

32 John Calvin, *The Epistles of Paul to the Romans and Thessalonians* (translated by R. Mackenzie; CNTC volume 8; Grand Rapids: Eerdmans, 1973), 1.

33 *Serm. Ps.* 119.5, cited in Lester De Koster, *Light for the City: Calvin's Preaching, Source of Life and Liberty* (Grand Rapids: Eerdmans, 2004), 81.

In basing his sermons on the *lectio continua* of the Bible, 'Calvin's purpose in preaching was to render transparent the text of Scripture itself.'[34]

The Reformation had to undo the untold damage caused by the decision made by leaders of the Roman Catholic Church that the Bible was too difficult for ordinary people, and was reserved for scholars; and that instead of the Bible, the ordinary people would have statues and paintings, 'the bibles of the uneducated'.[35] This policy produced generations of people who knew Bible images, but had no idea what they meant. Calvin and his colleagues ministered amidst biblical illiteracy. Expository preaching was one of their remedies.[36]

Susan Schreiner claims that his 159 sermons on the book of Job are an excellent example of expository preaching.[37] She comments that in his preaching of the whole book, 'Calvin had to respect the integrity of the complete text.'[38] Calvin's respect for the text reflected his respect for human authors and for God. He recognized the moral duty of the hearer and reader. In Kevin Vanhoozer's words, 'The Golden Rule, for hermeneutics and ethics alike, is to treat others—texts, persons, God—with love and respect.'[39] Dawn DeVries comments on Calvin's preaching: 'He moves constantly from text to meaning, from words to doctrine, and from doctrine to the contemporary problems of being a Christian in a sixteenth century Geneva.'[40]

Engage with theology

Reading biblical texts in context is a theological as well as a literary exercise. This is because the Bible is a book about God and because God's mind lies behind the coherence of the collection of Bible texts. John Leith comments on Calvin's preaching: 'The sermons are powerful precisely because Calvin explicated and applied the Scriptures word by word, verse by verse, within the framework of a vision of the Christian faith as a whole.'[41] Calvin's preaching gains strength from his theological engagement with the texts, his theological thinking more generally, and his theological critique of the Church and world of his generation. His theological engagement of the texts of Scripture not only

---

34 Leith, 'Calvin's Proclamation,' 214.

35 *Inst.* 1.11.5.

36 This was not his only style, as he preached sermons for church festivals, especially Christmas, Passiontide and Easter, and Pentecost, and also special wedding sermons—see Parker, *Calvin's Preaching*, 160-62, 165-68.

37 Susan Schreiner, 'Calvin as an interpreter of Job' in Donald McKim (ed.), *Calvin and the Bible* (Cambridge: CUP, 2006), 57, 59. See, also, Susan Schreiner, 'Through a Mirror Dimly: Calvin's Sermons on Job,' *CTJ* 21 (1986), 175-93.

38 Schreiner, 'Calvin as an interpreter of Job,' 58.

39 Kevin J. Vanhoozer, *Is there a meaning in this text?* (Leicester: Apollos, 1998), 32.

40 Dawn DeVries, *Jesus Christ in the Preaching of Calvin and Schleiermacher* (Louisville: Westminster John Knox, 1996), 41.

41 Leith, 'Calvin's Proclamation,' 224.

helps him avoid a superficial treatment of the texts of Scripture, it also helps him to see the relevance of the texts for the people to whom he preaches.

When we think about his theology, it is worth distinguishing between biblical theology and systematic theology, as both are present and both bring depth to his preaching. Biblical theology is the explanation of the theology which reflects the shape of the gradual unfolding of the biblical revelation throughout Old and New Testaments. It expresses the shape and extent and balance of the Bible, deals with its unity and diversity, and expresses its coherence. It is an account of the verbal revelation that accompanies salvation history: for as salvation history is an account of the saving works of God, biblical theology is an account of the saving words of God. Biblical theology is the study of the God-given interpretation of salvation history that is expressed in the Bible, its developing themes. While it is true that the formal study of biblical theology did not occur until the work of Gabler,[42] it is not possible to expound the Scriptures without some kind of biblical theology, implicit or explicit. Calvin did not write a biblical theology. Instead, he expressed his biblical theology in different ways in the *Institutes*, his commentaries and in his sermons. Calvin developed a strong and comprehensive biblical theology, which not only helped him interpret the Bible, but also helped him to preach and apply it.[43]

Systematic theology is the exposition of the coherence of Christian thought, which expresses and develops biblical thought in topics, and, also, shows the coherent connections between those topics. It brings together what the Bible as a whole teaches on a topic, and shows the balance, shape, coherence and implications of that teaching. It analyses what the Bible teaches and puts that teaching in the light of the intellectual history of the Church and of humanity. Calvin's focus was on knowing God and so, therefore, knowing ourselves. As Parker has pointed out, an aspect of the coherence of all his writing and preaching was that he kept on answering the questions: 'Who is God?' 'What is God like?'[44]He thought and wrote as a theologian. In the words of Steinmetz, 'The *Institutes* uncovered the architectonic structures of the Bible, the underlying plan of the whole, that placed the details in their proper context.'[45]

Calvin does not refer to the *Institutes* in his sermons,[46] yet his work in thinking and writing that is represented in the *Institutes* was fundamental to the power, relevance and application of his preaching of the Bible. For Calvin did not confuse academic presentation with intellectual clarity. He used his academic rigour to help achieve clarity of thought and presentation, but did not believe

---

42 M. Elliott, 'Gabler, Johan Philipp' in Donald K. McKim (ed.), *Dictionary of Major Biblical Interpreters* (Downers Grove: IVP, 2007), 452-57.

43 For a summary of Calvin's biblical theology, see Peter Adam, *Hearing God's Words: Exploring Biblical Spirituality* (Leicester: Apollos, 2004), 119-38.

44 Parker, *Calvin's Preaching*, 95-100.

45 Steinmetz, 'John Calvin,' 291.

46 Zachman, *Calvin as Teacher*, 155.

that intellectual clarity must always appear in academic garb. In fact, he wanted to use clarity of thought for the benefit of common people.

Calvin's engagement with biblical and systematic theology served his preaching well. Calvin's biblical and systematic theology helped to bring a unity of mind to his preaching,[47] and, also, helped him in his application of the Scriptures to his congregation.

Engage his humanity in his preaching

Calvin's commitment to the power and glory of God did not blind him to the fact that God uses human beings in his service and that he uses preachers to teach, edify, form and train his people. There are two reasons why some preachers diminish the humanity of the preacher and of the congregation. They might want to emphasize the presence and power of God: yet Calvin knew that the present and powerful God delighted to use humans in his gospel service. They might want to restrict the effects of sinful humanity: but this is to diminish the power and grace of God, who is able to achieve his gospel purposes through sinful humans and does so for his glory and their blessing. Calvin made neither mistake, because he knew that God's glory was not diminished by using humans and his power not diminished by using sinful humans in his service.

God uses the humanity of each preacher, and that humanity determines in part the style of the preaching. Preachers who are not self-aware will be blind to the ways in which their character and personality and interests may help or hinder their preaching, will be less able to adapt to serve the needs of the congregation, and will be less useful in training other preachers, as they will naturally try to create them in their own image.

If we need to know ourselves,[48] then the self-knowledge and self-awareness of the preacher will help in the effective communication of God's words to the congregation. Here are some examples of Calvin's particular humanity. He writes, 'I am naturally fond of brevity,'[49] and Steinmetz comments, 'Calvin's "lucid brevity" is one of his principal contributions to the intellectual heritage of the Reformation.'[50] His sermons benefit from his brevity, because by speaking briefly on each verse, he did not lose the meaning of the texts by endless ornamentation, distraction or amplification. However, Calvin, also, realized that brevity had its drawbacks, and that when people were hearing texts and ideas for the first time, they needed help to understand and absorb the words of the preacher. So, to complement his brevity, he added repetition, to help his congregation, for in order to serve his people, Calvin was willing to change his

---

[47] John H. Leith, 'Reformed Preaching Today,' *PSB* 10.3 (1989), 230.

[48] *Inst*. 1.1.1.

[49] *Inst*. 3.6.1.

[50] David Steinmetz, 'John Calvin on Isaiah 6. A Problem in the History of Exegesis,' *Int* 36 (1982), 158. See, also, R. Gamble, '*Brevitas* and *facilitas*: towards an Understanding of Calvin's Hermeneutics,' *WJT* 47 (1985), 1-17.

natural style.[51] As he wrote in his introduction to his commentary on Romans, 'I have tried to modify my style.'[52] So, in his preaching, brevity is complimented by explanation, exhortation and time to help the congregation to feel the significance of God's words in Scripture.[53]

Many of Calvin's skills in dealing with texts and words were honed in his humanist training. So Battles and Hugo note the following features of Calvin's expository style, even when used in his younger years to expound a pagan author. Calvin's 'aim is quite simple, to ensure that the reader will understand what Seneca is saying'.[54] This intention and ability requires the moral willingness to set aside one's own ideas to focus on the ideas of another, imaginative sympathy in understanding the text written by another person in a different historical context, and the ability to communicate to contemporary readers the ideas and significance of the original author. Finally, they observe Calvin's ability to paraphrase, to 'compress matter without loss of meaning,' and they comment on the fact that in paraphrasing he picks up 'the whole context and underlying spirit of Seneca's words'.[55] Calvin wrote of the value of this kind of training: 'How richly deserving of honour are the liberal sciences, which polish man, so as to give him the dignity of true humanity.'[56]

He was, also, aware of his weakness and sins, which lay deep within him. So, after a dispute, he wrote to Farel, 'There I sinned grievously in not having been able to keep within bounds for so had the bile taken possession of my mind that I poured out bitterness on all sides.'[57] He seems to speak of himself in these words: 'By nature we are too irritable, and Satan pushes us to an inhuman rigor under the pretext to strictness. As a result, wretched men, denied forgiveness, are swallowed up by grief and despair.'[58]

Calvin worried lest his ministry be counterproductive: 'That I am in danger of being unjust to God's mercy by laboring with so much anxiety to assert it, as if it were doubtful or obscure.'[59] No wonder Calvin advised those considering the call to be pastors: 'Let them therefore . . . when they offer themselves to preach the word of God, enter into themselves and seek out the bottom of their thoughts . . . that they seek nothing else but to give themselves to God in such a

---

[51] Parker, *Calvin's Preaching*, 149.

[52] *Comm. Rom.* 1.

[53] See Richard A. Muller, *The Unaccommodated Calvin* (Oxford: OUP, 2000), 143.

[54] Ford Lewis Battle and André Malan Hugo, *Calvin's Commentary on Seneca's* De Clementia, *with introduction, translation and notes* (Leiden: Brill, 1969), 62.

[55] Battles and Hugo, *Calvin's Commentary on Seneca*, 79.

[56] *Comm. 1 Cor.* 1.17, cited in Parker, *Oracles*, 66.

[57] Cited in Wallace, *Calvin, Geneva*, 295.

[58] *Comm. Matt.* 18.21, cited in William J. Bouwsma, *John Calvin. A Sixteenth Century Portrait* (New York: OUP, 1988), 228.

[59] *Comm. Ezek.* 9.3-4, cited in Bouwsma, *John Calvin*, 32.

way that they not be unprofitable, but build up the flock.'[60] And he warns against excessive zeal:

> Whenever, under the pretext of zeal for perfection, we cannot bear any imperfection either in the body or the members of the church, the devil's inflaming us with pride and seducing us through hypocrisy to abandon the flock of Jesus Christ.[61]

Reynolds asserts Calvin's strong emotional engagement with his people: 'Calvin sought to enter into an intimate dialogue with the congregation in order to enhance his emotional effectiveness.'[62] He claims that Calvin over-identifies with God, and with the Old Testament prophets, and uses sermons for his own needs, and reads his emotions into God and into the text.[63] The danger for Calvin was no inhuman remoteness but over-engaged humanity. Yet, as Reynolds comments, '[T]he congregation is kept on the edge of their seats; they are enticed to come back day after day to hear how the story turned out.'[64] It was Calvin the human in the pulpit by God's appointment, and God used his humanity in his preaching.

Engage with the congregation in the sermon

For Calvin, ministry preaching should be contextual, contemporary, engaged with the congregation. Timeless truths, remote Biblicism, disengaged ministry, or unapplied preaching are unsatisfactory.

> Many people would like me to preach with my eyes closed, not considering where I live, or in what locale, or in what time. As if those whose responsibility it is to proclaim God's message did not proceed the way it was done in the time of the apostles—as if the prophets did not apply the law of Moses to their day and time , as if the apostles did not follow the same practice![65]

For Calvin, 'Doctrine without zeal is either a sword in the hand of a lunatic, or lies cold and useless and serves a perverse ostentation.'[66] God accommodates himself to us in Christ, in the Scripture and in providing human preachers and teachers.[67] 'For it would be a cold way of teaching, if teachers do not carefully

---

60 *Serm.1 Tim.* 3.1-4 (240-41).

61 From Calvin, 'Against the Errors of the Anabaptists,' cited in Bouwsma, *John Calvin*, 228.

62 Blair Reynolds, 'Calvin's Exegesis of Jeremiah and Micah: Use or Abuse of Scripture?' (Proceedings Eastern Great Lakes and Midwest Biblical Societies, 11, 1991), 88.

63 Reynolds, 'Calvin's Exegesis,' 85-88.

64 Reynolds, 'Calvin's Exegesis,' 83.

65 *Serm. Acts* 6.1-6 (327).

66 *Comm. Acts* 18.25, cited in Bouwsma, *John Calvin*, 228.

67 Peter Adam, *Speaking God's Words: A Practical Theology of Preaching* (Leicester: IVP, 1996), 137-45; Ford Lewis Battles, 'God was accommodating himself to human capacity,' *Int* 31 (1977), 19-38.

consider the needs of the times and what is appropriate to the people, for in this matter nothing is more unbalanced than absolute balance.'[68]

As van der Walt comments, 'Calvin's style of exegesis as revealed in his sermons is true homiletical exegesis, which means that it is not simply exposition but exposition and application.'[69] Application must be clearly expressed: 'We rightly divide the word of God when we give such lessons as the hearers are able to bear, and each one received a portion that he or she is able to receive. It is like a father feeding his children, when he gives each one the right amount.'[70]

God accommodates to us through preachers, for 'imparting too much would only result in loss'.[71] Yet it is the task of preachers to challenge their hearers, 'it is the duty of a good teacher to be always moving higher, until perfection has been reached'.[72]

Calvin knew that the right use of language was essential:

> And so it came to pass in Papistry . . . that the Holy Scripture became as it were a strange language, which men call Divinity, not as doctrine common to all God's family, but as a craft or science for a few only. For what is true divinity? That which our Lord would have common to all his children both to small and great.[73]

For the Bible was addressed in the most part to the people of God and God expected the ordinary believers in Rome, at Corinth, at Thessalonica and Ephesus to be theologians, able to understand the Scriptures, as he had expected his people in Moab to receive Moses' preaching.[74]

Calvin used familiar and colloquial language. 'We always labour to make the Scriptures familiar, so that we may know that it is God who speaks to us.'[75] Calvin used the persuasive power of the Bible texts, including vivid contrasts, language and imagery.[76] T.F. Torrance commented that Calvin used 'a mode of persuasion which throws the reader back upon the truth itself and its inherent validity'.[77]

---

68 *Comm. Matt.* 3.7, cited in Bouwsma, *John Calvin*, 116.

69 van der Walt, A.G.P., 'John Calvin and the Reformation of Preaching' in *Our Formational tradition: a rich heritage and lasting vocation* (no editor named; Potchefstroom: Potchefstroom University of Christian Higher Education, 1984), 195.

70 *Serm. 2 Tim.* 2.14-15 (805).

71 *Comm. 1 Cor.* 3.1.

72 *Comm. 1 Cor.* 3.1.

73 *Serm. 1 Tim.* 1.3-4 (17).

74 Peter Ward, 'Coming to sermon: the practice of doctrine in the preaching of John Calvin,' *SJT* 58.3 (2005), 328-30.

75 *Serm. 1 Tim.* 1.3-4 (15).

76 See Parker, *Oracles*, 65-80; Parker, *Calvin's Preaching*, 131-49.

77 T.F. Torrance, *The Hermeneutics of John Calvin* (Edinburgh: Scottish Academic, 1988), 148; Leith, 'Calvin's Proclamation,' 221.

His homiletic was a comprehensive appeal to the mind, emotions, memory, will and actions.[78] Blair Reynolds writes,

> Thus, Calvin's goal in preaching is far more than merely expressing the cognitive characteristics of faith in order to ensure doctrinal purity, although he is often interpreted that way. Rather, his is essentially the aesthetic-affective quest to lure the congregation to greater depth and breadth of feeling. Although we are accustomed to defining Calvin as a theologian, this definition is too limiting; he was also a very talented artist and actor.[79]

Brevard Childs describes Calvin's ability to relate the message of the Bible to his own time as 'one of the most impressive aspects of Calvin's interpretation of Scripture'.[80] Calvin had what his publisher, Conrad Badius, described as the gift of prophecy.

> It exists for the purpose of clearly understanding and purely expounding to God's people the holy Scripture according to its *vray et naturel sens* and of understanding how to apply it properly to one's own time and in accordance with those with whom one has to do.[81]

This came out of his daily personal and pastoral engagement with his people. His contemporary, Colladon, described Calvin's life and ministry as follows:

> Calvin for his part did not spare himself at all, working far beyond what his powers and regard for his health could stand. . . . He never failed in visiting the sick, in private warning and counsel, and the rest of his numberless matters arising out of the ordinary exercise of his ministry.[82]

Effective, contextual and transformative preaching only comes about through sustained ministry with people. Skills are no substitute for loving, understanding and insight.

Engage with the congregation as hearers

One of the great traps for conscientious preachers is that they prepare full notes or texts of their sermons, but that these are designed to be read, not heard. They are in essay style, which is designed to be read, and is very difficult to hear read! Spoken language is very different to written language, because reading is very different to hearing.

---

[78] Zachman, *Calvin as Teacher*, 153-72; Michael Parsons, *Calvin's Preaching on the Prophet Micah: The 1550-1551 Sermons in Geneva* (Lewiston: Edwin Mellen, 2006), 7; Leith, 'Calvin's Proclamation,' 221; Ward, 'Coming to sermon,' 322.

[79] Reynolds, 'Calvin's Exegesis,' 82.

[80] Cited in Parsons, *Calvin's Preaching*, 11.

[81] Conrad Badius, cited in Benjamin W. Farley, *John Calvin's Sermons on the Ten Commandments* (Grand Rapids: Baker, 1980), 29.

[82] Cited in Parker, *Calvin's Preaching*, 62-63.

Calvin recognized the need for different styles of verbal communication. He had three styles of published writing, each with its intended purpose, genre and audience. The first was his theological writing, most notably the *Institutes*. Here he addressed the universal Church and responded to its issues. The genre was dense explanation of an outline of theological topics. The second style was exposition of the Bible in his commentaries, which were his lectures to students or ministers in written form. These were also intended for the universal Church. These two were originally in Latin, though Calvin then translated them into French.

The third style was that of his sermons. These were in vernacular French, oral in style, addressed to congregations in Geneva and responded to their issues. The genre was exposition and application of the books of the Bible. They were originally intended to be heard, rather than read, and were addressed to his own congregation. However, from 1549 his sermons were systematically recorded by shorthand and then published. Badius commented that at first '[Calvin] desired that his sermons should not extend further than his pastorate, both because they were preached especially for his sheep, to whose capacity he accommodated himself as best he could.'[83] Later, Calvin agreed to their publication for a wider audience. So sermons designed to be heard by the church at Geneva then became available for the wider people of God. We have much to learn from Calvin the preacher. Calvin had a specific style of communication in his sermons.[84]

He identified with the congregation. One striking feature of his homiletic was that he used 'we' and 'us,' rather than 'I' and 'you'. 'When we come to a sermon, if we do not understand all that is spoken to us, let us wait and, in the meanwhile, honour our God and reverence him in the things that are too high for our understanding to reach to.'[85] This meant that he and the congregation were joint recipients of God's words. This promoted solidarity with the congregation. He did this too when he used corporate monologue, in which he meditated with the congregation on shared experiences and struggles. He also articulated the instinctive responses that he knew people would have to the Scriptures.[86] So when he preached on giving to those in need, he added our common excuses: 'Thus we say, "Oh, I'll do that some other time, for if I give all away today, tomorrow when I am approached, I will have nothing left! It is best if I keep this for myself.'[87] He applies the Bible to the whole congregation, including himself. 'But since he has gathered into his flock, and united us in his

83 Conrad Badius, cited in John Calvin, *Sermons on the Epistle to the Ephesians* (translated by Arthur Golding; revised by Leslie Rawlinson and S.M. Houghton; Edinburgh: Banner of Truth, 1973), x.

84 Muller, *Unaccommodated Calvin*, 140-158.

85 *Serm. Eph*. 3.1-6 (237).

86 Adam, *Speaking*, 150-153.

87 *Serm. Gal*. 6.9-11 (622).

name, and since we call upon him with one voice as our Father, we must show brotherly love to one another.'[88]

Calvin's preaching style was designed to be heard, not read: it was for ears, not eyes. He had a rhetoric that he used for the *Institutes*[89] and a different oral rhetoric for his sermons. He preached to be heard, and usually preached for between 40 and 60 minutes.[90] He opposed grandiloquence that obscured the text, personal 'inspiration' that bypassed it, and misusing the text and so profaning it.[91]

Engage the congregation in training

Calvin preached not only to convert and transform, but also to train the congregation. This aspect of preaching is not always present today and churches suffer as a result.

to receive God's words in sermons

Some of Calvin's congregation were eager to hear his preaching; he still had to win over many to accept his model of ministry, and the Scriptures that he taught. So he had to train the congregation to hear sermons and to honour preachers. The wise believer will welcome the ministry of preachers. To hear the preacher is to hear Christ: '[F]or it is the will of Christ to exercise his ministry as Prophet by the mouths of those whom he ordains to be ministers among the faithful.'[92]

When so much had changed in church buildings, the pulpit remained: 'So the pulpit . . . has prominent place in the church building . . . so that the teaching which comes from the mouth of the preacher may be received with greater reverence, and everyone submit to it.'[93] Calvin wanted to train his people to hear God's words in sermons.

to read the Bible[94]

Calvin's aim was to ensure that lay people read and understood the Bible. 'When, therefore, we see that there are people from all classes making progress in God's school, we acknowledge His truth which promised a pouring out of his spirit on all flesh.'[95] This represented one of the most significant changes achieved by the Reformation, for before that time, as Calvin wrote to Cardinal Sadoleto, 'Among the people themselves, the highest veneration paid to the

88 *Serm. Gal.* 6.9-11 (627).

89 See Serene Jones, *Calvin and the Rhetoric of Piety* (Columbia: Columbia Theological Seminary, 1995).

90 Calvin, *Ephesians*, xv.

91 Marvin Anderson, 'John Calvin, Biblical Preacher,' *SJT* 42.2 (1989), 176-81.

92 *Serm. Deut.* 18.16-20 (674-75).

93 *Serm. 1 Tim.* 3.1-4 (243).

94 For this material I am indebted to Zachman, *Calvin as Teacher*, 55-76.

95 Cited in Zachman, *Calvin as Teacher*, 56-57.

Word was to revere it at a distance, as a thing inaccessible, and abstain from all investigation of it.'[96]

He trained lay people to assess what they heard by the Scriptures for, 'no doctrine is worth believing except as we perceive it to be based in the Scriptures . . . which makes it all the clearer that individuals are called to read the Scriptures.'[97] The need for ordinary believers to know their Bibles is even more evident when we see Calvin's expectations in terms of their ministries of the Word. In his sermons, he trained a ministry team which included all the laity.

to teach and convert others

In his 'Reply to Sadoleto' Calvin wrote, 'It certainly is the part of the Christian man to ascend higher than merely to seek and secure the salvation of his own soul.'[98] So Christians are to serve others, not just in ordinary matters of daily life, but also in sharing words of eternal life.[99]

> Although not all have the office of preaching the word of God, yet a private person who is a member of the church may beget spiritual children to God if he has the occasion and ability to win a poor soul and enlighten him with the faith of the gospel.[100]

He also warned of failing to take those opportunities:

> But when most people see that God provides an opening for them and a way to instruct the uninformed, they will remain silent, keep their mouths shut, and not say a word. . . . He will be guilty of other people's sin because he had the means to admonish them and did not.[101]

So Christians are to know their Bibles and be trained and active in teaching and exhorting others.

to serve God in the world

The congregation must learn to serve God in the world, by doing good works of daily work and voluntary service. 'So therefore it becomes every man to apply his vocation in such a way that he may do all he can for his neighbours. . . . [W]e must be ready to do all good works.'[102] To care for others is to express true and godly humanity.

> Since [God] has stamped his image upon us, and since we share a common nature, this ought to inspire us to provide for one another. The one who seeks to be ex-

---

[96] Cited in Zachman, *Calvin as Teacher*, 70.

[97] *Comm. Acts* 17.11, cited in Zachman, *Calvin as Teacher*, 70.

[98] Calvin, *Treatises*, 228.

[99] For a useful discussion of Calvin's missiology, see Parsons, *Calvin's Preaching*, 181-225.

[100] *Serm. Deut.* 25.5-12 (883).

[101] *Serm. Acts* 6.7-9 (337).

[102] *Serm. Titus* 3.1-2 (1208-1209).

> empt from the care of his neighbor is disfiguring himself and declaring that he no longer wishes to be a man. For whilst we are human beings, we must see our own faces reflected, as in a mirror, in the faces of the poor and despised . . . even if they are people who are most alien to us.[103]

The best good works include our daily tasks of 'digging earth . . . sewing and tailoring,'[104] for by these we honour God and benefit our neighbours.

Engage the congregation in taking part in God's global gospel plan

Calvin wanted the church in Geneva to have a global gospel vision, to take part in a strategy to convert the world to Christ in their own day, and also to make provision for gospel ministry in the future. For, 'God places no higher value on anything than the preaching of the gospel for he wants his kingdom to be dominant in the world, and preaching is the way to lead men to salvation.'[105] And the church in Geneva should work with God, 'To draw the world to God and to build up the Kingdom of our Lord Jesus Christ that he may rule among us.'[106] And all believers have this responsibility.

> For the knowledge of God must be known through the whole world, and every one must share in it, and we must take pains to bring all that wander. And we must think not only of our own time, but also of the time after our death. . . . [W]e must labour to make God known throughout the whole world.[107]

The gospel will go to the world as churches are planted and godly ministers are provided.

> The gospel cannot be maintained without the means of which Paul speaks, that there be ministers appointed in every town, for the means to maintain the church is by preaching . . . which is the incorruptible seed by which we are born of God, it is the milk of little children, and food of the great ones. So the Church cannot but decay and perish unless it be maintained by the preaching of the word of God.[108]

What are the implications of this? First, that civil and church leaders should take great care in the selection and appointment of ministers.[109] Second, that people should think strategically and sacrificially of the need for good ministers: 'But men have so little care to serve God and his Church that no man would have his son to be a preacher.'[110]

---

103 *Serm. Gal.* 6.9-11 (624).
104 *Serm. Gal.* 5.19-23 (550).
105 *Serm. Acts* 6.1-6 (325).
106 *Serm. 2 Tim.* 2.16-18 (808).
107 *Serm. 2 Tim.* 2.1-3 (747, 749).
108 *Serm. Titus* 1.5-6 (1064).
109 *Serm. 1 Tim.* 2.12-14 (244).
110 *Serm. 1 Tim.* 3.1-4 (240).

The congregation also needed to be conscious of the need to train preachers and what kind of preparation was appropriate. This was important for their support of their preachers and for those who were thinking of becoming teachers or pastors.

Engage in training up future preachers

Calvin wanted to train people to recognize the significance of the ministry of preaching, and he also wanted to train up future preachers. This process began in the Church and was completed in the Academy. Future preachers were formed by present sermons.

All this sets high standards for preachers who need to engage with the texts of Scripture, know how to help their congregations engage with God, how to think theology, and how to love and serve people. Here are some of the requirements God places on preachers.[111]

> Choose out the ablest in the world, yet they must acknowledge that they cannot speak of God with such majesty and reverence, unless God govern them and give them new speech, altering and reforming their tongues so that they may not speak after the manner of men but may show that it is the Holy Spirit who rules them.[112]

Preachers must be rigorous in orthodoxy, zealous in ministry, with a desire to honour God and to be an example to their people.

> The first thing that is required of those whom God send to preach his word is that they continue in pure doctrine, not ending in falsehoods or going astray from true religion, but maintaining true uprightness. It is not enough for us to teach people faithfully, unless we have a zeal to edify and care for the salvation of all, and do this with a desire to honour God and show the way, and be an example to those we lead.[113]

They must be able to do public and private ministry of the Word: 'And then, when a man will be a preacher, it is not just a question of making a sermon, to know that it is necessary to proclaim the Word of God both publicly and privately in order to edify, so that the word may be profitable.'[114]

Preachers must be students of God's Word: 'No man shall ever be a good minister of God's word unless he first be a student of it.'[115] They must be able to teach and preach: 'For though a man walk uprightly and have great and excellent virtues, yet if he does not teach, he may be a good Christian, but he is no

---

[111] For an excellent study of notions of preaching in Calvin's sermons on Micah, see Parsons, *Calvin's Preaching*, 147-80.

[112] *Serm. Deut*. 32.1-4 (1105).

[113] *Serm, 1 Tim*. 1.18-19 (239).

[114] *Serm. 1 Tim*. 3.1-4 (239).

[115] *Serm. Deut*. 5.23-27 (258).

minister.'[116] They must be willing to face hardship and suffering: 'not only diligent and indefatigable in pursuing the task of teaching, but . . . ready to undergo the danger of death for the defence of the doctrine'.[117] They must be able to rebuke sin: 'When the word of God is rightly applied, then there must be conflict and war against all vices. . . . So our Lord will have his word rightly applied.'[118] They must know how to serve people: 'We cannot serve God except by serving his people.'[119] They must avoid arrogance: 'One of the greatest virtues of those who have the charge of governing the Church and preaching the Word of God, is that they guard themselves from being puffed up and having a foolish arrogance which carries them away.'[120] They must be resilient enough to face the opposition of the world and of Satan: 'they cannot preach the word of God, but Satan on the one side will do what he can to hinder them, and the world will be in an uproar'.[121] They must know what condemnation they face if they betray their trust:

> If private people who run riot against God are worthy to be condemned, then [ministers of the gospel] who do this are rightly called devils. Jesus Christ called them so in the person of Judas. So therefore those who are called to so honourable an office should take heed to themselves, because God has chosen them in his service.[122]

Preachers must use their gifts to serve others, not themselves: 'Let them not seek to be esteemed for their brave babbling and lofty speech, for their subtleties, for the fine and sharp wits, for the passing bravery: all these things must be laid under foot, or else we can never serve God and his Church.'[123] They must realize the privilege and responsibility they carry: 'All they to whom God has appointed to be ministers of his word must realize that as keys of the kingdom are committed to them, so they must keep this treasure so that it does not perish.'[124]

Conclusion

Certainly, Calvin set a high standard for preachers. While one may be gifted in bringing people to meet God, in reading and communicating texts, in thinking theologically, in working with people, and in training, it is rare for any one person to have all these gifts. The lesson is not that sermon preparation is hard

[116] *Serm. 1 Tim.* 4.12-13 (411).
[117] *Comm. Acts* 15.25-26.
[118] *Serm. 1 Tim.* 1.8-11 (59).
[119] *Serm. 1 Tim.* 3.6-7 (293).
[120] *Serm 1 Tim.* 3.6-7 (289).
[121] *Serm. 1 Tim.* 1.18-19 (101).
[122] *Serm. 1 Tim.* 1.12-13 (71).
[123] *Serm. 1 Tim.* 6.20-21 (651).
[124] *Serm 1 Tim.* 6.20-21 (647).

work, though it is, but that preachers need to undergo rigorous and demanding preparation for their ministries, and need to maintain the equivalent standards throughout their ministries.

Calvin did not always meet the high standards that he set for himself.[125] His sermon on 1 Timothy 3.16 loses the shape and content of the text and focuses entirely on the topic of the divinity and humanity of Christ.[126] His usual pattern was to preach from 4-8 verses. This works well in texts that are theologically dense, but in extensive narratives it is less successful, as the momentum of the text is lost because he divides up the units of meaning. In his series on Job he cannot avoid the idea that after all Job must have sinned, and so favours Elihu that he is taken to speak as a Reformed believer.[127] Preaching from a harmony of Matthew, Mark and Luke, as Calvin did for his Sunday sermons from 1559-1564, was not the best way to present those three distinct texts. Sometimes Calvin moved so slowly through the text that its inherent momentum was lost. Yet it seems petty to throw stones, when Calvin preached so faithfully and effectively, and when he helped to set standards by which we might now judge him.

If we want to find a good model of preaching, we will not imitate Calvin's style in the *Institutes*, or in the commentaries, but the style of his sermons. The genius of Calvin's preaching is found in his nine engagements: he engaged with God who was present in preaching; he engaged with the texts of Scripture; he engaged with theology; he engaged his own humanity in his preaching; he engaged with the congregation; he engaged with them as hearers; he engaged in training them; he engaged in recruiting them in God's gospel plan for the world; he engaged in training up future preachers. This fine 'art of preaching' provided a striking model for Calvin's contemporaries, as it does for us today.

The creator and focus of preaching is God; the purpose is the conversion, transformation and training of the congregation, and the two means are the Scriptures and the preacher. May God raise up such able preachers for our Church and our world.

---

125 These comments are taken from my 'Preaching of a lively kind'.

126 *Serm. 1 Tim.* 3.16 (321-33).

127 Derek Thomas, *Calvin's Teaching on Job: Preaching the Incomprehensible God* (Geanies House: Mentor, 2004), 105-10; Schreiner, 'Calvin on Job,' 67-69.

CHAPTER 11

Contributions of the Brethren of the Common Life to the Reformation

Lloyd A. Harsch

The Reformation is one of the defining eras in the life of the church. Such monumental change does not materialize without others laying the groundwork. Several movements emerged in the century preceding the Reformation. Most students of church history are familiar with John Wycliffe's work in England and John Huss' in Bohemia (modern Czech Republic). However, there is another movement which was contemporary with these others that is largely overlooked. It was known as the Brethren of the Common Life.

The fourteenth century was a turbulent time. The Mongolian Golden Horde's waning strength did not prevent raids into Hungary during the first quarter of the century. The Ottoman Empire arose at the dawn of this century and soon moved into Europe. It captured Constantinople in 1453 and controlled much of the Balkans. A rising merchant class formed the Hanseatic League to protect its Baltic and Scandinavian trade routes, paving the way for capitalism to replace feudalism. The papacy moved to Avignon, France, in 1309, not to return to Rome for some 70 years. No sooner had it returned than rival popes were elected. It was during this unsettled time that the Brethren of the Common Life emerged.

The Brethren were a lay-led attempt at reforming the Church. They were not the first group to attempt such a task. Prior to their efforts, the Beguines (female) and the Beghards (male) brought some measure of reform to the church in the eleventh and the thirteenth centuries respectively.[1] In addition, several new monastic orders gained papal recognition in the thirteenth century. These included the Franciscans (1210), Dominicans (1220), Carmelites (1229) and Augustinian Friars (1256). However, the impact of their work faded as their followers lost the zeal of their founders. Other movements, such as the Waldensians and later the Lollards, emerged which were not welcomed by the Church in Rome and remained outside the ecclesiastical fold.

---

1 Samuel Kettlewell, *Thomas à Kempis and the Brothers of Common Life* (New York: G.P. Putnam's Sons, 1882), 1.160.

The Brethren movement was a revival of these earlier attempts at spiritual renewal and reform. While essentially a regional movement centered around Deventer and Zwolle in the Netherlands, Brethren schools and teachers could be found throughout Western Europe. The aim of these practical mystics was the reformation of the Church through the education of the youth and the instruction of the common people in the fundamentals of Christian living.[2]

The Christ-centered teachings and lifestyle of the Brethren greatly impacted the Church and the Reformation. Through their work, they either directly or indirectly influenced every major character on the Reformation stage. This chapter will highlight their contributions to the Reformation in three areas: personal piety, education and monastic renewal.

A movement is born

The acknowledged founder of the movement was Gerhard (Greete) Groote, (1340-1384). He was born into a wealthy family in Deventer. Deventer was the chief town of Overyssel, located in the central part of the Netherlands, and a leading city in the Hanseatic League. It was a center for trade and manufacturing. It was also noted as a place of learning and culture.[3]

Wealth brought Groote the advantage of education. He studied medicine, theology and canon law at the University of Paris, earning a Master of Arts degree in 1358 after three years of study. He continued his education for a brief time at Prague, but soon returned to Paris to study law. Astrology and magic were also interests of his at that time.[4]

The following years could be described as those of a wandering student/playboy, for Groote's parents had left him quite a fortune upon which to live.[5] So notorious was his conduct that a local priest refused to give him communion.[6] In spite of this, his political connection to the Church resulted in prebends in Utrecht and Aix.[7] When an illness put Groote on what he thought was his deathbed, he ordered his magic books burned and promised God a renewed life.[8] This new life lasted as long as the illness.

It was not until 1374, after several conversations with an old friend, Henry of Calcar, that Groote forsook the wanton lifestyle of his youth. He immediate-

---

2 Albert Hyma, *The Brethren of the Common Life* (Grand Rapids: Eerdmans, 1950), 113-14.

3 E.F. Jacob, 'Gerhard Groote and the Beginnings of the "New Devotion" in the Low Countries,' *JEH* 3 (1952), 45.

4 Hyma, *Brethren*, 16.

5 Hyma, *Brethren*, 18.

6 William R. Estep, *Renaissance and Reformation* (Grand Rapids: Eerdmans, 1986), 46.

7 J.M. Neale, *A History of the So-Called Jansenist Church of Holland; with a Sketch of Its Earlier Annals, and Some Account of the Brothers of the Common Life* (New York: AMS, 1970), 76.

8 Hymna, *Brethren*, 18.

ly surrendered his prebends and began allowing righteous women who were not under orders to live in his family's house. Groote kept but two rooms for himself.[9] The women began to share responsibilities and expenses, living as they thought the primitive Church of the New Testament had.

Groote spent five years struggling to overcome and atone for his previous way of life. The latter portion of this time he spent in the Carthusian monastery where Henry was prior. Here he adopted an ascetic lifestyle.[10] In December, 1379, Florentius van Wevelinckoven, the Bishop of Utrecht, ordained Groote as a deacon and allowed him to preach.[11] Groote embarked upon a preaching tour throughout the Netherlands. As he traveled, he was greatly disturbed by the lifestyles of the priests and monks. Their debauchery, reminiscent of his earlier years, became the focus of his preaching. Groote would address the priests in Latin and the common people in the vernacular because he believed that both the clergy and the laity needed deeper religious fervor.[12]

When he returned to Deventer, Groote gathered twelve disciples around himself and they met in the vicarage of the local priest, Florentius Radewijns (Floris Fadewijnzoon).[13] This was the beginning of the *devotio moderna*, or new devotion. In addition to their study sessions, the Brethren boarded young school boys.

Groote's preaching did not go unnoticed by the priests and monks. They were outraged both by the sermons and the exemplary lives led by Groote and his followers. Their protests and political maneuvering forced the Bishop to silence Gerhard.[14] He humbly submitted to the ban and retired to Woudrichem (Workum).[15] The short time he spent there was devoted to reflection and writing.

Supporters then came forward and wrote to Pope Urban VI (1378-1389 from Rome), asking that the ban on Groote's preaching be removed. Impressed with Groote's teachings and behavior, Urban agreed. Unfortunately, the plague claimed Groote's life before the Pope's answer arrived, a scant four years into his ministry.[16] The prime mover behind the establishment of the Brethren of the Common Life never saw the realization of his work.

Florentius Radewijn (1350-1400) built upon the foundation that Groote had laid. He was born in 1350 in Leerdam and later studied at Prague.[17] Florentius was not the scholar that Groote was and his frail constitution was prone to ill-

---

[9] Hyma, *Brethren*, 19.

[10] Hyma, *Brethren*, 19.

[11] Neale, *Jansenist History*, 76; Hyma, *Brethren*, 18.

[12] Albert Hyma, *The Youth of Erasmus* (Ann Arbor: University of Michigan Press, 1930), 22.

[13] Hyma, *Brethren*, 22.

[14] Neale, *Jansenist History*, 77.

[15] Neale, *Jansenist History*, 80.

[16] Hyma, *Brethren*, 24.

[17] Neale, *Jansenist History*, 82-83.

ness. His study of medicine often provided him with the means of his own survival.[18]

Florentius lived the simple life. He wore plain clothing, avoided dainty foods and read only those books that he believed would improve his character.[19] As the vicar of the altar of St. Paul in the church of St. Lebwin,[20] Florentius became famous for his preaching in the vernacular. So good were his sermons that it became customary for those who could write to copy down the sermons he preached.[21] People would come for miles either to hear him or one of his followers preach.

To defray the boarding costs of those wanting to study with Groote, students were assigned the task of copying books which were then sold. Groote's purposes in all this were to increase the number of good books available, to have a profitable means of housing poor youth and to influence them toward living a holy life through their contact with good literature.[22]

It was Florentius, concerned with the expenses of boarding the increasing number of copyists, who spearheaded the move toward living in common.[23] He came to Groote and asked if it was wrong for those who wished, to live in common, pooling their resources to meet their common needs.[24] Groote feared the reprisal from the monks for such a move and preferred that a monastery, associated with an existing order, be built instead. But Florentius' persistence prompted him to agree to lead such a group.[25]

With Groote's untimely death, it fell upon Florentius to organize the first communal home. It was called a brethren-house and was probably formed in the fall of 1384.[26] The first official residence, the 'House of Florentius,' was constructed in 1391. It also served as a clearing house for placing students into foster homes during their time at school.[27]

This semi-monastic living arrangement brought opposition from the mendicant orders who claimed that the Brethren had created a new, unsanctioned order. In response, the early organizers attempted to distinguish the brethren-house from a new monastic order. While each person agreed to contribute to the support of the community, no vows were made and members were free to leave the fellowship if they so chose.[28] Defending the Brethren, the Augustinian Canons Regular noted that they taught no heresy, had no secret society, wore

18 Neale, *Jansenist History*, 85.
19 Hyma, *Brethren*, 58.
20 Hyma, *Brethren*, 22.
21 Hyma, *Brethren*, 57-58.
22 Kettlewell, *Thomas à Kempis*, 1.154.
23 Kettlewell, *Thomas à Kempis*, 1.155.
24 Hyma, *Brethren*, 52.
25 Hyma, *Brethren*, 52-53.
26 Hyma, *Brethren*, 65.
27 Hyma, *Brethren*, 64.
28 Kettlewell, *Thomas à Kempis*, 1.156-58.

no new monastic garments and that Pope Gregory XI (1370-1378 from Avignon and Rome) had given his approval for their lifestyle.[29]

In 1398 the plague again visited Deventer. After a number of the brethren died, Florentius and some others fled to Amersfoort, leaving only a few to care for the house.[30] During this self-imposed exile, the pressure from the monks, especially the Dominicans, increased. They continued to accuse the Brethren of founding a new monastic order without permission and cited their common life as proof.[31] Florentius, homesick for Deventer, could not take the pressure. He surreptitiously returned to Deventer, in spite of the continuing plague, and left the fray.[32]

It fell upon a new member, Gerhard Zerbolt (1367-1398), to press the case. Zerbolt was born in Zutphen in 1367 and joined the community in 1384.[33] He was an avid scholar. Just prior to his death in 1398, Zerbolt wrote *On the Common Life*, in which he presented his defense of the Brethren.[34] This one-hundred-page treatise, using canon law to defend the Brethren, proved decisive in defending the movement.[35]

His first point was that it was allowable to practice religion privately as well as in a monastery. The Reformation teaching of the priesthood of the believer will later expand upon this point. Zerbolt also asserted that a group could meet for the purpose of addressing and encouraging one another and correcting each other's faults as equals. Brethren who were not ordained did not preach to the public nor did they consider their sessions as supplanting the need for oral confession to a priest.

Zerbolt's final argument was that the general public spent too much time reading worthless stories about myths and monsters. The laity should be encouraged to study religious works instead. It was for this reason that the Brethren spoke in the vernacular regarding religious matters and produced religious works in the vernacular. Zerbolt's defense and subsequent papal support finally slowed the attack upon the Brethren.[36]

---

[29] Hyma, *Brethren*, 67.
[30] Hyma, *Brethren*, 67-68.
[31] Hyma, *Brethren*, 67.
[32] Hyma, *Brethren*, 69.
[33] Hyma, *Brethren*, 69.
[34] Hyma, *Brethren*, 70-78.
[35] John Van Engen, *Devotio Moderna: Basic Writings* (New York: Paulist, 1988), 13.
[36] For Gabriel Biel's subsequent defense of the Brethren in Germany, see William M. Landeen, 'Gabriel Biel and the Brethren of the Common Life in Germany,' *CH* 20 (1951), 25-28.

Major contributions

Personal piety

The first major contribution of the Brethren of the Common Life was their emphasis on personal piety. The aim of the Brethren was to bring about a life of piety through a renewed devotion to Christ. This new devotion, or *devotio moderna*, had four primary emphases: living for Christ, studying Scripture, progressing in holiness and growing spiritually.[37]

True religion was to love God and to worship him. Jesus should have first place in one's heart.[38] Personal piety involved more than just following an outward form of religiosity. It involved choosing to turn toward Christ and devote one's life to him. This choice to live for Christ was open to all people.[39]

The Fall produced a bondage to sin, even corrupting human intellect and will. Contrary to the later reformers who held to a strict predestinarianism, the Brethren believed that just enough human will remained for a person to reject or respond to God's love in Christ.[40] They were not totally depraved. They were responsible for their choice.

Once the choice to live for Christ was made, a believer was to live a holy life. The laity were as obligated as the clergy to live a holy life. It was this conviction that led them into the common life, following the example they found in the New Testament. The Bible should be studied by both clergy and laity so that everyone would know how to live for God. The Brethren highly valued the New Testament in general and the Gospels in particular. The Old Testament was seen as less valuable.[41] Groote developed the foundational teachings of the *devotio moderna* using primarily the New Testament and the Fathers, especially Augustine and Jerome, as sources.[42]

The life of faith was not a one-time event that resided solely in a mystical, internal plane, but a life-long journey. There needed to be a continual progression in holiness. This desire for sanctification became more apparent the closer one came to death.[43]

Growing in holiness necessitated a change of behavior. Confession before a priest without repentance, including a change in behavior, was useless.[44] There needed to be both a personal faith and a public demonstration of that faith; an

---

[37] Van Engen, *Devotio Moderna*, 27.
[38] Hyma, *Brethren*, 63.
[39] Kenneth R. Davis, *Anabaptism and Asceticism: A Study in Intellectual Origins* (Scottdale: Herald, 1974), 252-53.
[40] Albert Hyma, *The Christian Renaissance* (Hamden: Archon, 1965), 519.
[41] Davis, *Anabaptism and Asceticism*, 259.
[42] Hyma, *Brethren*, 27-28.
[43] Hyma, *Erasmus*, 34.
[44] Hyma, *Brethren*, 36.

inward knowledge of self and an outward charity.[45] To the Brethren, love for God was more than simply fighting heresy and vice. It was a response to the love God had shown them. That love impelled them 'to apply in everyday life the religious inspiration derived from the mystical experience'.[46] Love, along with humility, was the crowning virtue.

Groote, Radewijns and Zerbolt all encouraged private meditation for spiritual growth. This allowed the person to examine themself, to contemplate Christ's love and to grow in their understanding of faith. These experiences and insights were often shared among the Brotherhood. Perhaps the most well-known devotional writing coming from the Brethren is the *Imitation of Christ*, attributed to Thomas à Kempis (ca. 1379-1471).

Thomas was born in 1379 in Kempen (approximately 70 miles south of Deventer). At 13 years of age he traveled to Deventer to follow in his older brother, Jan's footsteps and study with the Brethren. By this time, Jan had joined the monastery at Windesheim (see below) and by 1398 had become the prior to a new monastery near Zwolle at Mount Saint Agnes, associated with the Augustinian Canons Regular. It was here that Thomas became a candidate in 1399, took full vows in 1408 and was ordained a priest in 1414. Apart from the three-year span during which the region was under interdict, Thomas spent the remainder of his life at Mount Saint Agnes, dying at the age of 92.[47]

The *Imitation* is comprised of 114 devotionals, divided into four books. It was a particularly popular work among the middle class tradespeople.[48] A thorough knowledge of scripture is evident in the work. It contains over 1,000 direct scriptural references, representing almost all the books of the Bible and the Apocrypha.[49] The first book, comprised of 25 chapters, emphasizes a spirituality that goes beyond scholastic philosophy and explores a vital, personal dimension.[50] It is titled, 'Thoughts Helpful in the Life of the Soul.'[51] Book two, 'The Interior Life,' proceeds to describe the virtues of the spiritual life in 12 chapters. The third book, 'Internal Consolation,' is more than twice as long as any of the other three. In 58 chapters, the author explores the practical working application of the spiritual life. The final book is an 'Invitation to Holy Commun-

---

45 R.W. Scribner, 'The Social Thought of Erasmus,' *JRH* 6 (1970), 5.

46 Lewis W. Spitz, *The Renaissance and Reformation Movements* (Chicago: Rand McNally, 1971), 42.

47 Thomas à Kempis, *On the Passion of Christ: According to the Four Evangelists: Prayers and Meditations* (translated by Joseph N. Tylenda; San Francisco: Ignatius, 2004), 9-12.

48 Henry S. Lucas, *The Renaissance and the Reformation* (New York: Harper, 1934), 181.

49 J.E.G. De Montmorency, *Thomas à Kempis: his Age and Book* (New York: G.P. Putnam's Sons, 1906), 174.

50 Montmorency, *Thomas à Kempis*, 224.

51 All book titles are taken from Thomas à Kempis, *The Imitation of Christ* (translated by Aloysius Croft and Harold Bolton; Mineola: Dover, 2003).

ion' in 18 chapters. It is not until this final book that one encounters theology that is specifically Roman Catholic.[52] The preceding books are Christological in nature.

This focus on Christ did not bring an end to following church tradition. The Brethren continued to revere Mary, pray to the saints and believe in indulgences.[53] Purgatory, on the other hand, was not seen as a place of punishment for sin but rather the place where one's works would be tried by fire.[54] However, as Van Engen points out, 'this focus on the person of Jesus Christ was so total . . . that there was in effect, if not necessarily in conscious intention, something of a shift toward a more exclusively Christocentric form of piety'.[55]

Education

A second contribution of the Brethren was in the area of education. In order to achieve their goal of both clergy and laity living a holy life, the laity would have to be taught to read so that they could learn for themselves how to live in a holy manner. Probably the greatest accomplishment of the Brethren was their educational reforms.

The initial source of income for most brethren-houses was the copying of books that were then sold. The advent of the printing press reduced the demand for expensive, hand-written books, so the move to education was a natural progression.[56]

Most brethren-houses operated a school that was separate from the brethren-house. Often the brethren would teach at the city school.[57] Students were required to keep a notebook of Christian teachings called a *rapiarium*.[58] The teacher dictated the plainest and most helpful sayings from the Gospels and the New Testament in a loud clear voice, which the students copied into their notebooks. This facilitated the memorization of these passages by the students. When they finished school, many students returned to their homelands in Poland, Germany and the Netherlands, carrying with them the teachings of the *devotio moderna*. Other students provided ready recruits for the brethren-houses or monasteries associated with the Congregation of Windesheim (see below).

Groote was devoted to education and he influenced the great reformer of education, John Cele. Cele was a native of Zwolle, the site of one of the earliest brethren-houses. He came to Groote for advice on whether or not he should join

---

52 Philip McNair, 'Seeds of Reform' in *Eerdmans' Handbook to the History of Christianity* (Grand Rapids: Eerdmans, 1977), 355.

53 Hyma, *Brethren*, 144.

54 Kettlewell, *Thomas à Kempis*, 2.339.

55 Van Engen, *Devotio Moderna*, 25.

56 Hyma, *Erasmus*, 29.

57 Kenneth A. Strand, 'The Brethren of the Common Life: A Review Article of R.R. Post's *The Modern Devotion*,' *AUSS* 8 (1970), 65.

58 Hyma, *Brethren*, 93.

a monastery. Groote discouraged him from taking Orders by pointing to the vast need for education among both clergy and laity. Partly through Groote's influence, Cele obtained the rector's position in the city school in Zwolle. He would teach at Zwolle from 1374 or 1375 until 1417.[59]

It was Cele who originated and founded the secondary school system.[60] He divided the school into eight grades, with the last two presenting special studies for the students.[61] Cele taught the *quadrivium* of grammar, logic, ethics and philosophy, the latter including poetry, elocution, mathematics and physics.[62] He supervised the revival of learning among commoner and cleric alike. In the process, the center of the *devotio moderna* shifted from Deventer to Zwolle.[63]

Many of the students were lodged by the Brethren. At Zwolle, there were several houses available for students, depending on the student's financial footing. The 'House for Rich Boys' housed those boys with means. The 'Small House' sheltered the boys whose parents were not wealthy but were able to pay for the tuition. Those who paid only a part of their expenses stayed at the 'House for the Middle Classes'. Boys whose education was totally subsidized lived in the 'House for Poor Students'.[64] For many of these boys, Cele also provided paper and ink. In spite of all the generosity he showed, Cele made a good deal of money at the school.[65]

After 1475, the center of the *devotio moderna* shifted from Zwolle back to Deventer when Alexander Hegius took leadership of the school there. Hegius melded the teachings of the *devotio moderna* with humanist principles as part of the basis of the Northern Renaissance.[66]

While much of what the Brethren did and taught was absorbed by others, their work in education remains. It was the one enduring aspect of their reform, not only because of the advances in educational practices, but also in the lives of the students they taught who applied the lessons during the Reformation.

Monastic renewal

The third contribution of the Brethren to the Reformation was in monastic renewal. The impact of the Brethren on the monasteries began as a means of self-preservation. Groote preferred the establishment of a monastery, where brethren desiring a more disciplined lifestyle could live, to an independent organization. It was his hope that the establishment of a monastery, designed after an existing monastic order, would diffuse the complaints that a new unsanctioned monastic order was being created. He hoped that with some of their number in

---

[59] Hyma, *Brethren*, 45.
[60] Hyma, *Brethren*, 90.
[61] Hyma, *Brethren*, 92-93.
[62] Kettlewell, *Thomas à Kempis*, 1.109.
[63] Hyma, *Brethren*, 45.
[64] Hyma, *Brethren*, 105.
[65] Hyma, *Brethren*, 94.
[66] Hyma, *Brethren*, 118-19.

a traditional monastic setting, some measure of security would be provided for those who chose to remain in the brethren-house. While Groote was not as concerned about the structure of the movement as he was about reform of the Church, it was his desire that the Brethren would be a model of how the monastic life should be lived out.[67]

In 1386, two years after Groote's death, some of his followers built a monastery north of Deventer at Windesheim to avoid further persecution.[68] It was designed after the Augustinian Canons Regular and adopted the Rule of Saint Augustine in 1387,[69] but the initiates took only the three vows of poverty, chastity and obedience to the prior.[70] They swore no obedience to the bishop or any other ruler.

The formation of a monastery allowed the movement to proceed along two parallel tracks. Some brethren took orders as part of a monastic life. Others took no orders, but lived in common as an expression of personal piety. It also relieved some of the pressure on the movement.

Women who desired to live in common were called the Sisters of the Common life. The first group formed was the one that met in Groote's home. They supported themselves by working as seamstresses, producing lace and textiles.[71] A dozen years after the founding of Windesheim at Deventer, the women felt the need to establish a convent. Discipline and devotion had become lax under their first confessor, John Van der Gronde. Upon his death, John Brinckerinck became confessor and led in the organizing of a convent at Diepenveen in 1400.[72] Even though the women began living in common before the men, little source material of their work remains.[73]

One outstanding characteristic of the Brethren of the Common Life was their obedience to the hierarchy of the Church. This was in evidence during a period in which they were in a self-imposed exile from their monasteries.[74]

From the seventh century, Utrecht had been an independent see and controlled the right of choosing its own bishops. Trouble began in 1423 with the election of a new Bishop of Utrecht. The constituents elected Rodolph de Diepholt as bishop. Pope Martin V (1417-1431) who wanted to extend his control over the area in the wake of the papal schism (1378-1417), appointed Sweder de Culenborgh as bishop in place of Rodolph. When Rodolph's supporters

---

67 Kettlewell, *Thomas à Kempis*, 1.141.

68 Hyma, *Brethren*, 82.

69 Steven Ozment, *The Age of Reform (1250-1550): An Intellectual and Religious History of Late Medieval and Reformation Europe* (New Haven: Yale University Press, 1980), 96.

70 Hyma, *Brethren*, 84.

71 John Van Engen, *Devotio Moderna*, 14.

72 Hyma, *Brethren*, 87.

73 Hyma, *Brethren*, 18.

74 Kettlewell, *Thomas à Kempis*, 2.146.

evicted Sweder, Martin put the territory under interdict, forbidding all clergy from performing their functions.

At length, the people demanded that clerics perform their tasks in spite of the papal decree. This proved to be a problem for the Windesheim monastery which was located within the quarantined zone. While the Brethren believed that Martin had overstepped his authority, they had no wish to disobey their pontiff's decree. Nor did they want to make the people irate by obeying the pope and not providing ministry. Instead, they chose exile from the interdicted territory. In that way they could be obedient without causing offense. The situation was eventually resolved in 1432 when Martin's successor, Eugenius IV (1431-1447), worrying over the Council of Basel, allowed Rodolph to return and removed the interdict.

Initiates into either the brethren-house or monastery passed through several stages of probation. When one requested admission, he was first asked whether he ate well, slept well and was willing to yield obedience to the prior.[75] All three had to be answered affirmatively. This process eliminated those who had tendencies toward overly enthusiastic asceticism. The initiate was also asked if he could write and whether he liked to read. If all went well, he was allowed to stay for two or three months.[76] A second trial period of ten to twelve months followed. The initiate became a full member at the end of this time when, before a notary public and witnesses, he renounced to the Brotherhood all claim to his personal property.[77] If a member left or was expelled due to ill-behavior, he could not redeem his property.

The Brethren arose at three or four o'clock in the morning and had prayer and personal devotions on a prescribed passage or subject.[78] Next came daily mass, followed by time spent in manual labor. Since the Brethren preferred good works, either among themselves or toward others, to contemplation, all who could work were expected to do so. Before work, prayers against temptation were offered and afterward, prayers of forgiveness and thanksgiving.[79] While working, the men would chant the Canticles of David or one of the Psalms.[80]

During meals, a passage of the Bible was read and the Brethren ate in silence so that they could concentrate on what was being read.[81] Three days a week the men ate meat. Three other days, they were fed eggs, food prepared from milk and on Friday, they ate a Lenten meal.[82] After supper, there was free time spent

---

[75] Kettlewell, *Thomas à Kempis*, 1.384.
[76] Hyma, *Brethren*, 113.
[77] Hyma, *Brethren*, 113.
[78] Hyma, *Brethren*, 110.
[79] Kettlewell, *Thomas à Kempis*, 1.388.
[80] Kettlewell, *Thomas à Kempis*, 1.389.
[81] Hyma, *Brethren*, 111.
[82] Kettlewell, *Thomas à Kempis*, 1.382.

in one's room. At eight o'clock there was to be silence and then lights out at eight-thirty.

On Sundays and holidays, the Brethren would give informal addresses.[83] A passage of Scripture was read and a discussion on it would ensue. These were open to the public and would draw good crowds.

The garments worn by the Brethren were dark-grey with the length of the hem indicating the rank.[84] Priests wore them to the ankle and Laics to mid-calf. A black belt and hood completed the outfit. Each brethren-house contained between 12 and 20 persons. There were usually four priests, accompanied by eight clerks and other laymen.[85] With the laity in the majority, it was not uncommon to have a layman elected as rector.[86]

Windesheim became the center of the *devotio moderna*, or new devotion. Its influence spread well beyond the region. Of the forty brethren invested before 1424, half became rectors or priors of other monasteries.[87] With the flow of reformers streaming out of Windesheim to other monasteries, a desire arose to form a fellowship of these reforming centers. This resulted in the founding of the Congregation of Windesheim in the winter of 1394-1395.[88] This association grew first by individual monasteries and then by whole chapters. Over 100 monasteries in all joined the Congregation of Windesheim.[89]

The Congregation developed into six families of monasteries.[90] The most influential was the Belgian family, which included Deventer and Zwolle. These cities remained the leading centers throughout the duration of the movement. The other families were the German, Italian, Portuguese, Sicilian and Genoese.[91]

One of the Brethren converts, Johann Busch, a native of Zwolle, was called to head the monastery of Neuwark, near Halle. His efforts drew the attention of Pope Nicholas V (1447-1455). In 1451, he instructed Busch to supervise the reform of all the monasteries of the Augustinian Canons Regular in Saxony, Meissen and Thuringia. The influence of this reform extended beyond the Canons Regular to affect the Benedictine, Cistercian and Premonstratensian orders.[92]

The Franciscans also benefitted from the reform-minded Brethren. Francis of Assisi (ca. 1181-1226), founder of the Franciscan Order, tried to involve more

---

83 Hyma, *Brethren*, 112.
84 Kettlewell, *Thomas à Kempis*, 1.386.
85 Neale, *Jansenist History*, 96.
86 Spitz, *Renaissance and Reformation*, 42.
87 Hyma, *Brethren*, 85.
88 Hyma, *Brethren*, 129.
89 Hyma, *Brethren*, 130.
90 Neale, *Jansenist History*, 100.
91 See Landeen, 'Gabriel Biel,' for an informative description of the development of the Brethren in Germany.
92 Hyma, *Brethren*, 132-34.

lay people in the monastic movement by designing a lay category, known as the Third Order. It was open to men, women, bishop, priests, etc. who were not already members of a religious order.[93] Because of this emphasis on lay involvement, many Brethren became Third Order Franciscans.[94] By 1470, some 82 brethren-houses had associated with them.[95]

Even as late as the end of the fifteenth century, the Brethren were experimenting with new ways of living in common. Near the conclusion of his life of ministry among the Brethren Gabriel Biel (d. 1495) organized a new brethren-house in 1492 at Schoenbuch. This house intentionally placed men from all levels of society in one place to live in common. Each house was to have a

> prior as head and twelve canons secular living the common life, . . . and thirteen lay brothers from the noble or knightly estate, of legitimate birth, . . . and twelve lay brothers, to wit commoners, who all shall be members of the said church and house.[96]

While this egalitarian experiment broke down class walls, it reveals the challenge of a maturing movement. The grass-roots lay movement, begun without the assistance of the established Church, had become absorbed by the ecclesiastical hierarchy. A quota system was now in place upon the Brethren. By the time of the Reformation, the Brethren had separated themselves from the common people they initially sought to educate and became more contemplative. What had once been the stimulus of ecclesiastical learning and reform became a part of the religious structure.

Brethren and the Reformation

The influence of the Brethren and their desire for a holy life, scholarship and religion in the vernacular bore its greatest fruit in the lives of the figures associated with the Reformation. Every major reformer crossed paths with the Brethren. Cardinal Cusa (Cusanus), who exposed the Donation of Constantine as a forgery studied in a Brethren school.[97] The German humanists, Alexander Hegius, Wessel Gansfort and Jacob Wimpheling either studied or taught at Brethren schools. John Calvin, Martin Bucer, Johannes Oecolampadius, Ulrich Zwingli,[98] Philipp Melanchthon[99] and Johannes Agricola all were influenced by

---

93 N.F. Thompson, 'Third Order, Secular' in *The New Catholic Encyclopedia* (Catholic University Press of America, 2003), 909. Third Order members are lay members who are allowed to participate in ministry and wear the order's habit.

94 Davis, *Anabaptism and Asceticism*, 51.

95 Davis, *Anabaptism and Asceticism*, 245.

96 Landeen, 'Gabriel Biel,' 33.

97 Neale, *Jansenist History*, 99.

98 Kenneth A. Strand, 'Calvin and the Brethren of the Common Life: The Role of Strassburg,' *AUSS* 15 (1977), 46-49.

99 Hyma, *Brethren*, 90.

either the teachings of the *devotio moderna* or the educational reforms based upon them. Martin Luther studied at a Brethren school in Magdeburg and the monastery at Wittenberg was a member of the Congregation of Windesheim.[100] Even those who remained within the Roman Catholic fold were influenced by the Brethren. Erasmus studied at Deventer and Ignatius Loyola was influenced by Zerbolt, impacting the Jesuits.[101]

The most telling impact was the election of Adrian of Utrecht in 1522 as Pope Adrian VI. He followed Leo X (1513-1521), who had opposed Martin Luther. Adrian not only studied at a Brethren school, his see was an influential center of Brethren-inspired monastic reform. He moved to clean up corrupt abuses of power within the church, using the Vatican as a model. Unfortunately, he died in September 1523. Adrian's pontificate was too short to achieve his reformation agenda.[102]

The teaching of the Brethren whetted the appetite of those it touched for something more than formal religion. How the person sought to satiate that hunger differed. Some, like the Brethren themselves, attacked only abuses within the system and not the doctrines or dogma of the church.[103] Others openly sided with the reformers in attacking the papacy and scholasticism.[104] Whatever the case, the spirit of the Brethren lived on through their students.

The growing friction between the reform movements and Rome led to the decline of the Brethren. They were forced to choose between their loyalty to the Roman Church and the principles of reform and piety which were the basis of their existence.[105] While a number of the Brethren joined the ranks of the reformers, only one community joined it as a group.[106] Those remaining were either forced to accept the stricter, standard monastic discipline or were expelled from their monasteries under Jesuit pressure.[107]

Without Deventer and Zwolle to provide leadership, the movement collapsed. Brethren teachers in the city schools gradually attracted more students than the Brethren-run schools because they offered a broader range of subjects. The last brother-house was erected in 1505 and by 1579 the school at Zwolle had dropped from a high of 1200 students to 3.[108]

In 1559, the revenues of the Brethren-run monasteries were given to Pope Paul IV (1555-1559). The monks were later driven out of the Windesheim monastery in 1573 by troops fighting the Spanish, who controlled the country at

100 Hyma, *Brethren*, 129.
101 Hyma, *Brethren*, 168-71.
102 Lucas, *Renaissance and Reformation*, 629-30.
103 Hyma, *Brethren*, 34.
104 Hyma, *Erasmus*, 30.
105 Kettlewell, *Thomas à Kempis*, 2.442.
106 Spitz, *Renaissance and Reformation*, 43.
107 Kettlewell, *Thomas à Kempis*, 2.444.
108 Kettlewell, *Thomas à Kempis*, 2.446.

that time.[109] Within a span of two hundred years, the outward evidence of the Brethren of the Common Life arose and disappeared.

Conclusion

The Brethren of the Common Life undeniably impacted the fifteenth- and sixteenth-century Church. They were excellent copyists and educators. Yet their legacy resides not in the structures or programs that they left behind, but in the spiritual impact they had on both commoner and cleric alike.

First, the taste of spiritual water provided by the Brethren did not simply disappear once a person left the brethren-house or brethren-run school. The desire to continue to live in fellowship with the Author of one's faith must have driven at least some to press on with the life of simple piety taught by the Brethren. This personal reform would lead some to a push for a structural reform of the Church.

Secondly, the Brethren taught that a life of faith was not restricted to 'professional' Christians. The laity could experience a vital spiritual life without having to withdraw from daily life. This realization opened the door for reform among the laity. Finally, through education, the Brethren produced literate clergy and laity who could read and comprehend the ideas espoused by the emerging reformers.

The Brethren of the Common Life did not itself play an active role during the Reformation era. Yet it did provide the tools of scholarship, the training in their use and the personnel to carry out its aim of producing authentic Christianity. Their ministry reminds modern church leaders of the importance and vitality of an educated, empowered laity.

---

[109] Kettlewell, *Thomas à Kempis*, 2.447.

CHAPTER 12

Returning to Marburg to rethink Martin Luther

Matthew J. Kasper

The Marburg Colloquy of 1529 was a crucial moment in the infant stages of the Protestant Reformation. It presented an opportunity for Protestant leaders to consolidate efforts both theologically and politically, but it also possessed the potential to shatter Protestantism indelibly. This chapter explores two sets of issues. First, what was the Marburg Colloquy and what happened before and during this meeting to hinder the goal of Protestant unity? Second, it explores how historians have perceived the legacy of Marburg, and especially how we can understand Martin Luther's role at the Colloquy. Was the lack of agreement at Marburg a failure to consolidate Protestantism or was it a victory for those who stood on their convictions even at the expense of unity? How far reaching were the effects of Marburg?

The Marburg Colloquy was held on 1-4 October 1529 in the town of Marburg in the German state of Hesse. It was convened by Philip I, Landgrave of Hesse, to find compromise regarding essential Protestant tenets between Martin Luther, Swiss theologian Ulrich Zwingli, and other reformers.[1] Hermeneutical disagreements regarding the Eucharist had caused an especially acerbic literary skirmish between the reformers. Philipp I, therefore, arranged this meeting at Marburg so that the rival factions could discuss theological issues, especially the Eucharist, and forge unity between themselves. Philip's motives were both spiritual *and* political. He wanted to achieve a theological basis for unifying German cities against inevitable backlash from Rome and, militarily, from the Habsburgs.[2] German cities were torn between Luther's and Zwingli's positions

---

1 The other collocutors included Johannes Oecolampadius, Martin Bucer, Caspar Hedio, Justus Jonas, Philipp Melanchthon, Andreas Osiander, Stephanus Agricola, and Johannes Brenz.

2 Heiko A. Oberman, *Luther: Man Between God and the Devil* (New York: Doubleday, 1989), 236; Gottfried W. Locher, 'The Change in the Understanding of Zwingli in Recent Research,' *Church History* 34.1 (1965), 13; Thomas R. Schreiner and Matthew R. Crawford, *The Lord's Supper: Remembering and Proclaiming Christ Until*

concerning the Eucharist and, 'Wittenberg and Zürich were competing for the spiritual, as well as the political, allegiance of south German cities'.[3] Division among the reformers jeopardized the theological and political benefits that unity promised.[4]

Again, the chief issue at the Marburg Colloquy was the Eucharist, which was one of seven important rites according to Roman Catholics and one of two sacraments for most Protestants. It recalls the final meal celebrating Passover that Christ had with his disciples before his crucifixion, and this Last Supper is regularly re-enacted by many churches. A view of the Eucharistic known as transubstantiation developed during the middle ages and was accepted as dogma at the Fourth Lateran Council in 1215. Proponents of this view asserted that the bread and wine mysteriously, but ontologically, become the physical body and blood of Christ. They apply an unyieldingly literal hermeneutic to Jesus' statements, 'This is my body'[5] and 'He who eats my flesh and drinks my blood has eternal life.'[6]

The reformers of the early 1500s fought against what they perceived to be the superstition and corruption of Roman Catholicism. Specific grievances included the bloated ecclesiastical hierarchy, the peddling of indulgences, the amassing of papal authority, and, not inconsequentially, the transubstantiation view of the Eucharist. While all reformers rejected transubstantiation, they differed regarding the extent to which Jesus' presence was in the communion bread and wine or whether these elements stood as mere symbols of Christ's crucifixion and propitiation. A point of contention was the specific interpretation of the word 'is' in Jesus' statement, 'This is my body,' and whether that word should be taken literally, symbolically or spiritually. This was not a tangential issue for the reformers; they were 'convinced that to be right about the sacraments was to be right about salvation'.[7] In his 1523 work 'The Adoration of the Sacrament,' Luther declared of the Words of Institution, 'Everything

---

He Comes (Nashville: B&H, 2010), 216; James M. Kittleson, *Luther the Reformer: The Story of the Man and His Career* (Minneapolis: Augsburg, 1986), 222.

3 Esther Chung-Kim, *Inventing Authority: The Use of the Church Fathers in Reformation Debates over the Eucharist* (Waco: Baylor University Press, 2011), 19.

4 When the theological avenue did not unify the region as he had hoped, Philipp I and John Frederick I of Saxony formed the Schmalkaldic League in 1531. Philipp's concerns about the burgeoning antagonism toward Protestant lands by Holy Roman Emperor Charles V were not illegitimate; hostilities between the two forces came to fruition in a series of skirmishes between 1546 and 1547, referred to as the Schmalkaldic War.

5 See Mt. 26.26, Mk. 14.22, Lk. 22.19, and the slightly rearranged version in 1 Cor. 11.24. The over-literalization of these verses is odd and this interpretative method is applied inconsistently relative to similar metaphorical statements of Jesus.

6 Jn. 6.54.

7 Chung-Kim, 15. Similarly, Oberman asserts that Luther believed that 'Baptism and holy communion are the solid ground on which the certainty of a Christian's faith rests' (227).

depends on these words. . . . They are words of life and of salvation, so that whoever believes in them has all his sins forgiven through that faith.'[8] For Luther, Christ's presence in the Table elements is profoundly tied to hermeneutics, and hermeneutics to bibliology, to Christology, and, ultimately, to soteriology. Thus, Luther saw the interpretation of the Eucharist as a fundamental issue that justified 'rending Christian unity, love, and peace,'[9] if necessary.

Luther promoted what has come to be known as 'consubstantiation' suggesting that Christ's actual presence is mystically *with*, but not changed *into*, the bread and wine.[10] While trying to disavow transubstantiation, he refused to separate himself from transubstantiation's literalist hermeneutic. Zwingli, on the other hand, was influenced by the rationalism of his day and he and others championed a memorial or symbolic view of communion. In article 18 of his 67 articles of faith, published in 1523, Zwingli asserts: 'Christ, having sacrificed himself once and for all, is for all eternity a perpetual and acceptable offering for the sins of all believers, from which it follows that the mass is not a sacrifice, but a commemoration of the sacrifice and assurance of the salvation which Christ has given us.'[11] He asserted that it was foolish to assign any spiritual benefit to physical substances: 'As the body cannot be nourished by a spiritual substance, so the soul cannot be nourished by a corporeal substance.'[12] Zwingli also felt that Luther's consubstantiation was not sufficiently distinct from the former monk's previous Romanism. Philip I hoped that at the Marburg Colloquy Luther and Zwingli would peacefully resolve their differences.

Luther's relentless sectarianism prior to 1529 provides a clue for why unity at Marburg collapsed. His acerbic polemics relative to the Eucharist reached a climax in his 1527 work, 'That These Words of Christ, "This Is My Body", etc., Still Stand Firm Against the Fanatics,' and his 1528 treatise, 'Confession

---

8 *LW* 36.277.

9 *LW* 37.23.

10 For more nuance on Luther's view and the use of the word 'consubstantiation' see Herman Sasse, *This is My Body: Luther's Contention for the Real Presence in the Sacrament of the Altar*, Revised Edition (Adelaide: Lutheran Publishing House, 1977), 79-87.

11 Ulrich Zwingli, 'Sixty-seven Theses,' *A Reformation Reader: Primary Texts With Introductions* (translated by Denis Janz; Minneapolis: Fortress, 2008), 190. In his 1527 work 'On the Lord's Supper' Zwingli refers to Jesus' words 'Do this in remembrance of me' and comments, 'These words tell us why it is that he has instituted this symbolical bread, for the remembrance of Christ and his self-offering for us'—*Zwingli and Bullinger* (translated by G.W. Bromiley; Philadelphia: Westminster, 1953), 229. However, his view is more than merely a bare memorial view. Later in 'On the Lord's Supper' he emphasizes the sense of unity among believers that is encouraged by communion. Believers are 'the community of the body and blood of Christ' (237).

12 Ulrich Zwingli, 'An Account of the Faith of Zwingli,' *Readings in the History of Christian Theology* (translated by William John Hinke; Philadelphia: Westminster, 1988), 2.22. See Sasse, *This is my Body*, 117.

Concerning Christ's Supper.' More than the mere content and argumentation of these literary efforts, their tone demonstrates Luther's vicious divisiveness that sheds light on the failure at Marburg. In these works, Luther frequently uses invectives against his theological opponents such as '*schwärmer*' ('fanatics'), 'brazen impudent fellows,'[13] 'false prophets,'[14] 'deceivers,'[15] and 'fickle wind-bags,'[16] who 'flutter about and slobber something irrelevant'.[17] He compares his opponents to Judas the Betrayer,[18] to the early church heretic Marcion,[19] or simply to an 'arch-heretic'.[20] He labels their arguments as 'empty prattle'[21] or as 'sheer lies and slanders'[22] promoting 'poisonous, deceptive teaching'.[23] Furthermore, Luther often confuses civil theological debate with Satan's attempts to create dissention and he portrays opponents as lapdogs to the Accuser's wiles. Speaking of the efforts of reformers who espoused the memorial view Luther states: 'May God repay you, Satan, you damnable wretch, for the shameful and cocksure way you ridicule us!'[24] Later in that work, he castigates his *human* adversaries: 'Listen now, you pig, dog, or fanatic, whatever kind of unreasonable ass you are . . . go back to your pigpen and your filth'.[25] In 'Confession Concerning Christ's Supper,' he declares: 'I am through with them. I shall write no more to them, lest Satan become still more frantic and spew out still more lies and follies.'[26] He frequently accuses his opponents of blasphemy[27] and recurrently charges them of being in league with or motivated by the

13 *LW* 37.97.

14 *LW* 37.20.

15 *LW* 37.169.

16 *LW* 37.197.

17 *LW* 37.118.

18 *LW* 37.28.

19 *LW* 37.110.

20 *LW* 37.162. He refers to the memorial position as 'a shameful heresy' in 'That These Words' (*LW* 37.16; see also *LW* 37.169).

21 See *LW* 37.19, 82.

22 *LW* 37.87.

23 *LW* 37.107.

24 *LW* 37.48. There was a theological basis for this rhetorical tactic of harshly associating one's enemies with Satan, a tactic utilized by many Protestant and catholic theologians at the time, but used liberally by Luther. Constance M. Furey, 'Invective and Discernment in Martin Luther, D. Erasmus, and Thomas More,' *Harvard Theological Review* 98.4 (2005), 469-88, elaborates on this tactic: 'If Christ redeemed this human foulness, humans could oppose Satan with weapons as offensive as those of Satan himself. For Luther, therefore, the theology of the Incarnation seemed to justify the use of insults' (478).

25 *LW* 37.68.

26 *LW* 37.162.

27 *LW* 37.20, 26, 52, 67, 98, 115, 135, 139, 142, 147; *LW* 37.252, 280, 286.

Devil![28] He believes that his opponents 'blaspheme God and are giving the lie to the Holy Spirit, betray Christ, and seduce the world'.[29]

A brief literary comparison will help us to see that Luther's ruthless rhetoric was more than merely the product of his cultural milieu. An exhaustive survey of literature from the early sixteenth century or even just a survey of the writings of reformers in the 1520s is beyond the scope of this chapter.[30] However, it is valuable to provide some literary comparisons against which Luther may be assessed. On one hand, some other reformers claimed that their opponents—whether the pope, the Catholic priesthood, or other reformers—acted and spoke at the behest of the devil. Words like 'antichrist,' 'blasphemous,' 'foolish' and 'devilish' were bandied about with regularity, as were accusations that an author's detractors were heretics, liars and deceivers. Such rhetoric was a common convention utilized by both protestant and catholic theologians alike. Yet, even in this milieu of acceptable theological discourse Luther utilizes these invectives against his foes with exceptional frequency. Michael A. Mullett asserts that 'The demonization of opponents had certainly been evident in [Luther's] 'That those Words of Christ. . . ,' in which the figure of Satan put in about 77 appearances.'[31] Mark Edwards notes that 'In controversies among evangelicals, the accusations of demonic possession and the *ad hominem* abuse tended to come more from Luther than from his opponents.'[32] Luther's perspective that any of his enemies, whether papists or anti-papists, are antichrists and satanic is pervasive in his writings and forms the backbone of his polemics and thinking.[33] He seems to import this conviction into the proceedings at Marburg, which apparently motivates his persistent intransigence. In addition to the fre-

---

28 *LW* 37.13, 18, 21, 31, 33, 35, 37, 48, 73, 74, 89, 103, 147, 148, 150, 161, 162, 163, 164, 165, 168, 171, 179, 188, 189, 200, 203, 209, 233, 236, 238, 251, 261, 296, 270, 274, 285, 291, 310. By listing these references, I aim to demonstrate that Luther's view that his opponents were serving the opinion of Satan is not gleaned from merely a few passing references.

29 *LW* 37.26.

30 A broader literary survey would include Luther's international contemporaries, such as the English churchman Thomas More, Dutch humanist Desiderius Erasmus, French humanist François Rabelais and Italian political theorist Niccolò Machiavelli. Works like Erasmus' *The Praise of Folly* (1511), *On The Freedom of the Will* (1524), and More's *Utopia* (1516) contain biting wit, satire, and jabs at religious and civil authorities. However, the worst comments in these works seem tame relative to the Luther's vulgar and personal insults. For a helpful comparison of Luther, More and Erasmus, see Furey, 'Invective and Discernment'.

31 Michael A. Mullett, *Martin Luther* (London: Routledge, 2004), 197.

32 Mark U. Edwards, Jr., *Luther and the False Brethren* (Stanford: Stanford University Press, 1975), 197-98.

33 See Furey, 'Invective and Discernment'; Heiko Oberman, 'Teufelsdreck: Eschatology and Scatology in the "Old" Luther,' *Sixteenth Century Journal* 19.3 (1988), 443-46, 449-50.

quency of his taunts, however, Luther is also exceptional in his repeated use of vulgarity, crudity and personal insult.

For instance, Zwingli's 1527 treatise 'On the Lord's Supper' reflects obvious frustration, and yet, is far more measured and mature than Luther's Eucharistic works. Zwingli only rarely uses the words 'blasphemy,' 'foolish' or 'antichrist' and exhorts those who agree with him to meet their theological opponents 'with charity and truth'.[34] He calls on scholars, most likely Luther himself, to 'cease from unworthy tirades, and the pouring out and heaping up of abusive words' and urges for debate that focuses on truth that is not despoiled 'by unmeasured words which necessarily suggest arrogance'.[35] Indeed, he speaks firmly when he mentions 'the writings of certain scholars who have presented the whole matter in the most bad-tempered and shameless fashion' and who employ 'childish objections' and 'childish frolic'.[36] Recognizing the dangerous and divisive rhetoric he asserts that 'if we blacken our opponents with rough words, the stain may well become so great that the truth is lost . . . . [thus] as much evil will issue from the roughness of the words as good is wrested from their meaning and force'.[37] Zwingli chooses to temper his own rhetoric, and also urges others to do the same.

Andreas Karlstadt, another rival of Luther, provides an additional comparison. He also referred to his opponents as 'devilish' and 'antichrists', but rarely utilized the vulgar verbiage of Luther. In 'On Both Forms in the Holy Mass' from November 1521, for instance, Karlstadt, as often did Luther, reserves his worst invectives for the pope: 'I ask the laypeople simply to believe the gospel and to consider the pope as a heretic, who blabbers against the clear text of the gospel and says that the bread isn't the body of Christ.'[38] Later he exclaims, 'Listen to me, pope, and open your ears, you big hare! . . . You devil's head!'[39] But, these insults seem tame and innocuous compared to Luther's invectives toward the Pope or toward other reformers. In 'On the Priesthood and Sacrifice of Christ', published early in 1524, he utilizes terms like 'devil,' 'blasphemy,'

---

34 Ulrich Zwingli, 'On the Lord's Supper,' 218.

35 Zwingli, 'On the Lord's Supper,' 187.

36 Zwingli, 'On the Lord's Supper,' 187, 209, 224.

37 Zwingli, 'On the Lord's Supper,' 187. Erasmus also recognized the exceptional harshness of Luther's rhetoric in the debate on free will and therefore recommended: "Let us pursue the matter without recrimination, because this is more fitting for Christian men, and because in this way the truth, which is so often lost amid too much wrangling, may be more surely perceived"—'On The Freedom of the Will,' Luther and Erasmus: Free Will and Salvation (trans. by E. Gordon Rupp, Philip S. Watson; Philadelphia: Westminster, 1969), 36.

38 Andreas Karlstadt, 'On Both Forms in the Holy Mass,' *The Eucharistic Pamphlets of Andreas Bodenstein von Karlstadt* (translated by Amy Nelson Burnett; Kirksville: Truman State University Press, 2011), 54.

39 Karlstadt, 'On Both Forms,' 67, 73.

and 'foolishness' a bit more frequently.[40] In 'Against the Old and New Papistic Masses' (October 1524) he mentions the 'poor, stinking, impure, knavish' priests[41] and throws out the adjective 'devilish' a few more times.[42] In response to the sustained personal attacks of Luther's 'Against the Heavenly Prophets,' Karlstadt wrote three pamphlets, which seem both justified and mild relative to Luther.[43] In these works Karlstadt strongly defies Luther, saying that he 'staggers,'[44] 'encourages such disorderly grease-bellies,'[45] is 'mad and foolish'[46] and his writing is 'unscriptural and unchristian'.[47] In 'A Review' Karlstadt refers to Luther's 'devilish doctrines'[48] and 'wrangling spirit'.[49] But on the whole, his rhetoric appears imminently tamer that Luther's; it is mocking but measured, without the regular and frequent baseness and brutality of Luther's treatises.

A brief survey of other significant theological treatises by Luther himself, especially those written in the *beginning* of the decade, further demonstrates that while Luther's vitriolic and crude rhetoric seems exceptional *vis-à-vis* most other reformers, it is rather typical of him. Three works of Luther from 1520, namely, *To the Christian Nobility of the German Nation*, *The Babylonian Captivity of the Church* and *The Freedom of a Christian* arguably set the tone for theological discourse over the next decade. While space does not allow us to recount all of Luther's colorful statements in these works, a brief collage will reinforce the point.

In *To the Christian Nobility of the German Nation* Luther attempted to rally the Germanic princes to oppose the incursion of the Roman Catholic Church into civic authority structures. He refers to the 'knavery and wickedness' of the church and accuses Catholic canon law of being written by the 'chief devil

40 Andreas Karlstadt, 'On the Priesthood and Sacrifice of Christ,' *Eucharistic Pamphlets*, 99, 101, 103, 109.

41 Andreas Karlstadt, 'Against the Old and New Papistic Masses,' *Eucharistic Pamphlets*, 111, and again on 112.

42 Karlstadt, 'Against the Old and New Papistic Masses,' 113, 115.

43 Andreas Karlstadt, 'A Review of Some of the Chief Articles of Christian Doctrine in which Dr. Luther Brings Karlstadt under Suspicion through False Accusation and Calumny,' *Karlstadt's Battle With Luther: Documents in a Liberal-Radical Debate* (translated by Ronald J. Sider; Eugene: Wipf and Stock, 2001), 127-38; 'Explanation of 1 Corinthians 10, "The Bread That We Break, Is It Not a fellowship of the Body of Christ?"' *Eucharistic Pamphlets*, 219-37; and 'On the New and Old Testament Answer to the Saying, "The Cup, The new testament in my blood," etc., Luke 22, 1 Cor. 11,' *Eucharistic Pamphlets*, 238-57.

44 Karlstadt, 'A Review,' 133.

45 Karlstadt, 'A Review,' 136.

46 Karlstadt, 'Explanation,' 235.

47 Karlstadt, 'On the New and Old Testament,' 238.

48 Karlstadt, 'A Review,' 130.

49 Karlstadt, 'A Review,' 131.

himself'.[50] He asserts: 'At Rome, they build on this accursed and devilish foundation, and think that we should let all the world go to the devil rather than resist their knavery.'[51] Not content with this critique, he later suggests that, 'Today . . . there is such a swarm of parasites in that place called Rome, all of them boasting that they belong to the pope, that not even Babylon saw the likes of it.'[52]

Luther's *The Babylonian Captivity of the Church* (1520) also demonstrates the divisiveness and crudity of his tone. In response to one detractor, Luther says, 'The wiseacre imagines he is adoring his drivel with the multitude of his quotations. The rest I will pass over, lest I smother you with the filth of this vile-smelling cloaca.'[53] With a coloratura unique to Luther, he proclaims, of the 'insatiable bloodsucker' of the Roman Church: 'For these monstrous things we are indebted to you, O Roman See, and to your murderous laws and ceremonies, with which you have corrupted all mankind.'[54] Elaborating on some of the Catholic regulations on marriage, Luther declares: 'The Romanists of our day have through them become merchants. What is it they sell? Vulvas and genitals—merchandise indeed most worthy of such merchants, grown altogether filthy and obscene through greed and godlessness . . . [they] openly sell to men the pudenda of both sexes.'[55]

Luther's *The Freedom of a Christian* (1520) also utilizes unnecessary invectives beyond the standard insults and devilish associations in theological literature. In the preliminary letter to Pope Leo X, Luther states: 'I have truly despised your see, the Roman Curia, which . . . is more corrupt than any Babylon or Sodom ever was, and which, as far as I can see, is characterized by a completely depraved, hopeless, and notorious godlessness.'[56] Furthermore, Luther asserts that, 'The name of the Roman curia is today a stench throughout the world, papal authority languishes and notorious Roman ignorance is in ill repute.'[57]

Therefore, these two works of Luther related to the Eucharist that led up to the Marburg Colloquy, the 1527 treatise 'That These Words of Christ,' and the

---

50 Luther, 'To the Christian Nobility of the German Nation,' *Three Treaties* (translated by Charles M. Jacobs; Minneapolis: Fortress, 1990), 11, 18.

51 Luther, 'To the Christian Nobility,' 18.

52 Luther, 'To the Christian Nobility,' 30.

53 Luther, 'The Babylonian Captivity of the Church,' *Three Treaties* (translated by A.T.W. Steinhäuser) 129.

54 Luther, 'The Babylonian Captivity,' 216-17.

55 Luther, 'The Babylonian Captivity,' 226.

56 Luther, 'The Freedom of a Christian', *Three Treaties* (translated by W.A. Lambert), 268. While Luther directed this attack more toward the Roman Catholic *system* in general than the pope specifically, it would be understandably hard for Leo X—who had been a cardinal for 24 years and already had been Pope for seven—not to take these critiques personally, which he did.

57 Luther, 'The Freedom of a Christian,' 273.

1528 work 'Confession Concerning Christ's Supper,' were both representative of Luther's rhetoric and they did appear to stand out for their tone among the reformers. Many discourses of theological and literary lucidity are punctuated by petulance, arrogance, vulgarity, and slander. Regarding one argument made by his foes, Luther retorts, 'Oh, how the devil's pants stink here!'[58] At another point Luther suggests that the sermons of the 'fanatics' would be better used for toilet paper.[59] Regarding Zwingli's argumentation, Luther cries, 'The children should pelt it with dung and drive it away!'[60] Of his opponents, he comments, 'They are exactly like a person who, just as I was about to greet him, would turn around thunder with his backside and then walk away. Well, they will not run off so insolently and leave their stench behind them, if it be God's will!'[61] Certain sections of these works were perceived to be so repugnant that they were omitted from some subsequent editions.[62] Since such crudity and petulance was not uncharacteristic of Luther, honest historiography must concede that he was both a prolific and undeniably brilliant figure but he also seemed to be an unnecessarily acerbic and regrettably sectarian one. Other political and theological leaders of the infant Reformation were unsettled by Luther's rhetoric, and they recognized that his rancor could shatter the swelling momentum of the Protestant movement. There was hope that the Marburg Colloquy could heal these rifts and promote unity.

The Marburg Colloquy

Interpreting the accounts of Marburg is itself a challenge.[63] At Luther's request, and despite Zwingli's protest, Philip forbade anyone from taking minutes or notes of the meeting.[64] The seven versions of the proceedings come from the memory of those present, and some of these are from anonymous sources.[65] As a result, these reports are a summary-style presentation of specific discussion points, and therefore, are probably somewhat tempered in their retelling. However, one can glean clues from these summaries that demonstrate Luther's continued obstinacy, petulance and sometimes even eccentric behavior. For instance, Rudolph Collin, a colleague of Zwingli, reveals that, 'Before the colloquy began . . . Luther had written on his table, "This is my body," in order that he might not allow himself to be diverted from these words.'[66] He reflects that

---

58 *LW* 37.35.
59 *LW* 37.67.
60 *LW* 37.212.
61 *LW* 37.349.
62 *LW* 37.147, n.255.
63 For a 'harmony' of these divergent accounts, see Sasse, *This is my Body*, 178-220.
64 Sasse, *This is my Body*, 177.
65 Johannes Brenz reports, 'There is nothing that can be repeated by anyone about that colloquy except what has been securely retained in his memory' (*LW* 38.74).
66 *LW* 38.52, 64.

in his opening speech Luther 'testified in advance that he disagreed with the persons of the opposing party and that he would continue to do so'.[67] Casper Hedio concurs that in his first address Luther proclaimed his intransigence and demonstrated hopelessness regarding agreement.[68] An anonymous report says that Luther 'answered that he could hardly put up with' the remarks of Oecolampadius.[69] Hedio records that already on the first day, Luther proclaimed to Zwingli, 'Your logic is very poor; it is the kind of logic for which a schoolboy is caned and sent to the corner.'[70] According to the report by the pro-Luther scholar Andreas Osiander, when Luther was encouraged to provide proof for his views on the Eucharist, he replied, 'At the outset you volunteered to prove that [the real presence] was impossible and that our interpretation was false. You are obligated to prove this and cannot demand proof from us, for we do not owe you a proof.'[71] At one point, Luther told Zwingli to desist from continuing his argument, because its continuance would result in 'long, unnecessary, useless, and irksome chatter'.[72] When Philip urged both sides to come to some agreement, Luther replied, 'I know of no other means than that [the Swiss reformers] give the glory to God's word and believe as we do.'[73]

Nor could participants agree on the *tone* of the Meeting. Johannes Brenz reports that there was no mention of schism or heresy (contra the report of Hedio), and he suggests that a witness 'would have alleged that Luther and Zwingli were brothers'.[74] Osiander asserts that the meeting was 'friendly' and 'non-argumentative'.[75] But even Sasse attributes the friendly and Christian nature of this meeting more to the hospitality of its host, Philip I, than to the theologians who attended.[76] There was tension and stubbornness from *both* the Germans and the Swiss and Luther and Zwingli mutually admitted to using 'sharp words' with the other.[77] Collin recounts that relatively early in the proceedings both

---

[67] *LW* 38.52-53.

[68] *LW* 38.15. Hedio reports Luther's sentiment: 'What is lost, is lost . . . [we] might discuss at the close of the colloquy whether or not [we] can regard each other as brethren' (*LW* 38.21).

[69] *LW* 38.46.

[70] *LW* 38.25.

[71] *LW* 38.66-67. Apparently, Luther's rhetoric and tone had rubbed off on Osiander, who accuses Luther's opponents of being malicious and blasphemous (*LW* 38.71) as well as exhibiting apostasy and slander (*LW* 38.72).

[72] *LW* 38.64.

[73] *LW* 38.69-70. In a 20 October 1529 letter to Joachim Vadian, Zwingli refers to his opponent simply as 'the foolish and obstinate Luther'—*A Reformation Reader* (Minneapolis: Fortress, 2008), 196.

[74] *LW* 38.74.

[75] *LW* 38.63.

[76] Sasse, *This is my Body*, 174-75.

[77] *LW* 38.35. Zwingli, at least once responded to Luther 'indignantly' (*LW* 38.51).

Luther and Oecolampadius 'testified that they would persevere in their opinion, since neither of the two had convinced the other'.[78]

But, overall, Marburg seems to demonstrate divergent styles of theological debate and Christian leadership between Luther and his opponents. Luther's 'stubborn insistence on the literal word' was in sharp contrast, for instance, to Martin Bucer's 'burning, untiring zeal for the unity of the Church'.[79] One sees a more agreeable tone in Oecolampadius, who also demonstrated concern for unity, while Luther disparagingly remarked that he would pray that his opponents will 'come to a right understanding of this matter'.[80] Philip Melanchthon, though firm in his convictions, also appears more conciliatory vis-à-vis Luther.[81] Zwingli is portrayed as a rational thinker having a 'supremely calm and serene style'.[82] His background in political dealings with the Zurich city council had taught him the value of a conciliatory nature.[83] Yet he found himself having to call Luther out for being 'childish'[84] and 'quarrelsome'.[85] The various accounts demonstrate how the Swiss pleaded for unity and friendship, but were rebuffed by Luther and his colleagues,[86] and Luther reportedly refused even to shake hands with Zwingli.[87]

But Luther did not simply reject the opinion of the Swiss nor snub them socially. Rather, he affirmed what he had charged previously, specifically, that because of their stance on the Eucharist, they were unbelievers. He stated to the Swiss reformers, 'It is clear that we do not possess the same spirit,'[88] which was, essentially, an accusation that they were heretics.[89] Similarly, in 'Confession' he had declared: 'I testify on my part that I regard Zwingli as un-Christian'[90] and he prayed that God would convert his foes who diverged from him regarding the real presence of Christ in the communion elements.[91] Thus,

---

78 *LW* 38.54.

79 Locher, 'The Change in Understanding,' 13. Sasse, *This is my Body*, 155, refers to Bucer as 'the great negotiator'.

80 *LW* 38.35.

81 Later, Melanchthon broke with Luther over issues related to Christ's presence in the elements and regarding whether this was an issue that should divide Christians (Sasse, *This is my Body*, 252-55).

82 Locher, 'The Change in Understanding,' 4.

83 Mullett, *Martin Luther*, 197.

84 *LW* 38.55.

85 *LW* 38.61.

86 *LW* 38.21; Sasse, *This is my Body*, 216.

87 Mullett, 197; Sasse, *This is my Body*, 230.

88 *LW* 38.70-71. Luther had already concluded this by the end of 'That These Words' (*LW* 37.150). His allusion there to 1 Jn. 4.1-3 confirms that he is calling his opponents Satanically-driven heretics because they reject Christ's flesh in the communion elements.

89 See 2 Cor. 11:4, Gal. 1:6, 2 Thess. 2:2 and 1 Jn. 4:1.

90 *LW* 37.231.

91 *LW* 37.288.

Luther entered Marburg having made up his mind regarding the spiritual state of his rivals, and during the meeting he demonstrated no intention to modify that opinion.

It is amazing that the reformers agreed on as much as they did at Marburg. A concord was written and the collocutors affirmed 14 of 15 theological assertions.[92] However, the impasse regarding the Eucharist prevented the fuller unity that its conveners envisioned. In fact, the Marburg Articles were a thin veil over a pervasive wedge that would continue to divide the reformers. Brenz, representing the Luther faction, proclaimed,

> We who affirm the presence of the body of Christ [in the elements] would have gladly received our opponents into fellowship with us if they had turned away from their error. Since no kind of an agreement could be reached with them, we decided unanimously that they were outside of the fellowship of the Christian church and that we would not recognize them as brothers and members of the church.[93]

Brenz affirms, in what apparently seemed to him like a remarkably conciliatory act, that Luther and his associates 'were willing to acknowledge our opponents, Zwingli and Oecolampadius, as friends, but not as brothers and members of the church of Christ'.[94] Even Osiander reports that Zwingli 'shed tears' when the two sides had come to an impasse on the issue.[95] The Swiss begged Luther to accept them as Christian brethren and to celebrate the sacrament together, but the latter refused.[96] This makes the concord that concluded Marburg suspect relative to its intent and effect. Indeed, after Marburg the Eucharistic controversy continued to divide the Reformation traditions.

Historiographical issues

We now consider some historiographical issues of Marburg pertaining to how historians have perceived Marburg, generally, and Luther's involvement in this controversy, specifically. First, historians recognize that the Marburg Colloquy was a failure to achieve Protestant unity rather than a victory for those who remained true to their convictions. For example, scholars laud the stand that Luther took at the Diet of Worms in 1521. When repeatedly commanded by the Roman Catholic authorities to recant his writings Luther responded, 'I cannot and I will not recant anything, for to go against conscience is neither right nor

92 *LW* 38.85-89.
93 *LW* 38.78.
94 *LW* 38.79.
95 *LW* 38.70.
96 *LW* 38.72.

safe. God help me. Amen.'[97] Yet, scholars generally do not revere the resolve of Luther or the other participants at Marburg, and simply see obstinacy and failure. Reformation historian Diarmaid MacColloch, for instance, calls the Marburg Colloquy 'a great missed opportunity' and the 'first in a line of failures' to consolidate Protestantism.[98] Heiko A. Oberman asserts that 'Marburg marked a profound, painful turning point in Reformation history.'[99] The Colloquy is generally treated as a failure to find agreement, or at least toleration, regarding the Eucharist.[100]

Scholars differ, however, as to whom specifically is to blame for the failure at Marburg. Some recognize the propensity of all participants to speak past each other or to 'straw man' their opponents. In *Marburg Revisited*, Paul C. Empie declares that during the discussion over the Eucharist, 'Different terms and concepts were employed which . . . led to mutual misunderstanding and misrepresentation.'[101] Oberman suggests that, 'The general vilification of opponents [before and at Marburg] made it inconceivable for them to take each other's positions seriously.'[102] This tendency, however, is noted especially of Luther, who had refused to attend similar meetings previously and attended Marburg only reluctantly.[103] Gottfried Locher suggests that 'Luther's irritability breaks through repeatedly.'[104] Liturgical historian James White claims that Luther simply did not appreciate how Zwingli's interpretation complemented his own.[105] Thomas Schreiner asserts that Luther 'refused to budge' from what he had written previously about the Eucharist.[106] What was needed at Marburg more than sheer agreement was agreeability. The success of Marburg depended upon its participants wielding a measure of understanding and humility, neither of which Luther appeared to demonstrate to any great degree.

---

97 Martin Brecht, 'Luther, Martin,' *Oxford Encyclopedia of the Reformation* (translated by Wolfgang Katenz; New York: Oxford University Press, 1996), 2.60. Some versions add Luther saying, 'Here I stand. I cannot do otherwise.'

98 Diarmaid MacColloch, *The Reformation* (New York: Viking, 2005), 168.

99 Oberman, *Luther*, 244.

100 James F. White, *Protestant Worship: Traditions in Transition* (Louisville: Westminster John Knox, 1989), 58; Roland Bainton, 'Luther and the *Via Media* at the Marburg Colloquy,' *The Lutheran Quarterly* 1 (1949), 396; Mullett, *Martin Luther*, 197. Hastings Eells, 'The Contributions of Martin Bucer to the Reformation,' *Harvard Theological Review* 24.1 (January, 1931), 32, includes the 1530 Diet of Augsburg in his catalog of failures to unify.

101 Paul C. Empie, *Marburg Revisited: A Reexamination of Lutheran and Reformed Traditions* (Minneapolis: Augsburg, 1966), 103-104. Empie goes on to assert: 'Properly interpreted, the differing terms and concepts were often complementary rather than contradictory' (104).

102 Oberman, *Luther*, 244.

103 Schreiner and Crawford, *The Lord's Supper*, 216; Sasse, *This is my Body*, 155.

104 Locher, 'The Change in Understanding,' 12.

105 White, *Protestant Worship*, 59.

106 Schreiner and Crawford, *The Lord's Supper*, 217.

Another historiographical issue percolates from this analysis. A definitive bias can be detected from pro-Luther scholars relative to those who are perhaps more invested in the Reformation generally than in Luther particularly. Luther scholar Oberman asserts that, 'the tone [of Marburg was] only rarely acerbic' and that 'various transcripts show that the personal rancor between the two reformers [i.e., Luther and Zwingli] had subsided'.[107] Luther biographer Roland Bainton asserts that 'Luther . . . was not so intransigent throughout,'[108] and he blames the Swiss theologians for rejecting Luther's *via media*, or 'middle road,' between the two opposing viewpoints.[109] However, Luther proposed this middle road idea only after he had already written off his opposition and continued stubbornly to maintain his position.[110] Bainton further asserts that '[Luther] and his party took the initiative in proposing a formula of concord.'[111] Yet, it is commonly agreed that Luther presented this formula only *after* Philipp I assigned this task to him.[112] Some historians blame the meek Philip Melanchthon who allegedly suggested that he and Luther would jeopardize their relationship with the German Catholics if they conceded to Zwingli's views of the Eucharist.[113] It is hard, however, to find any other verification for Luther's conciliatory nature and for Melanchthon's non-conciliatory one.[114] Here again, one finds

---

[107] Oberman, *Luther*, 237. This is an odd conclusion considering in a letter to Vadian, 196, Zwingli himself summarizes the meeting by twice asserting that the opposing sides 'fought' during the Colloquy.

[108] Bainton, 'Luther and the *Via Media*,' 396.

[109] Bainton, 'Luther and the *Via Media*,' 395.

[110] *LW* 38.34. Luther's discussion and writings demonstrate that, in reality, he had little interest in a *via media*. In fact, on the very next page, Hedio reports, 'Luther wants to abide by his faith, nor can he yield' (*LW* 38.35). Luther apparently abandoned his *via media* sentiment quite quickly.

[111] Bainton, 'Luther and the *Via Media*,' 396.

[112] Schreiner and Crawford, *The Lord's Supper*, 218; Sasse, *This is my Body*, 175, 216; and further, it was a concord that Luther borrowed largely from work that he and fellow Wittenberg theologians had already done at Schwabach. Also, Osiander, whose pro-Luther bias we have previously observed reports that after the debates on 2-3 October, 'It was decided that Luther should list the chief articles of the faith' (*LW* 38.72). That is, this was a corporate decision and not one that came from Luther's initiative. Similarly, Brenz, who was sympathetically disposed to Luther, reports that 'Luther was given the assignment of drawing those articles' of concord (*LW* 38.79).

[113] Bainton, 'Luther and the *Via Media*,' 397, suggests, 'At Marburg Luther wanted to yield to the Swiss but Melanchthon would have none of it. Justo L. González, *The Story of Christianity* (San Francisco: Harper Collins, 1985), 2.52, hints at this as well. González adds, however, 'Some time later, when the break with Catholics was clearly irreversible, Melanchthon himself reached an agreement with the reformers from Switzerland and Strasbourg' (see n.81).

[114] Consider for instance, the charming, and even touching tone of Melanchthon's letter to Oecolampadius, dated 8 April 1529, just months before the Marburg Colloquy—*A Melanchthon Reader* (translated by Ralph Keen; New York: Peter Lang, 1988), 127-29. He remained firm in his own position, even suggesting that Oecolampadius has

the slant of Luther scholarship somewhat suspect; perspectives that attempt to release Luther from blame fit awkwardly into the historical record.

Despite the failure of Marburg, some *do* see its silver lining. While Oberman recognizes that Philipp I's purpose for the Marburg meeting did not come to fruition, he nevertheless praises the prime participants for their doctrinal principles, saying, 'The Marburg colloquy of 1529 attests to the fact that the reformers, Luther and Zwingli alike, were steadfast in their refusal to subordinate their convictions to the demands of political calculation.'[115] However, Oberman *does* concede later: 'In 1529 the dispute [regarding the Eucharist] prevented the formation of a unified Evangelical front.'[116] Some perceive Marburg as a 'breakthrough' even though it did not achieve what Philipp had intended.[117] The fifteen articles that Luther was asked to write at Marburg were adapted from the Schwabach Articles that he and other Wittenberg theologians crafted earlier in 1529 and these became the foundation for the prominent Augsburg Confession of 1530.[118] Yet, these are small successes relative to the overall failure of Marburg to reconcile divergent beliefs relative to the Eucharist and may be mere attempts to vindicate Luther despite his obstinacy and his rhetoric.

What hinders interpretation about Luther is the manner in which Reformation scholarship has, especially in the twentieth century, made Luther into a typical Reformation figure and the measuring rod by which others are judged. Locher summarizes his own perception of this tendency:

> Luther's inner development, his way and, finally, his conception of doctrine provide the standard for evaluating all Reformation efforts. Luther is made the normative Reformer. Whatever conforms to his picture is regarded as valid, but that which does not, is regarded as alien.[119]

Sasse is typical of this syndrome when he comments of Luther's theology of the hiddenness of God, 'One must keep in mind this character of Luther's theology in order to understand Zwingli.'[120] It is as though Zwingli's theology of the sacraments, or of anything, cannot be understood on its own merits without the lens of Luther's perspective. This is not to undermine how significant Lu-

---

adhered to many 'absurdities' (129). However, Melanchthon demonstrated a concern for the unity of the church and a goodwill toward Oecolampadius, personally. Additionally, Mullett, *Martin Luther*, 207, recognizes how the divergent approaches of Luther and Melanchthon resurface in 1530: 'There was, then, with Augsburg, a clear rift within Lutheranism and it pitched the intractable Luther against the conciliatory Melanchthon.'

[115] Oberman, *Luther*, 237, 240.

[116] Oberman, *Luther*, 243.

[117] Charles P. Arand, Robert Kolb and James A. Nestingen, *The Lutheran Confessions: History and Theology of the Book of Concord* (Minneapolis: Fortress, 2012), 94-95.

[118] Arand, Kolb and Nestingen, *Lutheran Confessions*, 96.

[119] Locher, 'The Change in Understanding,' 4.

[120] Sasse, *This is my Body*, 93.

ther was and how contemporary reformers perceived his groundbreaking role in the Protestant movement. But, Luther is often quoted by modern scholars with uncontested authority and venerated as the wise and gentle sage of the Reformation, who epitomizes homologous Protestant thought as the seminal theologian of this period.

However, Luther was anything *but* normative. He was exceptional in his literary output, prodigious in his hymn contribution, pioneering in his theological thought and seminal in his overall influence. Other reformers recognized this and were eager for his approval. However, Luther also stood out among other reformers for his verbal venom amidst theological discourse,[121] often providing an example that should be neither honored nor emulated. When scholarship attempts to *normalize* the exceptional Martin Luther, they white-wash him and thrust him to the historical foreground while the contribution of other reformers—whose views may be more typical of many Protestants today—are put to the back. That is, by hero-izing Luther as a typical or even reformer *par excellence*, scholarship does Luther, other reformers, and the Reformation *in toto* a disservice. Locher ponders: 'Here we can leave it an open question whether [by trying to normalize Luther] one thereby really honors Luther or even understands him.'[122]

The final historiographical issue is whether historians perceive that Marburg set a precedent in Protestantism for further fragmentation or if it is seen as a rather isolated event with minimal consequences. Only by speculation could we imagine the impact a unified reformational front may have had both for Europe of the sixteenth century or for evangelicalism today. One could only wonder how the propensity of evangelicalism to divide over non-essential issues—or even non-essential issues masquerading as essential issues—may have been quelled by the exemplar of a successful meeting at Marburg. Unfortunately, Marburg tells a tragic tale of what-is relative to what-could-have-been. Jill Raitt sees Marburg as the cause of the rift between Lutherans and the Swiss reformers that sent theological and political ripples throughout Europe.[123] Sasse suggests that this Eucharistic controversy between Luther and Zwingli has 'deeply influenced even the political and cultural development of Europe' and that Marburg specifically 'decided the history of Protestantism for centuries'.[124] Bainton admits that, 'there might in the long run have been more to be gained' had Luther bent even slightly toward Zwingli's memorial view.[125] White sees

---

[121] Despite Luther's 'brutal attacks on his evangelical opponents' Edwards, *Luther and the False Brethren*, 3, notes 'the reluctance of these opponents to respond in kind'. Edwards does concede, and I concur, that Thomas Müntzer was an exception to this and he often rivaled Luther in his vitriol and vulgarity.

[122] Locher, 'The Change in Understanding,' 4.

[123] Jill Raitt, *The Colloquy of Montbéliard: Religion and Politics in the Sixteenth Century* (New York: Oxford University Press, 1993), 50-51.

[124] Sasse, *This is my Body*, 3.

[125] Bainton, 'Luther and the *Via Media*,' 398.

that Marburg created a 'pattern . . . that has ever since been a prominent characteristic of Protestant worship—disparate traditions'.[126] The Colloquy is perceived to be a failure to consolidate and a precedent in Protestantism for further division over non-essential issues.

Conclusion

Standing in the middle of the melee at Marburg is Martin Luther, a man of extraordinary intellect and influence, but a man *also* with an indisputably destructive sectarian attitude. While he will always be revered for his influence on the Reformation by his contemporaries, and by historians, alike, academic integrity compels us to rethink Luther. Perhaps we should be less inclined to view him as a normative reformer, and less hasty to venerate him in light of some of his destructive tendencies. The Marburg Colloquy represents a moment when Protestantism could have grasped profound unity even in the midst of peripheral theological disagreement. Instead, Marburg entombs one of the greatest ironies of church history, namely, that Luther, one of the key individuals who *instigated* the Protestant Reformation was also one of the prime figures who shattered it.[127]

---

[126] White, *Protestant Worship*, 58.

[127] My thanks to Dr. Jared Poley of Georgia State University for his input on this project and also to my wife, Martha, for her editorial assistance.

CHAPTER 13

Calvin's circle of friends: propelling an enduring movement

David W. Hall

At any commemoration or historical review, it might be prudent for us to ask: How does one sustain a movement of ideas over time? And is something as non-cognitive as social friendship a factor? One historian of the Swiss Reformation noted that it would be impossible for a Calvin to be so dearly loved at his death if he had been a monster all his life. Not only was Calvin praised at his death (see below), but his many friends joined him in embracing similar ideas and sought to cultivate those. This survey reviews his friendships in different locales, during his student days, while in exile in Strasbourg, as evidenced among Genevan institutions, and at his death. Its goal is to consider the propulsion effect of friendships to cultivate longevity for an ideological movement.[1]

Rehabilitating an image

Even a cursory study of Calvin's letters reveals a pattern of friendship and collegiality.[2] As van den Berg observes, without a wide circle of friends providing a colorful palette for the canvass, students would not be acquainted with Calvin's finer points embedded within his extensive correspondence. To be sure, Calvin did not view himself as the only individual involved in these matters of reform. For the other side of the story, one should consult the short work, *The Humanness of John Calvin* by Richard Stauffer.[3] In the Foreword to that monograph, leading Calvin scholar J.T. McNeill chronicles how he had been led to

---

1 The 1997 Calvin Studies Society Colloquium featured essays on Calvin's friendship with Viret, Farel, Bullinger, Bucer, Melanchthon and the Budé family. See, also, Machiel A. van den Berg, *Friends of Calvin* (translated by Reinder Bruinsma; Grand Rapids, Michigan/Cambridge: Eerdmans, 2009), which includes vignettes of 24 friendships.

2 See the observations from these in Herman Selderhuis, *John Calvin: A Pilgrim's Life* (Wheaton: IVP, 2009).

3 Richard Stauffer, *The Humanness of John Calvin* (New York: Abingdon, 1971).

question the hearsay about Calvin, which depicted him as largely inhumane. As he perused Calvin's letters, he found, to the contrary, that Calvin was vividly humane, associated with rich and poor alike, exhibited a sturdy loyalty to friends, and attributed to Calvin the following traits: gentleness, warmth, tenderness, generosity, hospitable, and other well attested virtues.[4]

Richard Stauffer describes the 'calumny' that Calvin has received from his enemies and also how he has 'been misunderstood and misinterpreted by his great-grandchildren'.[5] Another historian noted that no other reformer generated more personal loyalty than Calvin. Emile Doumergue[6] put it this way: 'There were few men who developed as many friendships as he and who knew how to retain not only the admiration, but also the personal affection of these friends.'[7] Abel Lefranc expressed the same sentiment this way:

> The friendships which he inspired . . . among his teachers as well as among his colleagues, are strong enough testimonies to the fact that he knew how to combine with his serious and intense commitment to work, an affability and graciousness which won everyone over to him.[8]

Whether he was in a university setting or whether he drew on the experience of his teachers to assist him, Calvin was a more sociable man than sometimes thought. He was a habitual letter writer, corresponding with jurists, governors, common people and many ministers. These letters provide glimpses into the real Calvin. In these letters, he could refer to the affection he had for his teacher, Melchior Wolmar, and at the same time could mourn the passing of a ministerial friend as so staggering as to be burdened with grief.

The character and impulse of Calvinism (and Lutheranism as well) impacted the world through a fraternity of devoted and committed friends. American theologian, Douglas Kelly, confirms that the Calvinistic tradition wielded influence far beyond Switzerland and France. No individual could sow so many seeds; these victories were scored by a team of colleagues. Take for example, the area of political formulation.

Calvin was the premier but certainly not the only Protestant theorist; indeed, he absorbed much from his comrades. Other reformers, who were in his circle of friendship, briskly articulated theologies of the state, with the following seminal works appearing in rapid succession in less than thirty years: Martin Bucer's *De Regno Christi* (1551), John Ponet's *A Short Treatise of Political Pow-*

---

4 Stauffer, *The Humanness of John Calvin*, 9.

5 Stauffer, *The Humanness of John Calvin*, 19.

6 Emile Doumergue, *The Character of Calvinism: The Man, His System, The Church, The State* (1923; rpr. Neuilly [Seine]: La Cause, 1931), highlights the following as distinguishing attributes, among others, of Calvin's character: vivacity, joyishness, affection (Fr. *mignardise*, preciousness), nobility and a concern to pitch his written style for common understanding.

7 Stauffer, *The Humanness of John Calvin*, 47.

8 Stauffer, *The Humanness of John Calvin*, 51.

er (1556), Christopher Goodman's *How Superior Powers ought to be obeyed of their subjects; and wherein they may lawfully by God's word be disobeyed and resisted* (1558), Peter Viret's *The World and the Empire* (1561), Francois Hotman's *Francogallia* (1573), Theodore Beza's *De Jure Magisterium* (1574), George Buchanan's *De Jure Regni Apud Scotos* (1579) and Languet's *Vindiciae Contra Tyrannos* (1579). Each of these works legitimized the idea of citizen resistance against governmental expansion that exceeded proper limits. Interestingly, this corpus of political thought emanated from a tight circle of friends, most of whom were in direct contact with Calvin. It is hard to attribute such robust similarity of thought either to accident or to independent discovery.

Calvin's companionship with Theodore Beza is a model of friendship, and with all the heady intellectual issues of the day, still what greatly impressed Beza was Calvin's personal support and friendship. Thus Beza (and others) wrote about the camaraderie that Calvin shared with those around him. Calvin epitomized the modern notion of collegiality, and he was prudent enough to attract brilliant friends if at all possible. Once when Beza was ill, Calvin wrote about the 'fresh fear' that 'overwhelmed him with deep sorrow' upon learning of Beza's sickness. He was 'staggered . . . already weeping for him . . . grieved' and afraid of the loss that might come to the Church and to him personally. Fortunately, Beza recovered.

Moreover, there were many other friends beside Beza. The consensual strains of thought that flowed through the literary veins of Bullinger, Bucer, Viret and Calvin—soon to be supplemented by Knox, Beza, Hotman and Junius Brutus—formed an intellectual tradition with Geneva at its epicenter and Calvin its architect. His friendship with these scholars would prove to be the glue that held the movement together in its delicate infancy.[9] J.H. Merle D'Aubigne noted this mutual interchange of ideas in these words:

> The catholicity of the Reformation is a noble feature in its character. The Germans pass into Switzerland; the French into Germany; in latter times men from England and Scotland pass over to the Continent, and doctors from the Continent into Great Britain. The reformers in the different countries spring up almost inde-

---

9 Aurelio Garcia, 'Bullinger's Friendship with Calvin: Loving One Another and Edifying the Churches,' *Calvin Studies Papers (1997)* (Grand Rapids: CRC Product Services, 1998), 126, summarized the connection between the Zurich and Genevan reformers as follows: 'Very often Bullinger would transmit this information, or conversely, we will find Calvin inquiring about events. Geneva in turn, was particularly closely involved with events in France and was well-acquainted with the life of congregations there. Very closely related to this theme of current news, is the evaluation of events. By means of third parties or directly, appraisals of historical happenings, or the clarification of the validity of rumors, would be carried out. Routine and domestic issues would be taken care of, such as the arrival of students, entrusted by their parents to the care of either city's churches, by mediation of the pastors. On occasion, we find Bullinger and Calvin clarifying monetary accounts, usually in relation to the provision of some writing.'

> pendently of one another, but no sooner are they born than they hold out the hand of fellowship. . . . It has been an error, in our opinion, to write as hitherto, the history of the Reformation for a single country; the work is one.[10]

Calvin's associates served to stabilize and standardize an international movement. Their collective effort certainly led to its expansion.

Calvin, Farel and Peter Viret were called 'the tripod' or 'three patriarchs,' so well-known was their friendship. In Calvin's *Commentary on Titus*, he wrote that he did 'not believe that there have ever been such friends who have lived together in such a deep friendship in their everyday style of life in this world as we have in our ministry'.[11] Calvin, in that preface, referred to their 'friendship and holy union,' averring that their union, despite holding forth from different locales, aided the unity of the Church. Even when there were strong disagreements, Calvin was a paragon of friendship. When these reformers experienced family struggles or joys, Calvin shared those in his letters. These letters to various reformers are full of sympathy and quick to illustrate a healthy loyalty. Moreover, his correspondence with refugees exhibits his great compassion as well. He even built bridges to Luther's disciples after the German leader denounced him.

Calvin's acquaintance with Melanchthon began with correspondence to Bucer during Calvin's Strasbourg exile. Calvin first met Melanchthon in person, however, at the 1539 Diet of Frankfort. At this early stage of the Reformation, the winds of 'ecumenical optimism' blew freely among many reformers. Calvin thought that Melanchthon agreed with him on a wide range of doctrinal topics, thinking even that Melanchthon perhaps held the key to potential unity with Lutherans.[12] At this early stage of the Reformation, shortly after his arrival in Strasbourg, Calvin advised trying 'every remedy' that might affect unity, 'persever[ing] even to the last gasp'.[13] Despite the similarities in personality and scholarly bent—especially contrasted with their mercurial mentors, Luther and Farel—Calvin and Melanchthon never attained the unity first thought possible.

What began in Geneva with a multi-national cadre of colleagues, all seeking to extend the 'republic of Christ,' grew into a movement which featured theology, ideas and a unique view of history far surpassing the city of Geneva

---

[10] J.H. Merle D'Aubigne, *The History of the Reformation of the Sixteenth Century* (New York: American Tract Society, 1848), 3.416.

[11] Stauffer, *The Humanness of John Calvin*, 57.

[12] Randall C. Zachman, 'Restoring Access to the Fountain: Melanchthon and Calvin on the Task of Evangelical Theology,' *Calvin Studies Papers (1997)* (Grand Rapids: CRC Product Services, 1998), 207, notes that although their friendship was strained at times—with numerous epistolary rebukes—nevertheless, the friendship lasted until Melanchthon's death. Zachman highlights the difference in methodology between these two reformers, noting that the mutual admiration, however, remained. Calvin also thought that Melanchthon's differences with Luther on God's decrees might further ecumenical cooperation (211).

[13] Zachman, 'Restoring Access,' 209.

alone.[14] With their confidence in God's providence and divine election, this circle of friends urged civil rulers to adopt their religious views and political practices 'holding that no frontiers, no boundaries, no limits should confine the zeal of pious princes in the matter of God's glory and of the reign of Christ'.[15] To some, the theology of resistance maintained by this Genevan circle would appear politically subversive.

At times, as in any historic era, there were also disruptions of friendships.[16] Calvin had to assist church members with broken relationships and he had to deal with friction among the Protestant reformers. No leader should expect that all will always go smoothly in the area of friendship; however, Calvin learned to encourage others around him and he delegated certain responsibilities to his associates.

Richard Stauffer concluded that Calvin was far from

> the isolated hero or the lonely genius that has often been pictured. Throughout his career, he had relationships with friends who show him unfailing affection and indefatigable devotion. If he exerted such charm, it is certainly because he himself had been such an incomparable friend. . . . For the devotion which one showed him, he paid the tribute of unswerving loyalty.[17]

Following Calvin's death,[18] the continuing work of reformation was entrusted to his colleagues, Beza being the chief.

Calvin's early theological mentors and peers: friends in ideas

Calvin had to realize that massive change could only occur on strong foundations. He was also modest enough to avoid boasting that all good ideas percolated from his own mind. Calvin's admiration for those excellent theologians who had gone

---

14 *Calvinism in Europe, 1540-1610: A Collection of Documents* (translated and edited by Alistair Duke, Gillian Lewis and Andrew Pettegree; Manchester: Manchester University Press, 1992), 200. This internationality, to some degree, blunts the suggestion by Harro Hopfl, *The Christian Polity of John Calvin* (Cambridge: CUP, 1982), 56-57, that Geneva was unique in applying Calvinism because it was a relatively small political space in which the laws could be easily enforced.

15 *Calvinism in Europe*, 200.

16 Calvin had a 'huge capacity for friendship. He maintained some friendships from childhood years into adult life. Two of his closest friends were Viret and Farel, with whom he shared the highs and lows of the Reformation cause. Calvin chided Farel when at the age of sixty-nine he married a much younger woman. But this did not break their friendship. Calvin even urged restive members of Farel's church to bear with their pastor as the old warrior looked for the comforts of married life. Calvin also extended the hand of friendship to men whose opinion on theological matters was different to his own, amongst them Luther's deputy, Philip Melanchthon'—http://exiledpreacher.blogspot.com/2009/07/humanness-of-john-calvin-by-richard.html.

17 Stauffer, *The Humanness of John Calvin*, 71.

18 See the final section, below.

before him reflected his willingness to value the contributions of others—those he viewed as literary friends. He frequently referred to classic writings and he drew upon wisdom from the past. He did not believe that all new insights were necessarily correct or that he or his generation would be superior in wisdom to others. He was also happy to associate with other peers. Calvin knew better than to seek to re-create all parts of the wheel. He happily drew upon Augustine and built on him.[19] A host of other intellectual mentors to Calvin also laid the foundation for his work.

While at that University of Paris in 1521, Calvin studied rhetoric, logic and arts—common topics for the day—and received a classical education. He was also influenced by the work of the leading Roman Catholic progressive John Major[20]—a towering intellect—and Peter of Spain.[21] He also could not avoid the deluge of intellectual currents swirling through Paris at the time. Protestant professors and students alike, originally called 'Lutherans,' huddled together for protection against persecution, forming bonds of friendship that would endure. Calvin counted both Nicholas and Michael Cop as friends in Paris, with one study inferring: 'Such friendships testify both to the worth and the attractiveness of his character, and contradict the old legend that he was an unsociable misanthrope.'[22]

Calvin, like Melanchthon, was trained in three classic languages. Calvin's method, itself, was also likely shaped by exposure to Melanchthon's *Elemento-*

---

19 One scholar found that, of the sources Calvin quoted in the *Institutes*, Augustine is in a class of his own, being cited 228 times. The next most frequently cited authorities were Gregory I (39 times), Chrysostom (27 times), Bernard (23 times), Ambrose (18 times), Cyprian (14 times). The number of citations from Augustine compares to 9 from Cicero, 7 from Plato, 5 from Aristotle and 3 from Seneca. See Philip Schaff, *History of the Christian Church* (1910, rpr. Grand Rapids: Eerdmans, 1979), 8.539. The Reformation itself was, in the main, a return to Augustinianism and Calvin's thought can hardly be seen as an imitation of previous, secular models. Arthur Custance, *The Sovereignty of Grace* (Philipsburg: P&R, 1979), 27.

20 Some historians see a common pedagogical strain, insofar as it is likely that Calvin, Knox and Buchanan were all former students of John Major. J.T. McNeill, 'Calvinism and European Politics in Historical Perspective' in George L. Hunt (ed.), *Calvinism and the Political Order* (Philadelphia: Westminster, 1965), 15. Douglas Kelly, *The Emergence of Liberty in the Modern World* (Phillipsburg, NJ: P&R, 1992), chapter 1, sees Major's *History of Great Britain* as especially influential on Knox and Buchanan.

21 Alister McGrath, *A Life of John Calvin* (Cambridge, MA: Basil Blackwell, 1990), 34. For a recent evaluation of the place of Calvin, see, also, Alister McGrath, 'Calvin and the Christian Calling,' *First Things* 94 (June/July 1999), 31-35.

22 At Orleans, 'His friends here were Melchior Wolmar, a German schoolmaster and a man of exemplary scholarship and character, François Daniel, François de Connam and Nicolas Duchemin; to these his earliest letters were written.' See the article on John Calvin in the NNDB; http://www.nndb.com/people/507/000094225/

rum Rhetorices Libri Duo, frequently used during his Paris student days.[23] Calvin's humanist education[24] included enrollments at key education institutions at Paris,[25] Orleans, Bourges, Basle, and familiarization with other learning centers of the day. He was exposed to the thought of Erasmus, Le Fevre, Wolmar and Francois Rabelais, a veritable *Who's Who* of Western European education for his day.

Prior to taking up residence in Geneva in 1536, Calvin enjoyed a friendship with the neighboring Lausanne reformer, Peter Viret, extending back almost a decade to their Paris years. Both studied under the same professors at the College de Montaigu,[26] and both had a common friend/mentor in Guilluame Farel.[27] So close were Calvin and Viret that when it came time to return to Geneva from his Strasbourg exile, Calvin asked Viret to prepare the way for his *parousia*.[28] From that point on, whenever mediation was needed in Geneva, Calvin and the leaders often turned to Viret, who eventually settled there in 1559, following his own exile from Lausanne. So close were these friends that both were awarded full citizenship in Geneva on the same day, December 25, 1559.

Among Calvin's correspondents, Viret was one of the most voluminous (with almost 400 extant letters to him). Calvin and Viret would remain close until death took Calvin. Their shared traits of shyness, determination, sensitivity to sufferers and tireless labor are reflected in their correspondence. Their epistolary testimony indicates that they were close enough to give blunt rebukes and correction, while also 'commiserating with each other in their mutual grief

---

23 Zachman, 'Restoring Access,' 212-13. Alexandre Ganoczy also documents the influence of Melanchthon's 1521 *Loci Communes* on Calvin's initial edition of the *Institutes* in 1536 (See Zachman, 'Restoring Access,' 212).

24 The humanism of the day emphasized the classics. *Ad fontes*, or 'back to the sources,' became the rallying cry of the new educational model of the day.

25 McGrath, *A Life*, 21, notes that an inscription on the façade of the Bibliotheque Sainte-Genevieve in Paris lists Calvin, along with Erasmus and others, as an intellectual leader.

26 Jeannine Olson, 'The Friends of John Calvin: The Budé Family' in *Calvin Studies Papers (1997)* (Grand Rapids: CRC Product Services, 1998), 160, has noted the friendship with the brothers Budé (Jean, Francois and Louis) that extended back to Calvin's student days in Paris. She also observes, 'Viewing Calvin among his friends puts him, too, in a positive light. It also reveals how he accomplished as much as he did, for the people with whom he associated helped him with his work, especially his publications. Together they collectively shaped the Reformation from Geneva.'

27 Robert D. Linder, 'Brothers in Christ: Pierre Viret and John Calvin as Soul-mates and Co-laborers in the Work of the Reformation' in *Calvin Studies Papers (1997)*, 141. Linder, also, notes that Calvin broke with Farel after his mentor's marriage to a lady half his age in 1558.

28 The well-chosen term is from Linder, 'Brothers in Christ,' 155. David N. Wiley, 'Calvin's Friendship with Guillaume Farel' in *Calvin Studies Papers (1997)* (Grand Rapids: CRC Product Services, 1998), 192, believes that Calvin wanted Viret to assume the pastorate in Geneva, so that Calvin might stay in Strasbourg.

over the loss of spouses whom they described as beloved partners and companions'.[29] In terms of impact, Viret may even have wielded an influence far greater than previously known in terms of politics; he supported the right to resist magistrates more than any other of Calvin's friends early on and likely persuaded Calvin (if not his disciples) toward that radical idea.[30] Indeed, Robert Linder assessed the friendship to be so strong that to the four statues of Farel, Calvin, Beza, and Knox in Geneva's Parc de Bastions a statue of Viret should be added 'symbolically just behind his good friend John Calvin's left shoulder'.[31]

A Circle of Friends in Strasbourg

Beza's biography is perceptive enough to view this exile to Strasbourg as part of 'Divine providence,' enabling Calvin to train for greater effectiveness while employing his gifts to strengthen another city. After this initial brush with defeat in Geneva, his three years in Strasbourg would prove essential for his future.

Calvin's sojourn in Strasbourg from 1538 to 1541 proved providential, as he later claimed. It was in Strasbourg, a city that had already traveled further down the path of reformation than had Geneva at the time, that Calvin saw the full potential of reformed religion and politics. Under the powerful example of such leading educators of the Reformation as Johann Sturm (1507-1589) and Martin Bucer, Calvin received sound mentoring there—not to mention fellowship. He accompanied Bucer on diplomatic missions, taught in Sturm's freshly minted Academy that became a model for Geneva's own, and observed a harmonious relationship between Church and state.[32] Calvin also pastored 400-500 French Protestant refugees in Strasbourg.[33]

Willem Van 't Spijker has explored the impact of Bucer's friendship on Calvin in and after his time in Strasbourg.[34] Van 't Spijker reports that Calvin had recently rebuked Bucer only about three months prior to his April 1538 exile. Despite such, the magnanimity of Bucer is seen in his encouragement to young

[29] Linder, 'Brothers in Christ,' 150. And they were also close enough to differ on the selection of a new wife after Elizabeth Viret's death (152).

[30] Linder, 'Brothers in Christ,' 154, terms Viret's view 'more advanced and generous' toward the right of resistance than Calvin's. For more on this see Linder, 'Brothers in Christ,' 154, who terms Viret's view 'more advanced and generous' toward the right of resistance than Calvin's. For more on this see Robert Dean Linder, *The Political Ideals of John Calvin* (Geneva: Librairie Droz, 1964); David W. Hall, *Calvin in the Public Square* (Phillipsburg: P&R, 2009), chapter 4.

[31] Linder, 'Brothers in Christ,' 157.

[32] McGrath, *A Life*, 101.

[33] Schaff, *History of the Christian Church*, 8.368.

[34] Willem Van 't Spijker, 'Calvin's Friendship with Bucer: Did It Make Calvin a Calvinist?' in *Calvin Studies Papers (1997)* (Grand Rapids: CRC Product Services, 1998), 170-71.

Calvin to seek shelter in Strasbourg.[35] From that time on, Bucer was a larger influence over Calvin than Farel. Van 't Spijker states,

> A deep friendship developed between them, which continued as long as they lived and which made Calvin always talk about Bucer with deep appreciation, even after Bucer's death. When Calvin was called to return to Geneva in 1541, he consented only on the condition that Bucer was to accompany him to reform the Geneva church together.

Bucer, at least through his commentary on Romans (1536; Calvin's later in 1539), wielded a friendly and lasting influence over Calvin and his *Institutes*.

Just prior to returning to Geneva, Calvin became a citizen of Strasbourg and met a widow, Idelette De Bure, who became his wife. He also inherited Idelette's two daughters by a previous marriage, becoming solely responsible to care for them after her death in 1549. When Idelette died in 1549, Calvin faced an unparalleled grief. His letters to Farel and Viret reveal both his faith in God and his love for her. In this grief observed, those watching developed admiration. He paid high tribute to Idelette after her death, as one who was an excellent companion either in exile, sorrow, or death.

Calvin's exile ended in 1541 when he returned to Geneva 'contrary to [his] desire and inclination'. What motivated him to return to the place where he had been so rudely treated only a few years earlier? 'The welfare of this church . . . lay so near my heart,' he stated, 'that for its sake I would not have hesitated to lay down my life.' Competing with his natural diffidence, the weight of 'solemn and conscientious duty' was greater than his personal comfort. Still, it was with considerable grief, tears, anxiety and distress (not to mention 'a remarkable act of social pragmatism and religious realism'[36]) that he returned to Geneva.

The Company of Pastors

Not only was it venerable, but the Company of Pastors also formed a circle of friends. One of the things that Calvin insisted on upon returning to Geneva was that a presbyterate be formed. Rather than wishing for dictatorial rule, Calvin opted for collegiality in his fraternity of ministers. His *Ecclesiastical Ordinances* called for the establishment of a circle of ministers who would labor together, meeting frequently. Later, when the Academy was formed, this added another guild of friendships.

Calvin was prudent enough to draw on others and his past experiences—even his painful exile—for inspiration for the school. There were three dominant influences on Calvin as he established an enduring university; various leaders from different parts of Protestant Switzerland each made distinct contributions. First, Calvin profited from his friend Peter Viret's previously estab-

[35] Van 't Spijker, 'Calvin's Friendship,' 171.
[36] McGrath, *A Life*, 86.

lished Lausanne Academy, which actually had been founded two decades before Calvin's. In the 1540s, the Lausanne Academy (approximately 40 miles away from Geneva) was the leading French-speaking educational institution, featuring an All-Star faculty. The Lausanne influence on the Genevan Academy increased when some of those professors (Theodore Beza, Francois Hotman, and Peter Viret) came to teach in Geneva after 1559.[37] Rival leaders in Bern even accused Calvin of a 'brain-drain,' conspiring to steal an excellent faculty, but all this happened because of institutional disruption in Lausanne itself. Second, Calvin witnessed another excellent model in Johann Sturm's academy at Strasbourg during his exile from 1538 to 1541. Third, Calvin emphasized the Bible-centered, expository method of Zwingli, elevating the original texts of Scripture to the most authoritative platform possible. Most of the leading voices of the Reformation also became leaders in educational reform in Strasbourg, Zurich, Lausanne and Geneva—surely a local lesson with global implications for a perceptive leader. After its inception in 1558, however, Calvin's Academy soon far outpaced these other centers, and subsequently remained at the forefront of Protestant educational ventures for over two centuries.[38]

Following the St. Bartholomew's Day massacre (1572), Francis Hotman—one of the leading constitutional lawyers on the continent—arrived to teach at the Genevan law school. In addition to him, Denis Godefroy, who influenced Johannes Althusius, also was on the law faculty and was one of two Academy professors to become First Syndic (akin to a mayor) in Geneva while teaching. The presence of these two legal giants, Hotman (from 1573-1578) and Godefroy, gave Calvin's Academy one of the earliest Swiss legal faculties. The medical school, attempted shortly after Calvin's death, was not successfully established until the 1700s.[39] After education at Calvin's Academy, for example, Thomas Bodley returned to Oxford and established the Bodleian Library, perhaps the finest research library in the world. His action followed Calvin's educational mission. These bonds expanded the tentacles of the Reformed movement. The whole was greater than the sum of its parts.

After its founding, the Academy also helped nourish alternative power structures. As early as 1555 Geneva was unique in Switzerland in entrusting the power of excommunication to the Consistory (comprised of local ministers and elders), not the civil magistrate.[40] That was both progressive and restrictive of the civil power. That this structure was at the heart of Calvinism and its view of political reality is seen from the fact that wherever Calvinism spread, other

[37] See Marco Marcacci, *Historie de L'Universite de Geneve 1558-1986* (Geneva: University of Geneva, 1987), 20.

[38] According to Marco Marcacci, *Historie*, 23, under Beza, Geneva was known as a Christian state or a 'bibliocentric Republic'. The pastors and the students played a large role in supporting the city and liberty.

[39] Henry Martyn Baird, *Theodore Beza, The Counsellor of The French Reformation, 1519-1605* (New York: G.P. Putnam's Sons, 1899), 106, 113.

[40] Monter, *Calvin's Geneva*, 138.

'Venerable Companies of Pastors' developed, e.g., in Potiers (1555), Orleans (1557), La Rochelle (1558) and Nimes (1561).[41] Perhaps the influence of the Academy helps explain these similarities. These ecclesiastical governing authorities precluded civil magistrates from acting as the only lawfully ordained governors; power had to be shared with the private sphere. In contrast to other municipalities, one thing that contributed to Geneva's unique adherence to a consistent reformation was the creation of an institution that was rare for her day—the Consistory. The collegial religious body assumed numerous roles (i.e., moral correction, corporate guidance and censorship), which had once been the prerogatives of princely courts.[42] However, it is doubtful that Calvin's ideas would have been exported as quickly or in as sustained fashion without his ground-breaking work in the Genevan Academy.

Calvin even enjoyed amicable relationships with many rulers. The amount of concerted interaction among Calvin, his Company of Pastors, and the Genevan city council may unsettle modern readers. Although there was a purposeful separation of jurisdictions, these reformers did not think it was healthy for the leading spheres of influence, Church and state, to operate in strict isolation. The Genevan Senate and the Council of Two Hundred frequently consulted with the Genevan pastors. At times, the pastors suggested legislation or due processes that were approved by the civil council. While each power was to have 'autonomy of function, the relationship envisaged was one of harmony in which church and state cooperated fruitfully with each other to the glory of God'.[43]

Friends in correspondence and via dedications

It is customary to acknowledge friends in book dedications. It is also true that such dedications can, at times, be aspirational (more than accomplished) for friendships. However, Calvin dedicated the following volumes of his commentaries to these friends: Genesis to Henry (IV), Duke of Navarre, at the age of 10; Psalms to Edward, the 17th Earl of Oxford; Isaiah to Prince Edward VI and Queen Elizabeth of England; Jeremiah to Prince Frederick of Palatine; Ezekiel to Gaspar Coligny (posthumously in 1565 by Beza);[44] Daniel to all pious wor-

---

41 McGrath, *A Life*, 184.

42 See Ronald S. Wallace, *Calvin, Geneva and the Reformation* (Edinburgh: Scottish Academic, 1988), 36.

43 Philip E. Hughes (ed.), *The Register of the Company of Pastors in the Time of Calvin* (Grand Rapids: Eerdmans, 1966), 7.

44 In Beza's preface, he bemoans the rapid loss of many reformed leaders. While Bullinger, Farel and Viret survived, the Reformed church had recently lost Melanchthon, Peter Martyr, Musculus and Hyperius. Beza opined that while Calvin was still alive, these losses ('calamities') were offset. His friendship and admiration is seen, however, as he continues to speak of Calvin as 'that great man, far superior to others . . . and no one can estimate the loss which the Church has suffered, unless those who were eye-witnesses of his labors. For what did that man not achieve? Who was to be compared with him in Meetings, in Lecturing, and in Writings. Who was shorter in

shipers in France; the Minor Prophets, ending with prayers for best wishes to Prince Heric and Gustave's brothers, to King Gustave of Sweden; the Harmony of the Gospels to the Noblemen and Council of Frankfort; the Gospel of John to the Syndics and Council of Geneva (he praises these civic leaders for their hospitality); the Book of Acts to Prince Nicolas Radziwill, Duke of Lithuania, who is commended for withstanding public opposition for his faith; Romans to Simon Grynaeus (Calvin acknowledges that he writes this commentary after Melanchthon and Bucer, not mentioning Luther and Peter Martyr); 1 Corinthians to James of Burgundy; 2 Corinthians to Melchior Wolmar, as an apology for not writing in over 5 years; Galatians to Prince Christopher, Duke of Wirtemberg; 1 Timothy to Edward, Duke of Somerset; Titus to Farel and Viret; and the Catholic Epistles to Edward VI, King of England.

It may be debated, of course, as to how well Calvin knew each of these persons. However, in most of these dedications his familiarity with their situations seems obvious, indicating some level of intimacy. Moreover, the international affinities, at the very least, must be acknowledged.

Earlier, Calvin had dedicated his *The Bondage and Liberation of the Will* (1543) to Melanchthon, hoping to underscore the unity among reformers on this *loci*. Calvin's reasons for this dedication were numerous, including Melanchthon's own professed love for Calvin, as well as Calvin's commendation for Melanchthon's similar teaching, referring to Melanchthon in these halcyon years as a 'most zealous supporter' and 'a distinguished and very brave champion'.[45] Calvin, known for his love for brevity, clarity and simplicity (perhaps going back to Melanchthon's text on rhetoric used in Paris during Calvin's student days), commended Melanchthon similarly for his sharpness, perspicuity and simplicity.

Calvin's friends also included childhood friends who were publishers. One recent study states:

> No description of the international efforts of the Reform can omit to mention the contributions of the printer and scholar Robert Estienne, the printer and martyrologist Jean Crespin . . . or for that matter the lifelong and deliberate use of publication as a weapon on the part of Calvin and Theodore de Beze.[46]

Robert Estienne printed French editions by Calvin's disciples Beza, Hotman and Viret from Geneva. Jean Crispin, a groomsman at Beza's secret marriage,[47] published popular devotional material; moreover, a wide array of educational

teaching, and yet more solid—more happy in solving difficulties, more vehement in reproving, sweeter in consoling, and more correct in confuting errors?" (Calvin's *Commentary on Jeremiah*, 2.xxxix).

45 Zachman, 'Restoring Access,' 211. As early as 1539, Calvin also interpreted Melanchthon's differences with Luther on matters of the eternal decree as a point of contact (215).

46 *Calvinism in Europe*, 201.

47 Schaff, *History of the Christian Church*, 8.851.

material was produced for the burgeoning Academy. Bibles and theological texts flew off Genevan printing presses.

Friends to the end: a vignette from Calvin's death

Before concluding our survey of Calvin's life of friendship, one should pause to note the accolades given to him by contemporaries at this death. Calvin was revered by many in his own lifetime. The plaudits of his peers are an impressive correction to a faulty image.

On April 25, 1564, sensing the nearness of death, Calvin filed his final will. In it he pled his unworthiness ('Woe is me; my ardor and zeal have been so careless and languid, that I confess I have failed innumerable times'[48]) and thanked God for mercy. He appointed his brother, Anthony (whose reputation for divorcing an earlier wife due to adultery had been maliciously used to malign Calvin, himself), to be his heir, and in his will he bequeathed equal amounts to the Boys' School, the poor refugees, and his stepdaughters. He also left part of his meager estate to his nephews and their children. To vindicate Calvin against charges of greed, Beza reiterated what Calvin had stated earlier: 'If some will not be persuaded while I am alive, my death, at all events will show that I have not been a money-making man.'[49] When his will was notarized and brought to the attention of the Senate,[50] members of that council visited the declining Calvin to hear his final farewell personally. Calvin was not viewed by his contemporaries as a foe to be shunned.

Calvin's concluding relationship to the city leaders may be gleaned from his *Farewell Address to the Members of the Little Council.* [51] The members of this council had gone to his home to hear his advice and to express their appreciation for the 'services he has performed for the Seigneurie and for that of which he has faithfully acquitted himself in his duty'. A contemporary recorded his sentiments from April 27, 1564. In that chronicle, the dying Calvin first thanked these leaders for their support, cooperation, and friendship. Although they had engaged in numerous struggles, still their relationship was cordial.

He concluded by encouraging each one to 'walk according to his station and use faithfully that which God gave him in order to uphold this Republic. Regarding civil or criminal trials, one should reject all favor, hate, errors, commendations.' He also advised leaders not to aspire to privilege as if rank was a benefit for governors. 'And if one is tempted to deviate from this,' Calvin added, 'one should resist and be constant, considering the One who established us, asking him to conduct us by his Holy Spirit, and he will not desert us.'

---

[48] Theodore Beza, *Life of John Calvin*—in John Calvin, *Tracts and Treatises on the Reformation of the Church* (Grand Rapids: Eerdmans, 1958), volume 1, cxxv.

[49] Beza, *Life of John Calvin*, cxxxviii.

[50] Beza, *Life*, cxxii, refers to this Little Council as the 'senate'.

[51] Posted at http://capo.org/premise/99/jan/p990110.html.

Calvin's farewell to these political leaders was followed by his *Farewell Address to the Ministers* on April 28, 1564. From his chamber, Calvin reminded them poignantly:

> When I first came to this Church there was almost nothing. We preached and that was all. We searched out idols and burned them, but there was no reformation. Everything was in tumult. . . . I lived here through marvelous battles. I was welcomed with mockery one evening in front of my door by 50 or 60 rifle shots. Do you think that that could disturb a poor, timid student as I am, and as I have always been, I confess?

The farewell address continued to review his Strasbourg exile, the tensions he faced upon return, and some of his experiences with various councils. Calvin concluded by predicting that the battles would not lessen in the days ahead, warning,

> You will be busy after God takes me, even though I am nothing, still I know I prevented three thousand uproars that there might have been in Geneva. But take courage and strengthen yourselves, for God will use this Church and will maintain her, and be sure that God will keep her.

Calvin humbly confessed,

> I say again that all that I did has no value, and that I am a miserable creature. But if I could say what I truly wanted to, that my vices always displeased me, and that the root of the fear of God was in my heart, and you can say that what I was subjected to was good, and I pray that you would forgive me of the bad, but if there is anything good, that you conform yourselves to it and follow it.

He denied that he had written hateful things about others, and he confirmed that the pastors had elected Beza to be his successor. 'Watch that you help him [Beza],' exhorted the dying Calvin, 'for the duty is large and troublesome, of such a sort that he may be overwhelmed under the burden. . . . As for him, I know that he has a good will and will do what he can.' Further, he requested that senators not change anything in Geneva's structures and urged them 'not to innovate—we often ask for novelties—not that I desire for myself by ambition what mine remains, and that we retain it without wanting better, but because all change is hazardous, and sometimes harmful.' The advice from this leader is filled with layer upon layer of wisdom.

When Calvin passed away almost a month after making these comments on May 27, 1564, 'the whole State regretted' the death of 'its wisest citizen . . . a common parent'. He was interred in a common cemetery at Plein Palais, finally finding the anonymity he craved. That, one historian wrote, was characteristic of Calvin in life as in death.[52] The widespread notice and sadness at his death should serve to correct any faulty view that his contemporaries either despised him or underestimated his importance. He was mourned, and his large number of friends

---

[52] Doumergue, *The Character of Calvin*, 173.

would keep his memory alive far more than contemporaries would have predicted. This leader's successes were recognized and celebrated by others.

Conclusion

These kinds of friendship show how reformers strove for unity; at the same time, they did not withhold rebukes. Calvin could severely accuse Melanchthon of being timid, too quick to concede matters that were not adiaphoric, and as unwilling to draw orthodox lines at some *loci*. At the same time, Calvin wrote that, merely due to his reproofs (which Melanchthon gave him full liberty to issue), any construal that he and Luther's lieutenant were 'in opposition greatly wrongs both the one and the other, as well as the whole Church of God'.[53] Yes, these reforming friendships defended one another's reputations and sought to build bridges based on common belief; but, no, they were not always affirming. Still, as late as December 1558, Calvin would write to Melanchthon, urging him to let his zeal burn more brightly (noting that even 'pious friends' were criticizing his timidity) while cheering: 'Whatever happens, let us cultivate with sincerity a fraternal affection towards each other, of which no wiles of Satan shall ever burst asunder the ties.'[54]

Few, if any, social or theological movements will endure if led only by an individual. For lasting impact, a set of ideas must be attractive to more than one or a few. It is, thus, not accidental that faculties or 'schools' often have more longevity than even the finest individual thinkers of a generation. Barth would have little influence if there were no Barthians; the same is true for Luther and Lutherans. Interestingly, few identify themselves as generic Protestants; most of the living strands of Protestantism that thrive and survive anchor themselves in a Luther, a Calvin, or a Zwingli. And those same enduring Protestant traditions seem to have circles of friendship at their fonts.

---

53 Zachman, 'Restoring Access,' 224.

54 Zachman, 'Restoring Access,' 227. Nevertheless, Zachman also notes the deterioration of ecumenicity after Melanchthon's 1560 death, showing that Calvin began to view Lutheranism more negatively until his death—'I am carefully on the watch that Lutheranism gain no ground, not be introduced into France' (228).

CHAPTER 14

Edme Aubertin and the Eucharistic debates in seventeenth-century France

Martin I. Klauber

Edme Aubertin (1595-1652) was a French Reformed pastor and patristics scholar serving first at the Reformed Church at Chartres from 1621 to 1631 when he joined the staff at Charenton and spent the rest of his career there. He is best known for one major work, which he revised throughout his life, *L'Eucharistie de l'ancienne Église* (1633),[1] which was a direct refutation of the Roman Catholic polemicist, Cardinal Jacques-Davy Du Perron and to a lesser extent Cardinal Robert Bellarmine. Many of Aubertin's contemporaries believed he was quite successful in arguing that the Early Church of the first six centuries did not believe or teach the real presence of the doctrine of transubstantiation. One way of gauging the level of his success was that royal officials sought to arrest him for referring to himself as a '*ministre de l'Eglise*,' a term reserved for Roman Catholics, rather than using the phrase '*ministre de la Religion Prétendue Réformée*' when describing his position as a pastor. He was also accused of calling Cardinals Bellarmine and Du Perron enemies of the Church. Of course, these attempts to discredit him actually increased the sales of his books and made him even more popular. On his deathbed, Roman Catholic officials sent in a *curé* to hear his last rights, claiming that he wanted to die in fellowship with the Roman Church. The family tried to kick the priest out forcibly, but finally had to allow him to the bedside of the dying pastor where he reaffirmed his belief in the Reformed faith.[2]

---

1 Edme Aubertin, *L'Eucharistie de l'ancienne église ou Traitté auquel il est monstré quelle a esté durant les six premiers siecles depuis l'institution de l'Eucharisitie, la créance de l'Eglise touchant ce Sacrement: le tout deduit par l'examen des escrits des plus celebres Autheurs qui ont flory pendant ce temps, avec response à tout ce que les Cardinaux Bellarmin, Du Perron, et autres Adversaires de l'Eglise ont allegué sur ceste matiere* (Geneva: Pierre Aubert, 1633).

2 Eugène and Emile Haag, *La France Protestante: ou vies des protestants français qui se sont fait un nom dans l'Histoire depuis la premier temps de la réformation jusqu'à la reconnaissance du principe de la liberté des cultes par l'assemblée nationale* (Paris: Joël Cherbulier, 1857), 1.148-50.

Perron had bested the Huguenot leader, Philippe du Plessis-Mornay at the famed Conference at Fontainebleau, presided over by King Henri IV. The focus of the conference had been to determine the accuracy of Mornay's 5,000 citations from the Church Fathers over the nature of the Eucharist. Mornay claimed that transubstantiation had been a theological innovation, unknown in the Early Church. His use of patristic sources continued the trend that went back to the earliest days of the Reformation. Although the early reformers held to *sola scriptura*, they also believed that they had the testimony of the Fathers to support them and to show that Protestant theology was not new, but could trace its roots back to the New Testament era. Protestants had been using the Church Fathers for support from the early days of the Reformation and Theodore Beza made great use of them in reference to the Lord's Supper at the Colloquy of Poissy. Mornay's defeat at Fontainebleau threatened this narrative and his followers took up the pen to vindicate his honor.[3]

Several of Mornay's successors in the fight to defend the Calvinist view of the Eucharist were pastors at the famed Reformed church at Charenton, just a few miles outside of Paris. According to the Edit of Nantes, it was illegal for the Huguenots to worship within the city, so they constructed a massive 'temple' at Charenton for Parisian Protestants who made the trek to the outskirts of the city. Some 14,000 to 15,000 Huguenots worshipped there regularly. This church boasted some of the most prominent pastor/theologians in all of Europe. The famed Pierre du Moulin preached there, as did Michel le Faucheur, Jean Mestrezat, Jean Daillé and Jean Claude.[4]

What is interesting about this coterie of clergy was that every single one of them listed above composed a major treatise on the Lord's Supper and all of them were targeted, at least in part, directly against Du Perron. Aubertin's work was by all accounts the best of the lot and when Jean Claude (1619-1687) published the last of these works, he expressed his debt to Aubertin and boasted

---

[3] Studies on the conference at Fontainbleau include: Eugène Haag, 'La Célebre Conference de Fontainbleau entre Mornay et le Cardinal Du Perron,' *Bulletin de la Société de l'Histoire du Protestantisme français VI* (1858), 351-61; J.A. Lalot, *Essai historique sur la conférence tenue.à Fontainbleau entre Duplessis Mornay et Duperron le 4 Mai 1600* (Paris, 1889); Mack P. Holt, 'Divisions Within French Calvinism: Philippe Mornay and the Eucharist' in Mack P. Holt (ed.), *Adaptations of Calvinism in Reformation Europe: Essays in Honor of Brian G. Armstrong* (St. Andrews: Ashgate, 2007), 165-78; Michael Wolfe, 'Exegesis as Public Performance: Controversialist Debate and Politics at the Conference of Fontainbleau (1600)' in *Politics and Religion in Early Bourbon France* (New York: Palgrave Macmillan, 2009), 65-85. See also Henri Martin, *Livre Pouvoirs et Société à Paris au XVIIe Siècle (1598-1701)*, 2 volumes (Genève: Droz, 1969); Hugues Daussy, *Les Huguenots et le roi: le combat politique du Philippe Mornay (1572-1600)* (Genève: Droz, 2002).

[4] See Jacques Pannier, *L'Église Réformée de Paris sous Henri IV* (Paris: Librairie Ancienne Honoré Champion, 1911).

that Aubertin had never been and could never be refuted.[5] The son of Jean Daillé exclaimed: 'The great and incomparable work *L'Eucharistie* has outlived all the attacks of the other communion, no one of whom has ventured into open war with it, or, so to speak, dared to meet it *tête-à-tête*.'[6] Remi Snoeks calls it the most important work on the subject during this era. Aubertin's work served as an arsenal for other Protestants as they attempted to battle the Roman Catholics in the Eucharistic debates. It carried an aura of invincibility and would require a monumental effort to even try to refute it.[7]

This work was so influential that the Jansenist Antoine Arnauld specifically criticized Aubertin in his famous *La perpétuité de la foi de l'Église catholique touchant l'eucharistie* (1669) and devoted several chapters of the fifth section to Aubertin. The fact that the Roman Catholics were still trying to discredit Aubertin's arguments decades after he published his work on the Eucharist is a testimony to its enduring quality. It is also particularly interesting that Arnauld admitted that he could not do an adequate job refuting Aubertin point by point, so he limited himself to general derogatory comments without ever getting to the heart of the specific arguments. Arnauld asserted that it would be too difficult to do so and it would require a comprehensive work and a level of expertise that was beyond his ability.[8]

Arnauld was correct in noting that an adequate refutation would require an extensive essay over a thousand pages at least. Having read Aubertin, I would definitely agree so the scope of my essay will have to be restricted. I will focus on recounting the heart of Aubertin's arguments in defining the nature of the Lord's Supper and his treatment of the Eucharistic views of two specific western, ante-Nicene fathers, Justin Martyr and Irenaeus of Lyons. I am choosing these fathers specifically because they were dealing with specific heresies characterized by Docetism. Therefore, it would make sense that they would emphasize the physical character of Christ not only in his life, ministry and passion, but also in his resurrected state including his presence in the elements of the Lord's Supper. If Aubertin could show that these fathers rejected the real presence of Christ, it would go a long way in proving his major point that transubstantiation was a theological innovation.

---

5 Jean Claude, *Réponse au livre de M. Arnaud intitulé la Perpetuité de la foy de l'église catholique touchant l'eucharistie* défenduë (Rouen: Jean Lucas, 1670), 3.

6 Guillaume de Félice, *Histoire des Protestants de France depuis l'origine de la Réformation jusqu'au temps present* (Paris: Librairie protestante, 1850), 353.

7 Remi Snoeks, *L'Argument de tradition dans la controverse eucharistique entre catholiques et réformés français au XVIIe siècle* (Louvain: Publications Universitaires de Louvain, 1951), 133-34.

8 Antoine Arnauld, *La perpétuité de la foy de l'Eglise catholique touchant l'Eucharistie, deffendue contre le live du Sieur Claude, Ministre de Charenton* (Paris: Charles Savreux, 1669), 4.

L'Eucharistie de l'ancienne Église (1629)

The book is divided into three parts. In the first section Aubertin outlined the Scriptural and rational support for his views on the Eucharist. In the second section, he traced the development of the Early Church's practice of the Lord's Supper through the first six centuries. Lastly, he showed how the Roman Catholic position on the Eucharist developed with special emphasis on showing that the doctrine of transubstantiation was an innovation.

The preface to the book was addressed to the Roman Catholic faithful and here Aubertin attempted to convince the readers to have at least an open mind. Comparing the religious discord in France of the seventeenth century to that of the preceding one, Aubertin warned that Roman Catholic distortions and tricks were plaguing the Reformed faith more than ever before. He compared his era to the blooming of flowers that inevitably coincide with the birth of nasty insects that threaten their survival. The threats of his generation, he believed, were more subtle and pernicious than the fire and violence of the era of the Wars of Religion. The sophistries of the Roman apologists were very effective and more 'monstrous' than the overt attacks of the previous century. So the purpose of his work was to expose the falseness of their arguments and to warn the faithful against falling for their ruses. Aubertin compared their approach to the methods of the ancient heretics who attempted to confuse the orthodox by twisting their interpretation of Scripture. One of the main problems was the Roman Catholic view of the lack of clarity of Scripture. Since they argued that one could not truly understand the Bible without the authority of the Church, it would be extremely difficult for the average person to argue against official interpretations and see the clarity of the Reformed view. Aubertin, therefore, asked his Roman Catholic readers at least to listen to his explanation of the historical development of the doctrine of the Eucharist.[9]

Aubertin contended that Du Perron and his supporters held to three principles concerning the ancient church. First, the Church Fathers held a decisive authority on the controversies of the seventeenth-century French Church. Second, one accepts their authority when they are in agreement, seeing it as a kind of crime to depart from their views. Third, their entire beliefs were fully contained in the writings of the Fathers.[10]

He then responded to these three points as follows. First, he asserted that human authorities are not infallible, even the Church Fathers, while Scripture alone is infallible because it was inspired by God. Furthermore, Aubertin did not reject the teachings of the fathers out of hand but revered them as great individuals who by their writings and holy lives provided great light to the Church. One must therefore not reject their teachings lightly, but one must read them with judgment and discretion. He went on to note example after example

9 Aubertin, *L'Eucharistie de l'ancienne église*, 1-2.

10 Aubertin, *L'Eucharistie de l'ancienne église*, 2.

where Church Fathers commented on doctrine and issues that the Roman Catholic hierarchy of the seventeenth century deemed to be incorrect. For example, Jerome stated that the divine right of the priest and the bishops are the same while Bellarmine said he was wrong. Ambrose said that in cases of adultery it was permissible for a man to leave his wife and marry another while Sixtus of Sienna (1520-1569) said no.[11]

The author then went on to list doctrine after doctrine taught by the seventeenth-century Roman Church that the Early Church Fathers clearly did not believe, such as the notion that venial sins need not be confessed, that there is no salvation outside of the pope, that the saints serve as intercessors and are in some way our redeemers before God, that the papacy is the Roman Church and that one must follow it in all matters even when it is in error. He concluded:

> None of the early fathers believed one of these points and so many others that we will produce on the matter of the Eucharist taking citations from the writings of your popes, cardinals, archbishops, bishops, and theologians. And nevertheless you dare to say that the early fathers are for us and that you believe nothing different than they did in method or in fact. Oh ignorance, oh what extreme audacity![12]

He signaled out in particular Cardinal Du Perron whom he labeled a person of refined subtly, with skills that far surpassed his colleagues, who was able to use all kinds of ruses and tricks and sleights of hand to draw people to his positions. Aubertin vowed to examine every single important passage and every objection in order to expose the folly of Du Perron. He pledged not to truncate or misuse any citation from the Church Fathers as Du Plessis-Mornay had been accused of. His desire was to present the teachings of the Early Church in a clear way and he dared anyone to go back to the original texts to check his work.[13]

First of all the proper name of the sacrament is the *Cène du Seigneur* or Lord's Supper. This is what Jerome, among many other patristic figures, called it. The key in calling it the *Cène du Seigneur* was that it was a meal offered to all and to all together. So the word comes from the Greek word *κοινον* meaning 'common'.[14] The second term is the word 'Eucharist,' which was used for a couple of reasons. First the Lord gave thanks while instituting it. Second, when we partake we thank God for his grace, as did Origen who in his *Contra Celsum* said: 'the bread is called Eucharist, and is for us a symbol of the work of grace that he had rendered unto us'.[15] The third term is 'body and blood of Christ' which was a very common name for it. Augustine, among others, said, 'Almost all call the Sacrament his body.' Facundus of Hermiane, the sixth-

---

[11] Aubertin, *L'Eucharistie de l'ancienne église*, 8.

[12] Aubertin, *L'Eucharistie de l'ancienne église*, 15.

[13] Aubertin, *L'Eucharistie de l'ancienne église*, 16.

[14] Aubertin, *L'Eucharistie de l'ancienne église*, 17-18.

[15] Aubertin, *L'Eucharistie de l'ancienne église*, 19.

century African bishop also said: 'We call body and blood of Christ the sacrament of his body and his blood which is consecrated in the bread and in the cup. It is not that the bread is literally his body and the cup his blood, but it is holy because it contains in itself the mystery of his body and his blood."[16]

In the next chapter, the author discussed the meaning of the term 'sacrament'. He explained that the word *μψστεριον*, or 'mystery' in Greek, is the basis for the word 'sacrament' and carries its meaning of a sacred sign or a sign of secret virtue. Aubertin noted that there are three different types of signs. First are the ones that signify by analogy the things they represent such as a portrait, which represents its real subject by colors and shading. The second type confirms the connection such as a wax seal attached to the letters of the king. Lastly are signs that exhibit the thing itself such as the oil which is used in the crowning of a king or when the Old Testament prophets were invested with their office.[17]

Having defined the basic terms for the Lord's Supper, Aubertin went on to explore the writings of the Church Fathers of the first six centuries one by one, noting how they were in agreement with his own view. As I mentioned above, I am limiting my discussion here to Aubertin's treatment of two of them, Justin Martyr and Irenaeus of Lyons.

Justin Martyr

Justin Martyr (100-ca 165 AD) is best known for his treatment of Judaism and his apologetic works written to the emperor Antonius Pius in defense of early Christian practice. The key works in which he discussed the Eucharist were his *First Apology* (c 150 AD) and his *Dialogue with Trypho*. These were some of the earliest statements from the Church Fathers on the topic. The first passage Aubertin discussed was from chapter 46 of the *Dialogue with Trypho*:

> 'And the offering of fine flour, sirs,' I said, 'which was prescribed to be presented on behalf of those purified from leprosy, was a type of the bread of the Eucharist, the celebration of which our Lord Jesus Christ prescribed, in remembrance of the suffering which He endured on behalf of those who are purified in soul from all iniquity, in order that we may at the same time thank God for having created the world, with all things therein, for the sake of man, and for delivering us from the evil in which we were, and for utterly overthrowing principalities and powers by Him who suffered according to His will.'[18]

Aubertin argued that in this passage the offering of the flour was for the purpose of making bread, not the body of Christ. Du Perron had dismissed this

---

[16] Aubertin, *L'Eucharistie de l'ancienne église*, 19-20.

[17] Aubertin, *L'Eucharistie de l'ancienne église*, 17.

[18] Justin Martyr, *Dialogue of Justin with Trypho, a Jew* in A. Roberts, J. Donaldson and A.C. Coxe (eds), *The Ante-Nicene Fathers, Volume I: The Apostolic Fathers with Justin Martyr and Irenaeus* (Buffalo, NY: Christian Literature Company, 1885), 215.

interpretation saying that if the offering of fine flour is the figure of the bread of the Lord's Supper, the Eucharist is then the fulfillment of this offering. Furthermore, how could it be the fulfillment of the sacrifice of flour if it were not itself a sacrifice? This was an absolutely ridiculous explanation according to Aubertin. After all, we have water as the sign of baptism and one cannot have baptism without it.[19]

The second passage from Justin was also from the *Dialogue with Trypho*, interpreting the words of Isaiah 33.16:

> 'Bread shall be given to him, and his water [shall be] sure. Ye shall see the King with glory, and your eyes shall look far off. Your soul shall pursue diligently the fear of the Lord. Where is the scribe? Where are the counselors? Where is he that numbers those who are nourished,—the small and great people? With whom they did not take counsel, nor knew the depth of the voices, so that they heard not. The people who are become depreciated, and there is no understanding in him who hears.' Now it is evident, that in this prophecy [allusion is made] to the bread which our Christ gave us to eat, in remembrance of His being made flesh for the sake of His believers, for whom also He suffered; and to the cup which He gave us to drink, in remembrance of His own blood, with giving of thanks. [20]

Du Perron had commented that one of the great mysteries of the Eucharist was that, like the incarnation, the heavenly bread was made flesh and thereby became is the true image of the incarnation. Therefore, the earthly bread is made flesh just like the heavenly word is made flesh. Aubertin contended that Justin meant that the bread of the Eucharist is made a memorial of the body of the Lord, which he gave for us in his passion. The bread is a sign of the passion but not the passion itself. There is a difference between making the bread a memorial and a sign of his body and making it truly and properly his body. Therefore, Du Perron was mixing the sign with the thing signified. Aubertin went on to cite Augustine from his *Reply to Faustus* who said,

> Before the coming of Christ, the flesh and blood of this sacrifice were foreshadowed in the animals slain; in the passion of Christ the types were fulfilled by the true sacrifice; after the ascension of Christ, this sacrifice is commemorated in the sacrament."[21]

It would be ridiculous, therefore, to argue that the image is the image of itself. Du Perron then raised the example of manna or the rod of Aaron that were preserved in the Ark of the Covenant. These were actual things and not signs. Au-

[19] Aubertin, *L'Eucharistie de l'ancienne église*, 57-60.

[20] Justin Martyr, *Dialogue of Justin with Trypho*, 234.

[21] Augustine of Hippo, *Reply to Faustus the Manichæan* in P. Schaff (ed.), *A Select Library of the Nicene and Post-Nicene Fathers of the Christian Church, First Series, Volume IV: St. Augustine: The Writings against the Manichaeans and against the Donatists* (Buffalo, NY: Christian Literature Company, 1887), 262.

bertin responded that it was not for the purpose of providing an object of worship, but to remind the people of the faithfulness of God.[22]

The third passage comes from Justin's *First Apology*:

> And on the day called Sunday, all who live in cities or in the country gather together to one place, and the memoirs of the apostles or the writings of the prophets are read, as long as time permits; then, when the reader has ceased, the president verbally instructs, and exhorts to the imitation of these good things. Then we all rise together and pray, and, as we before said, when our prayer is ended, bread and wine and water are brought, and the president in like manner offers prayers and thanksgivings, according to his ability, and the people assent, saying Amen; and there is a distribution to each, and a participation of that over which thanks have been given, and to those who are absent a portion is sent by the deacons. And they who are well to do, and willing, give what each thinks fit; and what is collected is deposited with the president, who succours the orphans and widows, and those who, through sickness or any other cause, are in want, and those who are in bonds, and the strangers sojourning among us, and in a word takes care of all who are in need. But Sunday is the day on which we all hold our common assembly, because it is the first day on which God, having wrought a change in the darkness and matter, made the world; and Jesus Christ our Saviour on the same day rose from the dead. For He was crucified on the day before that of Saturn (Saturday); and on the day after that of Saturn, which is the day of the Sun, having appeared to His apostles and disciples, He taught them these things, which we have submitted to you also for your consideration.[23]

Aubertin saw this as a simple explanation of the common celebration of the Lord's Supper in the Early Church where the people gathered on Sunday for the preaching of the words of God and the giving of prayers and thanksgiving. All who attended participated and the bread and the cup were distributed to all, simply and without elevation, adoration, completely conforming to the Reformed liturgy of the seventeenth century.[24]

Du Perron had argued that Justin had affirmed simply that the bread was not common bread but the flesh of Christ and did not mention specifically that the bread was merely a sign or a figure. Given the fact that the work was an apology written to the emperor to counter the charge that the early Christians were cannibals, it seemed strange to Du Perron that Justin would not have clearly stated here that the elements were merely figures. Aubertin responded that one must look at this particular citation in the context of the entire *Apology*. In the section just preceding the citation above Justin declared:

---

22 Aubertin, *L'Eucharistie de l'ancienne église*, 60-61.

23 Justin Martyr, *The First Apology of Justin* in A. Roberts, J. Donaldson & A.C. Coxe (eds), *The Ante-Nicene Fathers, Volume I: The Apostolic Fathers with Justin Martyr and Irenaeus* (Buffalo, NY: Christian Literature Company, 1885), 186.

24 Aubertin, *L'Eucharistie de l'ancienne église*, 62.

> For not as common bread and common drink do we receive these; but in like manner as Jesus Christ our Saviour, having been made flesh by the Word of God, had both flesh and blood for our salvation, so likewise have we been taught that the food which is blessed by the prayer of His word, and from which our blood and flesh by transmutation are nourished, is the flesh and blood of that Jesus who was made flesh.[25]

It would not make sense to say that our bodies are nourished if we were eating actual flesh and drinking actual blood. Therefore, he must have meant that the elements were merely signs. Otherwise the entire purpose of the *Apology* would be in vain. Furthermore, why would he write the *Apology* at all if he did not want to dispel the charges of cannibalism?[26]

Irenaeus of Lyons

Aubertin then directed his attention to Irenaeus of Lyons (ca. 130-202 AD) who wrote about the Eucharist in the context of his attack against various gnostic and docetic heresies, most prominently those of Valentinus and Marcion. The first passage of discussion is from *Against Heresies* where the author was attempting to refute the heterodox idea that the father is different from the creator:

> For some, by maintaining that the Father is different from the Creator, do, when they offer to Him what belongs to this creation of ours, set Him forth as being covetous of another's property, and desirous of what is not His own. Those, again, who maintain that the things around us originated from apostasy, ignorance, and passion, do, while offering unto Him the fruits of ignorance, passion, and apostasy, sin against their Father, rather subjecting Him to insult than giving Him thanks. But how can they be consistent with themselves, [when they say] that the bread over which thanks have been given is the body of their Lord, and the cup His blood, if they do not call Himself the Son of the Creator of the world, that is, His Word, through whom the wood fructifies, and the fountains gush forth, and the earth gives 'first the blade, then the ear, then the full corn in the ear'.
>
> Then, again, how can they say that the flesh, which is nourished with the body of the Lord and with His blood, goes to corruption, and does not partake of life? Let them, therefore, either alter their opinion, or cease from offering the things just mentioned. But our opinion is in accordance with the Eucharist, and the Eucharist in turn establishes our opinion. For we offer to Him His own, announcing consistently the fellowship and union of the flesh and Spirit. For as the bread, which is produced from the earth, when it receives the invocation of God, is no longer common bread, but the Eucharist, consisting of two realities, earthly and heaven-

---

25 Justin Martyr, *The First Apology of Justin*, 185.

26 Aubertin, *L'Eucharistie de l'ancienne église*, 63.

ly; so also our bodies, when they receive the Eucharist, are no longer corruptible, having the hope of the resurrection to eternity.[27]

In this passage, Irenaeus was able to use the Eucharist as evidence in favor of the physical resurrection of Christ and of believers. Aubertin concluded that this passage teaches three things. First, the Eucharist is an offering to God not of the literal body and blood of Christ, but of the fruits of the earth. Second, the Lord honored the symbols (bread and wine) by calling them his body and blood, but without changing their nature. Third, the elements are not consecrated when the priest utters the words of institution, but only through prayer and the will of God himself.[28] Aubertin also objected to Du Perron's idea that after the consecration of the elements, they are a terrestrial thing that is the body of Christ and not the sacramental sign. By the heavenly reality it would mean the spirit of Christ rather than the body of Christ. If this were true it would follow that the Eucharist would not consist of a sacramental sign at all, which he believed absurd. The more obvious and correct reading would be to say that the Eucharist consists of two aspects. The first would be terrestrial, whereby the bread without changing its earthly substance is the sacrament of a heavenly thing. It could also mean, as Bellarmine asserted, that the bread is made both a heavenly and an earthly thing at the same time. In this case the bread is received by the faithful who are of the earth, but who are also heavenly because they are born of the Spirit. Aubertin preferred the former reading arguing that if the earthly thing is the body of Christ and the heavenly thing is the spirit of Christ, it would mean that the bread is changed into the body of Christ and also into the divinity of Christ, which makes no sense.

Du Perron contended that the context of *Against Heresies* was a refutation of the Valentinian idea that the body of Christ was really a heavenly and not an earthly body and that the Virgin Mary was a simple vessel through which Christ passed without inheriting anything from her. So it would make sense that when Irenaeus spoke of the body of Christ he would emphasize its earthly qualities. For Aubertin this line of argumentation was difficult but not impossible to resolve. First, just because Irenaeus was attempting to show elsewhere that the body of Christ was a physical body does not necessarily mean that in this passage he was referring to the elements of the Eucharist and not the actual body of Christ. He agued that this same earthly flesh communicated in the Eucharist to us who are of a similar substance, could also communicate Christ's immortality to the believer.[29]

The next passage is also from Irenaeus's *Against Heresies*:

---

[27] Irenaeus of Lyons, *Irenæus against Heresies* in A. Roberts, J. Donaldson & A.C. Coxe (eds), *The Ante-Nicene Fathers, Volume I: The Apostolic Fathers with Justin Martyr and Irenaeus* (Buffalo, NY: Christian Literature Company, 1885), 486.

[28] Aubertin, *L'Eucharistie de l'ancienne église*, 66.

[29] Aubertin, *L'Eucharistie de l'ancienne église*, 67.

> But if these indeed do not attain salvation, then neither did the Lord redeem us with His blood, nor is the cup of the Eucharist the communion of His blood, nor the bread which we break the communion of His body. For blood can only come from veins and flesh, and whatsoever else makes up the substance of man, such as the Word of God was actually made. By His own blood he redeemed us, as also His apostle declares, 'In whom we have redemption through His blood, even the remission of sins.' And as we are His members, we are also nourished by means of the creation (and He Himself grants the creation to us, for He causes His sun to rise, and sends rain when He wills). He has acknowledged the cup (which is a part of the creation) as His own blood, from which He bedews our blood; and the bread (also a part of the creation) He has established as His own body, from which He gives increase to our bodies.[30]

Here Aubertin pointed out that when Irenaeus said that the human body is sustained by the bread and the wine, which are created things, he meant that it is the bread and the wine which nourish the body. Otherwise, to say that the human body is nourished by eating the body and the blood would not make any sense.

We have to keep in mind, he reasoned, that Irenaeus was primarily countering the Valentinian belief that the creator and the father could not be one and the same being. Since the creator was the ultimate source of the fruits of the earth, the bread and the wine, the signs of the Lord's Supper would support the view that the creator and the father were one and the same.[31] Aubertin argued that Irenaeus viewed the Eucharist in two ways. The first was the actual elements, the fruits of the earth that nourish the body. The second would be for spiritual nourishment.[32] Furthermore, if the bread and the wine are symbols of the reality of Christ's flesh and blood, that would be a solid response to the Gnostic heretics who wanted to diminish the reality of Christ's physical body. The symbols would point to something real and physical.[33]

What we find in these brief selections of only a couple of Church Fathers is the difficulty of coming to a unanimous conclusion about their respective teaching on the Eucharist. Both sides were guided by their own rigid confessional views and there was no easy way to reconcile the two. Aubertin believed he had righted the ship from the Reformed side and that Du Perron had sunk at Fontainebleau. At the very least, he set the stage for the theological debates that would follow. The battle between the Jansenists Antoine Arnauld and Pierre Nicole and Aubertin's colleague Jean Claude, was particularly interesting because the Jansenists had two goals. One was to refute Claude, but a second was to prove that they were good Roman Catholics rather than the crypto-Calvinists that many of their Jesuit adversaries believed.

30 Irenaeus of Lyons, *Irenæus against Heresies*, 528.
31 Aubertin, *L'Eucharistie de l'ancienne église*, 67.
32 Aubertin, *L'Eucharistie de l'ancienne église*, 83.
33 Aubertin, *L'Eucharistie de l'ancienne église*, 85.

BIBLIOGRAPHY

PRIMARY WORKS

à Kempis, Thomas, *The Imitation of Christ* (translated by Aloysius Croft and Harold Bolton; Mineola, NY: Dover, 2003).

—. *On the Passion of Christ: According to the Four Evangelists: Prayers and Meditations* (translated by Joseph N. Tylenda; San Francisco: Ignatius, 2004).

Anselm, *Anselmi Cantuariensis In omnes Pauli Apostoli Epistolas enarrationes* (Coloniae: Gennepaeum, 1545).

Aquinas, Thomas, *Commentary on the Epistle to the Hebrews* (translated by Chrysostom Baer and O. Praem; South Bend, IN: St. Augustine's Press, 2006).

—. 'Expositio super Epistolam S. Pauli Apostoli ad Hebraeos.' In *Divi Thomæ Aquinatis ex ordine prædicatorum doctoris angelici In omnes d. Pauli Apostoli epistolas commentaria* (Leodii: Dessain, 1858), 3.191–406.

—. *Summa Theologica* (translated by the Fathers of the English Dominican Province; EWTN Online, 1947 Benziger Brothers); hypertext version edited by New Advent, 1995, 1996): http://www.newadvent.org/summa.

Arnauld, Antoine, *La perpétuité de la foy de l'Eglise catholique touchant l'Eucharistie, deffendue contre le live du Sieur Claude, Ministre de Charenton* (Paris: Charles Savreux, 1669).

Aubertin, Edme, *L'Eucharistie de l'ancienne église ou Traitté auquel il est monstré quelle a esté durant les six premiers siecles depuis l'institution de l'Eucharisitie, la créance de l'Eglise touchant ce Sacrement: le tout deduit par l'examen des escrits des plus celebres Autheurs qui ont flory pendant ce temps, avec response à tout ce que les Cardinaux Bellarmin, Du Perron, et autres Adversaires de l'Eglise ont allegué sur ceste matiere* (Geneva: Pierre Aubert, 1633).

Augustine, St. Bishop of Hippo, 'Confessions.' In *A Select Library of Nicene and Post-Nicene Fathers of the Christian Church*, series 1, volume 3 (edited and translated by Philip Schaff and Henry Wace; Grand Rapids: Christian Classics Ethereal Library, 2002). Online: http://www.ccel.org/ccel/augustine/confess.i_1.html

—. *Enarrationes in Psalmos* Patrologiae Latina [PL], volumes 36–37 (edited by J.P. Migne; Paris: Migne, 1865).

—. 'Enchiridion.' In *Opera Omnia*. Patrologiae Latina [PL] (edited by J.P. Migne; Paris: Migne, 1841), 40.231–288.

—. 'On the Catechizing of the Uninstructed.' In *A Select Library of Nicene and Post-Nicene Fathers of the Christian Church*, series 1, volume 3 (edited and translated by Philip Schaff and Henry Wace; Grand Rapids: Christian Classics Ethereal Library, 2002). Online: http://www.ccel.org/ccel/schaff/npnf103.iv.iii.html

—. 'John's Gospel.' In *A Select Library of Nicene and Post-Nicene Fathers of the Christian Church*, series 1, volume 7 (edited and translated by Philip Schaff and Henry Wace; Grand Rapids: Christian Classics Ethereal Library, 2002). Online: http://www.ccel.org/ccel/schaff/npnf107.iii.i.html

—. 'On the Good of Marriage.' In *A Select Library of Nicene and Post-Nicene Fathers of the Christian Church*, series 1, volume 3 (edited and translated by Philip Schaff and Henry Wace; Grand Rapids: Christian Classics Ethereal Library, 2002). Online: http://www.ccel.org/ccel/schaff/npnf103.v.ii.html

—. *Reply to Faustus the Manichæan* in P. Schaff (ed.), *A Select Library of the Nicene and Post-Nicene Fathers of the Christian Church, First Series, Volume IV: St. Augustine: The Writings against the Manichaeans and against the Donatists* (Buffalo, NY: Christian Literature Company, 1887).

Beza, Theodore, *Life of John Calvin*—contained in John Calvin, *Tracts and Treatises on the Reformation of the Church*, volume 1 (Grand Rapids: Eerdmans, 1958).

Bromiley, G.W., *Zwingli and Bullinger* (Philadelphia: Westminster, 1953).

Bugenhagen, Johannes, *Annotationes Io. Bugenhagij Pomerani in epistolas Pauli ad Galatas, Ephesios, Philippenses, Colossenses, Thessalonicenses primam et secundam, Timotheum primam et secundam, Titum, Philemonem, Hebraeos* (2nd ed. Basel: Adam Petri, 1525).

Bullinger, Heinrich, *A Confvtation Of the Popes Bull which was published more then two yeres agoe against Elizabeth the most gracious Queene of England, Fraunce, and Ireland, and against the noble Realme of England: together with a defence of the sayd true Christian Queene, and of the whole Realme of England.* London: John Day, 1572; STC (2nd ed.) / 4044. [Database online—subscription only]: Early English Books Online, http://eebo.chadwyck.com [13 August 2008].

—. *In piam et eruditam Pauli ad Hebraeos Epistolam* (Zurich: Christoph Froschauer, 1532).

Calvin, John, *A Harmony of the Gospels Matthew, Mark and Luke* (translated by A.W. Morrison; Calvin's New Testament Commentaries, volume 3; Grand Rapids: Eerdmans, 1972).

—. *Commentaries on the Book of the Prophet Isaiah*, 3 volumes (translated by William Pringle; Grand Rapids: Baker, 1979).

—. *Commentaries on the Catholic Epistles* (translated by John Owen; Grand Rapids: Eerdmans, 1948).

—. *Commentarius in Epistolam ad Hebraeos* (edited by T.H.L. Parker; Ioannis Calvini Opera Omnia, Series II, Opera Exegetica Veteris et Novi Testamenti, volume 19; Geneva: Droz, 1996). [Also COE II.19]

—. *Commentary on the Epistle of Paul the Apostle to the Romans* (translated and edited by John Owen; Grand Rapids: Baker, 1979.)

—. *Commentary on the Last Four Books of Moses Arranged in the Form of a Harmony* (edited and translated by Charles William Bingham; Grand Rapids: Baker, 2003).

—. *Concerning Scandals* (1550) (translated by John W. Fraser; Edinburgh: Saint Andrew Press, 1978).
—. *First Corinthians* (*Calvin's Commentaries* 20; edited and translated by John Pringle; Grand Rapids: Baker, 2003).
—. *Genesis* (edited and translated by John King; Grand Rapids: Baker, 2003).
—. *Institutes of Christian Religion*. Library of Christian Classics, vol. 21 (translated by Ford Lewis Battles, edited by John T. McNeill; Philadelphia: Westminster, 1960).
—. *Institutes of the Christian Religion* in P. Barth and G. Niesel (eds), *Joannis Calvini Opera Selecta*, volume 3 (Monachii in aedibus, Chr Kaiser, 1928).
—. *Ioannis Calvini Opera quae supersunt omnia*. 59 volumes (edited by G. Baum, E. Cunitz and E. Reuss; Brunswick & Berlin: C.A. Schwetschke, 1863-1900).
—. *Isaiah* (*Calvin's Commentaries* 8; edited and translated by William Pringle; Grand Rapids: Baker, 2003).
—. *John Calvin's Sermons on the Ten Commandments* (translated and edited by Benjamin W. Farley; Grand Rapids: Baker, 1980).
—. *Letters of John Calvin* (edited by Jules Bonnet; Philadelphia: Presbyterian Board of Publication, 1858)
—. *Letters of John Calvin* (Carlisle, PA: Banner of Truth, 1980).
—. *Philippians* (*Calvin's Commentaries* 21; edited and translated by William Pringle; Grand Rapids: Baker, 2003).
—. *Psalms 1-33* (*Calvin's Commentaries* 4; edited and translated by James Anderson; Grand Rapids: Baker Books, 2003).
—. *Psalms 93-150* (*Calvin's Commentaries* 6; edited and translated by James Anderson; Grand Rapids: Baker, 2003).
—. Reply to Sadoleto. In John C. Olin (ed.), *A Reformation Debate. Sadoleto's Letter to the Genevans and Calvin's Reply* (New York: Fordham University Press, 2000).
—. *Romans* (*Calvin's Commentaries* 19; edited and translated by John Owen; Grand Rapids: Baker, 2003).
—. *Sermons on Isaiah's Prophecy on the death and passion of Christ* (translated and edited by T.H.L. Parker; London: James Clarke, 1956).
—. *Sermons on the Beatitudes* (translated by Robert White; Edinburgh: Banner of Truth, 2006).
—*Sermons on the Epistle to the Ephesians* (translated by Arthur Golding; revised by Leslie Rawlinson and S.M. Houghton; Edinburgh: Banner of Truth Trust, 1973).
—. *The Acts of the Apostles*, volume 2 (translated by John W. Frazer; Calvin's New Testament Commentaries, volume 7; Grand Rapids: Eerdmans, 1979).
—. *The Epistle of Paul the Apostle to the Hebrews and the First and Second Epistles of St Peter* (edited by David W. Torrance and Thomas F. Torrance; translated by William B. Johnston; Calvin's New Testament Commentaries, volume 12; Grand Rapids: Eerdmans, 1994).

—. *The Epistles of Paul to the Romans and Thessalonians* (translated by R. Mackenzie; Calvin's New Testament Commentaries, volume 8; Grand Rapids: Eerdmans, 1973).

—. *The First Epistle of Paul to the Corinthians* (translated by John W. Fraser; Calvin's New Testament Commentaries, volume 9; Grand Rapids: Eerdmans, 1979).

—. *Theological Treatises* (translated by J.K.S. Reid; London: SCM, 1954).

—. *Tracts and Treatises on Reformation of the Church*, 3 volumes (translated and edited by Henry Beveridge; Edinburgh: Calvin Translation Society, 1851).

Calvinism in Europe, 1540-1610: A Collection of Documents (translated and edited by Alistair Duke, Gillian Lewis and Andrew Pettegree; Manchester: Manchester University Press, 1992).

Chrysostom, John, 'Homiliae XXXIV in Epistolam ad Hebraeos.' In *Tou en hagiois patros hēmōn Iōannou, Archiepiskopou Kōnstantinoupoleōs, tou Chrysostomou, ta ehyriskomena panta* (edited by J.P. Migne; translated by Mutianus Scholasticus; Patrologia Graece, volume 63; Paris: Migne, 1862). [Also PG 63]

—. *Homilies on the Gospel of St. John and the Epistle to the Hebrews* (edited by Philip Schaff; translated by T. Keble and Frederic Gardiner; Nicene and Post-Nicene Fathers First Series, volume 14; Peabody: Hendrickson, 1994). [Also NPNF[1]]

Claude, Jean, *Réponse au livre de M. Arnaud intitulé la Perpetuité de la foy de l'église catholique touchant l'eucharistie* défenduë (Rouen: Jean Lucas, 1670).

Cyril of Alexandria, 'Cyrilli Archiepiscopi Alexandrini Commentariorum in Epistolam Ad Hebraeos Fragmenta Quot Reperiri Potuerunt.' In *Sancti Patris Nostri Cyrilli Archiepiscopi Alexandrini Opera* (edited by P.E. Pusey; Oxford: Clarendon, 1872), 3.362–425.

Denis the Carthusian, 'In Epistolam ad Hebraeos.' In *In Omnes Beati Pauli Epistolas Commentaria* (Cologne: Peter Quentel, 1538).

Dorman, Thomas, *A Proufe of Certeyne Articles in Religion, Denied by M. Ivell* (Antwerp: Printed by John Latius, 1564; reprint, Ilkley, England: Scolar Press, 1976).

Erasmus, Desiderius. 'Annotationes in Epistolam Pauli Ad Hebraeos'. In *Novum Instrumentum Omne*, 584–601 (Basel: Froben, 1516).

—. 'Annotationes in Epistolam Pauli Ad Hebraeos'. In *Novum Testamentum*, 561–589 (3rd ed. Basel: Froben, 1522).

—. *In Epistolam ad Hebraeos paraphrasis* (Basel: Froben, 1523).

—. *Paraphrases Erasmi Roterodami in omnes epistolas Pauli germanas, & in omnes canonicas* (Basel: Froben, 1521).

Eusebius, *Church History* (Grand Rapids: Philip Schaff, 1890); NPNF[2] (Vol. 1) [Database online]: Christian Classics Ethereal Library, http://www.ccel.org [10 September 2009].

Ibn Ezra, Abraham ben Meïr, *Abraham Ibn Ezra's Commentary on the First Book of Psalms* (translated by H. Norman Strickman; Boston: Academic Studies Press, 2009).

Irenaeus of Lyons, *Irenæus against Heresies*. In A. Roberts, J. Donaldson & A.C. Coxe (eds), *The Ante-Nicene Fathers, Volume I: The Apostolic Fathers with Justin Martyr and Irenaeus* (Buffalo, NY: Christian Literature Company, 1885).

Jewel, John, *The Works of John Jewel* (edited by John Ayre: 4 vols: Cambridge: The University Press, 1845-50).

—. *An Apology of the Church of England* (translated by Lady Ann Bacon; edited by John Booty; New York: Church Publishing, 2002).

Karlstadt, Andreas, 'Against the Old and New Papistic Masses'. In *The Eucharistic Pamphlets of Andreas Bodenstein von Karlstadt* (translated by Amy Nelson Burnet; Kirksville: Truman State University Press, 2011), 110-115.

—. 'A Review of Some of the Chief Articles of Christian Doctrine in which Dr. Luther Brings Karlstadt under Suspicion through False Accusation and Calumny'. In *Karlstadt's Battle With Luther: Documents in a Liberal-Radical Debate* (translated by Ronald J. Sider; Eugene: Wipf and Stock, 2001), 127-138.

—. 'On Both Forms in the Holy Mass'. In *The Eucharistic Pamphlets of Andreas Bodenstein von Karlstadt* (translated by Amy Nelson Burnet; Kirksville: Truman State University Press, 2011), 49-77.

—. 'On the Priesthood and Sacrifice of Christ'. In *The Eucharistic Pamphlets of Andreas Bodenstein von Karlstadt* (translated by Amy Nelson Burnet; Kirksville: Truman State University Press, 2011), 89-109.

Kimhi, David, *Rabbi Davidis Kimhhi Commentarii in psalmos Davidis* (translated by Ambrosio Ianvier; Paris: Billaine, 1666).

—. *The Commentary of David Kimhi on the Fifth Book of the Psalms, CVII-CL* (edited by Jacob Bosniak; New York: Jewish Theological Seminary of America, 1954).

—. *The Commentary of Rabbi David Kimḥi on Psalms CXX-CL*, University of Cambridge Oriental Publications 22 (translated by Joshua Baker and Ernest W. Nicholson; Cambridge: CUP, 1973).

—.*The Longer Commentary of R. David Ḳimḥi on the First Book of Psalms (I-X, XV-XVII, XIX, XXII, XXIV)*, Translations of Early Documents IIII, volume 6 (translated by R.G. Finch; New York: Macmillan, 1919).

Lefèvre d'Étaples, Jacques, *Epistola ad Hebraeos* (Paris: Stephanus, 1512).

—. *Quincuplex Psalterium*, 1513 (reprint; Geneva: Librairie Droz, 1979).

Luther, Martin, 'Confession Concerning Christ's Supper'. In *Luther's Works* (translated by Robert H. Fischer; Minneapolis: Fortress, 1961), 37.161-372.

—. *De Servo Arbitrio* in *D. Martin Luthers Werke: Kritische Gesamtausgabe* [WA], vol. 18 (Weimar: Hermann Böhlaus Nachfolger, 1908).

—. *Lectures on Galatians 1535, chapters 1-4* in *Luther's Works* [*LW*], vol.26 (edited by Jaroslav Pelikan and Walter A. Hansen; St. Louis: Concordia, 1963).
—. *Lectures on Isaiah, chapters 1-39* in *Luther's Works* [*LW*], vol.16 (edited by Jaroslav Pelikan; St. Louis: Concordia, 1969).
—. *Lectures on Isaiah, chapters 40-66* in *Luther's Works* [*LW*], vol.17 (edited by Hilton C. Oswald; St. Louis: Concordia, 1972).
—. *Lectures on Titus, Philemon, and Hebrews* in *Luther's Works* [*LW*], vol. 29 (edited by Jaroslav Pelikan and Walter A. Hansen; St. Louis: Concordia / Philadelphia: Fortress, 1968).
—. *Letters, III*, WA, vol. 50 (edited by Helmut T. Lehmann: Philadelphia: Fortress, 1974).
—. *Luther: Letters of Spiritual Counsel* (edited and translated by Theodore G. Tappert; Vancouver: Regent College, 2003).
—. *Luther's Works* [*LW*] (edited by Jeroslav Pelikan [vols. 1-30] and Helmut T. Lehmann [vols. 31-55]; Philadelphia: Fortress, 1972).
—. *Martin Luther, Selections from his Writings* (edited by John Dillenberger; New York: Anchor, 1962).
—. *Sermons of Martin Luther*, vol. 1 (edited and translated by Eugene F.A. Klug, Erwin W. Koehlinger, James Lanning, Everette W. Meier, Dorothy Schoknecht and Allen Schuldheiss; Grand Rapids: Baker, 1996.)
—. 'That These Words of Christ, "This Is My Body", etc., Still Stand Firm Against the Fanatics' (translated by Robert H. Fischer) in *Luther's Works* (Minneapolis: Fortress, 1961), 37.13-150.
—. 'The Adoration of the Sacrament' (translated by Abdel Ross Tentz) in *Luther's Works* (Minneapolis: Fortress, 1959), 36.275-305.
—. *The Babylonian Captivity of the Church* in *Three Treatises* (translated by A.T.W. Steinhäuser; Minneapolis: Fortress, 1990), 123-260.
—. *The Bondage of the Will* in *Luther's Works* [*LW*], vol. 33, *Career of the Reformer: III* (edited by Philip S. Watson, translated by E. Gordon Rupp; Philadelphia: Fortress, 1972).
—. 'The Estate of Marriage' (translated by Walther I. Brandt; University of Oregon, no date). Online: http://pages.uoregon.edu/dluebke/Reformations441/LutherMarriage.htm
—. *The Freedom of a Christian* in *Three Treatises* (translated by W.A. Lambert; Minneapolis: Fortress, 1990), 262-316.
—. *To the Christian Nobility of the German Nation* in *Three Treatises* (translated by Charles M. Jacobs; Minneapolis: Fortress, 1990), 7-112.
Martyr, Justin, *Dialogue of Justin with Trypho, a Jew*. In A. Roberts, J. Donaldson and A.C. Coxe (eds), *The Ante-Nicene Fathers, Volume I: The Apostolic Fathers with Justin Martyr and Irenaeus* (Buffalo, NY: Christian Literature Company, 1885).

—. *The First Apology of Justin.* In A. Roberts, J. Donaldson & A.C. Coxe (eds), *The Ante-Nicene Fathers, Volume I: The Apostolic Fathers with Justin Martyr and Irenaeus* (Buffalo, NY: Christian Literature Company, 1885).

Melanchthon, Philip, *A Melanchthon Reader* (translated by Ralph Keen; New York: Peter Lang, 1988).

Meyer, Sebastian, *In apocalypsim Johannis Apostoli* (Zürich: Froschouer, 1539).

Nicholas of Lyra, *Textus Biblie cum Glossa Ordinaria et Expositione Lyre Litterali*, vol. 6 (Basel: Froben & Petri, 1508).

Oecolampadius, Johannes, *In Epistolam ad Hebraeos, ut ex ore praelegentis exceptae, per quosdam ex auditoribus digestae sunt* (Strassburg: Mathiam Apiarius, 1534).

Pellikan, Konrad, 'Commentarium in Epistolam D. Pauli Apostoli ad Hebraeos'. In *Commentaria Bibliorum*, vol. 7 (Zürich: Christoph Froschauer, 1539), 608-680.

Pratensis, Felix, *Biblia Rabbinica* (Venice: Bomberg, 1517).

Rashi. *Rashi's Commentary on Psalms 1-89 (Books I-III)*, South Florida Studies in the History of Judaism 161 (translated by Mayer I. Gruber; Atlanta: Scholars Press, 1998).

Tertullian, 'Against Marcion.' In *The Ante-Nicene Fathers: Translations of the Writings of the Fathers Down to AD 325* (*ANF*), vol. 3 (edited by Alexander Roberts and James Donaldson; Grand Rapids: Christian Classics Ethereal Library, 2002). online: http://www.ccel.org/ccel/schaff/anf03.v.html

—. 'Apologetic: On Idolatry.' In *The Ante-Nicene Fathers: Translations of the Writings of the Fathers Down to AD 325* (*ANF*), vol. 3 (edited by Alexander Roberts and James Donaldson; New York: Christian Literature, 1895).

—. 'Concerning Military Service.' In *The Ante-Nicene Fathers: Translations of the Writings of the Fathers Down to AD 325* (*ANF*), vol. 3 (edited by Alexander Roberts and James Donaldson; Grand Rapids: Christian Classics Ethereal Library, 2002). online: http://www.ccel.org/ccel/schaff/anf03.iv.iv.xix.html

—. 'On Baptism.' In *The Ante-Nicene Fathers: Translations of the Writings of the Fathers Down to AD 325* (*ANF*), vol. 3 (edited by Alexander Roberts and James Donaldson; Grand Rapids: Christian Classics Ethereal Library, 2002). online: http://www.ccel.org/ccel/schaff/anf03.vi.iii.html

Theodoret of Cyr, *Opera Omnia*, vols 80-84, Patrologiae Graeca [PG] (edited by J.P. Migne; Paris: Migne, 2004).

Vermigli, Peter Martyr, *Melachim, id est, Regvum Libri Dvo Posteriores et Commentariis* (Zurich: Christopher Froschouer, 1566); Zug, Switzerland: Inter Documentation Company, n.d., microfiche.

Zwingli, Ulrich, 'An Account of the Faith of Zwingli'. In *Readings in the History of Christian Theology* (translated by William John Hinke; Philadelphia: Westminster, 1988), 2.19-23.

—. 'In epistolam beati Pauli ad Hebraeos expositio brevis'. In *Epistolas aliquot Pauli, annotationes* (edited by Kaspar Megander; Zurich: Christoph Froschauer, 1539).
—. *On Providence and Other Essays* (edited by William John Hinke; Durham: Labyrinth, 1983).
—. 'On the Lord's Supper' in *Zwingli and Bullinger* (translated by G.W. Bromiley; Philadelphia, Westminster, 1953), 185-238.
—. 'Sixty-seven Theses'. In *A Reformation Reader: Primary Texts With Introductions* (Minneapolis: Fortress, 2008), 189-193.
—. 'Zwingli's Letter to Vadian (20 October 1529)'. In *A Reformation Reader* (Minneapolis: Fortress, 2008), 195-197.

SECONDARY WORKS

Adam, Peter, 'Calvin's Preaching and Homiletic: Nine Engagements, Part 1' *Churchman* 124.3 (2010), 201-216; 'Part 2' *Churchman* 124.4 (2010), 331-342.
—. *Hearing God's Words: Exploring Biblical Spirituality* (Leicester: Apollos, 2004).
—. '"Preaching of a lively kind"— Calvin's engaged expository preaching'. In Mark. D. Thompson (ed.), *Engaging Calvin* (Nottingham: Apollos, 2009), 13-41.
—. *Speaking God's Words: A Practical Theology of Preaching* (Leicester: IVP, 1996).
Alfeyev, Hilarion, 'The Patristic Heritage and Modernity,' *Ecumenical Review* 54.1 (2002), 91-111.
Allison, Gregg, 'Toward a Theology of Human Embodiment,' *Southern Baptist Journal of Theology* 13.2 (2009), 4-17.
Althaus, Paul, *The Theology of Martin Luther* (translated by Robert C. Schultz; Philadelphia: Westminster, 1966).
Anderson, Marvin, 'John Calvin, Biblical Preacher,' *Scottish Journal of Theology* 42.2 (1989), 167-81.
Arand, Charles P., Robert Kolb and James A. Nestingen, *The Lutheran Confessions: History and Theology of the Book of Concord* (Minneapolis: Fortress), 2012.
Backus, Irena, 'Calvin and the Greek Fathers'. In Robert J. Bast and Andrew C. Gow (eds), *Continuity and Change: the Harvest of Late Medieval and Reformation History* (Leiden: Brill, 2000), 253-76.
Bainton, Roland, H., *Hunted Heretic: The Life and Death of Michael Servetus 1511-1553* (Boston: Beacon, 1960).
—. 'Luther and the *Via Media* at the Marburg Colloquy,' *Lutheran Quarterly* 1 (1949), 394-398.
—. *The Reformation of the Sixteenth Century* (revised; Boston: Beacon, 1985).

Bardy, G., 'Divinisation [III Chez les pères latins]'. In M. Viller, F. Cavallera, J. De Guibert (eds), *Dictionnaire de spiritualité*, 17 vols (Paris: Beauchesne, 1935-95), 3.1390-98.

Barna Group, The, 'New Marriage and Divorce Statistics Released' (Ventura, Calif: The Barna Group. March 2008). Online: http://www.barna.org/family-kids-articles/42-new-marriage-and-divorce-statistics-released

Barnes, Michel René, 'De Régnon Reconsidered,' *Augustinian Studies* 26.2 (1995), 51-79.

Barnett, Paul, *The Second Epistle to the Corinthians* (NICNT; Grand Rapids: Eerdmans, 1997).

Battles, Ford Lewis, 'God was accommodating himself to human capacity,' *Interpretation* 31 (1977), 19-38.

—. and André Malan Hugo, *Calvin's Commentary on Seneca's* De Clementia, *with introduction, translation and notes* (Leiden: Brill, 1969).

Bender, John, and David Wellbery, *The Ends of Rhetoric: History, Theory, Practice* (Stanford: Stanford University Press, 1990).

Berkhof, Louis, *Systematic Theology* (Grand Rapids: Eerdmans, 1941).

Billings, J. Todd, *Calvin, Participation, and the Gift: The Activity of Believers in Union with Christ* (New York: Oxford University Press, 2007).

—. 'John Calvin: United to God through Christ'. In Michael J. Christensen and Jeffery A. Wittung (eds), *Partakers of the Divine Nature: The History and Development of Deification in the Christian Traditions* (Grand Rapids: Baker Academic, 2008), 200-218.

—. 'The Catholic Calvin,' *Pro Ecclesia* 20.2 (2011), 120-34.

—. 'The Contemporary Reception of Luther and Calvin's Doctrine of Union with Christ: Mapping a Biblical, Catholic, and Reformational Motif'. In R. Grant Holder (ed.), *Calvin and Luther: The Continuing Relationship* (Göttingen: Vandenhoeck & Ruprecht, 2013), 165-82.

—. 'United to God through Christ: Assessing Calvin on the Question of Deification,' *Harvard Theological Review* 98.3 (2005), 315-34.

Blocher, Henri, 'Calvin's Theological Anthropology.' In Sung Wook Chung (ed.), *John Calvin and Evangelical Theology: Legacy and Prospect* (Louisville: Westminster John Knox, 2009), 66-84.

Boersma, Hans, *Heavenly Participation* (Grand Rapids: Eerdmans, 2011).

Bonner, Gerald, 'Augustine's Conception of Deification,' *Journal of Theological Studies* 37.2 (1986), 369-86.

—. 'Deificare' in Cornelius Mayer (ed.), *Augustinus-Lexikon*. 2 Volumes (Basel: Schwabe, 1996), 265-66.

—. 'Deification, Divinization'. In Allan D. Fitzgerald (ed.), *Augustine Through the Ages: An Encyclopedia* (Grand Rapids: Eerdmans, 1999), 265-66.

Booty, John E., *John Jewel: Apologist of the Church of England* (London: SPCK, 1963).

Bornkamm, Heinrich, *Luther and the Old Testament* (translated by Eric W. and Ruth C. Gritsch; Philadelphia: Fortress, 1969).

Botterill, Steven, *Dante and the Mystical Tradition: Bernard of Clairvaux in the 'Commedia'* (Cambridge: Cambridge University Press, 1994).

Boulton, Matthew Myer, *Life in God. John Calvin, Practical Formation, and the Future of Protestant Theology* (Grand Rapids: Eerdmans, 2011).

Bouwsma, W.J., *John Calvin: A Sixteenth Century Portrait* (New York: OUP, 1988).

Brashler, James, 'From Erasmus to Calvin: Exploring the Roots of Reformed Hermeneutics,' *Interpretation* 63.2 (2009), 154–166.

Brecht, Martin, 'Luther, Martin' in *Oxford Encyclopedia of the Reformation*, vol. 2 (translated by Wolfgang Katenz; New York: Oxford University Press, 1996).

Burnett, Stephen G., 'The Strange Career of the *Biblia Rabbinica* Among Christian Hebraists, 1517–1620'. In Bruce Gordon and Matthew McLean (eds), *Shaping the Bible in the Reformation: Books, Scholars, and Their Readers in the Sixteenth Century* (Leiden: Brill, 2012).

Canlis, Julie, 'Calvin, Osiander and Participation in God,' *International Journal of Systematic Theology* 6.2 (2004), 169-84.

—. *Calvin's Ladder: A Spiritual Theology of Ascent and Ascension* (Grand Rapids: Eerdmans, 2010).

Casiday, Augustine, 'St Augustine on deification: his homily on Psalm 81,' *Sobornost* 23.2 (2001), 23-44.

Clark, R. Scott, '*Iustitia Imputata Christi*: Alien or Proper to Luther's Doctrine of Justification?' *Concordia Theological Quarterly* 70.3/4 (2006), 269-310.

Constable, Giles, *Three Studies in Medieval Religious and Social Thought* (Cambridge: Cambridge University Press, 1995).

Coontz, Stephanie, *Marriage, a History: From Obedience to Intimacy or how Love Conquered Marriage* (New York: Viking, 2005).

—. 'Taking Marriage Private,' *The New York Times* (op ed., Nov 26, 2007). Online: http://www.nytimes.com/2007/11/26/opinrion/26coontz.html?_r=2).

Carroll, Thomas K., *Preaching the Word: The Message of the Fathers of the Church* (Wilmington: Michael Glazier, 1984).

Childs, Brevard S., *Biblical Theology of the Old and New Testaments* (Minneapolis: Fortress, 1992).

—. *The Struggle to Understand Isaiah as Christian Scripture* (Grand Rapids: Eerdmans, 2004).

Chung-Kim, Esther, *Inventing Authority: The Use of the Church Fathers in Reformation Debates over the Eucharist* (Waco: Baylor University Press, 2011).

Cooper, John, *Body, Soul, and Life Everlasting: Biblical Anthropology and the Monism-Dualism Debate* (Grand Rapids: Eerdmans, 1989).

Cottret, Bernard, *Calvin. A Biography* (Grand Rapids: Eerdmans / Edinburgh: T. & T. Clark, 2000)

Cranfield, C.E.B. *Romans 1-8* (ICC; New York: T & T Clark, 1975).

Cross, Richard, 'Perichoresis, Deification and Christological Predication and John of Damascus,' *Mediaeval Studies* 62 (2000), 69-124.

Custance, Arthur, *The Sovereignty of Grace* (Philipsburg: Presbyterian and Reformed, 1979).

D'Aubigne, J.H. Merle, *The History of the Reformation of the Sixteenth Century* (New York: American Tract Society, 1848).

Daussy, Hugues, *Les Huguenots et le roi: le combat politique du Philippe Mornay (1572-1600)* (Genève: Droz, 2002).

Davis, Kenneth R., *Anabaptism and Asceticism: A Study in Intellectual Origins* (Scottdale, PA: Herald, 1974).

Davis, William, 'Calvin's Legacy in Philosophy.' In David W. Hall and Marvin Padgett (eds), *Calvin and Culture: Exploring a Worldview* (Phillipsburg: P & R, 2010), 114-141.

de Félice, Guillaume, *Histoire des Protestants de France depuis l'origine de la Réformation jusqu'au temps present* (Paris: Librairie protestante, 1850).

de Koster, Lester, *Light for the City: Calvin's Preaching, Source of Life and Liberty* (Grand Rapids: Eerdmans, 2004).

de Kroon, Marijn, *The Honour of God and Human Salvation* (translated by John Vriend and Lyle D. Bierma; Edinburgh: T & T Clark, 2001).

De Montmorency, J.E.G. *Thomas à Kempis: His Age and Book* (New York: G.P. Putnam's Sons, 1906).

Demura, Akira, 'Two Commentaries on the Epistle to the Romans: Calvin and Oecolampadius'. In *Calvinus Sincerioris Religionis Vindex* (Kirksville: Sixteenth Century Journal Publishers, 1997), 165–188.

DeVries, Dawn, *Jesus Christ in the Preaching of Calvin and Schleiermacher* (Louisville: WJKP, 1996).

Dragas, George Dion, 'Exchange or Communication of Properties and Deification: *Antidosis* or *Communicatio Idiomatum* and *Theosis*,' *Greek Orthodox Theological Review* 43.1-4 (1998), 377-99.

Doumergue, Emile, *The Character of Calvinism: The Man, His System, The Church, The State* (1923; rpr. Neuilly [Seine]: La Cause, 1931).

Eells, Hastings, 'The Contributions of Martin Bucer to the Reformation,' *Harvard Theological Review* 24.1 (January, 1931), 29-42.

Elliott, M., 'Gabler, Johan Philipp.' In Donald K. McKim (ed.), *Dictionary of Major Biblical Interpreters* (Downers Grove: IVP, 2007), 452-57.

Empie, Paul C., *Marburg Revisited: A Reexamination of Lutheran and Reformed Traditions* (Minneapolis: Augsburg, 1966).

Engel, Mary Potter, *John Calvin's Perspectival Anthropology* (Atlanta: Scholars Press, 1988).

Estep, William R., *Renaissance and Reformation* (Grand Rapids: Eerdmans, 1986).

Erickson, Millard J., *Christian Theology* (Grand Rapids: Baker, 2007).

Farley, Benjamin Wirt, *The Providence of God* (Grand Rapids: Baker, 1988).

Farrar, F.W., *History of Interpretation* (London: E.P. Dutton, 1886).

Fee, Gordon D., *Philippians* (NICNT; Grand Rapids: Eerdmans, 1995).

Finch, Jeffrey D., 'Neo-Palamism, Divinizing Grace, and the Breach between East and West'. In Michael J. Christensen and Jeffery A. Wittung (eds), *Partakers of the Divine Nature: the History and Development of Deification in the Christian Traditions* (Grand Rapids: Baker Academic, 2008), 233-249.

Forde, Gerhard O., *On Being a Theologian of the Cross. Reflections on Luther's Heidelberg Disputation, 1518* (Grand Rapids: Eerdmans, 1997).

Fracheboud, A., H-T. Conus and R-L. Oechslin, 'Divinisation [IV Moyen âge]'. In M. Viller, F. Cavallera, J. De Guibert (eds), *Dictionnaire de spiritualité*, 17 vols (Paris: Beauchesne), 3.1399-1445.

Fullerton, Kemper, 'The Reformation Principle of Exegesis and the Interpretation of Prophecy,' *American Journal of Theology* 12.3 (July 1908), 422-442.

Gäbler, Ulrich, *Huldrych Zwingli: His Life and Work* (Philadelphia: Fortress, 1983).

Gamble, Richard, '*Brevitas* and *facilitas*: towards an Understanding Calvin's Hermeneutic,' *Westminster Theological Journal* 47 (1985), 1-17.

—. 'Exposition and Method in Calvin,' *Westminster Theological Journal* 49 (1987), 153-165.

Garcia, Aurelio, 'Bullinger's Friendship with Calvin: Loving One Another and Edifying the Churches,' *Calvin Studies Papers (1997)* (Grand Rapids: CRC Product Services, 1998), 19-133.

Garcia, Mark A., 'Imputation and the Christology of Union with Christ: Calvin, Osiander, and the Contemporary Quest for a Reformed Model,' *Westminster Theological Journal* 68.2 (2006), 219-51.

Gazal, André A., *Scripture and Royal Supremacy in Tudor England: The Use of Old Testament Historical Narrative* (Lewiston, NY: Edwin Mellen, 2013).

Gibson, Michael, 'Either/Or: The Question of Identity and Eastern Orthodoxy in the Thought of Christos Yannaras'. Online: http://www.academia.edu/946991/) [accessed 1/11/2013].

Gilmont, Jean François, *John Calvin and the Printed Book*, Sixteenth Century Essays & Studies 72 (translated by Karin Maag; Kirksville: Truman State University Press, 2005).

Gilson, Etienne, *The Christian Philosophy of St. Thomas Aquinas* (New York: Random House, 1956).

Ginsburg, Christian D., *Introduction to the Massoretico-critical Edition of the Hebrew Bible* (London: Trinitarian Bible Society, 1897).

Godfrey, W. Robert, 'The Counselor to the Afflicted.' In Burk Parsons (ed.), *John Calvin. A Heart for Devotion, Doctrine and Doxology* (Lake Mary: Reformation Trust, 2008), 83-93.

González, Justo L., *The Story of Christianity*, vol. 2 (San Francisco: Harper Collins, 1985).

Gordon, Bruce, *Calvin* (New Haven: Yale University Press, 2009).

Gorham, George Cornelius, *Gleanings of a Few Scattered Ears* (London: Bell and Daldy, 1857).
Greer, Rowan A., *The Captain of Our Salvation: A Study in the Patristic Exegesis of Hebrews*. Beiträge zur Geschichte der biblischen Exegese [BGBE] 15 (Tübingen: Mohr, 1973).
Gregory, Brad S., *Salvation at Stake. Christian Martyrdom in Early Modern Europe* (Cambridge: Harvard University Press, 1999).
Grudem, Wayne A., *Systematic Theology: An Introduction to Biblical Doctrine* (Grand Rapids: Zondervan, 2000).
Haag, Eugène, 'La Célebre Conference de Fontainbleau entre Mornay et le Cardinal Du Perron,' *Bulletin de la Société de l'Histoire du Protestantisme français VI* (1858), 351-61.
Haag, Eugène and Emile, *La France Protestante: ou vies des protestants français qui se sont fait un nom dans l'Histoire depuis la premier temps de la réformation jusqu'à la reconnaissance du principe de la liberté des cultes par l'assemblée nationale* (Paris: Joël Cherbulier, 1857), 1.148-50.
Habets, Myk, '*Theosis*, Yes; Deification, No'. In Myk Habets (ed.), *The Spirit of Truth* (Eugene: Pickwick, 2010), 124-49.
Hagen, Kenneth. *A Theology of Testament in the Young Luther: The Lectures on Hebrews* (Leiden: Brill, 1974).
—. *Hebrews Commenting from Erasmus to Bèze, 1516-1598*. BGBE 23 (Tübingen: Mohr, 1981).
Hall, David W., *Calvin in the Public Square* (Phillipsburg, NJ: P & R, 2009).
Hansen, Gary Neal, 'Calvin as Commentator on Hebrews and the Catholic Epistles.' In Donald K. McKim (ed.), *Calvin and the Bible* (New York: Cambridge University Press, 2006), 257–281.
Harkness, Georgia, *The Providence of God* (New York: Abingdon, 1960).
Harnack, Adolf von, *History of Dogma*, 7 vols (London: Williams & Norgate, 1894-99).
—. *What is Christianity?* 5th ed. (translated by Thomas Bailey Saunders; Philadelphia: Fortress, 1986 [1900]).
Harris, Murray J., *The Second Epistle to the Corinthians* (NIGTC; Grand Rapids: Eerdmans, 2005).
Harris, Robert A., 'Medieval Jewish Biblical Exegesis.' In Alan J. Hauser and Daune F. Watson (eds), *A History of Biblical Interpretation* (Grand Rapids: Eerdmans, 2009), 2.141–171.
Heen, Erik and Philip Krey (eds), *Hebrews. Ancient Christian Commentary on Scripture: New Testament* 10 (Downers Grove, IL: InterVarsity, 2005).
Helm, Paul, 'Calvin (and Zwingli) on Divine Providence,' *Calvin Theological Journal* 29.2 (1994), 388-405.
—. *John Calvin's Ideas* (Oxford: Oxford University Press, 2004).
Henderson, Henry F., *Calvin in his Letters* (Eugene: Wipf and Stock, 1996).
Hesselink, I. John, 'Calvinus Oecumenicus: Calvin's Vision of the Unity and Catholicity of the Church'. In Eduardus Van der Borght (ed.), *Unity of the*

Church: A Theological State of the Art and Beyond. SRT 18 (Leiden: Brill, 2010), 69-93.

Hoekema, Anthony A., *Created in God's Image* (Grand Rapids: Eerdmans, 1986).

Holt, Mack P., 'Divisions Within French Calvinism: Philippe Mornay and the Eucharist.' In Mack P. Holt (ed.), *Adaptations of Calvinism in Reformation Europe: Essays in Honor of Brian G. Armstrong* (St. Andrews: Ashgate, 2007), 165-78.

Hopfl, Harro, *The Christian Polity of John Calvin* (Cambridge: Cambridge University Press, 1982.

Hughes, Philip E. (ed.), *The Register of the Company of Pastors in the Time of Calvin* (Grand Rapids: Eerdmans, 1966).

Hunter, Michael A., *The Teaching of Calvin: A Modern Interpretation* (London: James Clarke, 1950).

Hyma, Albert., *The Brethren of the Common Life* (Grand Rapids: Eerdmans, 1950).

—. *The Christian Renaissance* (Hamden: Archon, 1965).

—. *The Youth of Erasmus* (Ann Arbor: University of Michigan Press, 1930).

Jacob, E.F., 'Gerhard Groote and the Beginnings of the "New Devotion" in the Low Countries,' *Journal of Ecclesiastical History* 3 (January-April, 1952), 40-57.

Jelsma, Auke, *Frontiers of the Reformation. Dissidence and Orthodoxy in Sixteenth Century Europe* (Aldershot: Ashgate, 1998).

Jenkins, Gary W., *John Jewel and the English National Church. The Dilemmas of an Erastian Reformer* (Burlington, VT: Ashgate, 2006).

Johnson, Elizabeth A., 'Does God Play Dice? Divine Providence and Chance,' *Theological Studies* 57 (1996), 2-18.

Jones, Serene, *Calvin and the Rhetoric of Piety* (Columbia: Columbia Theological Seminary, 1995).

Kaplan, Benjamin J., *Divided by Faith. Religious Conflict in the Practice of Toleration in Early Modern Europe* (Cambridge: Harvard University Press, 2009).

Keating, Daniel A., *Deification and Grace* (Naples, Flor: Sapientia, 2007).

—. 'Divinization in Cyril: The Appropriation of Divine Life'. In Thomas G. Weinandy and Daniel A. Keating (eds), *The Theology of St Cyril of Alexandria: A Critical Appreciation* (London and New York: T & T Clark, 2003), 149-85.

—. *The Appropriation of Divine Life in Cyril of Alexandria* (Oxford: Oxford University Press, 2004).

Kelly, Douglas, *The Emergence of Liberty in the Modern World* (Phillipsburg, NJ: P & R, 1992).

—. 'The Transmission and Translation of the Collected Letters of John Calvin,' *Scottish Journal of Theology* 30.5 (1977), 429-437.

Kennedy, Daniel, 'Sacraments.' In *The Catholic Encyclopedia*, vol. 13 (New York: Robert Appleton, 1912). Online: http://www.newadvent.org/cathen/13295a.htm

Kettlewell, Samuel, *Thomas à Kempis and the Brothers of Common Life*, 2 vols (New York: G.P. Putnam's Sons, 1882).

Kirby, Torrance, *The Zurich Connection and Tudor Political Theology* (Leiden: Brill, 2007).

Kittleson, James M., *Luther the Reformer: The Story of the Man and His Career* (Minneapolis: Augsburg, 1986).

Koessler, John M., *True Discipleship: The Art of Following Jesus* (Chicago: Moody, 2003).

Kolb, Robert, 'God's Gift of Martyrdom: The Early Reformation Understanding of Dying for the Faith,' *Church History* 64.3 (1995), 399-411.

Köstlin, Julius, *The Theology of Luther in its Historical Development and Inner Harmony* (Whitefish, MT: Kessinger, 2010).

Kraus, Hans Joachim, 'Calvin's Exegetical Principles,' *Interpretation* 31 (1977), 8-18.

Lalot, J.A., *Essai historique sur la conférence tenue.à Fontainbleau entre Duplessis Mornay et Duperron le 4 Mai 1600* (Paris, 1889).

Lampe, G.W.H. (ed.), *The Cambridge History of the Bible* (Cambridge: CUP, 1969).

Landeen, William M., 'Gabriel Biel and the Brethren of the Common Life in Germany,' *Church History* 20 (March, 1951), 23-36.

Lane, A.N.S., 'Calvin's Attitude towards Catholicity'. In Herman J. Selderhuis (ed.), *Calvinus Clarissimus theologus*. RHT 18 (Göttingen: Vandenhoeck & Ruprecht, 2012), 206-27.

Leith, John H., 'Calvin's Doctrine of the Proclamation of the Word and Its Significance Today.' In Timothy George (ed.), *John Calvin & the Church: A Prism of Reform* (Louisville: WJKP, 1990), 206-229.

—. 'John Calvin—Theologian of the Bible,' *Interpretation* 25 (1971), 329-344.

—. *John Calvin's Doctrine of the Christian Life* (Louisville: Westminster/John Knox: 1989).

—. 'Reformed Preaching Today,' *Princeton Seminary Bulletin* 10.3 (1989), 224-257.

Linder, Robert D., 'Brothers in Christ: Pierre Viret and John Calvin as Soul-mates and Co-laborers in the Work of the Reformation". In *Calvin Studies Papers (1997)* (Grand Rapids: CRC Product Services, 1998), 134-158.

—. *The Political Ideals of John Calvin* (Geneva: Librairie Droz, 1964).

Locher, Gottfried W., 'The Change in the Understanding of Zwingli in Recent Research,' *Church History* 34.1 (1965), 3-24.

—. *Zwingli's Thought: New Perspectives* (Leiden: Brill, 1981).

Lubac, Henri de, *Medieval Exegesis: The Four Senses of Scripture*, 3 vols (Grand Rapids: Eerdmans, 1998).

Lucas, Henry S., *The Renaissance and the Reformation* (New York: Harper, 1934).

MacColloch, Diarmaid, *The Reformation* (New York: Viking, 2005).

MacKenzie, Cameron, 'The Origins and Consequences of Original Sin in Luther's *Bondage of the Will*,' *Concordia Journal* 31.4 (Oct 2005), 384–397.

Marcacci, Marco, *Historie de L'Universite de Geneve 1558-1986* (Geneva: University of Geneva, 1987).

Marrocco, Mary, 'Participation in Divine Life in the *De Trinitate* of St. Augustine,' *Augustinianum* 42.1 (2002), 149-85.

Martin, Henri, *Livre Pouvoirs et Société à Paris au XVIIe Siècle (1598-1701)*, 2 vols (Genève: Droz, 1969).

Matheson, Peter, *The Imaginative World of the Reformation* (Edinburgh: T. & T. Clark, 2000).

McCormack, Bruce L., 'Union with Christ in Calvin's Theology: Grounds for a Divinization Theory?' In David W. Hall (ed.), *Tributes to John Calvin* (Phillipsburg: P & R, 2010), 504-29.

McGowan, Andrew, 'Colossians 3: Deification, *Theosis*, Participation, or Union with Christ?' In R. Michael Allen (ed.), *Theological Commentary: Evangelical Perspectives* (London: T & T Clark, 2011), 154-71.

McGrath, Alister, *A Life of John Calvin* (Cambridge, MA: Basil Blackwell, 1990).

—. 'Calvin and the Christian Calling,' *First Things* 94 (June/July 1999), 31-35.

McGuckin, J.A., 'The Strategic Adaptation of Deification in the Cappadocians'. In Michael J. Christensen and Jeffery A. Wittung (eds), *Partakers of the Divine Nature: the History and Development of Deification in the Christian Traditions* (Grand Rapids: Baker Academic, 2008), 95-114.

McInerny, Ralph and John O'Callaghan, 'Saint Thomas Aquinas' in Edward N. Zalta (ed.), *The Stanford Encyclopedia of Philosophy* (Winter 2010 edition), URL = <http://plato.stanford.edu/archives/win2010/entries/aquinas/>

McNair, Philip., 'Seeds of Reform'. In *Eerdmans' Handbook to the History of Christianity* (Grand Rapids: Eerdmans, 1977).

McNeill, John T., 'Calvinism and European Politics in Historical Perspective'. In George L. Hunt (ed.), *Calvinism and the Political Order* (Philadelphia: Westminster, 1965), 1-20.

—. "The significance of the Word of God for Calvin," *Church History* 27 (1959), 131-146.

Meconi, David Vincent, *The One Christ: St. Augustine's Theology of Deification* (Washington: Catholic University of America Press, 2013).

Monter, William, 'Heresy Executions in Reformation Europe, 1520-1565.' In Ole Peter Grell and Robert W. Scribner (eds), *Tolerance and Intolerance in the European Reformation* (Cambridge: CUP, 1996), 48-64.

Moo, Douglas, *The Epistle to the Romans* (NICNT; Grand Rapids: Eerdmans, 1996).

Morse, Jennifer Roback, 'Privatizing Marriage Is Impossible,' *The Witherspoon Institute: Public Discourse on Ethics, Law and Common Good* (April 2-4, 2012). online: www.thepublicdiscourse.com/2012/04/5069

Mosser, Carl, 'The Earliest Patristic Interpretations of Psalm 82, Jewish Antecedents, and the Origin of Christian Deification,' *Journal of Theological Studies* 56.1 (2005), 30-74.

—. 'The Greatest Possible Blessing: Calvin and Deification,' *Scottish Journal of Theology* 55.1 (2002), 36-57.

Muller, Richard A., 'Biblical Interpretation in the Era of the Reformation: The View from the Middle Ages'. In Richard A. Muller and John L. Thompson (eds), *Biblical interpretation in the era of the Reformation: essays presented to David C. Steinmetz in honor of his sixtieth birthday* (Grand Rapids: Eerdmans, 1996), 3-22.

—. 'The Hermeneutic of Promise Fulfillment in Calvin's Exegesis of the Old Testament Prophecies of the Kingdom'. In David C. Steinmetz (ed.), *The Bible in the Sixteenth Century* (Duke Monographs in Medieval and Renaisssance Studies 11; Durham: Duke University Press, 1990), 68-82, 214-216.

—. *The Unaccommodated Calvin* (Oxford: Oxford University Press, 2000).

Mullett, Michael A., *Martin Luther* (London: Routledge, 2004).

National Center for Health Statistics, 'National Marriage and Divorce Rate Trends' (Atlanta, GA: Center for Disease Control and Prevention, 2012). Online: http://www.cdc.gov/nchs/nvss/marriage_divorce_tables.htm

Neale, J.M., *A History of the So-Called Jansenist Church of Holland; with a Sketch of Its Earlier Annals, and Some Account of the Brothers of the Common Life* (reprinted from Oxford: Henry and Parker, 1858; New York: AMS Press, 1970).

Niesel, Wilhelm, *The Theology of Calvin* (London: Lutterworth, 1956).

Oberman, Heiko A., *Luther: Man Between God and the Devil* (New York: Doubleday, 1989).

Odzak, Lazar, 'Marriage, History of.' *North Carolina Department of Cultural Resources* (Raleigh, NC: John Locke Foundation. no date). Online: http://www.northcarolinahistory.org/commentary/141/entry

Old, Hughes Oliphant, *The Reading and Preaching of the Scriptures in the Worship of the Christian Church*, vol. 3 (Grand Rapids: Eerdmans, 1999).

Ollerton, A.J., '*Quasi Deificari*: Deification in the Theology of John Calvin,' *Westminster Theological Journal* 73 (2011), 237-54.

Olson, Jeannine 'The Friends of John Calvin: The Budé Family'. In *Calvin Studies Papers (1997)* (Grand Rapids: CRC Product Services, 1998), 159-168.

Olson, Roger E., *Westminster Handbook to Evangelical Theology* (Louisville: Westminster John Knox, 2004).

Opitz, Peter, 'The Exegetical and Hermeneutical Work of John Oecolampadius, Huldrych Zwingli and John Calvin.' In Magne Sæbø (ed.), *Hebrew Bible,*

Old Testament: The History of Its Interpretation (Göttingen: Vandenhoeck & Ruprecht, 2008), 2.407–413

Oxford English Dictionary, The (edited by J.A. Simpson and E.S.C. Weiner; Oxford: Oxford University Press, 1989).

Ozment, Steven, *The Age of Reform (1250-1550): An Intellectual and Religious History of Late Medieval and Reformation Europe* (New Haven: Yale University Press, 1980).

Pak, G. Sujin, *The Judaizing Calvin: Sixteenth-Century Debates over the Messianic Psalms* (New York: Oxford University Press, 2010).

Pannier, Jacques, *L'Église Réformée de Paris sous Henri IV* (Paris: Librairie Ancienne Honoré Champion, 1911).

Parker, G.W.H., *The Morning Star: Wycliffe and the Dawn of the Reformation* (Grand Rapids: Eerdmans, 1965).

Parker, T.H.L., 'Calvin's Commentary on Hebrews.' In Geoffrey Bromiley, James E. Bradley and Richard A. Muller (eds), *Church, Word, and Spirit: Historical and Theological Essays in Honor of Geoffrey W. Bromiley* (Grand Rapids: Eerdmans, 1987), 135–140.

—. *Calvin's Old Testament Commentaries* (Edinburgh: T. & T. Clark, 1986).

—. *Calvin's Preaching* (Edinburgh: T. & T. Clark, 1992).

—. 'Commentary on the book of the prophet Isaiah,' *Evangelical Quarterly* 20 (1948), 297-298.

—. *John Calvin: A Full Scale Life of the Controversial Reformation Leader and Influential Theologian* (Batavia, IL: Lion, 1975).

—. *The Oracles of God: an Introduction to the Preaching of John Calvin* (London: Lutterworth, 1947).

Parsons, Michael, *Calvin's Preaching on the Prophet Micah: The 1550-1551 Sermons in Geneva* (Lewiston: Edward Mellen, 2006).

—. *Reformation Marriage. The Husband and Wife Relationship in the Theology of Luther and Calvin* (Eugene: Wipf and Stock, 2011).

Partee, Charles, *Calvin and Classical Philosophy* (Louisville: Westminster John Knox, 2005).

—. 'Predestination in Aquinas and Calvin,' *Reformed Review* 32 (1978), 14-22.

— 'The Soul in Plato, Platonism and Calvin,' *Scottish Journal of Theology* 22 (1969), 278-295.

—. *The Theology of John Calvin* (Louisville: Westminster John Knox, 2008).

Patrides, C.A., *The Cambridge Platonists* (Cambridge: Cambridge University Press, 1980).

Pattison, Bonnie, 'The suffering church in Calvin's *De Scandalis*: an exercise in Luther's *Theologia Crucis*? In Michael Parsons (ed.), *Since we are Justified by Faith. Justification in the Theologies of the Protestant Reformation* (Milton Keynes: Paternoster, 2012), 117-37.

Pelikan, Jaroslav, *Luther the Expositor: Introduction to the Reformer's Exegetical Writings* (St. Louis: Concordia, 1959).

Pettegree, Andrew, 'The spread of Calvin's thought.' In Donald K. McKim (ed.), *The Cambridge Companion to John Calvin* (Cambridge: Cambridge University Press, 2004), 207-224.

Posset, Franz, '"Deification" in the German Spirituality of the Late Middle Ages and in Luther: An Ecumenical Historical Perspective,' *Archiv für Reformationsgeschichte* 84 (1993), 103-26.

Potter, G.R. *Huldrych Zwingli* (New York: St. Martin's, 1977).

Poythress, Diane, *Reformer of Basel: The Life, Thought, and Influence of Johannes Oecolampadius* (Grand Rapids: Reformation Heritage Books, 2011).

Puckett, David L., *John Calvin's Exegesis of the Old Testament* (Louisville: Westminster John Knox, 1995).

Raitt, Jill, 'St. Thomas on Free Will and Predestination,' *Duke Divinity School Review* 43 (1978), 188-195.

—. *The Colloquy of Montbéliard: Religion and Politics in the Sixteenth Century* (New York: Oxford University Press, 1993).

Reynolds, Blair, 'Calvin's Exegesis of Jeremiah and Micah: Use or Abuse of Scripture?' (Proceedings Eastern Great Lakes and Midwest Biblical Societies, 11, 1991), 8-91.

Rilliet, Jean, *Zwingli: Third Man of the Reformation* (London: Lutterworth, 1964).

Rupp, E. Gordon, *Patterns of Reformation* (reprint; Eugene: Wipf & Stock, 2009).

Russell, Norman, *Fellow Workers with God: Orthodox Thinking on Theosis* (Crestwood: St Vladimir's Seminary Press, 2009).

—. *The Doctrine of Deification in the Greek Patristic Tradition* (Oxford: Oxford University Press, 2004).

—. 'Theosis and Gregory Palamas: Continuity or Doctrinal Change?' *St. Vladimir's Theological Quarterly* 50.4 (2006), 357-79.

Safley (ed.), Thomas M., *A Companion to Multiconfessionalism in the Early Modern World* (Leiden: Brill, 2011).

Sasse, Herman, *This is My Body: Luther's Contention for the Real Presence in the Sacrament of the Altar* (Adelaide: Lutheran Publishing House, 1977).

Sawyer, John F.A., *The Fifth Gospel: Isaiah in the History of Christianity* (Cambridge: Cambridge University Press, 1996).

Schaff, Philip, *History of the Christian Church*, vol. 8 (1910, rpr. Grand Rapids: Eerdmans, 1979).

Schreiner, Susan, 'Calvin as an interpreter of Job.' In Donald McKim (ed.), *Calvin and the Bible* (Cambridge: Cambridge University Press, 2006), 53-84.

—. 'Through a Mirror Dimly: Calvin's Sermons on Job,' *Calvin Theological Journal* 21 (1986), 175-193.

Schreiner, Tom, *Romans* (ECNT; Grand Rapids: Baker, 1998).

Schreiner, Thomas R. and Matthew R. Crawford, *The Lord's Supper: Remembering and Proclaiming Christ Until He Comes* (Nashville: B&H, 2010).

Scribner, R.W., 'The Social Thought of Erasmus,' *Journal of Religious History* 6 (June, 1970), 3-26.

Selderhuis, Herman, *John Calvin: A Pilgrim's Life* (Wheaton, IL: IVP, 2009).

Sheed, Frank J., *Theology and Sanity* (San Francisco: Ignatius, 1993).

Silva, Moises, *Philippians* (BECNT; Grand Rapids: Baker, 2005).

Simon, Uriel, *Four Approaches to the Book of Psalms: From Saadiah Gaon to Abraham Ibn Ezra* (Albany: State University of New York Press, 1991).

Slater, Jonathan, 'Salvation as Participation in the Humanity of the Mediator in Calvin's *Institutes of the Christian Religion*: A Reply to Carl Mosser,' *Scottish Journal of Theology* 58.1 (2005), 39-58.

Smith, James K.A., *The Fall of Interpretation: Philosophical Foundations for a Creational Hermeneutic* (Downers Grove, IL: InterVarsity, 2000).

Smith, Preserved, 'The Methods of Reformation Interpreters of the Bible,' *Biblical World* 38.4 (Oct. 1911), 235-245.

Smyth, Charles, *The Art of Preaching: 1747-1939* (London: SPCK, 1940).

Snavely, Iren, 'The Evidence of Things Unseen: Zwingli's Sermon on Providence and Colloquy of Marburg,' *Westminster Theological Journal* 56 (1994), 399-407.

Snoeks, Remi, *L'Argument de tradition dans la controverse eucharistique entre catholiques et réformés français au XVIIe siècle* (Louvain: Publications Universitaires de Louvain, 1951).

Southgate, W.M., *John Jewel and the Problem of Doctrinal Authority* (Cambridge, MA: Harvard University Press, 1962).

Speer, A., 'Vergöttlichung' in *Lexikon des Mittelalters*. 10 vols (Stuttgart: Metzler, [1977]-1999), 8.1531-1532; in *Brepolis Medieval Encyclopaedias - Lexikon des Mittelalters Online*.

Spitz, Lewis W., *The Renaissance and Reformation Movements* (Chicago: Rand McNally, 1971).

Staehelin, Ernst, Staehelin, Ernst. *Briefe und Akten zum Leben Oekolampads*. Reprint. QFR 10, 19. New York: Johnson, 1971.

—. *Das Theologische Lebenswerk Johannes Oekolampads*. QFR 21 (New York: Johnson, 1939).

—. *Oekolampad-Bibliographie*. 1918, 1928. Reprint. Nieuwkoop: B. De Graaf, 1963.

Stauffer, Richard, *The Humanness of John Calvin* (New York: Abingdon Press, 1971).

Steinmetz, David C. 'Calvin and Abraham: The Interpretation of Romans 4 in the Sixteenth Century,' *Church History* 57 (1988), 443-455.

—. 'Calvin as the Biblical Interpreter Among the Ancient Philosophers,' *Interpretation* 63 (2009), 142-153.

—. *Calvin in Context* (Oxford: Oxford University Press, 2010).

—. 'John Calvin as an Interpreter of the Bible.' In Donald McKim (ed.), *Calvin and the Bible* (Cambridge: Cambridge University Press, 2006), 282-291.
—. 'John Calvin on Isaiah 6. A Problem in the History of Exegesis,' *Interpretation* 36 (1982), 156-170.
—. *Luther in Context* (Grand Rapids: Baker, 1994).
—. *The Bible in the Sixteenth Century* (Durham: Duke University Press, 1990).
Stephens, W.P., 'Election in Zwingli and Bullinger: a comparison of Zwingli's *Sermonis de providentia Dei anamnema* (1530) and Bullinger's *Oratio de moderatione servanda in negotio providentiae, praedestinationis, gratiae et liberi arbitrii* (1536),' *Reformation and Renaissance Review* 7.1 (2005), 42-56.
—. *The Theology of Huldrych Zwingli* (Oxford: Clarendon, 1986).
Stiles, Margaret L., 'Theology, Anthropology and the Human Body in Calvin's *Institutes of the Christian Religion*,' *Harvard Theological Review* 74.3 (1981), 303-323.
Strand, Kenneth A., 'The Brethren of the Common Life: A Review Article of R.R. Post's *The Modern Devotion*,' *Andrews University Seminary Studies* 8 (January, 1970), 65-76.
—. 'Calvin and the Brethren of the Common Life: The Role of Strassburg,' *Andrews University Seminary Studies* 15 (Spring, 1977), 43-56.
Tamburello Dennis E., *Union with Christ: John Calvin and the Mysticism of St. Bernard* (Louisville: John Knox, 1994).
Tavard, George H., 'The Mystery of Divine Providence,' *Theological Studies* 64.4 (2003), 707-718.
Thomas, Derek, *Calvin's Teaching on Job: Preaching the Incomprehensible God* (Geanies House: Mentor, 2004).
Thompson, Mark, *A Sure Ground on Which to Stand: The Relation of Authority and Interpretive Method in Luther's Approach to Scripture* (Eugene: Wipf and Stock, 2006).
—. (ed.), *Engaging Calvin* (Nottingham: Apollos, 2009).
Thompson, N.F., 'Third Order, Secular' in *The New Catholic Encyclopedia* (2nd ed. Catholic University Press of America, 2003).
Torrance, T.F., *Calvin's Doctrine of Man* (Westport, CT: Greenwood, 1977).
—. *The Hermeneutics of John Calvin* (Edinburgh: Scottish Academic, 1988).
Tripp, Paul David, *Instruments in the Redeemer's Hands: People in Need of Change Helping People in Need of Change* (Phillipsburg: Presbyterian &Reformed, 2002).
van den Berg, Machiel A., *Friends of Calvin* (translated by Reinder Bruinsma; Grand Rapids, Michigan/Cambridge: Eerdmans, 2009).
van der Walt, A.G.P., 'Calvin on Preaching.' In B.J. van der Walt (ed), *John Calvin's Institutes: His Magnum Opus* Potchefstroom: Potchefstroom University for Christian Higher Education, 1986), 326-341.
—. 'John Calvin and the Reformation of Preaching.' In B.J. van der Walt (ed.), *Our Reformational tradition: a rich heritage and lasting vocation* (no editor

named; Potchefstroom: Potchefstroom University for Christian Higher Education, 1984), 192-202.

Vandunren, David, 'The Content of Natural Law: Calvin's Doctrine of the Two Kingdoms,' *Journal of Church and State* 46 (2004), 503-525

Van Engen, John, *Devotio Moderna: Basic Writings* (New York: Paulist, 1988).

Vanhoozer, Kevin J., *Is there a meaning in this text?* (Leicester: Apollos, 1998).

—. *The Drama of Doctrine: A Canonical-Linguistic Approach to Christian Theology* (Louisville: Westminster John Knox, 2005).

Van 't Spijker, Willem, 'Calvin's Friendship with Bucer: Did It Make Calvin a Calvinist?' In *Calvin Studies Papers (1997)* (Grand Rapids: CRC Product Services, 1998), 169-186.

—. *The Ecclesiastical Offices in the Thought of Martin Bucer* (translated by John Vriend and Lyle D. Bierma; Leiden: Brill, 1996).

van Vliet, Jason, *Children of God: The Imago Dei in John Calvin and his Context* (Gottingen: Vandenhoeck & Ruprecht, 2009).

Vatican, The *Catechism of the Catholic Church* (Vatican City: Par. 1131, no date). 'Online: http://www.vatican.va/archive/ENG0015/__P35.HTM

Usher, Brett, 'John Jewel Junked,' *Journal of Ecclesiastical History* 59 (2008), 501-11.

—. *William Cecil and the Episcopacy* (Aldershot, England: Ashgate, 2003).

Wallace, Ronald S. *Calvin, Geneva, and the Reformation* (Edinburgh: Scottish Academic, 1988).

Ward, Haruko Nawata, 'Martyrdom.' In David M. Whitford (ed.), *T & T Clark Companion to Reformation Theology* (Edinburgh: T. & T. Clark, 2012), 332-351

Ward, Peter, 'Coming to sermon: the practice of doctrine in the preaching of John Calvin,' *SJT* 58.3 (2005), 319-332.

Weinandy, Thomas G., 'The Supremacy of Christ: Aquinas' Commentary on Hebrews'. In Thomas Gerard Weinandy, Daniel A. Keating and John Yocum (eds), *Aquinas On Scripture: An Introduction to his Biblical Commentaries* (London: T & T Clark, 2005), 223–244.

Wendel, Francois, *Calvin: Origins and Development of his Religious Thought* (Grand Rapids: Baker, 1997).

Westerholm, Stephen, *Perspectives Old and New on Paul: The 'Lutheran' Paul and His Critics* (Grand Rapids: Eerdmans, 2004).

White, James F., *Protestant Worship: Traditions in Transition* (Louisville: Westminster John Knox, 1989).

Wilcox, Peter, 'Calvin as commentator on the Prophets'. In Donald McKim (ed.), *Calvin and the Bible* (Cambridge: Cambridge University Press, 2006), 107-130.

—. '"The Progress of the Kingdom of Christ" in Calvin's Exposition of the Prophets'. In Wilhelm H. Neuser and Brian G. Armstrong (eds), *Calvinus*

Sincerioris Religious Vindex: Calvin as Protector of the Purer Religion (Kirksville, Missouri: Sixteenth Century Journal Publisher, 1997), 315-322.

Wiley, David N., 'Calvin's Friendship with Guillaume Farel'. In *Calvin Studies Papers (1997)* (Grand Rapids: CRC Product Services, 1998), 187-204.

Willis, E. David, *Calvin's Catholic Christology* (Leiden: Brill, 1966).

Wippel, John F., *Metaphysical Themes in Thomas Aquinas*, volume 10, *Studies in the History of Philosophy* (edited by Jude P. Dougherty; Washington: The Catholic University of America Press, 1984).

Witte, John Jr., *From Sacrament to Contract: Marriage, Religion, and Law in the Western Tradition* (Louisville: Westminster John Knox, 1997).

—. 'The Reformation of Marriage Law in Martin Luther's Germany: Its Significance Then and Now,' *Journal of Law and Religion* 4.2 (1986), 293-351.

—. and Robert M. Kingdom, *Sex, Marriage, and Family in John Calvin's Geneva*, vol. 1: 'Courtship, Engagement, and Marriage' (Grand Rapids: Eerdmans, 2005).

Wolfe, Michael, 'Exegesis as Public Performance: Controversialist Debate and Politics at the Conference of Fontainbleau (1600)'. In *Politics and Religion in Early Bourbon France* (New York: Palgrave Macmillan, 2009), 65-85.

Wood, Arthur Skevington, 'Calvin'. In *The Principles of Biblical interpretation as enunciated by Irenaeus, Origen, Augustin, Luther, and Calvin* (Grand Rapids: Zondervan, 1967), 85-99.

Woodhead, Linda, 'Apophatic Anthropology'. In R. Kendall Soulen and Linda Woodhead (eds), *God and Human Dignity* (Grand Rapids: Eerdmans, 2006), 233-46.

Wulf, Maurice de, *The System of Thomas Aquinas* (New York: Dover, 1959).

Yearley, Lee H., 'St. Thomas Aquinas on Providence and Predestination,' *Anglican Theological Review* 49 (1967), 409-423.

Young, Davis, *Calvin and the Natural World* (Lanham, MD: University Press of America, 2007).

Zachman, Randall C., *Image and Word in the Theology of John Calvin* (Notre Dame, IN: University of Notre Dame 2007).

—. *John Calvin as Teacher, Pastor, and Theologian* (Grand Rapids: Baker Academic, 2006).

—. 'Restoring Access to the Fountain: Melanchthon and Calvin on the Task of Evangelical Theology'. In *Calvin Studies Papers (1997)* (Grand Rapids: CRC Product Services, 1998) 205-228.

INDEXES

Author index

Scripture index

Subject index